D0148837

Adam Smith's Moral Philosophy

Adam Smith is best known among economists for his book *The Wealth of Nations*, often viewed as the keystone of modern economic thought. For many, he has become associated with a quasi-libertarian laissez-faire philosophy. Others, often heterodox economists and social philosophers, on the contrary, focus on Smith's *Theory of Moral Sentiments*, and explore his moral theory. There has been a long debate about the relationship or lack thereof between these, his two great works.

This work treats these dimensions of Smith's work as elements in a seamless moral philosophical vision, demonstrating the integrated nature of these works and Smith's other writings. Although many practitioners today see the study of Smith as an antiquarian exercise, this book weaves Smith into a constructive critique of modern economic analysis (engaging along the way the work of Nobel Laureates Gary Becker, Amarty Sen, Douglass North, and James Buchanan) and builds bridges between that discourse and other social sciences.

Jerry Evensky is Professor of Economics and Laura J. and L. Douglas Meredith Professor for Teaching Excellence at Syracuse University. He coedited *Adam Smith and the Philosophy of Law and Economics* (1994) with Robin Malloy and is the author of the textbook *Economics: The Ideas, the Issues* (2004). Professor Evensky serves on the editorial board of *The Journal of the History of Economic Thought* and served on the Executive Committee of the History of Economics Society from 1997 to 2000. He has published articles in the *Journal of Economic Perspectives, History of Political Economy, Southern Economic Journal, American Journal of Economics and Sociology, Scottish Journal of Political Economy*, and *Research in the History of Economic Thought and Methodology*.

HISTORICAL PERSPECTIVES ON MODERN ECONOMICS

General Editor: Craufurd D. Goodwin, Duke University

This series contains original works that challenge and enlighten historians of economics. For the profession as a whole, it promotes better understanding of the origin and content of modern economics.

Other books in the series:

William J. Barber *Designs within Disorder: Franklin D. Roosevelt, the Economists, and the Shaping of American Economic Policy, 1933–1945*

William J. Barber *From New Era to New Deal: Herbert Hoover, the Economists, and American Economic Policy, 1921–1933*

M. June Flanders *International Monetary Economics, 1870–1960: Between the Classical and the New Classical*

J. Daniel Hammond *Theory and Measurement: Causality Issues in Milton Friedman's Monetary Economics*

Lars Jonung (ed.) *The Stockholm School of Economics Revisited*

Kyun Kim *Equilibrium Business Cycle Theory in Historical Perspective*

Gerald M. Koot *English Historical Economics, 1870–1926: The Rise of Economic History and Mercantilism*

David Laidler *Fabricating the Keynesian Revolution: Studies of the Inter-War Literature on Money, the Cycle, and Unemployment*

Odd Langholm *The Legacy of Scholasticism in Economic Thought: Antecedents of Choice and Power*

Philip Mirowski *More Heat Than Light: Economics as Social Physics, Physics as Nature's Economics*

Philip Mirowski (ed.) *Nature Images in Economic Thought: "Markets Read in Tooth and Claw"*

Mary S. Morgan *The History of Econometric Ideas*

Takashi Negishi *Economic Theories in a Non-Walrasian Tradition*

Heath Pearson *Origins of Law and Economics: The Economists' New Science of Law, 1830–1930*

Malcolm Rutherford *Institutions in Economics: The Old and the New Institutionalism*

Esther-Mirjam Sent *The Evolving Rationality of Rational Expectations: An Assessment of Thomas Sargent's Achievements*

Yuichi Shionoya *Schumpeter and the Idea of Social Science*

Juan Gabriel Valdés *Pinochet's Economists: The Chicago School of Economics in Chile*

Karen I. Vaughn *Austrian Economics in America: The Migration of a Tradition*

E. Roy Weintraub *Stabilizing Dynamics: Constructing Economic Knowledge*

Adam Smith's Moral Philosophy

A Historical and Contemporary Perspective on Markets, Law, Ethics, and Culture

JERRY EVENSKY

Syracuse University

CAMBRIDGE
UNIVERSITY PRESS

CAMBRIDGE UNIVERSITY PRESS
Cambridge, New York, Melbourne, Madrid, Cape Town, Singapore, São Paulo

Cambridge University Press
32 Avenue of the Americas, New York, NY 10013-2473, USA

www.cambridge.org
Information on this title: www.cambridge.org/9780521852470

First published 2005
Reprinted 2006 (twice)
First paperback edition 2007

Printed in the United States of America

A catalog record for this publication is available from the British Library.

Library of Congress Cataloging in Publication Data

Evensky, Jerry, 1948-
Adam Smith's moral philosophy / Jerry Evensky.
p. cm
Includes bibliographical references and index.
ISBN 0-521-85247-1 (hardcover)
1. Smith, Adam, 1723–1790. 2. Economics–Moral and ethical aspects. 3. Ethics.
4. Teleology. 5. Equality. 6. Smith, Adam, 1723–1790. Inquiry into the nature and
causes of the wealth of nations. 7. Smith, Adam, 1723–1790. Theory of moral sentiments.
8. Smith, Adam, 1723–1790–Criticism and interpretation. I. Title.
HB103.S6E93 2005
174′.4–dc22   2004030655

ISBN   978-0-521-85247-0 hardback
ISBN   978-0-521-70386-4 paperback

For Celia, Abby, and Jesse ... with love.

Contents

Preface

The realization of this book has been a long labor of love.

I began this research program in a graduate History of Economic Thought class taught at Syracuse University by Jesse Burkhead. Our interest piqued, Jesse offered a sequel to a small group of us. In that latter class, I focused on Adam Smith. I read, reflected, wrote, and through that process I began to develop a hypothesis regarding Adam Smith's moral philosophy and its relationship to the modern discourse. My commitment to the project grew and, with Jesse as my advisor, I wrote a dissertation titled "Expanding the neoclassical vision: a proposal for recapturing the lost legacy of Adam Smith."

With that graduate student beginning as a point of departure, my subsequent efforts have involved a constant process of iterative hypothesis development: refining my hypothesis regarding the logic of Smith's moral philosophy on one track, and on another developing my understanding of how that first track informs a constructive critique of the modern discourse in economics and its relationship to the larger domains of social science and social philosophy.

My ideas have evolved as follows. At every stage, I challenged my extant hypothesis regarding Smith's moral philosophy by reading and reflecting, always asking myself: Is it consistent with the original Smith texts, with what I've learned from the secondary literature on Smith, with Smith's historical context? As I challenged my hypothesis, new ideas emerged that changed or complemented that hypothesis.

At each new stage, with a revised hypothesis in mind, I returned to the literature with a new eye to challenge that new hypothesis. Each such iteration of rereading works and expanding the scope of my reading led to a continuous evolution in my thinking. With copious notes in hand, I would synthesize what I had learned from challenging my existing hypothesis and produce an article that almost invariably added new dimensionality and, I believe, more maturity to this evolving hypothesis. These articles would generate critiques from colleagues which, in turn, led to more reading and more reflection. Step by step, article by article, my comfort with my hypotheses regarding the content of Smith's moral philosophy and the relationship of that moral philosophy to the modern discourse has grown.

The year I spent writing this work was an intensely demanding and enjoyable immersion in this process of reading, reflecting, synthesizing, writing, and yet again reading, reflecting, synthesizing, writing, and yet again. . . . I thank Syracuse University for the sabbatical that afforded me the intellectual space to engage in this intensive process.

My goal for that year was to pull together all the pieces of my work along both lines of inquiry, Smith's moral philosophy and its relationship to the modern discourse, in order to produce a synthesis that offers an integrated, holistic representation of Smith's moral philosophy, weaves that analysis into a constructive critique of the modern economics discourse, and builds bridges between that discourse and the other social sciences. I promised myself that I would not submit my manuscript until I was very comfortable with the synthesis I had to offer. When I reached that point I submitted the manuscript. Now you hold the book.

I am responsible for this work, and you will judge to what degree I have achieved my goal. But whatever your judgment, I must acknowledge those who nurtured and encouraged me, and in doing so made it possible for me to produce this work.

First and foremost I must express my appreciation and love for the grandparents I knew and loved, Abe and Yetta Kapelow, and to my parents, Sylvia and Herbert Evensky. They ensured that I had the educational foundation to pursue my dreams and they nurtured me to do so. That alone would be wonderfully good fortune, but I was an especially lucky kid, for I had several families that made me theirs and offered me different dimensions of love and nurturing that have supported me and empowered me.

The Gilmans, the Kops, the Barkoffs, my Cohen cousins, my Uncle Nathan and Aunt Elsie, and the Kapelows . . . from my earliest days each of their homes was my home, each of their families was my family . . . and they still are. Since those days, I've been embraced by and have embraced more families that have enriched my life: the Frickes, the Fishers, the Trujillos, the Moiseyevs, the Franeys, the Robertsons, the O'Connors, the

El Hassan/McIntyres, the Kamps, the Jenkins, the Janks, the Hymans, the Malloys.

Along the way, I've had teachers and mentors who believed in me, cared for me, pushed me, and opened windows in my mind: Herbert Behrend, Margaret Grout, Norris K. Smith, Trout Rader, Lewis Hoffman, Max Wolfrum, Don Phares, Jerry Miner, Larry Samuelson, A. Dale Tussing, Bob Wolfson, Bill Stinchcombe. And of course there are the dear family, friends, and colleagues who have kept me smiling with the good times we share and have inspired me by their goodness and their good work: My brother and sister – Harold and Barbee – Martin Gilman, Rupert Barkoff, John Kops, and Charlie Carrera have been there for me since childhood. Bill Fricke became a dear friend in college. Since college, I've been blessed by sharing my path with Tom Franey, Vron Murphy, Jean LeLoup, Agnes Gregg, Paul O'Connor, Hussein Mirghani, Mazen Elhassan, Jeanne Hossenlopp, Barry Berg, Bob Diamond, Dee Ficarro, Don Dutkowsky, Robin Malloy, Jay Meacham, Joe Mercurio, Frank Wilbur, Jerry Edmonds, Robert Rubinstein, Mariana Lebron, the wonderful Syracuse University Project Advance teachers with whom I work, the ever helpful and caring Economics Department staff, my dear friends in the History of Economics Society with whom I enjoy a rendezvous once a year – Bert Barreto, Ross Emmett, Sherry Kasper, Neil Skaggs, Bo Sockwell, and many more wonderful HES colleagues including some thanked below for their specific help on this project – and, last but not least, the very nice women who greeted me in the Schine Student Center cafeteria each morning before I headed off to the library to work . . . with a smile, a kind word, and a cup of coffee.

Several people have been especially instrumental in helping me as I've developed my ideas for this work. I'm responsible for the ideas, but the support, encouragement, and invaluable feedback of these people have allowed me to realize this presentation of those ideas. First and foremost among these special people is Jesse Burkhead.

Jess was first my teacher, then my mentor, and finally my friend. He has passed away, but in his day he was everything I believe a scholar, in the finest sense of the word, should be: ever willing to learn, always wanting to learn, careful when he wrote, caring when he dealt with people, committed to making a contribution that made life better for the many, and committed to the integrity that makes life and liberty secure for all. As a scholar he is my role model.

Bob Heilbroner reviewed the first piece I ever submitted on Adam Smith. I know this because he allowed the editor to send me the full letter with his review, including his signature. Chutzpah demanded that I follow up, so I wrote to him thanking him for his valuable comments and asking a few questions. So began the many years of support and encouragement he offered me. I only met Bob once, briefly, in person. But the correspondence we shared allowed me to come to know him as a good and caring person, and an incredibly insightful scholar.

Warren Samuels has pushed and prodded and opened up opportunities to countless aspiring scholars. I am blessed to be in that number. Many years ago, when I wrote a lengthy commentary on a book for one of Warren's countless edited editions, after reviewing my draft he wrote me back with a very short charge: "Where's the Evensky in all of this?" That had a liberating effect on my mind. Warren invited me to find my own voice and I loved it. When I began my year of writing this work, the first person I turned to for feedback was Warren. He responded, and responded, and responded to countless queries on my part. I am deeply indebted to him for helping me get this project well underway.

In the course of developing this work, I've asked many folks for feedback and suggestions and I've benefited very much from the help I've received. A few of those whose feedback has been particularly valuable include: James Buchanan, Jerry Kelly, Avi Cohen, Robin Malloy, Edward Harpham, Leon Montes, Glenn Hueckel, Jeff Young, and James Alvey. I am also grateful for the excellent guidance I received from three anonymous reviewers.

Finally, I want to say a word about two editors with whom I've had the pleasure to deal in the course of this project.

Craufurd Goodwin is the editor of the journal *History of Political Economy* and is also the series editor for this book at Cambridge University Press. Most of my Smith work was developed in a series of articles in *HOPE*, so over the years I've had many an opportunity to interact with Craufurd as an editor. I cannot imagine a better person for that job.

Craufurd is the first and only editor of *HOPE*. Over the years, he has made the journal a treasure for those of us who choose to explore this dimension of ideas. His constant commitment to quality and care has earned *HOPE* the highest respect across the economics profession. Thus, he has built and sustained a respected outlet for our work in that realm of ideas. And as an added benefit for all of us, he's done this service with a wonderful wit and a ready warmth that makes it a pleasure to work with him.

Scott Parris is the Senior Editor for Economics and Finance at Cambridge University Press, Americas Region. I've known Scott for more than ten years. Many years ago, I told him of my planned project, and in an annual rite of early summer at each year's History of Economics Society Conference he would kindly ask me, "So how's the project coming, Jerry?" To which I would reply, in understatement, "Slow but sure."

When, finally, I had the prospect of a manuscript the following year, Scott gave me invaluable advice on how to think about the flow of my presentation vis-à-vis potential audiences and, given that a Cambridge acceptance was by definition a challenging prospect, he gave me advice on other houses to which I might consider submitting my manuscript. At every step of this process, Scott has been the consummate professional, and a kind and caring human being. It has been and remains a real delight to work with him.

Most of what you have here is new, but there are pieces from earlier work embedded in this work. I thank the journals *History of Political Economy* and the *Southern Economic Journal* for permission to use pieces from articles that previously appeared in those journals, and similarly I thank Kluwer Academic Publishers for permission to use pieces from a chapter I wrote for a book I co-edited with Robin Malloy. Chapter 10 is closely drawn from an article in the *Journal of Economic Education*. I thank the *JEE* for permission to use that piece.

Adam Smith's Moral Philosophy

PART ONE

ON ADAM SMITH'S MORAL
PHILOSOPHICAL VISION

ONE

Adam Smith's Vision

Imagination is more important than knowledge.

Albert Einstein

Philosophy is the science of the connecting principles of nature. Nature, after the largest experience that common observation can acquire, seems to abound with events which appear solitary and incoherent with all that go before them, which therefore disturb the easy movement of the imagination . . . Philosophy, by representing the invisible chains which bind together all these disjointed objects, endeavours to introduce order into this chaos of jarring and discordant appearances, to allay the tumult of the imagination, and to restore it, when it surveys the great revolutions of the universe, to that tone of tranquility and composure, which is both most agreeable in itself, and most suitable to its nature. Philosophy, therefore, may be regarded as one of those arts which addresses themselves to the imagination. . . .

Adam Smith
"History of Astronomy"

IMAGINATION, THE INVISIBLE HAND, AND PHILOSOPHY

Imagine that there is an order to the universe, an order that is the work of a deity as designer. Imagine further that somewhere beyond our sight that deity has a drafting table and on that table are the blueprints for that design. Those imagined blueprints are invisible to us, and so too the hand that drew them.

That hand is the invisible hand of Adam Smith's moral philosophy.

Smith uses the invisible hand image three times in his works. The first, in the "History of Astronomy," (hereafter, *HA*) refers to "the invisible

3

hand of Jupiter" (*HA*, 49), a clear connection between the image and a deity. However, this is a micro-managing deity of superstition. Smith's deity is a designer. His second and third usages of the invisible hand image (*The Theory of Moral Sentiments [TMS]*, 184; *An Inquiry into the Nature and Causes of the Wealth of Nations [WN]*, 456) reflect the power of that deity's design to guide the ultimate course of human events through, but independent of, humans' intentions.

Smith believes we can only imagine the invisible connecting principles designed by this hand. We cannot know them. His objective as a moral philosopher is to represent what he imagines these invisible principles to be, and to do so in a way that is persuasive to a thoughtful and observant spectator of human events and is instructive to the noble leader who seeks to contribute to humankind's progress. His system of moral philosophy is meant to be a guide, not a mandate. He would reject as insolent arrogance the assertion of anyone who claimed to know the design and to act on that knowledge with the self-assurance that he acts on behalf of the deity.[1]

Smith's analysis of the role of philosophy in humankind begins with the premise that although we cannot know the design, we do take comfort in the notion that there is a design, an order to our world. A child takes pleasure in offering a simple taxonomy of appearances "when it . . . ascertains to which of the two . . . classes of objects a particular impression ought to be referred; to the class of realities . . . which is (sic) calls *things*, or to that of appearances which it calls *nothings*" (*HA*, 38, emphasis in original). Adults do the same thing with the same purpose, but with more sophistication. "[W]hen something quite new and singular is presented [to us] . . . What sort of a thing can this be? What is that like? are the questions which . . . we are all naturally disposed to ask" (*HA*, 39). We do so out of a desire to "introduce order into this chaos of jarring and discordant appearances" (*HA*, 45–6).

As it is with the singular, so it is with "a succession of objects" or events (*HA*, 40). While we cannot observe the invisible connecting chain that gives rise to the succession we see, we are comforted when, through our imagination, we can conceive of principles that "seem" (*HA*, 41) to explain the order of the events we observe.

---

[1] Smith believes in the deity as designer but not in the "design argument" (Smith, Norris Kemp, 44): natural order as scientific proof of a deity. His belief is a matter of faith, not proof (more on this subsequently and in Chapter Four). In a eulogy to his father, Ron Reagan, Jr. offered a distinction that would suit Smith. Reagan, Jr. asserted that for his father, faith was "a responsibility, not a mandate. And there is a profound difference" (Reagan, 2004).

Customary successions are inherently comforting because such connections are easy to conceive:

There is no break, no stop, no gap, no interval. The ideas excited by so coherent a chain of things seem, as it were, to float through the mind of their own accord, without obliging it to exert itself.... (*HA*, 41)

Smith cites as an example of such thinking

the artisan [(e.g., "dyers, brewers, distillers") who] cannot conceive what occasion there is for any connecting events to unite those appearances ["to us very strange and wonderful"], which seem to him to succeed each other very naturally. It is their nature, he tells us, to follow one another in this order. In the same manner bread has, since the world began, been the common nourishment of the human body, and men have so long seen it, every day, converted into flesh and bones, substances in all respects so unlike it, that they have seldom had the curiosity to inquire by what process of intermediate events this change is brought about. (*HA*, 44)

It is the philosopher who, spurred by "anxious curiosity" (*HA*, 40), explores the invisible connecting chains that form those links that others take for granted.

[A] philosopher, who has spent his whole life in the study of the connecting principles of nature, will often feel an interval betwixt two objects, which, to more careless observers, seem very strictly conjoined. By long attention to all the connections which have ever been presented to his observation ... [the philosopher] has, like the musician, acquired, if one may say so, a nicer ear, and a more delicate feeling with regard to things of this nature. (*HA*, 45)

Adam Smith was a moral philosopher and, as Isaac Newton had done for natural philosophy, so Smith sought to do for moral philosophy: to imagine and represent those invisible connecting principles designed by the deity that determine the course of nature. Newton's natural philosophical realm encompassed all in nature that envelopes humankind. Smith's moral philosophical realm was humankind.

As philosophers who shared a belief in the deity as designer, both Newton and Smith faced the same challenge: How do we see into that windowless workshop of the designer? How do we know the design without access to the blueprints? As Smith writes:

Who wonders at the machinery of the opera-house who has once been admitted behind the scenes? In the Wonders of nature, however, it rarely happens that we can discover so clearly this connecting chain. With regard to a few even of them, indeed, we seem to have been really admitted behind the scenes.... (*HA*, 42–3)[2]

---

[2] Smith writes of "the various appearances which the great machine of the universe is perpetually exhibiting, with the secret wheels and springs which produce them...." (*TMS*, 19).

Nature's "Truth" lies "behind the scenes." No philosopher has the privilege, as an opera patron might, of going behind the scenes to observe
those "concealed connections" (*HA*, 51). No philosopher can see what
the invisible hand has drawn on those inaccessible blueprints. But while
Smith knows he cannot "see" the invisible, he believes he can imagine
it.[3] Based on what he can see, the visible effects from the work of that
invisible hand, he imagines the connecting principles of the design and
represents them.

Smith appreciates that he is not describing Truth, but rather he is offering his best approximation of what he imagines Truth to be. Even the
work of Sir Isaac Newton, whom Smith admires as the greatest philosopher of all time, is, in Smith's opinion, a representation, not a Truth. In
the closing paragraph of his "History of Astronomy," after expressing his
awe at Newton's accomplishments, Smith reminds us:

And even we, while we have been endeavouring to represent all philosophical
systems as mere inventions of the imagination ... have insensibly been drawn in,
to make use of language[4] expressing the connecting principles of this one, *as if*
they were the real chains which Nature makes use of to bind together her several
operations. (*HA*, 105, emphasis added)[5]

Not even Newton had found a window into the workshop of the deity.

Philosophy ... [only] *pretends* to lay open the concealed connections that unite
the various appearances of nature. (*HA*, 51, emphasis added)

---

[3] Lovejoy quotes Voltaire: "'the imagination takes pleasure in seeing....'" (Lovejoy, 252).

[4] On language and imagination in Smith evolutionary analysis: "Smith in 'Considerations
[Concerning the First Formation of Languages]' describes the evolution of language along
a line from particularity to generality, from simplicity to complexity, and from concreteness
to abstraction ... [and] language, as he sees it, ... must be taken as the starting point in
any analysis either of concrete or ideological phenomena. The analysis of language must
be undertaken in order to perceive the connection between a developing language and
the progress of society, for he assumes that they are related.... The power of language
to propel science and society, whose progress depends on science, is ultimately based on
man's ability to generalize [an act of imagination]. This capacity, in turn, is a gift that
the developed language bestows on its users.... The sign of relation is the preposition,
he notes, whose invention follows upon man's attainment of a relatively high capacity
for abstract thinking. By this extraordinary device we are enabled to express general
and abstract connections between substantive events or objects. Empiricist that he is, he
is most careful to observe that the connections themselves are never and can never be
directly perceived: '... relations never are the ... objects of our external senses.' He has
the extraordinary sophistication to see that it is the signs of the relations, and the signs
only, that are sensed directly" (Becker, J., 15–6).

[5] "While Smith wrote with real enthusiasm about Newton's contribution ... [he took] the
bold and novel step, in an age dominated by Newton, of reminding his readers that the
content of that system was not necessarily 'true'" (Skinner, 1979, 32, 36).

The difference between the stories of superstition and the representations of philosophy lies not in the distinction between fiction and truth. Neither represents Truth with a capital T. Both are fiction, both are products of the imagination. The difference lies in how the imagination forms the stories to be told.

The stories of superstition are *ad hoc*, a new piece (e.g., a new god) added whenever there is an apparent anomaly to be explained, and they are often designed to be fantastic in order to intimidate others into belief. The representations of philosophy are based on rich, systematic observation in search of patterns that may approximate the invisible connecting principles. A philosophical analysis that can represent the observed patterns in a familiar, elegant and simple way is compelling to Smith because it meets his standard of philosophical excellence: It is persuasive to a well-educated, open mind.[6]

FROM NATURAL TO MORAL PHILOSOPHY

Smith is a proud disciple of Newton, but he appreciates that there is a significant difference between Newton's natural and his moral philosophical enterprise. This derives from a fundamental difference between the human condition and the natural world that surrounds it.

---

[6] "Smith argued that a system of thought will only prove acceptable [persuasion is the standard] if it is capable of providing a coherent account of *observed* appearances (thus soothing the imagination), and in so far as the principles on which it relies are *plausible*" (Skinner, 1972, 310, emphasis in original) and reflect "simplicity" (Skinner, 1972, 312). "The desire of being believed, the desire of persuading, of leading and directing other people, seems to be one of the strongest of all our natural desires. It is, perhaps, the instinct upon which is founded the faculty of speech, the characteristical faculty of human nature. No other animal possesses this faculty, and we cannot discover in any other animal any desire to lead and direct the judgment and conduct of its fellows" (*TMS*, 336).

Smith believed that demonstrating probability is key to persuasion. In describing the theory of sound, for example, he writes that "[t]here are not many philosophical doctrines, perhaps, established upon a more probable foundation.... [And] this great probability is still further confirmed by the computations of Sir Isaac Newton ... (Of the External Senses, 147). In a moral philosophical context, rejecting Mandeville, he writes that "[t]hese, ["appearances in human nature"] described and exaggerated by the lively and humorous, though coarse and rustic eloquence of Dr. Mandeville, have thrown upon his doctrines an air of truth and probability which is very apt to impose upon the unskillful" (*TMS*, 308). This last point brings us to the issue of audience. Smith believed that, for a philosopher, the most significant audience is composed of those who possess "superior reason and understanding, by which ... [they] are capable of discerning the remote consequences of ... actions, and of foreseeing the advantage or detriment which is likely to result from them" (*TMS*, 189).

Morrow cites the "empirical persuasive fashion" in which Smith presented his principles (Morrow, 1927, 323).

The subjects of natural philosophy – the planets, the plants, the tides, and so on – these things do not imagine or reason, they simply follow the design of nature. Not so the subjects of moral philosophy; humans imagine, they reason, *and* they suffer "human frailty" (*Correspondence*, 221).[7] That "frailty" makes humankind unique in nature. We are the unnatural dimension of nature. Our vices can distort the "regular and harmonious movements" of the design:[8]

Human society, when we contemplate it in a certain abstract and philosophical light, appears like a great, an immense machine, whose regular and harmonious movements produce a thousand agreeable effects. As in any other beautiful and noble machine that was the production of human art, whatever tended to render its movements more smooth and easy, would derive a beauty from this effect, and, on the contrary, whatever tended to obstruct them would displease upon that account: so virtue, which is, as it were, the fine polish to the wheels of society, necessarily pleases; while vice, like the vile rust, which makes them jar and grate upon one another, is as necessarily offensive. (*TMS*, 316)

In Smith's analysis, the nexus of human imagination, reason, and frailty puts humankind in a peculiar and problematic position. Our imagination and reason[9] give us dominion over the earth and the capacity to develop natural resources into wealth far beyond our requirements for survival. But that imagination and reason, when wedded to frailty, also sets the stage for destructive interpersonal conflict when some seek to capture a larger share of the human bounty for themselves.

This dilemma was brought into sharp focus by the moral philosophers of the first ages of liberal society, who, including Smith, struggled with the "cohesion question": If the productive potential of liberal society derives from individuals' freedom to pursue their own interests (the

---

[7] He also refers to "the frailty of human nature" (*LJA*, 36). There are two sets of *Lectures on Jurisprudence* from Adam Smith. The earlier of these is referred to as "Report of 1762-3" and the other as "Report dated 1766". Following standard usage I will reference the first as *LJA* and the second as *LJB*.

[8] While this "noise" adds a dimension of complexity to moral philosophy, there is one sense in which moral philosophy is more likely to be reliable: "A system of natural philosophy may appear very plausible, and be for a long time very generally received in the world, and yet have no foundation in nature, nor any sort of resemblance to the truth. . . . But it is otherwise with systems of moral philosophy, and an author who pretends to account for the origin of our moral sentiments, cannot deceive us so grossly, nor depart so very far from all resemblance to the truth" (*TMS*, 313–14).

[9] "Man has received from the bounty of nature reason and ingenuity, art, contrivan<c>e, and capacity of improvement far superior to that which she has bestowed on any of the other animals, but is at the same time in a much more helpless and destitute condition with regard to the support and comfort of his life" (*LJA*, 334).

Physiocrats' "laissez-faire"), how can such a society avoid a Hobbesian war of all against all?[10] What cohesive force can constrain the destructive dynamic of unbridled self-interest and hold liberal society together so that its potential – a materially satisfactory, secure, tranquil life for each individual and the greatest possible wealth for the nation – can be realized?[11]

In order to answer this question Smith examines the history of humankind.[12] He culls from that history[13] the contours of those invisible connecting principles that have guided humankind through the twists and turns of distortions caused by our frailty, and that guide a more harmonious case where those distortions are diminished.[14] The framework of analysis he develops is evolutionary.[15]

---

[10] How, in modern terminology, does a liberal society avoid degenerating into a "rent-seeking society"? (Buchanan, et al., 1980).

[11] Locke envisioned a social contract. The Physiocrats advocated a "despotisme legal."

[12] "Smith and his contemporaries did not disregard the experience of ages and clearly accepted Aristotle's dictum that we can only understand what presently exists by first considering 'the origins from which it springs'" (Skinner, 1972, 317). "Smith's inclination in the study of any subject was to approach it historically in the first instance and then to form his own ideas from reflections on past history" (Raphael, 1997, 18).

[13] I use the term "cull" here in the same spirit as did Wordsworth in the Prelude, Book XIII, where he wrote of "wandering on from day to day where I could meditate in peace, and cull knowledge that step by step might lead me on to wisdom...." (Wordsworth, 248).

[14] Muller describes Smith's use of history to imagine this dynamic very nicely. He writes that Smith's method "entailed an inductive attempt to discover regularities in social life through observation and comparison, for which history provided much of the raw data. Finally, it called for an examination of the ways in which human propensities were shaped and molded into particular character types by historically changing social, political, and economic structures" (Muller, 1993, 48–9). "While Smith explored the more or less constant passions of the individual, he was more concerned with the degree to which historically developed institutions channel those passions in directions which are morally desirable and adapted for social survival" (Muller, 1993, 115).

[15] It is important to distinguish humankind's evolution from human evolution. The former is about societal constructs and their "organic" change, whereas the latter is about the change in the human organism. Smith does not ascribe humankind's progress to "better" humans, but to more constructive societal constructs built on the experience and progress of the past. He makes this point with respect to philosophers when he asserts "Let us not despise those ancient philosophers...[who held what we consider immature ideas. We have] no superior sagacity," just the advantage of time and chance (*History of Ancient Physics*, 109). In what follows, when I use the term "more mature" I mean it in that sense of more developed based on the advantages of time.

For Smith, human nature is universal and constant. Smith writes: "Man is perpetually changing every particle of his body; and every thought in his mind is in continual flux and succession. But humanity, or human nature, is always existent, is always, the same...." (*History of Ancient Logics and Metaphysics*, 121).

HUMANKIND'S EVOLUTION

Humankind has been evolving, according to Smith,[16] through stages. This process began in a rude state of human existence and has progressed from that rude state of hunting and gathering through stages of pasturage and agriculture to commerce.[17] This progress from stage to stage occurs because there is an intrasocietal dynamic that generates change within a society, and an intersocietal process of natural selection at work.

Intrasocietal change is driven by human imagination and reason. These give individuals the power to intentionally or unintentionally affect their inherited social construction. These choices, along with chance and

---

[16] "Smith has an evolutionary view of history and economic and political development" (Werhane, 50). Skinner writes that "[a]s Lester Crocker put it: 'The rise of relativism in ethics and social thought as evidenced in the writings of Montesquieu, Diderot and others, is a complementary part of a general evolutionist view of the universe, which embraced the cosmos, life, and societies.' Smith's interest in the general problem of historical change was clearly not a peculiarly Scottish phenomenon" (Skinner, 1975B, 172). Lovejoy notes that "the general notion ... of an evolutionary advance ... was becoming familiar in very widely read writings before the middle of the eighteenth century. ... In, roughly, the third quarter of the [eighteenth] century theories which may, in a broad sense, be called evolutionistic multiplied" (Lovejoy, 262, 268). Griswold cites Edward "Gibbon['s ...] tribute to Smith's work on the evolution of society. ..." (Griswold, 1999, 7–8) Charles Clark identifies an evolutionary dimension in Smith's work, but then asserts that "Smith's natural law preconceptions ... ultimately tie him down to a static theory" (Clark, 839). I disagree.

[17] "Within Scotland there were regions at very different stages of social and economic development, creating what one scholar has described as a 'social museum at Edinburgh's back door.' ... With such a multiplicity of political, economic, and social forms so close at hand, it is no wonder that Scottish intellectuals in Edinburgh and Glasgow were given to reflecting on the 'stages' of society and the role of government and commerce in the movement from one stage to another" (Muller, 1993, 22, 23). "Meek, 1976, remains a valuable study of four-stages theory, but is flawed by an overlong search for the first appearance of the theory in its most developed form. It is now recognized that various versions of the stadial sequence were common property among European scholars, and were developed by various authors in various ways" (Pocock, 1999, 315).

Meek considers it, as the names of the stages imply, a materialist history (Meek, 1976, 242). Richard Teichgraeber rejects this materialist interpretation, writing that "[s]urely the point of this entire line of inquiry [Smith's "four stages scheme" (Teichgraeber, 143)] is missed if we represent the arguments as parts of a materialist view of history. Smith's main concern was not to grasp a story whose underlying factors are predominately economic. It was, instead, to furnish his students with an answer to the philosophical question of how human sentiments come to shape our understanding of the purpose of law and government" (Teichgraeber, 144). Winch, after exploring all the twists and turns in Smith's stages, writes that "the whole unlinear stadial sequence begins to seem highly contingent on circumstances that are by no means traceable merely to economic causes" (Winch, 1983, 258–9). I generally agree with Teichgraeber and with Winch. To ascribe either a materialist or jurisprudential purpose to the four stages analysis is to miss Smith's purpose in using it as frame for analysis. As we will see, his representation is of a simultaneous system in which social, political, and economic dimensions evolve interdependently, with no one dimension being deterministic.

circumstance, determine the course of a society's changes. As more mature, productive social constructs emerge, these more mature constructs have the capacity, *ceteris paribus*, to be stronger than less mature constructions (e.g., *ceteris paribus*, pastoral societies have the means to dominate hunting and gathering societies, agricultural to dominate pastoral, and commercial to dominate agricultural). Thus there is a natural selection bias among humankind's societies toward increasing maturity in social constructions.

Evolution and natural selection are terms used in many domains, so before proceeding it is important to distinguish Smith's analysis of natural selection and evolution through stages from some other versions of natural selection/evolution and stages analysis – specifically Herbert Spencer, Charles Darwin, and Karl Marx.

With respect to Spencer, Smith's analysis is different because it is not a story of genetic superiority or of elites as representative of what is best in humankind.[18] Quite to the contrary, although elites can, and often do, play an instrumentally valuable role in Smith's analysis, they are not "superior" in any metaphysical sense. Smith believes that all human beings are made of the same "coarse clay" (*TMS*, 162). For Smith the ultimate measure of a society's progress is not to be found in the wealth of the elite, but rather in the well being of the least among the working class.

With respect to Darwin, Smith's analysis of natural selection is different in two significant ways.

- Darwin's biological evolution is not a function of the choices made by the members of the species involved. Smith's evolution of humankind is. Chapter Two describes the co-evolution of individual and society, a process in which the individual is initially socially constructed, but then as that individual grows, his unique biography,[19] his imagination, and his reason combine and empower him to conceptualize changes that reshape, intentionally or unintentionally, the social construction that initially shaped him.

---

[18] Social Darwinism "presupposes natural inequalities among individuals, which result in a stratified social organization which is also 'natural.' If moral attributes are biological facts and if the measure of morality is the control of property, then it is 'natural' that propertied individuals should exist at the expense of the propertyless; further, the social structure must be stratified according to 'natural' principles. Since inheritance does not involve variation, it follows that in a 'natural' and therefore, presumably good society, the system of social stratification should be perpetuated" (Tax and Krucoff, 404).

[19] "It is because he is a member of many ... groups that the complexity of the individual's life arises, for countless combinations of sympathies may be influencing him at any given moment" (Morrow, 1923, 56).

- Darwinian biological natural selection is about *divergence*. There is increasing biodiversity as new species fill ever-finer niches in the biosphere. Smith's societal natural selection is about *convergence*. He envisions humankind as moving through stages toward a single social construction. In this respect Smith's analysis is similar to Marx's.

In Marx, there is an inherent conflict, and thus an internal contradiction, in any mode of production that is structured on social relations that include an unproductive class that controls the means of production and a productive class that provides the labor for production. This contradiction gives rise to quantitative changes that ultimately resolve themselves as a qualitative change – a transformation into a new mode of production. Each new mode (e.g., feudalism, slavery, capitalism) embodies a new, albeit different, contradiction so long as the new social relations still embody a class conflict.

In Marx, convergence is realized at the end of the capitalist mode, when the internal contradiction, the opposition between the capitalists and the working class, is resolved into a classless society. With sweet irony Marx sees this resolution as inherent in the concentration of capital that is inevitable in the capitalist mode. Hand in hand with this concentration of capital goes the increasing organization of the working class, and that organization becomes the key to revolution:

The advance of industry, whose involuntary promoter is the bourgeoisie, replaces the isolation of the labourers, due to competition, by their revolutionary combination, due to association.... What the bourgeoisie, therefore, produces, above all, are its own grave-diggers. Its fall and the victory of the proletariat are equally inevitable ... (Marx, 715, fn.1, quotation cited from "Manifest der Kommunistischen Partei")

Marx's materialist philosophy tells a story of history that converges toward a classless communism. Smith's story of history is also convergent, but the destination he envisions is very different.

ON EVOLUTIONARY CONVERGENCE: THE LIBERAL PLAN
AS THE HUMAN PROSPECT

Smith imagines humankind's progress through stages as converging on an ideal limiting case[20]: "the liberal plan of equality, liberty and justice" (*WN*, 664).

---

[20] One hears Smith's conception of an evolution that allows humans to approach an ideal as limit in spite of their frailty in his eulogy for his dearest friend David Hume: "Thus

For Smith this ideal society is one in which the least of the working class are "tolerably well fed, clothed, and lodged":[21]

Servants, labourers, and workmen of different kinds, make up the far greater part of every great political society. But what improves the circumstances of the greater part can never be regarded as an inconveniency to the whole. No society can surely be flourishing and happy, of which the far greater part of the members are poor and miserable. It is but equity, besides, that they who feed, clothe, and lodge the whole body of the people, should have such a share of the produce of their own labour as to be themselves tolerably well fed, clothed, and lodged. (*WN*, 96)

Smith believes that the liberal plan is the best constitution for the working class because it produces the greatest wealth for the nation and distributes that wealth most justly. That plan is the most materially productive because the freedom and security it affords each individual encourages the most productive use of resources. As every resource holder allocates his labor and stock to the most advantageous option, all are

---

died our most excellent, and never to be forgotten friend. . . . Upon the whole, I have always considered him, both in his lifetime and since his death, as approaching as nearly to the idea of a perfectly wise and virtuous man, as perhaps the nature of human frailty will permit" (Correspondence, 221). As Hume the individual, his human frailty notwithstanding, could approach the ideal limiting case of the perfectly wise and virtuous man; so too, Smith believed, humankind as a whole could approach an ideal limiting case.

[21] Haakonssen cites Smith's concern for "poor people in any society" (Haakonssen, 1981, 141). Griswold writes that "[h]is outlook encompasses a passionate commitment to commutative justice and to the betterment of the lot of the ordinary person" (Griswold, 1999, 360). Muller writes that "Smith was less concerned with the welfare of the social and political elite than with the welfare – both material and moral – of the vast majority of society" (Muller, 1993, 8). Young asserts that "in more than one place Smith virtually equates the common good with the welfare of the lowest members of society" (Young, 165). From Sowell, we read that "Adam Smith . . . invariably sided with the 'underdogs' whenever he took sides between rich and poor, between businessmen and their employees, or between masters and their slaves" (Sowell, 3). Winch: "[T]he advance of civilization goes hand in hand with an improvement in the standard of material comfort enjoyed by the labouring classes, who comprise the bulk of society. Smith explicitly stated that such standards, and not merely rising *per capita* incomes, were the most appropriate measure of economic welfare" (Winch, 1978, 87). It should be noted that Smith is keenly aware of the potential for technical advancement in production to numb the mind of workers: "In the progress of the division of labour, the employment of the far greater part of those who live by labour . . . comes to be confined to a few very simple operations. . . . He naturally looses, therefore, the habit of such exertion, and generally becomes as stupid and ignorant as it is possible for a human creature to become. . . . [I]n every improved and civilized society this is the state into which the labouring poor, that is, the great body of the people, must necessarily fall, *unless government takes some pains to prevent it* (*WN*, 781–2, emphasis added). In Chapter Nine, we will see how Smith recommends government address this issue.

engaged in a competition for opportunities that eliminates advantages and requires efficiency for survival:

The whole of the advantages and disadvantages of the different employments of labour and stock must, in the same neighbourhood, be either perfectly equal or continually tending to equality. If in the same neighbourhood, there was any employment evidently either more or less advantageous than the rest, so many people would crowd into it in the one case, and so many would desert it in the other, that its advantages would soon return to the level of other employments. This at least would be the case in a society where things were left to follow their natural course, where there was *perfect liberty*, and where every man was perfectly free both to choose what occupation he thought proper, and to change it as often as he thought proper. Every man's interest would prompt him to seek the advantageous, and to shun the disadvantageous employment. (*WN*, 116, emphasis added)

The competition among workers is most keen under this plan because workers are most free and independent, and for Smith independence is a key to human dignity and personal maturity.[22] So too, the competition among capitals is most keen under this plan, and that competition, according to Smith, generates a distribution that allows workers to be "tolerably well fed, clothed, and lodged."

As will be described in Chapter Six, when capital is flowing in this secure world of "perfect liberty," it returns from every circuit of its flow expanded. Thus, the continuing circulation of capital creates an ever-deepening pool of capital that competes for labor. As a consequence, in the perfectly competitive markets of the liberal plan wages rise, and the rate of profit falls until it just covers the cost of superintendence.[23] In short, Smith believes that under the liberal plan, the least among the working class will do best, and the distance from top to bottom will be diminished.

However, it is not the freedom or the independency or the material fruits of the liberal plan that Smith values most. These are instrumental in approaching the ideal limiting case that he envisions:[24] a society in which

---

[22] "Nothing tends so much to corrupt and enervate and debase the mind as dependency, and nothing gives such noble and generous notions of probity as freedom and independency. Commerce is one great preventative of this custom," "the custom of having many retainers and dependents" (*LJA*, 333).

[23] In which case very few could live off accumulated capital. More on this in Chapters Six and Twelve.

[24] Smith's view of material goods relates closely to Sen's concept of capability: "If we value the capability to function, then that is what we do value, and the possession of goods with the corresponding characteristics [that allow us to function] is only instrumentally valued and that again only to the extent that it helps in the achievement of the things that we

all citizens have the opportunity to enjoy a life of "secure tranquility" (*TMS*, 215).

Tranquility represents, for Smith, peace of mind, "that equal and happy temper, which is so necessary to self-satisfaction and enjoyment" (*TMS*, 23).

One can suffer physical deprivation or even harm and still enjoy tranquility. Smith cites, for example, the "savages in North America" and the "negro[s] from the coast of Africa" who suffer the tortures and indignities of their oppressors with a "magnanimity and self-command . . . [that] are almost beyond the conception of Europeans" (*TMS*, 206). However, the ideal of human life is not tranquility in the face of oppression, it is secure tranquility, that peace of mind that one enjoys along with peace of body. The latter does not require wealth, only a sufficient subsistence for a satisfactory existence.[25]

In the most glittering and exalted situation that our idle fancy can hold out to us, the pleasures from which we propose to derive our real happiness, are almost always the same with those which, in our actual, though humble station, we have at all times at hand, and in our power. Except the frivolous pleasures of vanity and superiority, we may find, in the most humble station, *where there is only personal liberty*, every other which the most exalted can afford; and the pleasures of vanity and superiority are seldom consistent with perfect tranquility, the principle and foundation of all real and satisfactory enjoyment. (*TMS*, 150, emphasis added)

Smith fully appreciates that the liberal plan and the secure tranquility it can afford individuals is a limiting case that can never be fully achieved, but he believes that this ideal can be ever more closely approximated. The raison d'e'tre of his moral philosophy is therefore

- to lay out his vision of the ideal, and
- to persuade his readers
  - that this is an ideal that humankind can approximate,
  - that his moral philosophical system represents the contours of the

do value (viz. capabilities)" (Sen, 1984, 85). Sen notes: "I am not under any illusion that the capability approach to the standard of living would be very easy to use" (Sen, 1984, 87). Smith would certainly agree. Indeed, for Smith the well being of the least among the working class is a gross standard by which to measure a society's position in the course of humankind's progress. *Ceteris paribus*, by this standard, if it appears that the least among the working class are afforded a better standard of living, this is *prima facie* evidence that that society represents progress in the evolution of humankind.

[25] "The whole benefit of wea<l>th and industry is that you either employ a greater number or give those already employed a more comfortable subsistence" (*LJA*, 391, notation follows text).

ideal and highlights the obstacles that impede progress toward the ideal, and

- that his system is, therefore, an instructive, worthwhile guide for a public policy aimed at pursuing this ideal.

These goals present Smith with a complex challenge.

SMITH'S CHALLENGE AND THE ROLE OF "THEORETICAL OR CONJECTURAL HISTORY" IN HIS APPROACH

Given his vision of humankind's evolution through a process of natural selection toward a limit, Smith's challenge is twofold.

First, he must identify those natural, general principles that, he imagines, guide progress. This is a daunting task because, given the endless variety of distortions that frailty wedded to imagination and reason makes possible, humankind's evolution unfolds as a multiplicity of natural experiments (societies) simultaneously developing along different paths. These experiments take many peculiar turns due to circumstance, they often intersect and affect one another, and due to our frailties . . . stagnation, decline, and collapse have been the rule. There is no single example that reflects inexorable progress from the origin, so there is no case that clearly and simply represents the general principles that lead to progress.[26]

In order to establish that there are general principles to be found among all the particular cases, Smith looks beyond the experience of any given society and examines the nature of human nature and the flow of humankind's history as a whole. With self-reflection,[27] his own observations, reports of other societies, and the accounts of history as his empirical base, he develops a *ceteris paribus* story of the natural history of humankind

---

[26] "Smith would certainly be skeptical of any straightforward progressivist history . . . [H]istory's 'logic' [is] often opaque . . ." (Griswold, 1999, 353).

[27] " 'Every one is conscious of them in himself; and men's words and actions will satisfy him that they are in others.' [(Locke quoted by Bryson.)] What more indubitable objects of observation could empiricism demand? Here, it seemed to them, was the rock-bottom start for the study of man. As they looked into their own minds and found there ideas of benevolence, fear, vanity, justice, love, as well as ideas conveying information about the physical world; when they saw other people behaving as if they, too, experienced these same ideas and inclinations, it seemed to them that they had discovered not only an observable basis for the science of man, but one so universal that it embraced all the laws of nature at work in and for man. Hence, the organizing principles for making a science of man became for them human nature itself" (Bryson, 18). Sincere thanks to Glenn Hueckel for directing me to this quotation.

and identifies those general principles that he imagines guide humankind's natural progress.[28]

Then, given that "man is naturally disposed to reverse the natural" (Cropsey, 40),[29] Smith applies his general principles to particular cases in history in order to demonstrate that if we adjust for the fact that *ceteris* is never *paribus* and consider the workings of these general principles in the context of particular, distorted circumstances, then these general principles are consistent with all the twists, turns, stagnations, reversals, and collapses of humankind's actual history.

In effect, Smith tells two stories of humankind's history:[30]

- He presents a "theoretical or conjectural history" (Stewart, 293) that describes the undistorted course humankind's evolution would naturally follow according to his principles, and
- He offers an analysis of the course of recorded history explaining why the unnatural twists, turns, stagnations, and declines of societies do not represent violations of his general principles but, rather, reflect peculiar distortions of those principles caused by human frailty. As Smith tells the story, humankind's narrative history reflects his general principles because although individual societies have emerged, stagnated, and declined, the overall flow of humankind's history is consistent with his natural, conjectural story: evolution through four stages and progress toward the limit.

Smith's two histories thus complement one another. His conjectural history demonstrates the power of his principles to explain the broad flow of humankind's evolution,[31] while his analysis of narrative history

---

[28] J. G. A. Pocock writes that the civil jurisprudence tradition of Smith's Scottish intellectual milieu represented "the attempt to establish the principles of social living by empirically establishing the principles of human nature. Since human society could now be studied in much geographical and historical diversity, the way lay increasingly open to studying these principles as manifest in variety, change, process, and even development ... [and so it] became a science of man and society, founded on the unity of human nature in the diversity of human history ..." (Pocock, 1983, 246).

[29] Dugald Stewart, reflecting on Smith's thought in a 1793 biographical essay, wrote: "[P]aradoxical as the proposition may appear, it is certainly true, that the real progress [of human events] is not always the most natural" (Stewart, 296).

[30] "The sequences narrated in conjectural history were deemed to be *typical* [natural], whereas the sequences of narrative documentary history were *unique* and *particular*" (Hopfl, 23, emphasis in original). Hopfl offers a very nice analysis of the role of conjectural history in Smith's analysis.

[31] "Smith took a vast historical sweep and produced a theory (admittedly incomplete) which was designed to give coherence and order to what otherwise appeared as a chaos of unconnected events" (Skinner, 1975B, 168).

demonstrates the power of those same principles to explain peculiar, unnatural events when that analysis is adjusted for the presence of distortions.[32]

Smith employs precisely this "two history" strategy in the first three Books of his *Inquiry into the Nature and Causes of the Wealth of Nations*. Having laid out the general principles that guide the progress of opulence in Books I and II, including the general principle that progress begins in agriculture and proceeds from there to the cities, with commerce then expanding its boundaries; the first chapter of Book III reviews that "natural Progress of Opulence" (*WN*, 376) and then concludes:

> But though this natural order of things must have taken place in some degree in every such society, it has, in all the modern states of Europe, been, in many respects, entirely inverted. The foreign commerce of some of their cities has introduced all their finer manufactures, or such as were fit for distant sale; and manufactures and foreign commerce together have given birth to the principal improvements of agriculture. The manners and customs which the nature of their original government introduced, and which remained after that government was greatly altered, necessarily forced them into this unnatural and retrograde order. (*WN*, 380)

Smith then proceeds in the remainder of *WN* Book III to explain how the oppressive system of feudal government precluded progress in the countryside, while, thanks to the unintended consequences of political maneuvering by kings and cities' leaders,

> [o]rder and good government, and along with them the liberty and security of individuals, were . . . established in cities at a time when the occupiers of land in the country were exposed to every sort of violence. . . . [M]en in this defenceless state naturally content themselves with their necessary subsistence; because to acquire more might only tempt the injustice of their oppressors. On the contrary, when they are secure of enjoying the fruits of their industry, they naturally exert it to better their condition, and to acquire not only the necessaries, but the conveniencies and elegancies of life. That industry, therefore, which aims at something more than necessary subsistence, was established in cities long before it was commonly practised by the occupiers of land in the country. (*WN*, 405)

---

[32] Macfie writes: "To them [the eighteenth century writers including Smith] the history of society was a philosophy of history. They took the view, without questioning it, that a philosophy of society must in method be historical. For societies themselves were natural growths in their own unique environments, and interpreting that growth implied a theory of growth" (Macfie, 14).

This description of the evolution of events in Europe is doubly significant. First it highlights what Smith imagines are the contours of the general principles that lead to the progress: "the liberty and security of individuals." "[T]he liberal plan of equality, liberty and justice" is clearly the natural limiting point of this process. Second it represents a historical narrative in which distortions caused the course of particular events to be very "unnatural and retrograde" and yet, as we will see in Chapter Seven, through a convoluted process, those general principles that lead to the progress - liberty and security – emerged and made progress possible in the countryside as well.

Smith writes his "two histories" story because he believes that if, based on principles that seemed plausible, he can represent the broad flow of human experience as well as the particular experiences of individual societies in a manner that seems persuasive,[33] this will serve to establish the authority of his moral philosophical system as a valuable guide for public policy.[34]

SOME ISSUES IN THE SMITH SCHOLARSHIP

There are two issues in Smith scholarship that it is worthwhile to address at this point because doing so provides a valuable context for what is to come.

- Is there an "Adam Smith Problem"?, and
- Does Smith really believe in a deity?

---

[33] Smith describes a case in law as "gain[ing] a considerable strength by the appearance of probability and connection so that it is difficult afterwards to wrest our belief from them. And by this means tho we can prove but a very small part of the facts yet those which we have proved give the others by the close connection they have with them a great appearance of truth and the whole Story has the appearance, at least, of considerable probability" (*Lectures on Rhetoric and Belles Lettres, hereafter LRBL*, 178). This is very much what he does in his construction of conjectural history.

[34] Apropos of his own approach, Smith writes that: "[t]he design of historicall writing is not merely to entertain; ... besides that it has in view the instruction of the reader. It sets before us the more interesting and important events of human life, points out the causes by which these events were brought about and by this means points out to us by what manner and method we may produce similar good effects or avoid Similar bad ones" (*LRBL*, 90). Later, in the course of describing the evolution of histories, Smith writes that "[t]he Historians again made it their aim not only to amuse but by narrating the more important facts and those which were most concerned in bring about great revolutions, and unfolding their causes, to instruct their readers in what manner such events might be brought about or avoided" (*LRBL*, 111).

Is there an "Adam Smith Problem"?

In his "Historicizing the 'Adam Smith Problem,'" Laurence Dickey (1986) offers an excellent review of the Adam Smith Problem (hereafter ASP) in the literature.[35]

He writes that "the basic contours of the ASP have not really changed since August Oncken gave rather full expression to them in 1898.... In this form, the ASP seems to turn on two issues: the relation between *TMS* (1759) and *WN* (1776), and that of continuity and change in Smith's thought as it developed between the two books" (Dickey, 581–2).

Dickey offers the following taxonomy of Smith scholarship vis-à-vis the ASP:

- "the argument for continuity...
- the argument for change...and
- the argument for continuity and change" (Dickey, 583).

According to Dickey each of these arguments is problematic.

The continuity argument advocated by the Glasgow editors[36] takes the *TMS* as the point of departure for and the constant frame of reference in Smith's analysis. So, to use Dickey's terminology, in this continuity argument the *TMS* is the "motivating center" of Smith's work.[37] Dickey rejects the continuity "treatment of the ASP [because although it explains away any problem, it does so by a strategy that] refused to allow Smith fundamentally to change his mind about things.... [Dickey refers to this as] an unhistorical view of Smith as a thinker" (Dickey, 585).

The argument for change "emphasizes the lack of continuity between *TMS* and *WN*. One of the key spokesmen for this view is [Jacob] Viner" (Dickey, 585). This, the classic ASP argument, asserts that in response to his contact with the Physiocrats the sanguine *TMS* based on "wishful thinking about 'a system of natural liberty,' [gave way to a *WN* in which] Smith posited specific institutional agencies for correcting 'flaws' that developed within the 'system'" (Dickey, 585–6). In this case the *WN* is

---

[35] Montes (2003) offers an excellent history of the ASP.

[36] "The editors' introduction to the Glasgow edition of *TMS* is a fine example of the continuity argument. There are editors insist for several reasons on a basic similarity between *TMS* and *WN*" (Dickey, 583).

[37] Dickey cites "Alec Macfie, one of the Glasgow editors,...[who w]riting elsewhere... claimed that 'it would appear that the *WN* is simply a special case – the economic case – of the philosophy implicit in the *TMS*'" (Dickey, 584). Ergo the *TMS* as motivating center.

the motivating center of Smith's work. Dickey rejects this version of ASP, accepting the Glasgow editors' position that this "change" ASP argument is not consistent with the historical development of Smith's ideas.[38]

The continuity and change argument represented in the work of Fred Hirsch "tries to reconcile these two modes of historiographical discourse ... by accepting the *TMS* and *WN* as 'rival centers of meaning' in Smith's thought" (Dickey, 586). The result is two motivating centers that "are taken as complementary for historical rather than logical reasons" (Dickey, 587). Dickey rejects this as an ad hoc explanation.

Finding all three of these ASP arguments lacking, Dickey offers his own multiple motivating center version of the ASP. It derives from his belief that, contrary to the view of the Glasgow editors,[39] the revisions Smith made to the *TMS* in 1790 are very significant. Based on that assertion Dickey identifies not one, not two, but three motivating centers in Smith's works.

Dickey sees the 1790 revisions to *TMS* as a third motivating center because he believes Smith transforms his thought on prudence in particular and on virtue in general from a self-oriented concept to a civic concept. He suggests that this is motivated by Smith's concern about the "men of "middling virtue['s] ... tendency to opt for selfish 'bourgeois' rather than 'liberal' high minded values" (Dickey, 599).

Dickey does Smith scholarship a great service with his analysis of the 1790 revisions, but I disagree that there is an ASP here. There is a problem and there is a change in Smith, but the problem is not one of consistency in Smith and the change is not in his fundamental frame of analysis, his vision.

The "problem" that motivates the most significant changes in the 1790 *TMS* text is Smith's growing concern that the mercantile interests are controlling government policy, and the change is that Smith moves to a progressively more civic humanist rhetoric of active virtue. It is Smith's constant commitment to his larger vision, the liberal ideal as limit, that

---

[38] "[T]he editors of the Glasgow edition are quick to dismiss it as a problem because there is much evidence to suggest that Smith had already formulated the argument in the *WN* long before his trip to France" (Dickey, 582).

[39] "[T]he editors [of the Glasgow edition of *TMS*] arrive at the following conclusion: 'Smith's account of ethics and human behavior *is basically the same* in edition six of 1790 as in edition one of 1759. There is development but no alteration.' Coming from two fine Smith scholars, this conclusion would seem to be decisive. If, however, one looks closely at the text, it will become apparent that this is clearly not the case" (Dickey, 588, emphasis in original).

motivates him to take on the mercantile system and to adopt the civic humanist language as instrumental in his attack.

There is, as Dickey writes, a "'dramatic action' within the 1790 text," and Dickey is absolutely right that "it is clear from Smith's moral tone ... [that] he is urging upon his reader" a more active virtue (Dickey, 595). His audience is not, however, the "men of 'middling virtue ... [and their] tendency to opt for selfish 'bourgeois' rather than 'liberal' high minded values" (Dickey, 599). His audience is present and future leaders who must live by those "'liberal' high minded values" if they are to resist the power of well financed interests, in this case the mercantile interests, to seduce and/or intimidate them.

Smith delayed the initial publication of the *WN* to address his growing concern with mercantile influence. His language in the 1784 revisions to *WN* represents a much more virulent attack on the mercantile system than the original edition. His 1790 revisions to *TMS* are largely motivated by this deepening concern. Chapter Eight describes this sharpening focus in Smith's work by tracing the evolution of his voice on this issue. But while Smith's voice does evolve in response to the mercantile system, his vision has a constant and coherent logic that is consistent throughout that evolution.[40] In Dickey's terms, Smith's motivating center, his liberal vision, is constant, so by Dickey's standard there is no Adam Smith Problem. That is not to say, however, that there are no problems with Smith's work. There are.

A significant problem is that, given his focus on a sweeping, dynamic natural selection/evolution/limit analysis, he is all too often maddeningly imprecise or sloppy in his use of terms as he represents his vision.[41] However, as Thomas Sowell puts it very nicely:

[Smith] was very consistent in his use of terms throughout any given chain of reasoning, so that his conclusions were unaffected by his inconsistent use of terms between one set of reasoning and another. (Sowell, 11)[42]

---

[40] "My working assumption is that Smith's thought is relatively coherent ..." (Muller, 1993, 9). Citing the "principle of charity," Griswold writes that "I am assuming that Smith's works, whether taken singly or collectively, possesses organic unity" (Griswold, 1999, 26–7) in contrast to Vivian Brown (Griswold, 1999, 27fn40). I follow Griswold and Muller in principle and in the challenge: "[I]t cannot be denied that Smith forces the reader to do the labor of unification" (Griswold, 1999, 30).

[41] "[T]he systematic character of the theory [in *WN*] is a matter of showing connections rather than focusing upon a single explanatory principle ..." (Raphael, 1997, 9–10).

[42] Coats writes that "certain features of Smith's style and mode of presentation make it virtually impossible to determine the precise meaning and significance of his ideas. Among these is the conspicuous lack of that species of small-mindedness which makes a virtue of

The terms Smith uses must always be read relative to their context because he is not always consistent in usage across contexts. What is consistent across contexts is the vision that ties all of the pieces of Smith's analysis together. This consistency relates to his faith in a deity.

Does Smith really believe in a deity?

I began with the assertion that the invisible hand of Adam Smith's moral philosophy is the hand of a deity as designer. D. D. Raphael suggests that although "Smith was probably a deist.... [Nevertheless] Smith's account of natural processes can be read...with no need for an underpinning from theology" (Raphael, 1997, 37), and "Smith's image of the invisible hand is not a piece of theology.... He uses the phrase for vivid effect..." (Raphael, 1997, 66).

I entirely agree with the assertion that the logic of Smith's moral philosophy does not require a deity.[43] And certainly Smith appreciated full well Hume's withering, compelling attack on the design argument in the *Dialogues Concerning Natural Religion*.[44] However, Smith did have faith in a deity[45] and that faith did matter in his moral philosophy.

---

consistency..." (Coats, 218). See also Haakonssen (1981, 123). Sowell adds that "Smith's shifting use of terms provided many pitfalls for later classical writers, but Smith himself did not fall into these pits" (Sowell, 11).

[43] Others have made this same point. Knud Haakonsen suggests that the deity as "'leap-of-faith'" (Haakonssen, 1981, 77) may be Smith's view, but he continues: "The really important thing...is that it is irrelevant whether one wants to take the leap or not as far as moral theory and understanding are concerned. Nothing hinges on teleological explanations and thus on a guarantor of a teleological order." (Haakonssen, 1981, 77) T. D. Campbell writes: "[I]t is possible to remove the theological terminology and Smith's reflections about a benevolent Deity and not affect the empirical content of his work" (Campbell, 1971, 61). Campbell suggests that Smith's analysis of efficient causes is, in effect, independent of his identification of the "teleological" final cause (Campbell, 1971, 70).

[44] Smith was intimately involved in the events that led to its publication (Ross, 338–41), and, as Griswold writes, Smith does not adhere to "the argument from design, whose fallacies Smith had...learned from Hume" (Griswold, 1999, 333).

[45] "Adam Smith's reasons for believing in the reality of this 'natural order' were partly empirical, but mainly, it is safe to say, *a priori*.... The real foundation of Adam Smith's faith in the ultimate harmony of the conflicting interests of individuals is to be found in his theology" (Morrow, 1927, 333). "[W]hile we may admit that Smith's theology led him to expect nature to exhibit the signs of a creator, we should regard his faith as a consequence, and not as a cause, of his study of nature" (Campbell, 1971, 60) He had faith, but consequence or cause? I don't think it's something we can know. What we can say is that it wasn't based on the design argument or on revelation.

For Smith, the prospect of human progress that he envisioned was thanks to the benevolence of that deity, a benevolence reflected in the deity's design:[46]

The happiness of mankind... seems to have been the original purpose intended by the Author of nature... No other end seems worthy of that supreme wisdom and divine benignity which we necessarily ascribe to him.... (*TMS*, 166)[47]

However, this is only a prospect[48] and it is one that is approached more slowly or quickly depending in part on the actions of individual human beings. Superstition, ignorance and faction impede progress. Enlightenment speeds progress.

Smith along with his contemporaries expected the world to become more intelligent, more tolerant, and more humane with the decline of superstition and the advance of knowledge.... Smith was undeniably a 'progressivist'... Yet progress was not automatic. He did not look to Providence for direct aid in the economic and moral improvement of mankind. Man had to act on his own behalf... Smith's own work as economist and philosopher were (sic) intended, most probably, as contributions toward this progress. (Bittermann, 1940B, 733–4)

I, too, believe this was Smith's intention.[49]

Indicative of his commitment to this intention was his long battle against the sophistry of the mercantile interests, described in detail in Chapter Eight. Smith had no financial or reputational need for this effort. When he made his revisions to the *WN* and the *TMS* his income and his reputation were long since secure. His purpose was to expose the

---

[46] Griswold writes of "the Deity, understood [in Smith] as a benevolent designer... Hence natural religion provides us with a holistic context..." (Griswold, 1999, 323). In reflecting on the four stages analysis that he had explored in earlier work, Meek says that "I would now wish to place more emphasis on the important connection between the 'four stages' theory and the concepts of progress and the perfectibility of mankind..." (Meek, 1971, 24). In France, "Bossuet had claimed that although God makes history, He very seldom does this by intervening directly: He would act through 'chains of particular causes' and, as Bossuet put it, 'prepares the effects in the most distant causes'" (Meek, 1971, 26). I would suggest this is Smith's deity.

[47] Notice the use of "seems," Smith does not claim to know but only to imagine the deity's intention.

[48] Smith was optimistic but he was not Voltaire's Candide. David Spadafora's *The Idea of Progress in Eighteenth Century Britain* offers an excellent presentation of this Scottish reasoned hope, which he contrasts with a more romantic British attitude. "[I]f Smith did notice many defects of modern society, and some of the problems which were to arise in the future [as he indeed did!], the general tenor of his argument must be said to be broadly optimistic..." (Skinner, 1975B, 178).

[49] "Smith was not a believer in perfection... What he did believe was that we can always do better..." (Haakonssen, 1981, 97).

sophistry of a system that served no one but those who advocated it, and to appeal to current and future leaders to be models of civic virtue: to see through the sophistry, to rise above the influences and intimidations of faction, and to govern for the good of society as a whole. His motivation was his commitment to humankind's progress, and his belief in the possibility of that progress derived from his faith in a deity.

This connection between Smith's faith in a deity and his hopeful moral philosophy is also reflected in the role of and relationship between justice and instrumental institutions in his work. Anthony Waterman highlights this connection beautifully, as follows:

Every religion that acknowledges a God who is all-powerful, all-wise, all-knowing, and perfectly good faces the so-called problem of evil. How is the abundant evidence of unwilled suffering in sentient beings (physical evil), and of human wickedness and its consequences (moral evil), to be reconciled with the divine attributes? (Why does God allow cancer, war, injustice, and so on?) Answers that diminish any of the attributes are rejected as heterodox.... An inquiry that seeks to demonstrate the possible coexistence of all the divine attributes is known as *theodicy*....

By far the most influential theodicy in the Christian West is that of St. Augustine of Hippo ... Augustine began with the Pauline doctrine of Original Sin and the Fall of Man and attributed all moral evil, and most if not all physical evil, to that single cause. What then does God do about it? Augustine's answer was complex and not entirely satisfactory.... But his account of political society is suggestive. The state and its institutions are a self-inflicted *punishment* for human sin.... Moreover, without *justice*, the state is an unmitigated evil.... And because of human sin, true justice is never fully obtainable.... Yet some degree of justice remains possible; therefore, God allows the self-regarding acts of sinful human beings to bring the state into existence because its institutions ... are also a *remedy* for sin. By means of the state, the evil in human life may be constrained to that minimum that must result from freedom of the will in fallen humanity. I wish to suggest that there are parallels between this aspect of St. Augustine's theodicy and the account we may read in W[*ealth of Nations*] of ... "the wisdom of nature." (Waterman, 916, emphasis in original)

The parallels between the theodicy of St. Augustine and that of Smith are, I believe, even richer than Waterman suggests, because they are not limited to *The Wealth of Nations*. As Chapters Three and Four highlight, Smith's analysis of natural selection driving humankind's evolution toward an ideal limiting case is a tale of humankind's struggle with the immense evils born of human frailty and of the instrumental role of institutions in that struggle. As in "Augustine's answer," in Smith's analysis justice is essential, perfection is impossible, but the deity has made improvement achievable and institutions are instrumental in that improvement.

THE PLAN OF THE WORK

For more than two centuries, scholars have studied and offered rich analyses of the economic, political, social, legal, religious, and moral dimensions of Smith's moral philosophy, and some have explicitly focused on the connections between various dimensions, such as morals and economics (Young, 1997) or law and economics (Malloy, 1994). However, for Smith, the whole is much greater than any one connection or of the sum of these parts.

That whole is what he finds in history. By examining the course of humankind's history Smith develops his understanding of how these particular parts interact in a general dynamic evolving system. Unlike Marx, who gives priority to the material, there is no priority of place in Smith among the dimensions of his analysis. His is a simultaneous system in which all dimensions – social, political, and economic – are codetermined and constantly co-evolving. Thus to fully appreciate Smith's moral philosophy, it must be examined through the general frame he used to represent that dynamic simultaneous system: the natural selection/evolution/limit frame.

This chapter has laid out the logic of that frame. Subsequent chapters demonstrate how Smith applies that frame to his analysis of humankind, its narrative history and its prospect. Along the way, I will make the case that much of the best literature on Smith can be enhanced by setting it into Smith's natural selection/evolution/limit frame of analysis. Briefly, the story I tell here flows as follows:

Central to Smith's representation of humankind's evolution is the co-evolution of individuals and their societies. The latter shape the coarse clay of the individuals born into them but, in turn, those individuals grow into a unique perspective that, given human capacities for imagination and reason, makes it possible for them to reshape, intentionally or unintentionally, their society...and so it goes with every generation. As societies change, natural selection leads to the progress of humankind through stages, because progress is, *ceteris paribus*, a source of power that sustains itself. This analysis of the nature of human nature and the dynamics of social construction, change, and natural selection is presented in Chapter Two.

These evolving societal constructs are three-dimensional structures of social, political, and economic institutions. These institutions form a dynamic simultaneous system so, as in an ecosystem, change anywhere effects, to varying degrees, change everywhere, with attendant feedback effects. For a societal structure to function harmoniously these dimensions must complement one another such that the whole of the frame is internally consistent and coherent.[50] Thus sustainable change in any one dimension requires a complementary and consistent change in the other two. Chapters Three and Four present Smith's analysis of the instrumental role of political institutions (positive law) and social institutions (religion) respectively in the maturation of this simultaneous dynamic system.

The natural course of humankind's evolution is progress through stages toward a limiting case: "[T]he liberal plan of equality, liberty and justice" (*WN*, 664). Smith's conjectural or theoretical history is the story of that natural process. Instrumental in that process is the progress of opulence because material progress is a source of power and therefore the advantage that makes natural selection possible. Smith's analysis of the progress of opulence is the subject of his *Inquiry into the Nature and Causes of the Wealth of Nations*. Chapters Five through Nine examine the role of that *Inquiry* in Smith's moral philosophical enterprise.

My *WN* analysis is not meant to be either topical or encyclopedic. A topical approach highlights a few selected pieces of special interest at the expense of the whole. Encyclopedias cover the whole as a series of alphabetized pieces of information that are rarely, and then only barely, connected to one another. While both of these approaches can be useful, my goal is to demonstrate that the *WN* constitutes an integrated, consistent analysis that is, itself, an integral part of a larger moral philosophical analysis, all of which is diminished to the degree that it is deconstructed.

Chapter Five, drawn largely from *WN* Book I, lays out the premises Smith makes for the analysis to follow, focusing in particular on

- the division of labor as the source of productivity gains,
- functional distribution, given that the wage, profit, interest, and rent concepts become central to the analysis that follows, and
- the initial stages of the progress of opulence that establish the resource base for the accumulation of the capital that makes possible and fuels progress in the commercial stage.

Chapter Six describes the natural dynamic of capital accumulation, capital deepening, and flows of capital in the commercial stage as told in *WN* Book II. That analysis introduces Smith's concepts of productive

---

[50] "Smith had very modest expectations concerning people and the power of sheer reasoning to impose itself on a complex system of changing relationships. Yet he saw no chaos in the absence of such heroic feats of the intellect and will. Human society evolved its own balances, much like the ecological systems of nature" (Sowell, 7).

and unproductive labor, self-expanding circuits of capital, and the role of properly managed fiat money in facilitating international capital flows. It is the dramatic deepening of capital and the expansion of its flows in the commercial stage that would, if the natural course was undistorted, lead to significant growth in the wealth of the nation and a distribution that Smith considers just – one that allows the least among the working class to be "tolerably well fed, clothed, and lodged" (*WN*, 96).

Humankind's real story is not, however, one of an inexorable march of progress toward the limiting case because, given human frailty, human beings naturally distort the natural. Chapter Seven presents Smith's classic example of distortions ultimately giving way to natural progress: Europe's escape from feudalism described in *WN* Book III. In this case, as always in Smith's analysis, progress is not primarily a consequence of human reason applied to realize humankind's improvement, but rather it is largely the unintended consequence of choices made in pursuit of particular interests. Often distorted by human frailty, the ingenious design of the invisible hand nevertheless prevails. So it was that as Europe moved from feudalism to the commercial stage, it seemed to be more by serendipity than by reason. And for reasons described in Chapter Three, Smith believes that among these European nations Great Britain had progressed the most.

However, even as he writes admiringly of Britain's advanced constitution, Smith fears that institutional distortions caused by particular interests – the mercantile interests – are impeding and might even destroy Britain's achievement. In Chapter Eight Smith's *WN* Book IV attack on this mercantile system is explored in detail.

As noted earlier, this attack evolved. The evolution of Smith's views on the mercantile system is reflected in the transformation of his rhetoric in successive editions of *WN* and in his last revisions of *TMS*. Those *TMS* revisions include a civic humanist appeal to leaders to resist the seduction and pressures of partial interests and "assume the greatest and noblest of all characters, that of the reformer and legislator of a great state; and, by the wisdom of his institutions, secure the internal tranquility and happiness of his fellow-citizens for many succeeding generations" (*TMS*, 232). It may seem an irony that Smith begins to see civic humanist leadership as the best hope for maintaining Britain's advancement toward a classical liberal ideal, but while Smith is an idealist, he is also a realist and a pragmatist.

As a pragmatist, Smith believes that if the British system is to progress the government needs not only to escape the mercantile distortions, it needs to follow policies that encourage progress. Chapter Nine describes Smith's vision, largely laid out in *WN* Book V, of what a good government should do and should avoid doing in order to serve its society.

Chapters One through Nine present Smith's moral philosophy. On the face of it this might seem to be an antiquarian exercise in which the old work of a fellow long dead is studied as one might study the design of a nineteenth century steam engine – a fascinating innovation in a march toward progress that has passed it by. I don't see it that way. I believe Smith's conceptions of

- human nature and the co-evolution of individual and society, and of
- human society as a multidimensional, simultaneous, evolving system

offer a rich source of alternative ways of thinking at a time when economic analysis begins with *homo economicus* and the social sciences have become thoroughly departmental. Chapters Ten, Eleven, and Twelve bring the moral philosophy of Adam Smith into the modern discourse on economics, the social sciences, and social philosophy.

Chapter Ten argues that the Chicago paradigm, as represented by Gary Becker's *Economic Approach to Human Behavior*, which, according to Becker, "provides a valuable unified framework for understanding all human behavior" (Becker, 14), does not offer a satisfactory resolution to a dilemma of liberal society that has challenged liberal philosophers since the first experiments in liberal order began to emerge, the "cohesion question": If the productive potential of liberal society derives from individuals' freedom to pursue their own interests, how does such a society exploit that potential without also unleashing a Hobbesian war of all against all? As will be clear by the time we reach Chapter Ten, Smith's moral philosophy is largely constructed to resolve this dilemma because, absent such a resolution, there is no "liberal plan" in the human prospect.

Two modern, Nobel Prize winning scholars who richly address this "cohesion question" are Amartya Sen and James Buchanan. Chapter Ten examines Sen's resolution to this question. It requires relaxing the modern *homo economicus* assumption and allowing for the dynamic development of social values. It is a solution that is very much in the Smithian tradition.

Buchanan is the source of Sen's conception of the dynamic development of social values. In his "Constitutional Economics" Buchanan moves modern analysis from two dimensions – a political/economic institutional analysis represented by the New Institutional Economics and Buchanan's constitution – to a constrained three-dimensional analysis, one that includes a marginal consideration of change in social institutions and, in particular, civic ethics. Chapter Eleven traces this contribution by Buchanan and argues that it is enhanced by moving beyond the margin, from a constrained three-dimensional institutional analysis to a full Smithian dynamic three-dimensional institutional analysis.

In the original Preface to his *Principles of Political Economy*, John Stuart Mill writes:

For practical purposes, political economy is inseparably intertwined with many other branches of social philosophy. Except on matters of mere detail, there are perhaps no practical questions, even among those which approach nearest to the character of purely economical questions, which admit of being decided on economical premises alone. And it is because Adam Smith never loses sight of this truth; because in his applications of Political Economy, he perpetually appeals to other and often far larger considerations than pure Political Economy affords – that he gives that well-grounded feeling of command over the principles of the subject for the purposes of practice... (Mill, 4–5)

It is this dimensionality of Smith's thinking and its fruitfulness that I seek to represent here.

Chapter Twelve examines an issue that was a nascent concern of Smith's, lay at the heart of Marx's critique of liberal economics, was a very important issue to John Stuart Mill and John Maynard Keynes, and yet only lurks on the periphery of modern mainstream economic analysis: the perverse effect on a liberal system of an increasing concentration of control over capital that empowers the capital holders to extort advantages in pursuit of even greater returns on their capital. Exploring this issue makes it clear that any resolution to the cohesion question must address issues of commutative and distributive justice simultaneously.

An Epilogue offers a reflection on the human prospect.

A CAVEAT: ON KNOWING SMITH'S MIND

There are those who believe that because we cannot know Smith's mind we should not presume to ascribe a purpose to his work.[51] Instead

---

[51] Vivienne Brown writes that "[t]he 'commonsense' view of language put forward in *LRBL* is ... one that grounds the meaning of a text in the intended meaning of the author ... The reading of Adam Smith's discourse to be presented in this book ... does not attempt to apply the model of communication described in *LRBL*. In particular, it does not lay claim to uncovering or recovering Smith's own intentions in his lectures and writing. Such a claim could only be strictly justified if there existed independent evidence, over and above the text themselves, to which an appeal might be made concerning Smith's intentions. This would constitute objective external evidence against which the textual

we should simply examine Smith's texts as freestanding documents to which *we* give meaning. I think this is not only the wrong approach to Smith; I think it would disappoint him. I believe he wrote out of a commitment... with purpose, with intention... and he would not like the thought that his purpose died on the page.

So how do I respond to the argument that I cannot know the mind of a writer, in this case Smith's, and that it is arrogant of me to suggest that I can?

I think of myself as relating to Smith as I believe he related to the deity. Smith did not claim that he could know the mind of the deity.[52] I know I cannot know the mind of Adam Smith. However, Smith believed that the deity had a purpose, that that purpose was embodied in the design,[53] and that by observing the product of the deity's hand – nature – he could imagine, at least in general contours, the shape of that design and, in turn, its purpose.[54] I believe that Smith had a purpose, a design; and I believe that by observing the product of Smith's hand – his works – I can imagine, at least in general contours, the shape of that design and, in turn, his purpose.

In a letter celebrating the life of his recently deceased, very dear friend, David Hume,[55] Smith offers a description of his last conversation with Hume. Smith reports that in the course of their conversation he made note of Hume's "cheerfulness" and said to Hume that he "could not help entertaining some faint hopes" that Hume might survive his malady. Hume's response: "'Your hopes are groundless'" (*Correspondence*, 218).

Hume then went on to say that with this sense of inevitable death in mind he had been reading Lucian's *Dialogues of the Dead* and reflecting

exegesis could be tested, but no such evidence or higher court exists.... [I]nferences [of an author's meaning] are commonplace in the secondary literature in intellectual history as a result of the widespread assumption that the meaning of a text is governed by authorial intentionality, the assumption that underlies *LRBL*, and such claims function powerfully in commanding support for particular recoveries and discoveries of their author's intentions" (Brown, 19). Clearly Brown intends to suggest that what I propose to do is not possible.

[52] Indeed, as noted earlier, he would dismiss such a claim as arrogant beyond measure.

[53] "Smith's natural law implies a propensity working to accomplish its purpose. This animism is strictly in keeping with eighteenth-century deism, with which nature became the polite word for God" (W. Dunn, 335). "'Nature' is almost always viewed teleologically in W[*ealth of Nations*]. It exists for and with a purpose, and part of that purpose is human welfare" (Waterman, 918).

[54] Smith's "principles were not 'natural laws,' they were inferences, sometimes unwarranted, from the regularity of phenomena" (Bittermann, 1940B, 733).

[55] A letter to William Strahan (publisher of Smith's and of Hume's work) written at Kirkaldy, Fifeshire (Smith's home) on 9 November 1776 (*Correspondence*, 217–21).

on excuses he might make to Charon for not entering the boat to cross the river Styx into the realm of the dead. Smith's letter continues:

[A]mong all the excuses which are alleged to Charon for not entering readily into his boat, he [(Hume)] could not find one that fitted him; he had no house to finish, he had no daughter to provide for, he had no enemies upon whom he wished to revenge himself.... [Hume concluded:] "I, therefore, have all reason to die contented." He then diverted himself with inventing several jocular excuses, which he supposed he might make to Charon, and with imagining the very surly answers which it might suit the character of Charon to return to them. "Upon further consideration," said he, "I thought I might say to him, 'Good Charon, I have been correcting my works for a new edition. Allow me a little time, that I may see how the Public receives the alterations.' But Charon would answer, 'When you have seen the effect of these, you will be for making other alterations. There will be no end of such excuses; so, honest friend, please step in the boat.' But I might still urge, 'Have a little patience, good Charon, I have been endeavouring to open the eyes of the Public. If I live a few years longer, I may have the satisfaction of seeing the downfall of some of the prevailing systems of superstition.' But Charon would then lose all temper and decency. 'You loitering rogue, that will not happen these many hundred years. Do you fancy I will grant you a lease for so long a term? Get into the boat this instant, you lazy loitering rogue.'" (*Correspondence*, 218–9)

This shared moment contemplating the end of a life's work as a philosopher reflects a central element in the character of both Smith and Hume: These were scholars who wrote with purpose. Both wanted to make a contribution to humankind's betterment.[56] These were humble scholars.[57] Both knew their work was, at best, a contribution, not the last word.

---

[56] For Smith: "The natural order of society is the ideal moral order, and Smith seems to imply that there is an ideal that morality, society and even the political economy should emulate.... There is, then, a built-in teleology in human nature, an ideal to which we all do and should strive" (Werhane, 50–1). Coats sees a commitment, albeit more limited: "Although the prevailing theories and practices of government fell far short of his ideal – which he realized was unattainable in practice ... – he certainly hoped that his magnum opus would contribute to the reform of present discontents" (Coats, 223–4).

Griswold, borrowing from Haakonssen, is correct in saying that Smith rejects "'Burkean' quietism" (Griswold, 1999, 304). "It should be clear by now that we ought not to make the old mistake of inferring from the political open-endedness of Smith's 'utopia' that his politics is merely quietist" (Griswold, 1999, 307). Smith sees contours of constructive path and "[h]is insistence on the moral defensibility of the conceptions of liberty and justice ... provides a normative basis for social and political action" (Griswold, 1999, 307).

[57] "In all the liberal and ingenious arts, in painting, in poetry, in music, in eloquence, in philosophy, the great artist feels always the real imperfection of his own best works, and is more sensible than any man how much they fall short of that ideal perfection of which he has formed some conception, which he imitates as well as he can, but which he despairs of ever equalling. It is the inferior artist only, who is ever perfectly satisfied with his own performances" (*TMS*, 248).

And so it is with my work on Smith. I imagine the vision of Adam Smith's moral philosophy and I present my representation of that vision in what follows. I know mine is not the last word; I simply hope to make a contribution.

In Charles Griswold's excellent contribution on Smith, he writes that the "plausibility of my reconstruction of his basic framework rests primarily on its fit with his work" (Griswold, 170). Plausibility, fit, persuasiveness . . . these are standards right out of Smith, so they are the standards by which my work, too, should be measured.

TWO

On Human Nature, Social Norms, Co-Evolution, Natural Selection, and the Human Prospect

ON SYMPATHY, SENTIMENTS, AND SELF-COMMAND

Adam Smith's *Theory of Moral Sentiments* begins by making the point that we are, by our nature, social beings:

How selfish soever man may be supposed, there are evidently some principles in his nature, which interest him in the fortune of others, and render their happiness necessary to him, though he derives nothing from it except the pleasure of seeing it. (*TMS*, 9)

This connection is made through our capacity for "sympathy ... [which] denote[s] our fellow-feeling with any passion whatever" (*TMS*, 10). We feel sympathy with another when we, as spectator, step into that other's being and experience his circumstance as we imagine it is to him.[1] Sympathy is not simply, as is often the connotation, about "pity or compassion" (*TMS*, 9) for one who is experiencing sorrow. It is about the fellow-feeling we conceive with another in any and all of the circumstances that life presents (love, death, hunger, injury, kindness ...).

As I emphasized in Chapter One, imagination is central to Smith's moral philosophy. I described there how, according to Smith, it is through

---

[1] "[S]ympathy is very properly said to arise from an imaginary change of situations with the person principally concerned, yet this imaginary change is not supposed to happen to me in my own person and character, but in that of the person with whom I sympathize. When I condole with you for the loss of your only son, in order to enter into your grief ... I not only change circumstances with you, but I change persons and characters. My grief, therefore, is entirely upon your account, and not in the least upon my own. It is not, therefore, in the least selfish" (*TMS*, 317).

imagination that a philosopher pretends to enter into the mind of the deity. It is also through imagination that a philosopher or any individual pretends to enter into the mind of another person. And just as a philosopher imagines the invisible connecting principles of the deity's design that give rise to the unfolding nature we observe; similarly, one individual observing another imagines the invisible sentiments that give rise to the unfolding actions of that other whom he observes.

Sentiments are those "affection[s] of the heart, from which any action proceeds" (*TMS*, 18). There are three broad categories of sentiments in Smith's representation of human nature: self-love, justice, and benefi-cence.[2] Self-love is the spring for action in a human being. It is self-love that motivates in each of us "the hope of bettering his condition" (*WN*, 99). Justice is the legitimate right and expectation all persons have of redress for any injury.[3] Beneficence is the kindness and generosity, the warmth of the human heart, we bestow upon others.[4]

These sentiments are expressed through the passions. We feel sympa-thy with another to the degree that the balance of sentiments we imagine he should feel in any circumstance – the proportions of self-love, justice, and beneficence that should motivate him – is the balance that we imagine he does feel given the passions we observe.[5]

When the original passions of the person principally concerned are in perfect concord with the sympathetic emotions of the spectator, they necessarily appear to this last just and proper, and suitable to their objects; and, on the contrary, when, upon bringing the case home to himself, he finds that they do not coincide with what he feels, they necessarily appear to him unjust and improper, and un-suitable to the causes [the circumstances] which excite them. To approve of the passions of another, therefore, as suitable to their objects, is the same thing as to observe that we entirely sympathize with them; and not to approve of them

---

[2] "Concern for our own happiness recommends to us the virtue of prudence [a dimension of self-love]; concern for that of other people, the virtues of justice and beneficence; of which, the one restrains us from hurting, the other prompts us to promote that happiness" (*TMS*, 262).

[3] "[T]he violation of justice is injury: it does real and positive hurt to some particular persons, from motives which are naturally disapproved of" (*TMS*, 79).

[4] In his 1790 revisions to the *TMS*, Smith includes the words: "Kindness is the parent of kindness..." (*TMS*, 225). This seems to be indicative of Smith the person. See Stewart's description of his beneficence (Stewart, 326, fn*).

[5] Smith writes in *LJA* of "being overbalanced by a selfish motive" (*LJA*, 94). On Balance as the Standard: "By *propriety* Smith means something very like a kind of balance" (Skinner, 1979, 43, emphsis in original). "The standard Smith sets for the proper direction of our passions is an internal balance among the passions themselves...." (Fleischacker, 121).

as such, is the same thing as to observe that we do not entirely sympathize with them. (*TMS*, 16)

The degree of sympathy one feels with the passions and, thus, with the underlying sentiments that motivate another determines, according to Smith, the propriety or impropriety of that person's action. In contrast, the merit or demerit of another's action is determined by the consequences of that action:

[T]he sentiment or affection of the heart, from which any action proceeds, and upon which its whole virtue or vice depends, may be considered under two different aspects, or in two different relations: first, in relation to the cause or object which excites it; and, secondly, in relation to the end which it proposes, or to the effect which it tends to produce: that upon the suitableness or unsuitableness, upon the proportion or disproportion, which the affection seems to bear to the cause or object which excites it, depends the propriety or impropriety, the decency or ungracefulness of the consequent action; and that upon the beneficial or hurtful effects which the affection proposes or tends to produce, depends the merit or demerit, the good or ill desert of the action to which it gives occasion. (*TMS*, 67)

In a perfect world, intention is the only issue in moral judgment.[6] Thus, in assessing the behavior of another,

[t]he only consequences for which he can be answerable, or by which he can deserve either approbation or disapprobation of any kind, are those which were someway or other intended, or those which, at least, show some agreeable or disagreeable quality in the intention of the heart, from which he acted. To the intention or affection of the heart, therefore, to the propriety or impropriety, to the beneficence or hurtfulness of the design, all praise or blame, all approbation or disapprobation, of any kind, which can justly be bestowed upon any action, must ultimately belong. (*TMS*, 93)

In this perfect world where only intentions matter, the standard against which we must assess these intentions is that ideal balance of sentiments that would be in harmony with the deity's design. In order to make such

---

[6] This is because of the effect of fortune: "The consequences which actually, and in fact, happen to proceed from any action, are, if possible, still more indifferent either to praise or blame, than even the external movement of the body. As they depend, not upon the agent, but upon fortune, they cannot be the proper foundation for any sentiment, of which his character and conduct are the objects.

"The only consequences for which he can be answerable, or by which he can deserve either approbation or disapprobation of any kind, are those which were someway or other intended, or those which, at least, show some agreeable or disagreeable quality in the intention of the heart, from which he acted" (*TMS*, 93).

an assessment we would have to be:

- a perfectly impartial spectator,
- with a transparent window into the real sentiments ("the intention[s] of the heart" (*TMS*, 93)) of the one we observe, and
- a full knowledge of that ideal balance that is consistent with the design.[7]

If we could make an imaginary leap into such an ideal spectator position, from that perspective we could assess not only the morality of others, but also of ourselves. Such a self-assessment is the foundation, according to Smith, of perfect virtue. Add to that the self-command necessary to maintain that ideal balance in oneself, and you have Smith's image of perfect virtue:

The man who acts according to the rules of perfect prudence, of strict justice, and of proper benevolence, may be said to be perfectly virtuous. (*TMS*, 237)[8]

This is the character of those beings who would inhabit Smith's ideal liberal society. It would be a society in which all could enjoy liberty secured by the rule of justice. It would be a society in which there would be no need for institutional government to enforce that justice because, in this perfect world, citizens know the ideal measure of justice and have the self-government, the self-command, to enforce it upon themselves. As Smith writes:

What institution of government could tend so much to promote the happiness of mankind as the general prevalence of wisdom and virtue? All government is but an imperfect remedy for the deficiency of these. (*TMS*, 187)

But, alas, as Smith appreciated all too well, we don't live in this prefect world.

The Theory of Moral Sentiments . . . expounds a detailed psychology according to which human action is motivated by a less-than-perfect balance of 'sentiments': self-love, justice, and beneficence or benevolence. (Waterman, 912–13)

---

[7] The representation of this ideal by Firth is much more analytically refined than Smith would care to worry about and, in the process, creates an image that is, in fact, inconsistent with Smith's heuristic image. I agree with Raphael's rejection of Firth's extreme version of the ideal impartial spectator (Raphael, 1975, 95).

[8] The centrality of these three sentiments and the role of self-command in the character of virtue is clearly evident in the structure of the new Part VI, "Of the Character of Virtue" (*TMS*, 212) that Smith adds to the *TMS* in 1790. Section I covers self-love, Section II covers justice and beneficence, and Section III deals with self-command.

Perfection is, indeed, beyond our reach, but progress toward the limit is nevertheless possible:

> [In] situations which bear so hard upon human nature, that the greatest degree of self-government, which can belong to so imperfect creature as man, is not able to stifle, altogether, the voice of human weakness . . . though it [one's behavior] fails of absolute perfection, it may be a much nearer approximation towards perfection than what, upon such trying occasions, is commonly either to be found or to be expected. (*TMS*, 25–6)

Explaining how individuals become more ethical is an essential chapter in Smith's general story of humankind's progress because that general progress is contingent on a multitude of particulars: the ethical maturation of individual human beings.

We saw a moment ago a parallel between the role of imagination in Smith's general vision and in his particular analysis of virtue. In his general vision, imagination allows us to pretend to enter the mind of the deity. In his particular analysis of virtue, imagination allows us to pretend to enter the mind of another person. Now we see another parallel between his general vision and his particular analysis of virtue. Both offer normative reference points, limiting cases. In Smith's general vision, the liberal plan is the ideal norm, the limiting case of humankind's constitution. In the case of virtue, that perfect virtue just described is the ideal norm, the limiting case of individual human character.

These parallels are no coincidence. It is the evolution at the level of particulars that drives the evolution at the level of the general. Thus, to understand his general natural selection/evolution/limit story of humankind, we must examine its particulars. This chapter is about Smith's representation of the evolution of ethics.[9] The two chapters that follow examine the instrumental role that political and social institutions – positive

---

[9] In *Adam Smith's Marketplace of Life*, James Otteson offers a marketplace conception of ethical development in Smith's moral philosophy. As he describes Smith's logic, "human morality . . . display[s] four central substantive characteristics: it is a system that arises unintentionally from the actions of individuals, it displays an unconscious and slow development from informal to formal as needs and interests change and progress, it depends on regular exchange among freely associating people, and it receives its initial and ongoing impetus from the desires of the people who use it. . . . [These are] the same four structural elements [that] can be found in the system of unintended order described in Smith's *Wealth of Nations*" (Otteson, 124). I will argue that socialization is better than "exchange" as an analytical frame for understanding moral development in Smith's analysis.

A market is simply an amoral coordination mechanism that, given extant tastes and values, equilibrates exchange among autonomous individuals based on a flexible price signal. So where do the tastes and the values that participants bring to this autonomous

law and religion, respectively – play in Smith's general representation of humankind's evolution and the particular role these institutions play in the evolution of ethics. From these social and political dimensions we turn, beginning in Chapter Five, to Smith's analysis of the economic dimension of progress, his story of *The Nature and Causes of the Wealth of Nations*.

I begin with the evolution of ethics because this is the thread that ties Smith's analysis together. Understanding this evolution is best achieved in steps. First we'll examine Smith's analysis of the evolution of the individual being as he is shaped by his society. This representation of individual evolution will then be woven into a larger analysis of how the actions of the evolving individuals reshape, intentionally or unintentionally, the social construction that shaped them. This woven analysis is about the co-evolution of individual and society. The representation of this co-evolution then becomes the material from which the analysis of evolving social and political institutions and the progress of opulence can be developed.

ON THE ETHICAL EVOLUTION OF THE INDIVIDUAL

Human Nature and the Ties that Bind: the Power of Socialization

Sympathy, that fellow-feeling, is a universal human capacity: Even the "greatest ruffian, the most hardened violator of the laws of society, is not altogether without it" (*TMS*, 9). Thus, each of us knows what it is to feel sympathy with, to feel this fellow-feeling with, another person. We know that to sympathize with another is to feel approval of his sentiments. This approval, this approbation, is something we desire ourselves. So our capacity for sympathy awakens in us a desire for its reciprocation. Each of us "longs for ... the entire concord of the affections of the spectator with ... [our] own" sentiments (*TMS*, 22).

[N]othing pleases us more than to observe in other men a fellow-feeling with all the emotions of our own breast; nor are we ever so much shocked as by the appearance of the contrary. (*TMS*, 13)

---

exchange come from? I will argue that in Smith's model, these are socially constructed, the current norms generated by a multigenerational process of societal evolution. I agree with much of Otteson's excellent analysis, but I don't think his general frame, the marketplace, captures the fullness of Smith's moral philosophical vision. In Chapter Eleven, I deal with the market argument for the emergence of morality in detail.

The reciprocal nature of this fellow-feeling is the tie that binds us to other human beings. They desire our approval, our approbation, and so too we desire theirs. In pursuit of this approbation, we each adjust our behavior to please those spectators whose approval we value and desire. It is this dynamic, our willingness to adjust our behavior in pursuit of the approval of others, that, according to Smith, makes it possible for our society to shape, to socialize us:

This natural disposition to accommodate and to assimilate, as much as we can, our own sentiments, principles, and feelings, to those which we see fixed and rooted in the persons whom we are obliged to live and converse a great deal with, is the cause of the contagious effects of both good and bad company. (*TMS*, 224)

The Elementary Social Construction of Being and the Inculcation of Duty

The coarse clay of which the bulk of mankind are formed,[10] cannot be wrought up to ... perfection. There is scarce any man, however, who by discipline, education, and example, may not be so impressed with a regard to general rules, as to act upon almost every occasion with tolerable decency, and through the whole of his life to avoid any considerable degree of blame. (*TMS*, 162–3)

A significant part of Smith's career was devoted to teaching about ethics and his views on how education shapes individual ethics are well developed. According to Smith, ethics education starts early, in the home. A young child is the perfect student for a lesson in ethics because

[i]ts precepts, when ... [properly] dressed and adorned, are capable of producing upon the flexibility of youth,[11] the noblest and most lasting impressions, and as they fall in with the natural magnanimity of that generous age, they are able to inspire, for a time at least, the most heroic resolutions, and thus tend both to

---

[10] Smith believes that the properties of this clay, of our being, are constant: Skinner cites as one of Hume's influences on Smith the notion that mankind must be studied empirically and "that the study of man, thus constituted, would yield the conclusion that 'there is a great uniformity among the actions of men, in all nations and ages, and that human nature remains still the same, in its principles and operations' (*Inquiry Concerning Human Understanding* ...)" (Skinner, 1979, 15).

[11] This "flexibility" derives from Smith's view that "[t]here seems to be in young children an instinctive disposition to believe whatever they are told. ... [They] put implicit confidence in those to whom the care of their childhood, and of the earliest and most necessary parts of their education, is intrusted" (*TMS*, 335).

establish and confirm the best and most useful habits of which the mind of man is susceptible. (*TMS*, 329)

In this earliest stage of socialization, the home instills "domestic morals" (*TMS*, 222): Be respectful of your parents, be kind to your siblings. What better place to learn basic ethical standards than at home because there one is in the context of the lessons to be learned, and there one desires more than anywhere else to be approved of, to belong, to be beloved.

Self-command, on the other hand, is a lesson in virtue that, in Smith's view, is most likely learned once one has left the safe haven of home.

A very young child has no self-command... [and a child is unlikely to acquire this self-command w]hile it remains under the custody of such partial protectors [as parents].... When it is old enough to go to school, or to mix with its equals, it soon finds that they have no such indulgent partiality. It naturally wishes to gain their favor, and to avoid their hatred or contempt. Regard even to its own safety teaches it to do so; and it soon finds that it can do so in no other way than by moderating, not only its anger, but all its other passions, to the degree which its play-fellows and companions are likely to be pleased with. It thus enters into the great school of self-command. (*TMS*, 145)[12]

As students get older the process of ethical education becomes more complex, because as young adults they develop both a skepticism about the values of society and a greater ability to reason. Their skepticism expresses itself, according to Smith, through a rejection of society's assertion that certain values are *naturally* good and worthy of respect:

We frequently hear the young and the licentious ridiculing the most sacred rules of morality... Upon this account we generally cast about for other arguments, and the consideration which first occurs to us, is the disorder and confusion of society which would result from the universal prevalence of such practices. (*TMS*, 89)

Thus we use the capacity for reason that these young people are developing to persuade them of the utility of the rules of ethics that we seek to have them adopt.[13] The heuristic is different but, as with the young child,

---

[12] Smith suggests a slightly different timing in *LJA* (*LJA*, 142).

[13] For Smith, this utility argument is an educational strategy, not the original basis for our ethical systems. Smith specifically and repeatedly rejects the argument that ethics are derived from some sort of reasoned argument. Indeed, he argues that most philosophers and statesmen who endeavor to present representations of the order or suggest arrangements for the human order do so more for the aesthetics of the utility their representation or arrangements embody. The utility in and of itself is not their motive force. (See *TMS*, 188, 210, 263, 298–9, 306, 317.)

the motive we exploit in our attempt to teach virtue is the same. When students are willing to listen to this reasoning, it is out of a desire for approbation from a respected instructor and/or the admiration of their fellows.

Education is an important part of the process through which social values are inculcated in a new generation,[14] but Smith recognizes that there are other forces at work on the psyche of individuals that also influence their moral development. There is, for example: Example.

In Smith's view, modeling is a powerful socialization tool. Education exposes one not only to ideas, but also to examples or role models, and these models can significantly influence one's development. There are also many models experienced outside of education, and Smith sees these as extremely important in an individual's moral development. We are, for example, very likely to become like the company we keep. The power of that company over our being derives from our desire for the approbation of those who matter to us. Recall "the contagious effects of both good and bad company" (*TMS*, 224).

Obviously, the best company to keep is "really good company," those who practice "justice, modesty, humanity, and good order" (*TMS*, 200). Keeping such company encourages one to develop like qualities and to be "shocked with whatever seems to be inconsistent with the rules which those virtues prescribe" (*TMS*, 200). Unfortunately, not all company is good company.

As with our company, those we serve set an example for us. "[T]he servant who shapes his work according to the pattern which his master prescribes for him, will shape his life too according to the example which he set him" (*WN*, 612). The master's claim to esteem as a model rests on his accomplishments as a man of the world, but he has no higher claim. Not so the religious man who "never acts deliberately but as in the presence of that Great Superior who is finally to recompense according to his deeds. A greater trust is reposed, upon this account, in the regularity and exactness of his deeds" (*TMS*, 170). The religious leader, therefore, represents an especially powerful role model.

In Smith's analysis, the primary power of company or models derives from the psychic benefits and costs associated, respectively, with accepting or rejecting the company or the leader. From one's company one receives

---

[14] Smith writes that even "[t]he most vulgar education teaches us to act, upon all important occasions, with some sort of impartiality between ourselves and others..." (*TMS*, 139).

the following signal: If you become like us, you will become one of us – you will belong; and if you become a model of the behavior we admire, we will admire you. Conversely, if you do not choose to be like us, you will not be accepted among us – you will be ostracized.[15] From a leader as model one receives a signal that says: If you follow my lead you will have access to the benefits I am in a position to bestow, be they worldly (fame or material goods) or other worldly (access to heaven); turn away and you will be denied. The more significant the benefits/costs, the more powerful the attraction/sanction of the model, and the more likely it is to be accepted.

Example shapes us, education shapes us, and so too, according to Smith, "discipline" shapes us. By discipline Smith has in mind primarily those difficult challenges of life that, as the expression goes, build character. The particular element of an individual's nature that Smith feels is enhanced by discipline is the capacity for self-command. "Hardships, dangers, injuries, misfortunes are the only masters under whom we can learn the exercise of this virtue" (*TMS*, 153).

The education, example, and discipline of individuals' formative years instill an unrefined set of behavioral standards in the "bulk of mankind" (*TMS*, 163). These shared standards are unrefined because they represent an unreflective adoption of the inherited standards, but they are essential for social cohesion because they serve to stifle the more coarse inclinations that our human frailty would otherwise unleash:

Nature . . . has not left this weakness [our human frailty], which is of so much importance, altogether without a remedy; nor has she abandoned us entirely to the delusions of self-love. Our continual observations upon the conduct of others, insensibly lead us to form to ourselves certain general rules concerning what is fit and proper either to be done or to be avoided. . . .

The regard to those general rules of conduct, is what is properly called a sense of duty, a principle of the greatest consequence in human life, and the only principle by which the bulk of mankind are capable of directing their actions. . . .

[U]pon the tolerable observance of these duties, depends the very existence of human society, which would crumble into nothing if mankind were not generally impressed with a reverence for those important rules of conduct. (*TMS*, 159, 161–2, 163)

---

[15] In good company, a man who is "the proper object of the resentment and indignation of mankind, and of what is the natural consequence of resentment, vengeance and punishment . . . dares no longer look society in the face, but imagines himself as it were rejected, and thrown out from the affections of all mankind. . . . Ever thing seems hostile . . . [b]ut solitude is still more dreadful than society" (*TMS*, 84).

Duty is the coarse form that we impress on our coarse clay in order for social order to be possible, but we are capable of a more refined shape.

Were it possible that a human creature could grow up to manhood in some solitary place, without any communication with his own species, he could no more think of his own character, of the propriety or demerit of his own sentiments and conduct, of the beauty or deformity of his own mind, than of the beauty or deformity of his own face. All these are objects which he cannot easily see, which naturally he does not look at, and with regard to which he is provided with no mirror which can present them to his view. Bring him into society, and he is immediately provided with the mirror which he wanted before. It is placed in the countenance and behaviour of those he lives with, which always mark when they enter into, and when they disapprove of his sentiments; and it is here that he first views the propriety and impropriety of his own passions, the beauty and deformity of his own mind. (*TMS*, 110)

It is the reflection of society that offers each of us our first norms, but it is self-reflection that refines those norms. Smith's analysis of the maturation of individual values explains how that refinement takes shape.

The Development of Autonomous Being: From Duty to Imagination and Impartial Spectator as Guide

In following the dictates of duty, we listen to the judgments of real spectators from whom we desire approbation as they offer their assessment of our behavior based on those dictates. In our unrefined state, we accommodate our behavior to their judgments because we desire most of all their approbation. As we begin to develop an autonomous sense of self,[16] however, all too often we feel that these assessments are ill informed because these real spectators do not fully appreciate our circumstances. We still listen, but "we often appeal from the judgment of the actual spectators of our action to the judgment of future better informed spectators, or to what the judgment of the present spectators would be if they knew

---

[16] "In the same manner [as with our physical appearance] our first moral criticisms are exercised upon the characters and conduct of other people; and we are all very forward to observe how each of these affects us. But we soon learn, that other people are equally frank with regard to our own. We become anxious to know how far we deserve their censure or applause, and whether to them we must necessarily appear those agreeable or disagreeable creatures which they represent us. We begin, upon this account, to examine our own passions and conduct, and to consider how these must appear to them, by considering how they would appear to us if in their situation. We suppose ourselves the spectators of our own behaviour, and endeavour to imagine what effect it would, in this light, produce upon us. This is the only looking-glass by which we can, in some measure, with the eyes of other people, scrutinize the propriety of our own conduct" (*TMS*, 112).

all the circumstances. We appeal to the sympathies of the impartial spectator, who is freed from the limitations of their knowledge and personal situation" (Morrow, 1923, 32).

This emerging autonomous impartial spectator position[17] is a source of solace when we find that our behavior, behavior we feel is worthy of praise, is nevertheless, generally criticized by others who, we feel, do not understand and appreciate our circumstance. We can escape from the dictates of the general clamor because, according to Smith, although we seek praise, we also value the thought of being praiseworthy.[18] This independent assessment of worthiness through the perspective of an imagined impartial spectator makes the progress of individuals toward greater virtue possible:

Nature, when she formed man for society, endowed him with an original desire to please, and an original aversion to offend his brethren. She taught him to feel pleasure in their favourable, and pain in their unfavourable regard. She rendered their approbation most flattering and most agreeable to him for its own sake; and their disapprobation most mortifying and most offensive.

But this desire of the approbation, and this aversion to the disapprobation of his brethren, would not alone have rendered him fit for that society for which he was made. Nature, accordingly, has endowed him, not only with a desire of being approved of, but with a desire of being what ought to be approved of; or of being what he himself approves of in other men. The first desire could only have made him wish to appear to be fit for society. The second was necessary in order to

---

[17] "How, then, does the superior tribunal acquire its independence?" (Raphael, 1975, 91). Raphael describes this process of moral maturation beautifully. The key is: We can't please all the real spectators and none of them knows the situation as we do, so out of necessity we begin to construct our own reference point – our impartial spectator; taking a different perspective puts things into more real proportions, as with the view from his window (see Raphael, 1975, 91–2). Smith writes of this perspective issue: "In my present situation an immense landscape of lawns, and woods, and distant mountains, seems to do no more than cover the little window which I write by and to be out of all proportion less than the chamber in which I am sitting. I can form a just comparison between those great objects and the little objects around me, in no other way, than by transporting myself, at least in fancy, to a different station, from whence I can survey both at nearly equal distances, and thereby form some judgment of their real proportions. Habit and experience have taught me to do this so easily and so readily, that I am scarce sensible that I do it . . ." (*TMS*, 135–6).

[18] "Man naturally desires, not only to be loved, but to be lovely; or to be that thing which is the natural and proper object of love. He naturally dreads, not only to be hated, but to be hateful; or to be that thing which is the natural and proper object of hatred. He desires, not only praise, but praiseworthiness; or to be that thing which, though it should be praised by nobody, is, however, the natural and proper object of praise. He dreads, not only blame, but blame-worthiness; or to be that thing which, though it should be blamed by nobody, is, however, the natural and proper object of blame" (*TMS*, 113–14).

render him anxious to be really fit. The first could only have prompted him to the affectation of virtue, and to the concealment of vice. The second was necessary in order to inspire him with the real love of virtue, and with the real abhorrence of vice. In every well-formed mind this second desire seems to be the strongest of the two. (*TMS*, 116–17)

As we depend more on this internal assessment, we become more autonomous in our ethical judgments. From the imagined impartial spectator position, things begin to look different. From this position, we are invariably led to imagine not only what would be the socially acceptable response to the circumstance – what would be our duty – but also whether there is another response that seems more reasonable to us. This application of reason and imagination[19] is the dynamic that leads to individual standards based on our unique, independent perspective.[20] Thus our autonomous perspective leads to the development of autonomous standards.[21] Griswold offers an excellent description of this process:

[T]he impartial spectator ultimately defines the standards, but only after a process of reflection on and refinement of what is given. This is just what Smith says in referring to these standards as "the slow, gradual, and progressive work of the great demigod within the breast"; in shaping them, the wise and virtuous person "imitates the work of the divine artist" ... Since spectators' moral sentiments are woven into the world – into practices, traditions, and institutions, for example – and since the impartial spectator is a reflective refinement of the exchanges of ordinary life, moral evaluation typically begins with established rules and standards. The impartial spectator's judgments culminate a process of often complex reasoning that determines the relevant relations of "propriety." (Griswold, 1999, 145–6)[22]

---

[19] "His theory ... insists on a place for agency or self-determination. By means of the imagination's capacity to reflect on self from the standpoint of the spectator, and to identify with that standpoint, one can direct one's actions and shape one's character" (Griswold, 1999, 115).

[20] "The impartial spectator in each individual began as an external observer and then to some extent became internalized over time. .... The 'just and wise man,' which was Smith's phrase for a highly evolved individual, would give assent only to the internalized ideal ..." (Fitzgibbons, 64).

[21] "The all-wise Author of Nature has, in this manner, taught man to respect the sentiments and judgments of his brethren; to be more or less pleased when they approve of his conduct, and to be more or less hurt when they disapprove of it. He has made man, if I may say so, the immediate judge of mankind ...

"But though man has, in this manner, been rendered the immediate judge of mankind, he has been rendered so only in the first instance; and an appeal lies from his sentence to a much higher tribunal, to the tribunal of their own consciences, to that of the supposed impartial and well-informed spectator, to that of the man within the breast, the great judge and arbiter of their conduct" (*TMS*, 128–30).

[22] Jerry Muller offers a very nice description of this process in his Chapter 8, where he writes: "*The Theory of Moral Sentiments* ... [presents] a theory of the development of

This description of the emergence of an autonomous conscience[23] is, as I said, excellent, but there is one point in this description of ethical refinement that, I believe, needs to be refined.

Griswold asserts that "[t]he impartial spectator's judgments culminate a process of often complex reasoning that determines the relevant relations of 'propriety.'" The terms "culminate" and "determines" imply that there is an end to the process. There is no culmination, there is no final determination in Smith. Ethical maturation is an ongoing process because the ideal is a limit – we can forever refine our values as we approach it, but we can never achieve it.

[In assessing the behavior of another] though ... [that] behavior ... fails of absolute perfection, it may be a much nearer approximation towards perfection,

conscience through the internalization of social norms, as well as a theory of how the morally developed individual is able to ascend from moral conformity to moral autonomy" (Muller, 1993, 100).

Haakonssen (1981) also offers a very thoughtful analysis of this process in his Chapter 3: "[W]e are led to ask whether, according to Smith, the socially accepted and necessary is all there is to morality, or whether parts of morality can gain some independence of the commonly received, that is whether moral ideals are possible. A theory to explain this must be able to account for how moral ideals develop out of social morality, since the latter is the empirically given morality. ...

"It is exactly such a theory Smith is proposing" (Haakonssen, 1981, 55–6). Haakonssen proceeds to describe how we begin to become self-reflective in our ethical judgments. We initially use a spectator position to reflect on how "real" others would see us as we adjust our behavior in pursuit of their praise, but this independent spectator position can evolve into an independent position of assessment based on our own evolving sense of ethics. If it does, then we seek to please that imagined spectator in pursuit of praiseworthiness. "In this way it is *possible* for men to detach their morality, at least to some extent, from the social circumstances which created it" (Haakonssen, 1981, 56, emphasis in original). Such "independence" (Haakonssen, 1981, 57) becomes a new frame for effecting change.

23 This emergence of the autonomous ethical individual is Smith's representation of the emergence of our conscience. "Conscience ... is the mechanism whereby the individual comes to adopt the standpoint of the spectator in order to assess and guide his own conduct ..." (Campbell, 1971, 147). "The rudimentary stage of the virtue of self-command, found in the child or the man of weak character, depends on the feelings of actual spectators. The higher stage, reached by the man of constancy, depends entirely on conscience. ... [T]his distinction ... [contrasts] the normative ideals of conscience with the positive facts of social life" (Raphael, 1975, 94). Raphael suggests that this analysis of the evolution of our moral refinement, in fact, was a development that unfolded in the evolution of Smith's own refinement of his moral philosophy: "Smith began to stress the impartiality of the spectator only when he came to theorize about the effect on the agent of the reactions of spectators" (Raphael, 1975, 89). In the first edition of *TMS*, Smith's construction suggested that "conscience reflects actual social attitudes ... [but this construction] faces a difficulty: if this were correct, how could conscience ever go against popular opinion, as it clearly sometimes does? This must have been the objection put to Smith by Sir Gilbert Elliot" (Raphael, 1975, 90–1) because a letter from Smith to Elliot

than what, upon such trying occasions, is commonly either to be found or to be expected.

In cases of this kind . . . we very frequently make use of two different standards. The first is the idea of complete propriety and perfection, which, in those difficult situations, no human conduct ever did, or ever can come up to; and in comparison with which the actions of all men must for ever appear blameable and imperfect. The second is the idea of that degree of proximity or distance from this complete perfection, which the actions of the greater part of men commonly arrive at. (*TMS*, 26)

Here, we hear Smith explicitly reflecting on perfect virtue as a limit. We can approach a "much nearer approximation towards perfection, than what, upon such trying occasions, is commonly either to be found or to be expected." We can move beyond the current norms of society.[24] But we can never reach the limit.

The wise and virtuous man directs his attention to the . . . standard . . . of exact propriety and perfection. There exists in the mind of every man, an idea of this kind, gradually formed from his observations upon the character and conduct both of himself and of other people. . . . He endeavours as well as he can, to assimilate his own character to this archetype of perfection. But he imitates the work of the divine artist, which can never be equaled. (*TMS*, 247)

To the degree that an individual transcends the current societal norms in the approximation of perfection, that is to be esteemed. But societal

that includes his proposed revisions to *TMS* on this topic clearly demonstrates that he is addressing this issue in the next (second) edition of *TMS*. (See Raphael, 1975, 91.) That proposed revision included the term "developed conscience" (Raphael, 91), but it was not in the actual revisions.

Harpham describes this process as follows: "By starting with the basic idea of a spectator who is impartial and adding a variety of qualifying words or phrases to further identify the evaluative position desired, Smith uses the idea of impartial spectatorship to solve a number of different moral and philosophical problems in the world. His philosophical intentions in developing the idea started with a general concern over sociability in the first edition, to one over conscience in the second edition [in response to Elliot], to one of moral autonomy in the final edition [in response to his concern over the human prospect]" (Harpham, 2001, 144). Smith clearly took Elliot's criticisms very seriously: "I thought myselfe infinitely obliged to you for the objection which you made to a Part of my system" (Correspondence, 48); and on 10 Oct. 1759, Smith writes to Elliot about the refinement of the impartial spectator position in the revised presentation: "You will observe that it is intended both to confirm my Doctrine that our judgments concerning our own conduct have always reference to the sentiments of some other being, and to shew that, notwithstanding this, real magnanimity and conscious virtue can support itselfe under the disapprobation of all mankind" (Correspondence, 49).

[24] "A virtuous individual possessing self-command is not only someone who has internalized the moral norms of his community; he is someone who has learned to improve upon them. . . . [He] strives to achieve the ideal" (Harpham, 2000, 235).

progress is not made when one individual transcends the norm. It is made when the norm itself, and thus the common standard of civic ethics, progresses. Refined individuals can contribute to this progress, but the process of progress is larger than any one individual. To the degree that an individual can move the societal norms along with his own, he moves the standard for the next generation. If some in that next generation do as he has done, then over time, the approximation moves progressively nearer to the ideal. This process of inheriting norms, acting on them, and setting a new standard for the subsequent generation is the story of co-evolution that I turn to now.

ON THE DYNAMIC OF SOCIETAL CHANGE: CUSTOM AND THE CO-EVOLUTION OF INDIVIDUAL AND SOCIETY

Custom and the Golden Mean

In Smith's analysis, every society is a unique social construction with its own well-established norms that are peculiar to its particular time, place, and circumstance.[25] Smith refers to the set of social norms of a given society as its "golden mean":

Every age and country look upon that degree of each quality, which is commonly to be met with in those who are esteemed among themselves, as the golden mean of that particular talent or virtue. And as this varies, according as their different circumstances render different qualities more or less habitual to them, their sentiments concerning the exact propriety of character and behavior vary accordingly. (*TMS*, 204)

"[T]he chief causes of the ... opinions which prevail in different ages and nations concerning what is blamable or praise-worthy ... are custom ["the habitual arrangement of our ideas" (*TMS*, 194)] and fashion [the custom "of a high rank, or character" (*TMS*, 194)]" (*TMS*, 194).[26] Lacking perspective on time and place, most people consider custom as

---

[25] "In general, the style of manners which takes place in any nation, may commonly upon the whole be said to be that which is most suitable to its situation" (*TMS*, 209).

[26] "Every morall duty must arise from some thing which mankind are conscious of ... [yet] it is very seldom that one has a distinct notion of the foundation of their duties, but have merely a notion that they have such and such obligations.... [I]ndeed it will but seldom happen that one will be very sensible of the constitution he has been born and bred under; everything by custom appears to be right or at least one is but very little shocked at it." (*LJA*, 321–2).

representing the natural order of things:

> Few men have an opportunity of seeing in their own times the fashion in any of these arts change very considerably. Few men have so much experience and acquaintance with the different modes which have obtained in remote ages and nations, as to be thoroughly reconciled to them, or to judge with impartiality between them, and what takes place in their own age and country. Few men therefore are willing to allow, that custom or fashion have much influence upon their judgments concerning what is beautiful, or otherwise, in the productions of any of those arts; but imagine, that all the rules, which they think ought to be observed in each of them, are founded upon reason and nature, not upon habit or prejudice. (*TMS*, 195)

Because each of us is born into just such an extant social construction, our birthright includes, by custom, a particular "natural order of things" that is confirmed for us as Truth by the language and behavior of all of those who surround us. Indeed, we often become so enamored of our own society's Truth that we see it as evidence of our society's superiority over other societies. Smith cites as an example of this sociocentrism the absurdity of European arrogance with respect to definitions of beauty:

> What different ideas are formed in different nations concerning the beauty of the human shape and countenance? A fair complexion is a shocking deformity upon the coast of Guinea. Thick lips and a flat nose are a beauty. In some nations long ears that hang down upon the shoulders are the objects of universal admiration. In China if a lady's foot is so large as to be fit to walk upon, she is regarded as a monster of ugliness. Some of the savage nations in North-America tie four boards round the heads of their children, and thus squeeze them, while the bones are tender and gristly, into a form that is almost perfectly square. Europeans are astonished at the absurd barbarity of this practice, to which some missionaries have imputed the singular stupidity of those nations among whom it prevails. But when they condemn those savages, they do not reflect that the ladies in Europe had, till within these very few years, been endeavouring, for near a century past, to squeeze the beautiful roundness of their natural shape into a square form of the same kind. And that, notwithstanding the many distortions and diseases which this practice was known to occasion, custom had rendered it agreeable among some of the most civilized nations which, perhaps, the world ever beheld. (*TMS*, 199)

Smith asserts that such norms "concerning the beauty of the human shape and countenance" are not bounded by any natural standards, but norms of behavior are different. There are common elements in those latter norms across all societies because there are some natural standards that are essential for the cohesion of any social construct. Smith cites for example the universal abhorrence of wanton murder.

But whereas there are norms of ethical behavior that seem to be generally accepted (murder is evil), there are particular variations on these norms that are quite dramatic, "particular usages ... capable of establishing, as lawful and blameless, particular actions, which shock the plainest principles of right and wrong" (*TMS*, 209). The power of custom creates these particular variations and thus customs are "the chief causes of the many irregular and discordant opinions which prevail in different ages and nations concerning what is blameable or praise-worthy" (*TMS*, 194).

Smith cites, as an example of the power of custom to preserve some very abhorrent variations on the natural norms of ethics, the case of infanticide in Greece:

Can there be greater barbarity, for example, than to hurt an infant? ... Yet the exposition, that is, the murder of new-born infants, was a practice allowed of in almost all the states of Greece, even among the polite and civilized Athenians; and whenever the circumstances of the parent rendered it inconvenient to bring up the child, to abandon it to hunger, or to wild beasts, was regarded without blame or censure. This practice had probably begun in times of the most savage barbarity. (*TMS*, 209–10)

Smith imagines that in the most desperate of savage states there might have been a circumstance that warranted this unnatural horror – abandoning a child to certain death – because the alternative might have been more horrific; the death of the entire tribe.[27] However, when what in a very particular situation was an extreme remedy for extreme conditions becomes custom, this is unconscionable. Given human nature, however,

---

[27] Smith recognizes that, even in his own day, social necessity may warrant actions that seem unnatural. "A centinel, for example, who falls asleep upon his watch, suffers death by the laws of war, because such carelessness might endanger the whole army. This severity may, upon many occasions, appear necessary, and, for that reason, just and proper. When the preservation of an individual is inconsistent with the safety of a multitude, nothing can be more just than that the many should be preferred to the one. Yet this punishment, how necessary soever, always appears to be excessively severe. The natural atrocity of the crime seems to be so little, and the punishment so great, that it is with great difficulty that our heart can reconcile itself to it. Though such carelessness appears very blamable, yet the thought of this crime does not naturally excite any such resentment, as would prompt us to take such dreadful revenge. A man of humanity must recollect himself, must make an effort, and exert his whole firmness and resolution, before he can bring himself either to inflict it, or to go along with it when it is inflicted by others" (*TMS*, 90).

it is not unimaginable:

> The imaginations of men had been first made familiar with it [infanticide] in that earliest period of society, and the uniform continuance of the custom had hindered them afterwards from perceiving its enormity.... When custom can give sanction to so dreadful a violation of humanity, we may well imagine that there is scarce any particular practice so gross which it cannot authorise. Such a thing, we hear men every day saying, is commonly done, and they seem to think this a sufficient apology for what, in itself, is the most unjust and unreasonable conduct. (*TMS*, 210)

Custom shapes the extant social construction of each society and because each society has a unique history and circumstance, so, too, each has a unique set of norms for individual behavior. There are natural, general principles that shape these norms, but each society's actual norms embody particular variations around those natural principles that can be, as in the Greek case, dramatic and significant.[28]

Each society's unique set of norms, the golden mean of that particular time and place, is considered the natural order of things among those in the then and there. These norms are thus treated as tacit knowledge,

---

[28] Although Smith abhors this case of infanticide as "most unjust and unreasonable conduct," his criticism is more for the society that would sanction such a custom than for the individuals who are shaped by it. Whereas we can condemn those who lived by these customs, it is arrogant to think that we would have done better if born in that time and that place, so as we judge them we should be careful to avoid the arrogance of 20:20 hindsight. Smith cites, for example, Cato, who was, by the standards of his own time, by his society's golden mean, "a man of the most severe virtue and the strictest observer of the morall rules then in fashion..." (*LJA*, 181). With that caveat, Smith looks back from the eighteenth century and condemns Cato's treatment of his slaves. In *LJA*, he writes: "Nothing was more common then (sic) to turn out the old or diseased slaves to die, as we would a dying horse. Cato, who was a man of the most sever virtue and the strictest observer of the morall rules then in fashion, used frequently to do this and confessed it without shame; and this he would not have done if it had been contrary to the practise of the times" (*LJA*, 181). Based on the lessons he has drawn from his reading of humankind's history, Smith believes there are some principles for which a persuasive case can be made that they should be absolutes. The evils of slavery and of infanticide are two such principles.

Haakonssen writes that the case of slavery "clearly demonstrates that there is no automatic harmony between even the most basic rights of men...[because it] constitutes...[a] conflict between one man's right to personal liberty and another man's property right. We can now see that the former takes priority, and hence that the latter is no right at all when the two conflict, that is when property-right is claimed in persons. But many generations have to be schooled in humane respect the individual before we reach a state of impartiality in which we always recognize injury in this respect as more severe than injury to property" (Haakonssen, 140–1). This "many generations" logic is very much in keeping with Smith's evolutionary story.

rarely questioned, and thus inherently inert. But change in social norms can and does occur. Indeed, for Smith's natural selection/evolution/limit story of humankind to make sense, not only change but progress must occur, for the maturation of ethical norms is essential if humankind is to approach the human prospect.

Smith's representation of this process of progress involves two levels of analysis. The foundation is at the level of the particular, in intrasocietal change. This is a story of the co-evolution of individuals and their society. This co-evolution story then sets the scene for Smith's general analysis of intersocietal change. It is at this intersocietal level that natural selection leads to a maturation of norms as humankind evolves toward the limiting case of the liberal plan.

The Co-Evolution of Individual and Society: On Choice, Chance, Circumstance, and Natural Selection

As the transgenerational depository of core values and understandings, society, in the form of its institutions, has an organic existence that transcends and shapes each new individual.[29] The ability of any individual to change or even to question this societal structure is constrained by his initial existential acceptance of this inherited status quo.[30] Yet while Smith's beings are social, the process of socialization that shapes each being is entirely consistent with the sovereignty of the individual: "[I]n the great chess-board of human society, every single piece has a principle of motion of its own..." (*TMS*, 234).

In Smith's analysis, individuals are social beings *and* they are sovereign beings, each motivated by a unique balance of sentiments. The character of that balance originates in socialization, but even as the individual is

---

[29] "Institutions further imply historicity and control. Reciprocal typifications of actions are built up in the course of a shared history. They cannot be created instantaneously. Institutions always have a history, of which they are the products.... [A system of these are the] agglomerations of institutions that we call societies" (Berger and Luckmann, 54).

[30] I paraphrase Buchanan's expression, "existential acceptance of the status quo" (Buchanan 1991, 20). "With the acquisition of historicity, these formations... acquire...[a] crucial quality...: this quality is objectivity. This means that the institutions that have now been crystallized...are experienced as existing over and beyond the individuals who 'happen to' embody them at the moment. In other words, the institutions are now experienced as possessing a reality of their own, a reality that confronts the individual as an external and coercive fact" (Berger and Luckmann, 58).

shaped by society, the uniqueness of his personal biography gives him a singular perspective from which he can act on and affect the extant social constructs,[31] including the social definition of ethical balance, the "golden mean."[32] His imagination and reason equip him to do so.

Smith is conservative in his approach to change:

The love of our country seems, in ordinary cases, to involve in it two different principles; first, a certain respect and reverence for that constitution or form of government which is actually established . . . (*TMS*, 231)

Yet he also sees the need for change because the world we inherit is never perfect. Thus this quotation continues:

and secondly, an earnest desire to render the condition of our fellow-citizens as safe, respectable, and happy as we can. (*TMS*, 231)

So although he is wary of radical change,[33] Smith admires those who seek reasoned incremental, constructive change. Such a person is, for Smith,

[t]he man . . . [of] public spirit[,] . . . prompted altogether by humanity and benevolence, [who,] . . . like Solon, when he cannot establish the best system of laws, . . . will endeavour to establish the best that the people can bear. (*TMS*, 233)

Smith cites as examples of such admirable men:

Edward the 1ˢᵗ, one of the most prudent of our kings . . . [who] saw the danger [of concentrated judicial power and] . . . divided the business of the Justiciary into

---

[31] "Identity is, of course, a key element of subjective reality, and like all subjective reality, stands in a dialectical relationship with society. Identity is formed by social processes. Once crystallized, it is maintained, modified, or even reshaped by social relations. The social processes involved in both the formation and the maintenance of identity are determined by the social structure. Conversely, the identities produced by the interplay of organism, individual consciousness and social structure react upon the given social structure, maintaining it, modifying it, or even reshaping it. Societies have histories in the course of which specific identities emerge; these histories are, however, made by men with specific identities.

"If one is mindful of this dialectic one can avoid the misleading notion of 'collective identities' without having recourse to the uniqueness . . . of individual existence" (Berger and Luckmann, 174–5).

[32] "Individual judgments are, ultimately, constitutive of social norms, but social norms are also an indispensable source for individual judgments. Indeed, the process of moral judgment is the means by which individuals most deeply build the views of their society into themselves. Paradoxically, it is precisely by doing this that they can also most fully express their individuality" (Fleischacker, 49). "Individually free action and social construction of the self are compatible, for Smith, even dependent on one another" (Fleischacker, 51).

[33] "No government is quite perfect, but it is better to submitt to some inconveniences than to make attempts against it. . . . [But even radical change can sometimes be justified:] K. James, on account of his encroachments on the body politic, was with all justice and equity in the world opposed and rejected" (*LJB*, 435–6).

three different courts .... (*LJA*, 276; *LJB*, 422) ... [and] Henry 2nd, who of all our kings excepting Edwd.1^s. had the greatest legislative capacity (*LJA*, 283) [and established the foundation of the independent jury system.]

But individual intention is not, in Smith's analysis, the only or even the primary source of the societal change. Most change in any society is the unintended consequence of actions by individuals seeking some much narrower objective. Smith cites as an example of this the case of Elizabeth I:

> Elizabeth, who always affected popularity, was continually unwilling to impose taxes on her subjects. In order to supply her exigencies she sold the royal demesnes ... Her successors therefore standing in need of frequent supplies were obliged to make application to Parliament. The Commons were now to become very considerable, as they represented the whole body of the people, and as they knew the king could not want, they never granted him any thing without in some degree infringing his priviledges. At one time they obtained freedom of speech, at another they got it enacted that their concurrence should be necessary to every law. The king on account of his urgent necessities was forced to grant whatever they asked and thus the authority of the parliament established itself. (*LJB*, 420–1)

So, as the institutions of society construct individuals, so too those individuals, intentionally or unintentionally, reconstruct society's institutions.[34] This co-evolution is an essential element in Smith's representation of societal change, but it, too, has to be contextualized.

The actions of individuals are shaped not only by the extant societal structure within which they function, but also by the larger geopolitical context of that society. So, for example, in Smith's analysis, England's evolution is driven by the intended and unintended consequences of the Edwards, the Henrys, the Elizabeths, to name a few; but those actions and their consequences were in turn shaped by the fact that England is an island across a Channel from France and the rest of the European continent. Smith appreciates that this geopolitical context has implications for the internal trajectory of societal change. He writes, for example, that after the Union with Scotland in 1707, because Britain is an island,

> [t]he Union put them out of the danger of invasions. They were therefore under no necessity of keeping up a standing army; they did not see any use or necessity for it. ... [As a consequence] a system of liberty has been established in England before the standing army was introduced ... (*LJA*, 265, 269)

---

[34] Warren Samuels: "Smith used two analytical procedures: the method of regarding society as a derivative of the individual *and* that of regarding the individual as a product of society" (Samuels, 1984B, 199–200).

Smith's story of the English/British experience is indicative of his larger theme: Societal evolution is a quirky process of the chance, circumstance, and the intended and unintended consequences of the actions of individuals. Reason plays an important instrumental role in this dynamic, but reason is neither the original source of our moral understandings[35] nor the ultimate determinant of the trajectory of events. Individual human beings can affect the course of events,[36] but they cannot effect that course. The human condition is far too complex to be directed by the weak powers of human reason. There is, Smith believed, a greater and ultimately more benign power guiding the course of human events.

In Smith's story of humankind's history and its prospect, individuals, circumstances, and chance drive as well as distort or perturb the natural course of events causing the rise and fall of nations and empires. But through it all, the power of the design (the deity, nature) determines the long-term course of the human experience. That course is progressive in a normative sense because more mature societies are, *ceteris paribus*, more capable of sustaining themselves. Thus, while individual societies may grow, stagnate, and decline, natural selection gives rise to a continuously closer approximation of the ideal human prospect, the liberal plan.

In this story, human nature is constant (we are not "better" than our predecessors), but human character evolves along with human institutions, and these have the capacity to mature toward the ideal.

Moral Relativism, Institutions as Instrumental, and the Invisible Absolute

Girswold writes that "there is no *a priori* Smithian dogma" on the content of civic virtue, "*what* mix is appropriate will depend on the historical circumstances" (Griswold, 1999, 295, emphasis in original). Indeed, this

---

[35] "[T]hough reason is undoubtedly the source of the general rules of morality, and of all the moral judgments which we form by means of them; it is altogether absurd and unintelligible to suppose that the first perceptions of right and wrong can be derived from reason, even in those particular cases upon the experience of which the general rules are formed. These first perceptions, as well as all other experiments upon which any general rules are founded, cannot be the object of reason, but of immediate sense and feeling. It is by finding in a vast variety of instances that one tenor of conduct constantly pleases in a certain manner, and that another as constantly displeases the mind, that we form the general rules of morality" (*TMS*, 320).

[36] "[D]iversity of moral judgment that is critically reflective... may be the engine that propels humankind forward.... Conversations both with others and with oneself push the Enlightenment project forward" (Harpham, 2001, 144–5).

moral mix is a part of what evolves historically and thus it is appropriate to the circumstance. But that is not to say that there are no absolutes. Quite to the contrary, the premise of Smith's moral philosophy is that there are absolutes.[37]

Smith's approach to ethics can be described as moral relativism and invisible absolutes. It parallels his approach to philosophy more generally. There are invisible connecting principles that are absolute because they are the work of the deity, but we cannot know those absolutes – including the absolutes of morality. Our inability to "know" does not, however, abrogate our responsibility to imagine. We can, if Smith's premise of progress is correct, intuit the contours of these absolutes by observing the course of humankind's history.[38] By imagining and approximating these invisible absolutes we can hope to help humankind approach the ideal human prospect.[39]

Recall that according to Smith, humankind is evolving through stages and each stage represents a step in progress. By observing how norms change with progress, we can identify the normative principles that seem

---

[37] "Smith, like Hume, had no philosophical belief in absolutes, only a 'cool' hope in a very gradual, if stumbling improvement" (Macfie, 57). Progress implies some normative sense of better. Smith didn't presume to know the blueprints of the absolute, perfect design, but "'cool' hope in a very gradual, if stumbling improvement" was premised for Smith by an invisible absolute – the design case.

[38] Campbell cites a quotation from *TMS* (164–5) suggesting the "authority of moral rules . . . linked to the assertions that the moral faculty does in fact arbitrate within and between all other faculties, and this, in turn, is vindicated by the claim that this is a function which the Deity intended it to fulfill. This train of argument rests on the assumption that the world is a unified mechanism and on the belief that the justification of its constituent parts consists in demonstrating their place within the whole. Unfortunately for Smith, such an argument has to take for granted the goodness of the mechanism as a whole, and since this cannot be done without drawing on the very moral principles which he is required to justify, the argument is, in the end circular" (Campbell, 1971, 224). No – the deity justifies the final cause, but the emergence of moral systems that realize this end is part of the efficient causes and the dynamic of this evolution, not the absolute content of the ideal morality, is what he is describing. "[T]eleology in Smith's philosophy should be seen . . . not [as] a description of how the world is but a proposition of the harmony we yearn for it to have. It is therefore a regulative ideal . . ." (Griswold, 332–3).

[39] "The moralist in Smith would like to be able to claim that, for all of us, the judgments of the impartial spectators in our respective breasts are the same, irrespective of the experiences to which we have been exposed; but as a social theorist, he explains the impartial spectator as a construct that each of us makes from his own experience. In looking for a coherent reading of Smith, we may sometimes have to choose whether to give priority to his social theory or to his morality, to his assumptions or to his conclusions" (Sugden, 84). These are not conflicting conceptions; these are dimensions of Smith – the being in the process of the individual/humankind evolution (relative) v. the ideal, limiting case (absolute).

to be consistent with progress and in turn intuit what the contours of the ideal normative principles might be.

Recall also that institutions play an essential, instrumental role in this process because they are the transgenerational organic system through which this evolution unfolds. If, as we identify the cases of constructive progress in norms, we also identify how institutions have contributed to or have impeded that progress, this may offer guidance for shaping current institutions to play an instrumental role in pursuit of further progress . . . or so Smith hoped. To that end, he offered just such an analysis of the role of

- positive law and
- religion

in his story of humankind's evolution. Those instrumental institutions are the subject of the next two chapters.

THREE

On the Role of Positive Law in Humankind's Evolution

ON JUSTICE

Justice . . . is the main pillar that upholds the whole edifice . . . of human society. (*TMS*, 86)

In the first lecture we have from Adam Smith's 1762–63 series of *Lectures on Jurisprudence* (28 January 1762), he begins by asserting that "[t]he first and *chief* design of every system of government is to *maintain justice* . . ." (*LJA*, 5, emphasis added).

In an ideal world, perfectly virtuous citizens know and enforce perfect standards of justice upon themselves. But absent perfect virtue, if society is to cohere, it is essential that government emerge to define and enforce standards of justice. According to Smith, without government's enforcement of justice there would be chaos, and without government's instrumental role in the refinement of justice there would be no progress.

Smith's analysis of the emergence of government and of the instrumental role government plays in the refinement of justice as humankind evolves is not a story of the genius of human reason, but rather of the ingenious, benevolent design of the deity.

The very existence of society requires that unmerited and unprovoked malice should be restrained by proper punishments; and consequently, that to inflict those punishments should be regarded as a proper and laudable action. . . . [Y]et the Author of nature has not entrusted it to his [man's] reason to find out that a certain application of punishments is the proper means of attaining this end; but has endowed him with an immediate and instinctive approbation of that very application which is most proper to attain it. The *oeconomy of nature* is in this respect exactly of a piece with what it is upon many other occasions. With regard to all those ends which, upon account of their peculiar importance, may be regarded, if such an expression is allowable, as the favourite ends of nature, she has constantly in this manner not only endowed mankind with an appetite for the end which she proposes, but likewise with an appetite for the means by which this end can be brought about.... (*TMS*, 77, emphasis added)

Nature, as part of her "oeconomical" arrangement, has endowed humans with a natural sentiment of resentment in response to injustice,[1] and it is from this sentiment that the evolution of justice begins. In the rude state of society, where "there is properly no government at all" (*LJB*, 404), individuals impose a rough justice on one another as they personally avenge their own resentment of injustice.[2] However, as society begins to evolve, this rough justice is not sufficient for progress to proceed, because allowing individuals to define and enforce justice in a progressively more complex society would lead to chaos. It is then that government emerges in order to "maintain justice."[3]

As the violation of justice is what men will never submit to from one another, the public magistrate is under a necessity of employing the power of the commonwealth to enforce the practice of this virtue. Without this precaution, civil society would become a scene of bloodshed and disorder, every man revenging himself at his own hand whenever he fancied he was injured. To prevent the confusion which would attend upon every man's doing justice to himself, the magistrate, in all governments that have acquired any considerable authority, undertakes to do justice to all.... (*TMS*, 340–1)

Government authority emerges to establish order in society, but government is neither the original source of order nor the locus of control that establishes order in the ideal state. Order begins and ends with the individual citizen. In the beginning, a rude order is established by retribution based on a self-defined sense of justice. In the end, in the limit, a refined order is established by a common acceptance of social norms, civic ethics, among citizens with the self-command, the self-government, to enforce

---

[1] "Resentment seems to have been given us by nature for defence, and for defence only. It is the safeguard of justice and the security of innocence.... [Injustice] is, therefore, the proper object of resentment, and of punishment, which is the natural consequence of resentment.... [M]ankind [can] go along with, and approve of the violence employed to avenge the hurt which is done by injustice ..." (*TMS*, 78).

[2] "Among equals each individual is naturally, and antecedent to the institution of civil government, regarded as having a right both to defend himself from injuries, and to exact a certain degree of punishment for those which have been done to him" (*TMS*, 80).

[3] "In the first stages of society, when government is very weak, no crimes are punished [by government]; the society has not sufficient strength to embolden it to intermeddle greatly in the affairs of individualls.... But when the society gathers strength ... [government can and does impose] punishment" (*LJA*, 129–30).

those norms upon themselves. Between this beginning and this end, in the course of humankind's evolution from the rude state toward the ideal, the internal and external systems of governance – norms and positive laws, respectively – shape one another as systems of justice evolve.

ON POSITIVE LAW, SOCIAL NORMS, AND THE EVOLVING SYSTEM OF JUSTICE

In the nascent stage of humankind's evolution, the first steps in the progress of opulence give rise to the first holdings of valuable private property. This in turn creates more complex issues of property rights. As a consequence, justice becomes a more complicated concept. To preserve social order, civil government emerges to define and maintain justice by establishing and enforcing laws regarding property rights. For this new institution of civil government to function, however, it must have a source of authority.

Civil government supposes a certain subordination. But as the necessity of civil government gradually grows up with the acquisition of valuable property, so the principal causes which naturally introduce subordination gradually grow up with the growth of that valuable property. (*WN*, 710)

Subordination emerges with civil government because as property ownership increases so, too, does the distinction of ranks between those who have more and less property. This distinction nurtures subordination because there is a natural "disposition of mankind, to go along with all the passions of the rich and the powerful ... [While o]ur deference to their inclinations [is not] founded chiefly, or altogether, upon a regard to the utility of such submission, and to the order of society, which is best supported by it" (*TMS*, 52), there is nevertheless utility in this authority. It is instrumental in establishing order.

As the complexity of society increases, civil government takes on more responsibilities and the authority of civil government becomes institutionalized.[4] This institutional authority is, in turn, instrumental in shaping social norms, for if the authority of the civil government is seen as legitimate, this gives rise to allegiance. Allegiance can, in turn, inspire a sense of duty because the "duty of allegiance seems to be founded [in part] on ... the

---

[4] "In pastoral countries, and in all countries where the authority of law is not alone sufficient to give perfect security to every member of the state, all the different branches of the same family commonly chuse to live in the neighbourhood of one another.... In commercial countries, where the authority of law is always perfectly sufficient to protect the meanest man in the state, the descendants of the same family, having no such motive for keeping together, naturally separate and disperse, as interest or inclination may direct" (*TMS*, 222–3).

principle of authority" (*LJA*, 318). As we saw in Chapter Two, duty is the first ethical form our coarse clay takes from our community.

[I]t is very seldom that one has a distinct notion of the foundation of their duties, but have merely a notion that they have such and such obligations.... [I]ndeed it will but seldom happen that one will be very sensible of the constitution he has been born and bred under; everything by custom appears to be right or at least one is but very little shocked at it. (*LJA*, 321–2)

Thus, the mere weight of the government's authority, where that authority is seen as legitimate, tends to inculcate the standards embodied in its laws as personal standards among the people. That "[a]uthority [also serves as]... the foundation of that... utility or common interest" (*LJA*, 322) to which men appeal when persuading others of the virtue of the law. In this manner, positive law serves as an active tool for the inculcation of values. As Smith writes: "[W]hat forms the character of every nation... is the nature of their government..." (*WN*, 586).

Smith cites ancient Rome as an example of this interdependence of positive law and civic ethics. According to Smith, Rome was, in contrast to Greece, a state where respect for the institutions of justice nurtured good citizens:

The superiority of character in the Romans[5] over that of the Greeks, so much remarked by Polybius and Dionysius of Halicarnassus, was probably owing to the better constitution of their courts of justice ["The attention, to practice and precedent, necessarily formed the Roman law into... [a] regular and orderly system..."], than to any other circumstances to which those authors ascribe it. Romans are said to have been particularly distinguished for their superior respect to an oath. But the people who were accustomed to make oath only before some diligent and well-informed court of justice, would naturally be much more attentive to what they swore, than they who were accustomed to do the same thing before mobbish and disorderly assemblies. (*WN*, 779)

Smith believes that the English experience also reflects this salutary effect of more mature positive law on the character of the citizenry. As he makes the case for Roman civic maturity by contrasting it with Greece, so too Smith makes the case for English civic maturity by contrasting it with France. In particular, he contrasts the safety of London and Paris, asserting that the necessity of police to insure personal security in these two cities is not proportional to population but rather to the "nature of the manners of the people" (*LJA*, 332).

---

[5] "[T]he whole tenor of the Greek and Roman history bears witness to the superiority of the publick morals of the Romans" (*WN*, 773).

"Upon the whole it is the custom of having many retainers and dependents which is the great source of all the disorders and confusion of some cities; and we may also affirm that it is not so much the regulations of police which preserves the security of a nation as the custom of having in it as few servants and dependents as possible" (*LJA*, 333). The large number of "retainers and dependents" in Paris gives rise to the necessity of a large police force there because "[n]othing tends so much to corrupt and enervate and debase the mind as dependency, and nothing gives such noble and generous notions of probity as freedom and independency. Commerce is one great preventive of this custom. ["The establishment of commerce and manufactures . . . brings . . . independency, [and] is [therefore] the best police for preventing crimes" (*LJB*, 486–7).] . . . Hence it is that the common people of England who are alltogether free and independent are the honestest of their rank any where to be met with" (*LJA*, 333). And hence it is that while in Paris "hardly a night passes . . . without a murther or a robbery in the streets, . . . in London there are not above 3, 4, or 5 murthers in a whole year" (*LJA*, 332).

Thus, superior probity of the common people of England relative to those of France goes hand-in-hand with the formers' freedom and independence. That freedom and independence have evolved hand-in-hand with commercial progress. But, as we will see, that commercial progress goes hand-in-hand with the unique and very constructive development of the English legal system. So the maturation of the citizenry and the maturation of positive law go hand-in-hand. Indeed, everything in Smith's analysis goes hand-in-hand because in his moral philosophical system, these social, economic, and political dimensions form a simultaneous, evolving system.

Next, we turn to Smith's story of how the progress of positive law evolved into that legal system he considered the most mature in human history, that in England, and the relationship of this maturation to the progress of opulence that England enjoyed.

SETTING THE SCENE FOR THE ENGLISH STORY: POSITIVE LAW AND THE FOUR STAGES

Smith opens his Wednesday, February 23, 1763 lecture on jurisprudence with the following words:

In the last lecture I endeavoured to explain to you more fully that form of government which naturally arises amongst mankind as they *advance in society, and in what manner it gradually proceeded.* (*LJA*, 215, emphasis added)

We know where he is going – to that English model that he admires. But his purpose is not simply admiration. It is to analyze and explain why this model works so well so that he can cull from this example the lessons of progress. In order to do this, he needs to analyze and explain how this progress unfolded. That is why he tells his students that his course is about "advance in society, and in what manner it gradually proceeded." It is an investigation of humankind's evolution, that evolution as progress, and the principles (the design) that guide that progress.

This investigation begins, as did humankind, in the most unrefined or rude state of society, where "there can be very little government of any sort..." (*LJA*, 201). What judicial or executive power there is in that stage resides in the community as a whole.[6] Internal issues and decisions regarding intratribal disputes are resolved by consensus. "The legislative power can hardly subsist in such a state; there could be occasion but for very few regulations, and no individual would think himself bound to submit to such regulations as were made by others, even where the whole community was concerned" (*LJA*, 202).

The reason for this simple form of governance is the simple state of the society. The size and nature of tribal life makes communal meetings possible whenever necessary, and the number of potential disputes is small because the conception of property is very limited: "Among savages property begins and ends with possession, and they seem scarce to have any idea of anything as their own which is not about their own bodies" (*LJB*, 460).

Things become more complex in the next, shepherding stage of society. "Among shepherds the idea of property is further extended" (*LJB*, 460). "Those animalls which are most adapted for the use of man ... are no longer common but are the property of certain individualls. The distinctions of rich and poor then arise" (*LJA*, 202). This expanding domain and differential distribution of "[p]roperty makes it [(government)] absolutely necessary. ... [for property is] the grand fund of all dispute" (*LJA*, 208). Government must exist to maintain the property rights of the rich against the poor, and to insure that the poor "must either continue poor or acquire wealth in the same manner as they [(the rich)] have done" (*LJA*, 208–9). Thus, "[t]he age of shepherds is that [stage] where government properly first commences" (*LJA*, 202). But the legislative function

---

[6] "[I]n the early periods of every society ... trials were ... carried on by the assembly of the whole people ..." (*LJA*, 87–8).

of government, the institutionalization of positive law, is still missing:

> With regard to laws and the legislative power, there is properly nothing of that sort in this period. There must indeed be some sort of law as soon as property in flocks commences, but this would be but very short and have few distinctions in it, so that every man would understand it without any written or regular law. It would be no other than what the necessity of the state required. Written and formall laws are *a very great refinement of government*, and such as we never meet with but in the latest periods of it. (*LJA*, 213, emphasis added)

The emergence of civil government in the shepherding stage is a refinement, an advancement, in human society; but there is much greater refinement to come.

If it is in the age of shepherds that "government properly first commences" (*LJA*, 202), it is in the age of agriculture that government becomes properly legislative. This is due to the fact that in the age of agriculture "property receives its greatest extension" (*LJB*, 460), and with this extension begins the complex task of settling issues regarding those means, beyond possession, by which one can acquire property: accession,[7] prescription,[8] or succession.[9]

The complexity of the issues involved is very significant. As Smith writes with regard to the first of these: "Tho the opportunities of accession are but very few in the age of shepherds, yet they multiply to a number almost infinite when agriculture and private property in land is introduced" (*LJA*, 28). With this growing complexity it is no longer possible for law to be "very short ... [with] few distinctions in it, so that every man would understand it without any written or regular law." The complexity requires that the system of laws be regularized, institutionalized. Hence, it is in this stage that the establishment by government of a system of formal positive law begins.

The contours of the story Smith is telling are emerging: Economic progress, the movement from stage of production to stage of production, creates more complex issues of ownership and this, in turn, brings the need for a more complex legal system. If the legal system meets these needs, the security it affords leads to more economic progress. More economic progress leads to more complexity in economic ownership and intercourse, which, in turn, requires more development of positive law ... and

---

[7] See (*LJA*, 28) or (*LJB*, 460).
[8] See (*LJA*, 36) or (*LJB*, 461).
[9] See (*LJA*, 37) or (*LJB*, 462).

so it goes. Thus, progress depends on the harmonious, simultaneous development of the economic and legal dimensions of society.

As the burden grows on positive law to provide the security that comes with the enforcement of justice, the maturation of civic ethics can begin to bear some of this burden. Indeed, as Smith makes clear in his example comparing the policing of London and Paris, maturing civic ethics is an essential dimension of societal progress. Absent such civic ethics, order can only be established by countless police enforcing endless dictates of positive law, and this is inimical to the very freedom that is necessary for progress to proceed into the more advanced stages of society.

Smith clearly feels that a key reason for England's commercial progress beyond the rest of Europe was its escape from many of the illiberal positive laws that constrained those other nations. His story of this escape is not a story of superior English reason building a superior system, but rather one of the serendipitous unfolding of chance, circumstance, and the intended and unintended consequences of individuals' choices. In this process, individuals and institutions are co-evolving because, as we will see, even as individuals are shaped by the extant institutional structure, they are reshaping it.

PARTICULAR UTILITY AND GENERAL PROGRESS – THE ENGLISH STORY

Smith's analysis of the evolution of the English court system is a classic case of the "oeconomy of nature" at work: Pursuits of particular utility (self-interest) in particular geopolitical circumstances lead to an unintended but desirable general outcome, the maturation of justice and the progress of opulence. Smith reviews this evolution in his March 1763 lectures on jurisprudence:[10]

The judiciall power in the kingdom was first given ... [to a] Chief Justiciary ... ["All these three different parts of the judiciall power were united in the Great Justiciary" (*LJA*, 276):] the power of judging in all civill causes, ... [of trying] all criminall causes; ... [and of trying] fiscall [disputes] ... betwixt the sovereign and the subjects. (*LJA*, 275–6)

[The first] defalcation made on the power of the Justiciary [occurred] in the time of King John.... [A]s the Justiciary attended the king in his progresses thro the kingdom to execute justice, and his court followed that of the kings, it was found

---

[10] He covers the same subject in his 1766 lectures. He offers this analysis yet again in less detail in Book V, Part II "Of the Expence of Justice" in *WN* (*WN*, 708).

necessary to separate one of these powers from him, which was given to the Court of Common Pleas. (*LJA*, 276)

The reason for this change was entirely utilitarian. Because the resolution of civil suits was much slower than criminal suits,[11] following the Great Justiciary around the country as he in turn followed the king was a burden on the people. "This inconvenience was very soon perceived to require a remedy; it was therefore provided by the Magna Charta in King Johns time that" "Common pleas shall not follow the King's Court but be held in one fixed place" (*LJA*, 278, 278fn). The power of the Great Justiciary was not much abated by this change, however. In fact, that power was such that it was a threat to the king's own power, and so the king responded:

We see . . . that the Mayers de Palais [(the French equivalent to the English Great Justiciary)] during the two first races of the kings of France usurped the kingdom. . . . [But in England] Edward the Ist, one of the most prudent of our kings, who seems to have known what he did as well as any one, dreading least the Great Justiciary should serve him in the same way as the Mayer de Palais had done the French kings, abolished his authority all together. (*LJA*, 276)

This marked the point at which, according to Smith, the evolution of the English judicial system departed from that found on the continent.[12] This parting of the ways was not based on Edward's philosophical attachment to the notion of courts as impartial or independent, or on any intention to construct those institutions that became admirable in the mature English judicial system. It simply reflected Edward's prudence in the face of a potential threat to his power.

Edward Ist divided the business of the Justiciary into three different courts *vizt*

  The Court of King's Bench
  The Court of Exchequer
  The Court of Common Pleas

In the last all civil suits were tried. In the first all criminal ones, and to it lay the appeal from the Court of Common Pleas; . . . [and t]he Court of the Exchequer judged in all affairs between the king and his subjects. . . . The Court of Chancery was originally no court at all. The Chancellor was no more than a keeper of breives or writs according to which justice was done. What gave occasion to the keeping of these breives shall now be considered. (*LJB*, 422–3)

---

[11] A point that Smith finds ironic and consistent with his conception of punishment. See (*LJA*, 276–7).

[12] "[I]n every country but England he became as powerfull as the king. But Edward the first saw the danger and got it prevented" (*LJB*, 422).

At this point in his lectures Smith has explained the transformation in the structure of the judiciary. Now, with the language of evolution, he prepares his students to move on to the next chapter in his story describing how this new structure evolved and matured. As with the first, this new chapter is about particular utility guiding choices that cause unintended, but socially desirable, consequences.

When Edward had thus broke the judicial power, the persons whom he appointed as judges were generally of the meanest sort of no fortune or rank, who had been bread to the knowledge of the law, and very frequently these were clergy men.... [B]eing all low men who depended on the will of the king, they would be very unwilling and afraid in any shape to go beyond the meaning of the law or any ways to alter it; and therefore in all cases breives and writts were drawn out according to which they decided justice, and exact records of all proceedings were kept in the officina brevium. (*LJA*, 278–9)

This standard of exactness was pushed further by the fact that men of low station were vulnerable to "bribery and corruption. [In fact,] Edward himself levi'd at one time by fines for bribery about £100,000 . . . so that the bribery must have been very excessive. They were therefore ordered to judge by the strict law, and were to be tried in their proceedings by their own records . . ." (*LJA*, 279).

Thus, we see that pursuing their particular utility in a strategic game with one another, the judges and the king were each led to make choices that had very desirable, unintended consequences. The judges, being of "the meanest sort," turned to precedent as protection from the possible wrath of the king, and the king required scrupulous record keeping (essential for a system based on precedent) as protection from the corruption of the judges. Ironically, two characteristics that Smith would normally abhor in a court – low sorts as judges and lack of independent judges – gave rise to another, more permanent characteristic of the court that Smith found most essential to the sure administration of justice.

[One] thing which greatly confirms the liberty of the subjects in England . . . [is] the little power of the judges in explaining, altering, or extending or correcting the meaning of the laws, and the great exactness with which they must be observed according to the literall meaning of the words.... (*LJA*, 275)[13]

Having examined the causes that "gave occasion to the keeping of these breives" and the salutary effects of this evolution, Smith then turns

---

[13] "[I]t may be looked upon as one of the most happy parts of the British Constitution tho introduced merely by chance...." (*LRBL*, 176)

to the particular utility that gave rise to the professionalization of the courts.

Another thing which tended to support the liberty of the people and render the proceedings in the courts very exact, was the rivalship which arose betwixt them. (*LJA*, 280)

Smith describes how, through various methods, the several courts were able to encroach upon each other's jurisdiction. This process was encouraged by the fact that

the whole profits of the courts ... depended on the numbers of civill causes which came before them, [thus] they would all naturally endeavour to invite every one to lay his cause before their court, by the precision, accuracy, and expedition (where agreable) of their proceedings, which emulation made a still greater care and exactness of the judges. (*LJA*, 281)

Ultimately, as a consequence of this competition,

it came, in many cases, to depend altogether upon the parties before what court they would chuse to have their case tried; and each court endeavoured, by superior dispatch and impartiality, to draw to itself as many causes as it could. The present admirable constitution of the courts of justice in England was, perhaps, originally in a great measure, formed by this emulation.... (*WN*, 720)

Again we see the particular utility of the institution and its members leading to a general, unintended, but very desirable consequence, the professionalization of its work. And the evolution continues: There was, after all, the issue of filling gaps in the existing precedents.

Again, to England's good fortune, the process is directed by unintended consequences of particular utility toward the intended ends of the deity, the creation of the conditions necessary for a harmonious commercial society.

[When] the wrong complained of agreed not with any single brief but was comprehended under any two or more, he [(the Chancellor)] should cause the clerk to make out a new brief in that form.... In this manner he was as it were the judge of the *point of law*, and the courts had only the matter of fact to examine. Many causes would however occurr in which there was no fact disputed, in which case there could be no use or necessity to carry it before the courts ... In these cases the Chancellor could give a sufficient remedy. And in this manner it was that the equitable Court of Chancery began....

The Chancellor ... soon began to consider those cases which the common law did not comprehend. The first thing he did in this way was to order specifick performance of contracts. These were not sustaind by the common law ... This however a man was bound in honor to perform, and the Court of Chancery, which was considered as a court of conscience with the Chancellor at the head who was generally a clergy man skilled in the cannon law, began to give action on this head. (*LJA*, 281–2, emphasis in original)

Thus it was that an essential piece of the legal foundation of a commercial society, contract enforcement, came into being. This evolution of Chancellor's duties[14] was driven by particular utility, but clearly it filled an important role in the maturation of society.

In the story Smith tells of the evolution of the English courts, we see the "oeconomy of nature", the design, at work. We see it again in his story of the evolution of what he clearly believes is the most significant and mature element of the English judicial system: the jury. The jury "curbs the power of the judge . . . [because] in all causes . . . [t]he matter of fact is left intirely to their determination" (*LJA*, 283).

Note the phrase: "The matter of fact is left intirely to their determination." This focus on juries and adjudication based on facts weaves very nicely into Smith's larger story of the benevolent intentionality of the deity's design.

Recall from Chapter Two that in an ideal world, assessment of another is based on the intention of the actor (propriety or impropriety) rather than the consequences of the act (merit or demerit). Smith recognizes, however, that this is a dangerous prospect in real world assessment because we can never know the intention so well as the observed consequences of an action, the observed facts. Happily for England, nature's design has given rise to the evolution of a jury system based on "matter of fact," an essential compensation for humans' inability to function in the ideal.

Nature . . . when she implanted the seeds of this irregularity in the human breast [(assessing the behavior on consequences rather than intentions)], seems, as upon all other occasions, to have intended the happiness and perfection of the species. If the hurtfulness of the design, if the malevolence of the affection, were alone the causes which excited our resentment, we should feel all the furies of that

---

[14] The beauty of the new Court of Chancery is that, unlike those unfettered new courts Smith deplores ("All new courts are a great evil, because their power at first is not precisely determined and therefore their decisions must be loose and inaccurate" (*LJB*, 426)), the Court of Chancery joined an existing system of justice that could act, to a significant degree, as a constraint on any arbitrary judgment it might make. "[T]he Chancellor is certainly as arbitrary a judge as most. But neither is he very dangerous to the liberty of the subject, as he can not try any causes besides those which have no remedy at common law. Nor can he in any case act directly contrary to any method of proceeding laid down by the courts of common law. And from this court as from all others appeals may be carried before the House of Lords" (*LJA*, 283).

passion against any person in whose breast we suspected or believed such designs or affections were harboured, though they had never broke out into any action. Sentiments, thoughts, intentions, would become the objects of punishment; and if the indignation of mankind run as high against them as against actions; if the baseness of the thought which had given birth to no action, seemed in the eyes of the world as much to call aloud for vengeance as the baseness of the action, every court of judicature would become a real inquisition. There would be no safety for the most innocent and circumspect conduct.... Actions, therefore, which either produce actual evil, or attempt to produce it, and thereby put us in the immediate fear of it, are by the Author of nature rendered the only proper and approved objects of human punishment and resentment.... [This, as with] every part of nature, when attentively surveyed, equally demonstrates the providential care of its Author, and we may admire the wisdom and goodness of God even in the weakness and folly of man. (*TMS*, 105–6)

In Smith's view, the English system of justice was, as of his day, the most refined system in the world, and juries for determining fact were the crown jewel of that system.

The law of England, always the friend of liberty, deserves praise in no instance more than in the carefull provision of impartial juries.... Nothing can be a greater security for life, liberty, and property than this institution. The judges are men of integrity, quite independent, holding their offices for life, but they are tied down by the law. The jurymen are your neighbours who are to judge of a fact upon which your life depends. (*LJB*, 425)

As with the courts, the evolution of this English jury system was a serendipitous unfolding of chance, circumstance, and the intended and unintended consequences of individuals' choices:

In the beginnings of the allodial and feudall governments...the person prosecuted came into court with twelve others; and if he swore he was innocent and these 12 swore also that they believed him to be so, he was acquitted. (*LJA*, 283)

This method was ultimately undermined by the resentment among the nobles at the fact that they could get no satisfaction of an abridgement of their rights from such a partial process. As a result, they turned back to a more traditional method of settlement: "judiciall combat" (*LJA*, 283).

The first person to remedy these inconveniencies was Henry 2[d], who of all our kings excepting Edwd. I[s]. had the greatest legislative capacity. He ordered that instead of [the current system]...the sheriff should appoint 12 juratores who should be made acquainted with the cause, and having considered it should give in their opinion or verdict, to which the judge should adhere, and pronounce the sentence accordingly from the law.... Nothing can be more carefull and exact than the English law in ascertaining the impartiality of the jurers. (*LJA*, 283–4)

This impartial jury system was, in part, an unintended consequence of resentment of the nobles, but it was also the intended consequence of a choice by a wise leader. Henry 2nd put in place a mechanism for English justice to approximate the perspective of an impartial spectator, the very perspective that lies at the heart of Adam Smith's conception of justice in particular and of moral assessment in general.

Smith did not see the English judicial system of his day as perfect,[15] but he did believe it was the most mature example of jurisprudence human society had produced as of his lifetime. And he clearly believed that it was the good fortune of secure circumstance (being an island), wise leadership (e.g., Edward Ist and Henry 2nd), serendipitous unintended consequences, and the time to mature[16] that made the system more closely approximate his image of the ideal than any other.[17] This maturation had, in turn, he believed, provided the security necessary for England to enjoy the most robust progress of opulence in the world.

ON JUSTICE AND THE PROGRESS OF OPULENCE

The ultimate motive for pursuing justice is not utility. It is a sentiment, resentment. And the development of positive law is not driven for the most part by reason in pursuit of a desirable general outcome; but rather, as we have just seen, by chance, circumstance, and the pursuit of particular utility. Nevertheless, there is general utility, there are positive general outcomes, where justice is advanced, however it is advanced. One such positive general outcome is the progress of opulence.

Only where there is justice is there an incentive to establish a herd, to plant a crop, to accumulate stock. The herds of the pastoral stage, the crops of the agricultural stage, the stock of the commercial stage . . . these each require a sense of security among the shepherds, the farmers, and the merchants, respectively. That sense of security is only possible where

---

[15] For example, he criticizes the fact that juries must reach unanimous decisions as a significant defect in the system. See (*LJA*, 285).

[16] "It takes time and repeated practise to ascertain the precise meaning of the law or to have precedents enough to determine the practise of a court" (*LJA*, 287).

[17] I have focused on the evolution of the English judicial system as representative of Smith's view that the evolution of humankind is a rather quirky process of chance, circumstance, and the intended and unintended consequences of individuals' choices. There are many more examples to be found in Smith that reflect the same process. For example, he sees such a process in the emergence of the House of Commons (*LJB*, 420), in the evolution of contract law (*LJA*, 89), and in treatment of aliens (*LJA*, 307).

those who herd, or plant, or accumulate feel that there is a system of justice to protect them.[18] As Smith writes:

In the infancey of society, as has been often observed, government must be weak and feeble, and it is long before it's authority can protect the industry of individuals from the rapacity of their neighbours. When people find themselves every moment in danger of being robbed of all they possess, they have no motive to be industrious. There would be little accumulation of stock, because the indolent . . . would live upon the industrious, and spend whatever they produced. . . . In this manner it is next to impossible that any accumulation of stock can be made. . . . *Nothing can be more an obstacle to the progress of opulence.* (*LJB*, 522, emphasis added)

The progress of opulence through stages must, therefore, go hand-in-hand with a complementary evolution of a system of justice embodied in positive laws and civic ethics.

It is easy to see that in these severall ages of society, the laws and regulations with regard to property must be very different. . . . [W]here the age of hunters subsists . . . [a]s there is almost no property amongst them . . . [f]ew laws or regulations will [be] requisite . . . But when flocks and herds come to be reared property then becomes of a very considerable extent . . . [so] there are many opportunities of injuring one another . . . In this state many more laws and regulations must take place . . . In the age of agriculture . . . there are many ways added [to theft or robbery] in which property may be interrupted . . . The laws therefore . . . will be of a far greater number than amongst a nation of shepherds. In the age of commerce, as the subjects of property are greatly increased the laws must be proportionally multiplied. The more improved any society is and the greater length the severall means of supporting the inhabitants are carried, the greater will be the number of laws and regulations necessary to maintain justice. . . . (*LJA*, 16)

In Smith's analysis of humankind's evolution through these stages, there is a duality of limits. There is the ultimate limit set by the deity – that ideal liberal society of independent beings enjoying perfect liberty, making the most for all, and doing well for the least. This is the point of reference, the norm against which all societies can be compared to determine their level of advancement. Then there is the artificial limit a society imposes upon itself by "the nature of its laws and institutions" (*WN*, 111). Smith highlights the consequences of different "laws and institutions" when he compares China, where the laws and institutions have caused it to stagnate, and the "present [declining] state of Bengal", where "[w]ant, famine, and mortality" prevail, with the wonderful progress of opulence in the British American colonies.

---

[18] "[T]he liberty, reason, and happiness of mankind . . . can flourish only where civil government is able to protect them" (*WN*, 803).

Both China and Bengal began their progress deep in antiquity with many inherent advantages: Much fertile ground to till and, thanks to a system of navigable rivers,[19] an extensive market within reach.

China has been long one of the richest, that is, one of the most fertile, best culti- vated, most industrious, and most populous countries in world. It seems, however, to have . . . long [ago] . . . acquired that full complement of riches *which the nature of its laws and institutions permits it to acquire.*[20] (*WN*, 89, emphasis added). . . . But this complement may be much inferior to what, with other laws and institutions, the nature of its soil, climate, and situation might admit of. (*WN*, 111)

So, what about China's laws and institutions undermined its progress? They have created precisely the problem that constructive laws and insti- tutions are supposed to eliminate: insecurity.[21]

In a country . . . where, though the rich or the owners of large capitals enjoy a good deal of security, the poor or the owners of small capitals enjoy scarce any, but are liable, under the pretence of justice, to be pillaged and plundered at any time by the inferior mandarins, the quantity of stock employed in all the different branches of business transacted within it can never be equal to what the nature and extent of that business might admit. In every different branch, the oppression of the poor must establish the monopoly of the rich, who, by engrossing the whole trade to themselves, will be able to make very large profits. Twelve per cent accordingly is said to be the common interest of money in China, and the ordinary profits of stock must be sufficient to afford this large interest. (*WN*, 111–12)

As we will see in Chapter Six, the accumulation and the free flow of cap- ital are essential for the growth of commerce. If small capitals are always at risk, there will only be accumulation by large holders. If large holders monopolize capital, it will, all too often, not flow to ready opportunities

[19] "The improvements in agriculture and manufactures seem likewise to have been of very great antiquity in the provinces of Bengal, in the East Indies, and in some of the eastern provinces of China; though the great extent of this antiquity is not authenticated by any histories of whose authority we, in this part of the world, are well assured. In Bengal the Ganges and several other great rivers form a great number of navigable canals in the same manner as the Nile does in Egypt. In the Eastern provinces of China too, several great rivers form, by their different branches, a multitude of canals, and by communicating with one another afford an inland navigation much more extensive than that either of the Nile or the Ganges, or perhaps than both of them put together" (*WN*, 35).

[20] Indicative of his values, Smith sees the most significant consequence of this political failure to be "[t]he poverty of the lower ranks of people in China [which] far surpasses that of the most beggarly nations in Europe" (*WN*, 89).

[21] They also constrained access to the market: "A country which neglects or despises foreign commerce, and which admits the vessels of foreign nations into one or two of its ports only, cannot transact the same quantity of business which it might do with different laws and institutions" (*WN*, 112).

because the small number of larger holders can never have such a wealth of information about fruitful opportunities as a large number of small holders.

Furthermore, if concentrated control leads to constrained access to capital, capital will be inordinately expensive, so fewer opportunities can be exploited.[22] The twelve percent return Smith cites is indicative of a monopoly premium on the cost of capital when control over capital is concentrated and access is constrained. Elsewhere in *WN*, he writes that "[a]t present the rate of interest, in the improved parts of Europe, is nowhere higher than six per cent, and in some of the most improved it is so low as four, three, and two per cent" (*WN*, 335).

The consequence of these distortions in China is stagnation, but things are even worse in Bengal:

China, ... though it may perhaps stand still, does not seem to go backwards. . . . But it would be otherwise in a country where the funds destined for the maintenance of labour were sensibly decaying. . . . [There, w]ant, famine, and mortality would . . . prevail . . . This perhaps is nearly the present state of Bengal, and of some other of the English settlements in the East Indies. . . . [A] fertile country . . . where subsistence, consequently, should not be very difficult, and where, notwithstanding, three or four hundred thousand people die of hunger in one year. (*WN*, 90–1)

As in China, the source of Bengal's suffering is the perverse "laws and institutions" by which it is governed. In contrast to China, however, the laws and institutions governing Bengal are not imposed from within, but rather by the East India Company as the agent empowered with a largely free hand by the British government to run colonial Bengal.

As sovereigns, Smith asserts, the interest of the company should be to grant the greatest freedom and security to the people because this would generate the greatest wealth for the nation and "[t]he greater the revenue of the people . . . the greater the annual produce of their land and labour, the more they can afford to the sovereign" (*WN*, 637).

But a company of merchants are, it seems, incapable of considering themselves as sovereigns, even after they have become such. Trade, or buying in order to sell again, they still consider as their principal business, and by a strange absurdity regard the character of the sovereign as but an appendix to that of the merchant, as something which ought to be made subservient to it, or by means of which they may be enabled to buy cheaper in India, and thereby to sell with a better profit in Europe. They endeavour [therefore to stifle competition.] . . . Their mercantile habits draw them in this manner, almost necessarily, though perhaps insensibly, to

---

[22] In Chapter Twelve, I will return to this issue of concentrated control over capital.

prefer upon all ordinary occasions the little and transitory profit of the monopolist to the great and permanent revenue of the sovereign, and would gradually lead them to treat the countries subject to their government nearly as the Dutch treat the Moluceas [imposing "so perfectly destructive a system" (*WN*, 636)].... As sovereigns, their interest is exactly the same with that of the country which they govern. As merchants their interest is directly opposite to that interest. (*WN*, 637–8)

This merchant's focus on short-term gain has generated "[t]he great fortunes so suddenly and so easily acquired in Bengal [where] money ... [is] lent to the farmers at forty, fifty, and sixty per cent and the succeeding crop is mortgaged for the payment" (*WN*, 111). It has also led to the decline of Bengal.

This decline due to the absurd "laws and institutions" imposed on that colony by the East India Company makes a particularly stark and useful comparison for Smith because it is so very different from those other British colonies, the ones in North America:

The difference between the genius of the British constitution which protects and governs North America, and that of the mercantile company which oppresses and domineers in the East Indies, cannot perhaps be better illustrated than by the different state of those countries. (*WN*, 91)

"Plenty of good land, and liberty to manage their own affairs their own way, seem to be the two greatest causes of the prosperity of all new colonies" (*WN*, 572), but nowhere are those principles more closely approximated than in the British American colonies. There, the citizens enjoy the same system of justice as that which has benefited the citizens of England and, under that umbrella of security, those colonies have flourished. So, notwithstanding all the mercantile regulations that constrain the commerce of North American colonial farmers and merchants, the liberty and justice that they enjoy has afforded them security. Thanks to that security, capital has been accumulated. If, because of mercantile policies, that capital cannot flow entirely freely, it can at least flow safely.

That security which the laws in Great Britain give to every man that he shall enjoy the fruits of his own labour, is alone sufficient to make any country flourish, notwithstanding these [mercantile impediments] and twenty other absurd regulations of commerce ... The natural effort of every individual to better his own condition, when suffered to exert itself with freedom and security, is so powerful a principle, that it is alone, and without any assistance, not only capable of carrying on the society to wealth and prosperity, but of surmounting a hundred impertinent obstructions with which the folly of human laws too often incumbers its operations ... In Great Britain [and the American colonies] industry is perfectly secure; and though it is far from being perfectly free, it is as free or freer than in any other part of Europe [and certainly much more so than in Bengal]. (*WN*, 540)

Again and again in Smith's work he comes back to this nexus among laws, institutions, and the progress of opulence. The theme is always the same: Justice secured by positive law and civic ethics goes hand-in-hand with the progress of opulence. Where there is progress:

- It is primarily a consequence of the serendipitous unfolding of chance, circumstance, and the choices of individuals based on peculiar utility.
- It depends on the security that comes with refinement of justice.
- It is generally "by very slow degrees" (*WN*, 391).[23]

The evolution of this simultaneous system toward the human prospect can be encouraged, however, by the applied reason and persuasion of philosophers. Smith wrote with just such a purpose.

THE SCIENCE OF THE LEGISLATOR AND THE LESSONS OF HISTORY

In the closing words of the *TMS*, Smith writes:

Every system of positive law may be regarded as a more or less imperfect attempt towards a system of natural jurisprudence ... Sometimes what is called the constitution of the state, that is, the interest of the government; sometimes the interest of particular orders of men who tyrannize the government, warp the positive laws of the country from what natural justice would prescribe.... In no country do the decisions of positive law coincide exactly, in every case, with the rules which the natural sense of justice would dictate. Systems of positive law, therefore, though they deserve the greatest authority, as the records of the sentiments of mankind in different ages and nations, yet can never be regarded as accurate systems of the rules of natural justice. (*TMS*, 340–1)

But while history offers no example that represents perfection – the standards that "natural justice would prescribe"[24] – history is nevertheless

---

[23] For example, Smith traces the emergence of entail and primogeniture and the dependency of tillers. Then he traces the English case describing how tillers acquired "by very slow degrees" (*WN*, 391) more independency and security and how this process led to the unintended consequence of enhancing the grandeur of England: "Those laws and customs so favourable to the yeomanry have perhaps contributed more to the present grandeur of England than all their boasted regulations of commerce taken together" (*WN*, 392).

[24] Bittermann describes the essence of natural law doctrine as follows: "[T]here was an ethical law of nature, discoverable by reason alone, that was uniform through time and place; that this law was an ideal pattern to which positive laws, public policy, and individual conduct should conform; that this law had a divine origin; and that conformity to it was essential for accomplishing the divine plan" (Bittermann, 1940A, 492). Smith would buy most of this except for the "discoverable by reason alone" idea.

very valuable because by examining it we can learn how positive law has evolved and in some places progressed in the course of humankind's history. This in turn is an invaluable resource, because from that history we can cull those principles that seem to go hand-in-hand with progress, and thus we can imagine the contours of natural jurisprudence. The quotation just cited continues:

> It might have been expected that the reasonings of lawyers, upon the different imperfections and improvements of the laws of different countries, should have given occasion to an inquiry into what were the natural rules of justice independent of all positive institution. It might have been expected that these reasonings should have led them to aim at establishing a system of what might properly be called natural jurisprudence, or a theory of the general principles which ought to run through and be the foundation of the laws of all nations. But though the reasonings of lawyers did produce something of this kind . . . it was very late in the world before any such general system was thought of, or before the philosophy of law was treated of by itself, and without regard to the particular institutions of any one nation. (*TMS*, 341)

One would expect that this culling of general principles from the history of positive law would have been done long ago, because the lessons learned can be very valuable in establishing something approximating a system of natural jurisprudence and thereby encouraging progress. But only very recently have philosophical inquiries stepped out of the particular and taken that broad historical perspective, the course of humankind's history, that is necessary if those general principles are to be separated from the particulars of any given society. As he makes clear in the last words of the *TMS*, this is precisely what Smith hoped to do as a part of his larger moral philosophical enterprise:[25]

> I shall in another discourse endeavour to give an account of the general principles of law and government, and of the different revolutions they have undergone in the different ages and periods of society, not only in what concerns justice,[26] but in what concerns police, revenue, and arms, and whatever else is the object of

---

[25] Smith writes to Lord Hailes on 5 March 1769 that "I have read the law entirely with a view to form some general notion of the great outlines of the plan according to which justice has [been] administered in different ages and nations: and I have entered very little into the detail of Particulars . . ." (*Correspondence*, 141).

[26] Justice comes first because it is only once those institutions have secured "what we may call the internall peace, or peace within doors . . . [that] the government . . . [can turn to another of its functions:] promoting the opulence of the state . . . [by] what we call police" (*LJA*, 5) or regulation.

law. I shall not, therefore, at present enter into any further detail concerning the history of jurisprudence.[27] (*TMS*, 340–2)

He wrote the work on "the principles of law and government...in what concerns of police, revenue, and arms." That is the subject of his *Inquiry into the Nature and Causes of the Wealth of Nations*. He never wrote the book on justice, however.

What I have described is Smith's effort to work out some of his thoughts on "what concerns justice" as he lectures to his students at Glasgow. From those lectures and from sections of the *TMS* and *WN* that address these issues, some of "the general principles [regarding justice] which [he thought] ought to run through and be the foundation of the laws of all nations" are clear. These include:

- a professional judiciary – independent of the executive,[28] generally bound to precedent, and paid "[f]ixed salaries " (*WN*, 718)[29];
- an impartial jury system,
- the power to impeach (*LJA*, 272),
- a Habeas Corpus Act (*LJA*, 272; *LJB*, 480),
- reasonable frequency of elections (*LJA*, 273), and
- expanded suffrage (*LJA*, 274).

All of these contribute to the liberty and security of the English subjects, and that liberty and security is certainly the purpose of natural jurisprudence.

Knud Haakonssen puts it perfectly when he writes that the "failings throughout human history can show the character and the magnitude

---

[27] "The principles upon which those rules either are, or ought to be founded, are the subject of a particular science, of all sciences by far the most important, but hitherto, perhaps, the least cultivated, that of natural jurisprudence..." (*TMS*, 218).

[28] "This Separation of the province of distributing Justice between man and man from that of conducting publick affairs and leading Armies is the great advantage which modern times have over antient, and the foundation of that greater Security which we now enjoy both with regard to Liberty, property and Life. It was introduced only by chance and to ease the Supreme magistrate of this most Laborious and least Glorious part of his Power, and has never taken place until the increase of Refinement and the Growth of Society have multiplied business immensely" (*LRBL*, 176).

[29] On fixed salaries for judges: In the *WN* Smith notes how in the process of creating a regular and determinate tax revenue stream, the irregular compensation for justice based on presents was abolished and "[f]ixed salaries were appointed to judges" (*WN*, 718). This didn't significantly diminish the cost of justice given that much of that cost was to cover the fees of lawyers. It did, however, separate the judges' compensation from their judgments, and so it was hoped it would "prevent the corruption of justice" (*WN*, 719).

of the task for natural jurisprudence...[Studying these failings] can also suggest to a philosopher like Smith the foundation of such a discipline...When the principles are applied to the task, the contemplation of a philosopher turns into the science of a legislator" (Haakonssen, 1981, 189). This philosophical enterprise in pursuit of this science was very much Smith's purpose. I find Haakonssen's work compelling, so I will spend a few pages on how I believe the story I tell here relates to his work.

THE RELATIONSHIP OF THIS ANALYSIS TO KNUD HAAKONSSEN'S
THE SCIENCE OF A LEGISLATOR

Haakonssen writes, in describing Smith's standard of moral evaluation, that, as he reads Smith,

the description of the impartial spectator is a description of the criteria which mankind must use in deciding whether an action or character is morally valuable or not.... If we read Smith in this way his science of morals...assume[s] a genuine normative significance. For although the impartial spectator does not supply us with positive moral rules, the spectator principles do show us how moral judgments can be critically discussed and tested. Those moral judgments which do not comply with the principles embodied in the impartial spectator can, at least for the time being, be discarded....By supplying such principles Smith's science of morals becomes more than a science, it becomes a tool. This aspect of Smith's science is of great significance – not least for a full understanding of that branch of it called jurisprudence. (Haakonssen, 1981, 136)

So the "spectator principles" don't provide "mankind" with rules, but they do "give evaluation concrete form [and thereby inform] practical reasoning" (Haakonssen, 1981, 137) as we go about making moral assessments. Carrying this logic into the *Lectures on Jurisprudence*, Haakonssen writes that although critical analysis is not the purpose of those *Lectures*, Smith does use the spectator tool to pass judgment on legal constructions as he presents historical cases:

When we look at the lectures as reported in the students' notes, it is...[not the critical, but] the historical and analytical approach which predominates. They were not meant to be an agenda for systematic law-reform – how could they be? – but an introduction to the basic principles of the law as it is. Nevertheless, throughout the lectures there are a number of examples of how Smith would use the test of natural justice [the spectator principle] to criticize existing law.... (Haakonssen, 1981, 138)

This reflects the "close and necessary connection between the critical and the historical aspects of Smith's jurisprudence" (Haakonssen, 1981, 138): The critical eye of the impartial spectator position allows us to apply "the test of natural justice to criticize existing law" in various historical cases. Indicative of this conception of the connection, Haakonssen describes the progress of "[p]roperty law ... [as] based upon spectator approval refined over generations ..." (Haakonssen, 1981, 142).

After reviewing a number of examples of Smith's own application of "jurisprudential criticism" (Haakonssen, 1981, 146), Haakonssen writes that while "[t]his discussion of concrete legal criticism in Smith's work is hardly complete ... it is complete enough to show the critical capability which he thought his jurisprudence had" (Haakonssen, 1981, 147).

I agree with Haakonssen's assertion that Smith felt competent to offer a "systematic programme" of jurisprudential criticism. And I agree that this application of reason can be instrumental in the process of progress.[30] But as Haakonssen recognizes, his construction raises a puzzling question:

Smith's legal criticism obviously presupposes that the negative and precise virtue of justice is 'natural' in the sense that it is *somehow* outside the grip of social change. But we know that justice consists in the verdict of the impartial spectator on what is properly considered injury in concrete situations ... This would seem, however, to make the impartial spectator dependent upon the situation in which he judges: He cannot be purely and simply impartial – he must be impartial in relation to actual and particular people and circumstances. This raises the question of whether his verdict in itself is not dependent upon, or relative to, the situation? In which case, what becomes of the idea of natural justice?

We can understand how Smith avoided the horns of this dilemma in the following way. Some parts of the impartial spectator's verdict are universal – and in that sense 'natural' – while others are dependent upon the situation in which he judges. (Haakonssen, 1981, 147–8, emphasis in original)

I agree with Haakonssen that "natural justice is ... an ideal standard" (Haakonssen, 1981, 149), but I don't believe his attempt to escape from

[30] Though only instrumental: Smith believed that chance, circumstance, and the intended and unintended consequences of individuals' choices (reason being instrumental in this last category) are the real determinants of progress. And clearly Haakonssen agrees:

With phenomena as complex as those of human society there will nearly always be a number of directions which things can develop, and which direction is taken will depend upon a multiplicity of factors, ranging from 'hard' determining factors, like the absence of sea transport for a country, to 'soft' determining factors, like an individual's decisions about how to act. This means that although in our social and historical explanations we shall often be unable to point out the necessary and sufficient conditions of events, we shall yet be able to make these events intelligible by pointing out some of the more or less necessary conditions. (Haakonssen, 1981, 186)

the horns of this moral relativism dilemma is satisfying. It requires us to imagine a rather schizophrenic impartial spectator with "parts" at odds. It is not clear how this poor soul would resolve this internal conflict to arrive at a singular judgment that was at one and the same time relative and universal.

Setting Haakonssen's spectator principle into the natural selection/evolution/limit framework presented here can, I believe, resolve the issue more neatly. In this framework the questions become:

- Where did the extant "spectator principles" come from?
- How are they becoming more refined (as in the case of property law)?
- If refinement implies a normative ideal, what is that ideal?

The responses to these questions are, as laid out in Chapter Two:

- The extant "spectator principles" are a part of that "golden mean... [that] varies, according...[to society's] different circumstances" (*TMS*, 204).
- These principles change intrasocially as individuals and their social constructs co-evolve. They become more refined through an intersocial process of natural selection.[31]
- The ideal is not observable, but its existence is implicit in and its contours can be imagined by observing the historical process of refinement.

Setting Haakonssen's analysis into this larger frame is beneficial in another way as well. It contextualizes his analysis of Smith's history of law in Smith's more general story of the history of humankind. For example, Haakonssen notes in his presentation of Smith's analysis of "[t]he development of modern law" (Haakonssen, 1981, 171) that "[b]y far the most important changes here [with respect to property] were to the laws of succession" (Haakonssen, 1981, 172). Smith believed, as Haakonssen describes it, that after the fall of Rome, primogeniture was a natural response to the insecurity of the times: "Whatever order and stability there were depended wholly upon the strength of the local lord..." (Haakonssen, 1981, 172). According to Smith, however, the institution outlived its usefulness because it "was still pervasive" (Haakonssen, 1981,

---

[31] Haakonssen writes that "[n]atural justice has...been with men since the beginning of time and has been developed through men's reactions in particular circumstances.... [T]he rules of natural justice are rules which emerge unintentionally from such reactions in particular situations..." (Haakonssen, 1981, 150). "Emerge unintentionally" describes precisely this evolution/natural selection/limit process, albeit in a larger frame.

173) even after "[s]ecurity for property and all other rights was . . . derived from civil government . . ." (Haakonssen, 1981, 172).

Haakonssen has this exactly right. This is another piece of a classic contribution to the Smith literature. But again, I believe setting this analysis into Smith's larger frame can enhance this contribution. Haakonssen's focus is the evolution of law.[32] In Smith's work this evolution is an important but instrumental development in a larger analysis of humankind's evolution.

As Smith analyzes the evolution of the law, his primary focus is on security. Where that evolution made possible greater and broader security, the prospect for society's progress was enhanced because greater and broader security makes possible larger accumulation. This in turn provides the fuel for the progress of opulence, and, as demonstrated previously, this progress has feedback effects on the maturation of the law and civic ethics. In Smith's moral philosophy, law is a part of an evolving simultaneous system of institutions and individuals.

Smith's analysis of the history of law is constantly oriented by the question: How, at each stage in humankind's evolution, did positive law contribute to or impede progress? From this focus, he hoped to cull some insights that would help him imagine the direction the development of the positive law must take to maintain and spur progress toward natural jurisprudence and the human prospect: The liberal plan.

In closing his work, Haakonssen writes

Few of Smith's expressions have been as misleading as his insistence on the importance of a "regular *administration* of justice." The regular administration is a guiding ideal, an ideal of perfection, which can lead and direct a political process; but given the usual condition of human society, it will necessarily turn out to be less a realized ideal than a rough approximation. It is therefore a genuine misreading of Smith if his concept of a system of natural justice is taken as merely an 'administrative' matter, and his 'science of a legislator' thus seen as an impoverishment of political theory. The system of natural jurisprudence was in itself a political challenge, and Smith had no illusions about its magnitude. . . . [The] failings throughout human history can show the character and the magnitude of the task for natural jurisprudence . . . [Studying these failings] can also suggest to a philosopher like Smith the foundation of such a discipline . . . When the principles

---

[32] Similarly, Haakonssen's description of the evolution of contract law (Haakonssen, 1981, 174) is brief and is not put into a larger context. His analysis of the evolving legal relationship between lords and villains is brief and doesn't fully develop the evolutionary context: extension of the market, increased security, independence, productivity, accumulation . . . (Haakonssen, 1981, 176–7).

are applied to the task, the contemplation of a philosopher turns into the science of a legislator. (Haakonssen, 1981, 188–9, emphasis in original)

Again, beautifully said. Smith did conceive of the real as only "a rough approximation" of the ideal. He did study the history of our failings, as well as our successes, to imagine the contours of the ideal as a guide for policy. He did appreciate that turning the "contemplation of a philosopher...into the science of a legislator" is a daunting task. As I will describe in more detail in Chapter Eight, his sense of the challenge became ever more keen as he grew older, but his commitment never wavered. He saw political institutions as important instruments for societal change, and he wanted to help shape those instruments so their effect would be progressive.

Robin Paul Malloy writes in his excellent piece on "Adam Smith and the Modern Discourse of Law and Economics" that "Smith offered a dynamic and contextual understanding of the relationship between law and economics" (Malloy, 114). I believe Malloy has it right. But this "dynamic and contextual...relationship between law and economics" is only a part of a larger simultaneous system. Positive law is only one of the extremely important institutions in this simultaneous, evolving system. Religion is another.

FOUR

On the Role of Religion in Humankind's Evolution

There are some striking and significant parallels between the instrumental role of positive law and that of religion in Smith's analysis of the evolution of humankind. Both emerge to provide security in a very insecure, marginal state of human existence. Both grow from insignificance to powerful institutions. Both can, but do not always, play a constructive role in humankind's evolution, including facilitating the progress of opulence. In both cases, institutional inertia can transform what was, at one point, a useful construction into an impediment. Finally, for humankind to approach the limiting case, both the justice enforcement mechanisms of positive law and the power of institutional religion must wither because under the liberal plan, citizens enforce justice upon themselves and the ethics they share as citizens are not religious but civic.

There are also, of course, some important differences between institutions of positive law and religion in Smith's analysis. For example, positive law emerges to bring order to human society as it becomes too complex for the informal, individual enforcement of justice. In contrast, religion emerges as a means of allaying the fears humans share in the face of inexplicable and awesome displays of nature, as well as fears about their individual and collective prospect.

Beyond these distinct origins, these institutions begin to intersect. As religion becomes institutionalized, it takes on the role of ethical authority and enforcer, a power that can be exerted as a substitute for positive law if there is a political vacuum or as a complement to existing positive law. It is also possible, however, that the power of religion can conflict with, compete with, and impose upon and shape positive law to suit its particular interests.

To fully appreciate the role and relationship of legal and religions institutions in Smith's analysis, they must both be contextualized in his larger natural selection/evolution/limit frame. We've looked at positive law in that context; now we turn to religion.

ON THE EMERGENCE AND EVOLUTION OF RELIGION

Developing Religious Belief and Order

In the rude state, humankind is so vulnerable to the inconstancies of its marginal existence and is, at the same time, by virtue of human nature, so desperately in need of an explanation of the magnificent but terrifyingly inexplicable, that it turns to stories of "intelligent, though invisible causes" to make sense of them (*HA*, 46):

> Mankind, in the first ages of society, before the establishment of law, order, and security, have little curiosity to find out those hidden chains of events which bind together the seemingly disjointed appearances of nature.... Many ... smaller incoherences, which in the course of things perplex philosophers, entirely escape his [any individual's] attention. Those more magnificent irregularities, whose grandeur he cannot overlook, call forth his amazement. Comets, eclipses, thunder, lightning, and other meteors, by their greatness, naturally overawe him and he views them with a reverence that approaches to fear. His inexperience and uncertainty with regard to every thing about them, how they came, how they are to go, what went before them, what is to come after them, exasperate his sentiment into terror and consternation. But our passions, as Father Malbranche observes, all justify themselves; that is, they suggest to us opinions which justify them. As those appearances terrify him, therefore, he is disposed to believe every thing about them which can render them still more the objects of his terror. That they proceed from some intelligent, though invisible causes, of whose vengeance and displeasure they are either the signs or the effects, is the notion of all others most capable of enhancing this passion, and is that, therefore, which he is most apt to entertain. (*HA*, 48)

These invisible players who treat us as pawns in their game that is our life strike fear in our hearts, for they can, with no warning and for no reason but whim, move us into harm's way.

> But all the irregularities of nature are not of this awful or terrible kind. Some are perfectly beautiful and agreeable. These, therefore, from the same impotence of mind, would be beheld with love and complacency, and even with transports of gratitude; for whatever is the cause of pleasure naturally excites our gratitude. A

child caresses the fruit that is agreeable to it, as it beats the stone that hurts it. The notions of a savage are not very different. (*HA*, 48–9)

Here we see Smith's understanding of the evolution of human society and his understanding of social psychology woven together. As it is with a child, so it is with human society: Both begin in a very immature state with very little sophistication vis-à-vis appearances. As it seems to a child that all the joys and stresses of life are the result of ad hoc decisions of those more powerful beings who control his life, so too for the "savage." For the child, those powers are visible beings – parents in particular, adults in general. For the "savage," those powers are also beings, but in this case they are invisible: They are the gods.

Hence the origin of Polytheism, and of that vulgar superstition which ascribes all the irregular events of nature to the favour or displeasure of intelligent, though invisible beings, to gods, deamons, witches, genii, faires. For it may be observed, that in all Polytheistic religions, among savages, as well as in the early ages of Heathen antiquity, it is the irregular events of nature only that are ascribed to the agency and power of their gods. Fire burns, and water refreshes; heavy bodies descend, and lighter substances fly upwards, by the necessity of their own nature; nor was the invisible hand of Jupiter ever apprehended to be employed in those matters. But thunder and lightning, storms and sunshine, those more irregular events, were ascribed to his favour, or his anger. Man, the only designing power with which they were acquainted, never acts but either to stop, or to alter the course, which natural events would take if left to themselves. Those other intelligent beings, whom they imagined but knew not, were naturally supposed to act in the same manner.... And thus, in the first ages of the world, the lowest and most pusillanimous superstition supplied the place of philosophy. (*HA*, 49–50)

"In the first ages of the world," those living at the margin take "the natural course of things" (*HA*, 44), that is nature and its order, as a given, seamless reality that requires no explanation. What require explanation are the apparently ad hoc interruptions of nature, and those explanations are supplied by analogy: As the hands of humans only act on nature to interrupt its natural course, so, too, it must be the invisible hands of the gods (e.g., "the invisible hand of Jupiter") that account for those magnificent and often terrifying "irregular events" we observe in nature at large.

This polytheistic view not only "explains" the apparently ad hoc events of nature; it also serves humankind in that less mature stage by giving "sanction to the rules of morality...[and] thus enforc[ing] the natural sense of duty":

During the ignorance and darkness of pagan superstition, mankind seem to have formed the ideas of their divinities with so little delicacy, that they ascribed to them, indiscriminately, all the passions of human nature, those not excepted which do the least honor to our species, such as lust, hunger, avarice, envy, revenge. They could not fail, therefore, to ascribe to those beings, for the excellence of whose nature they still conceived the highest admiration, those sentiments and qualities which are the great ornaments of humanity, and which seem to raise it to a resemblance of divine perfection, the love of virtue and beneficence, and the abhorrence of vice and injustice.... These natural hopes and fears, and suspicions, were propagated by sympathy, and confirmed by education; and the gods were universally represented and believed to be the rewarders of humanity and mercy, and the avengers of perfidy and injustice. And thus religion, even in its rudest form, gave a sanction to the rules of morality, long before the age of artificial reasoning and philosophy. That the terrors of religion should thus enforce the natural sense of duty, was of too much importance to the happiness of mankind for nature to leave it dependent upon the slowness and uncertainty of philosophical researches. (*TMS*, 164)

This is classic Smith. The deity designed not only the limiting case of the ideal liberal society, the deity endowed human nature with properties that, by the deity's design and with no human intent, lead in the course of humankind's evolution to the development of institutional instruments that shape the coarse clay of human nature in ways that allow for the progressive evolution of humankind. In the earliest stage of societal development, cohesion requires a common sense of duty. Religion defines and instills that sense.

As society matures, so too does the story of the divine, and a medium for that maturation is philosophy.

Philosophy, by representing the invisible chains which join together all these disjointed objects, endeavours to introduce order into this chaos of jarring and discordant appearances, and to allay this tumult of the imagination.... (*HA*, 45–6)

The philosophic vision implies that nature is a coherent whole, that there is nothing ad hoc about its "jarring and discordant appearances." As philosophy develops our conception of nature as a singular system, theology no longer focuses on the stops of nature but on its wholeness. With this new frame a new explanation is required. Ironically, that new explanation is supplied by the same analogy, human action, but with a different image ... not as the ad hoc actor, but as the designer:

As soon as the Universe was regarded as a complete machine, as a coherent system, governed by general laws, and directed to general ends, viz. its own preservation and prosperity, and that of all the species that are in it; the resemblance which it evidently bore to those machines which are produced by human art, necessarily impressed those sages with a belief, that in the original formation of the world there must have been employed an art resembling the human art, but as much superior to it, as the world is superior to the machines which that art produces. The unity of the system, which, according to this ancient philosophy, is most perfect, suggested the idea of the unity of that principle, by whose art it was formed; and thus, as ignorance begot superstition, science gave birth to the first theism... (*History of Ancient Physics*, (hereafter *HAP*), 113–4)[1]

But, even as philosophy emerges and religion evolves, religion continues to play a central role in humankind's progress.

Religious Order and the Progress of Opulence

The organizing, institutionalizing, and regulating of individual behavior that come with religion complement a simultaneous development in human activity: the division of labor.

The division of labor is "derived" from a "propensity [in all individuals] to truck, barter, and exchange one thing for another" (*WN*, 25). Clearly, only through exchange is it possible for individuals to enjoy the gains from trade that are the fruits of the division of labor. However, as Smith emphasizes again and again, production for exchange requires a sense of security. To the degree that religion establishes and enforces rules that create that sense of security, it facilitates the development of the division of labor.

As the division of labor progresses, issues of property ownership emerge. This necessitates, as described in Chapter Three, rudimentary legal systems to provide the terms that codify and the magistrates that enforce nascent concepts of private property. Religion, by inculcating a moral framework for societal intercourse, can complement and reinforce these legal definitions and sanctions. The security provided by a complementary nexus of religious and legal institutions makes possible accumulation. As Chapters Five and Six describe, the emergence of accumulation is central to Smith's story of the progress of opulence because it is accumulation that provides the capital necessary for an ever-finer division of labor. This increasing division of labor generates even greater surpluses and ever more complex issues of interdependence and ownership, issues that necessitate the evolution of religious and legal systems. As long as religious and legal institutions mature in harmony with the

---

[1] As Spencer Pack writes: "It is philosophy itself that generates the belief in monotheism" (Pack, 302).

process of production, those institutions are instrumental in encouraging the progress of opulence that comes with the ever-finer division of labor.

Among the emerging divisions of labor made possible where religion and positive law provide the security necessary for the progress of opulence is the philosophical reflection necessary for a further systematizing of society's worldview:

[W]hen . . . order and security [are established], and subsistence ceases to be precarious, the curiosity of mankind is increased, and their fears are diminished. The leisure which they then enjoy renders them more attentive to the appearances of nature, more observant of her smallest irregularities, and more desirous to know what is the chain which links them together. That some such chain subsists betwixt all her seemingly disjointed phenomena, they are necessarily led to conceive; and that magnanimity, and cheerfulness, which all generous natures acquire who are bred in civilized societies, where they have so few occasions to feel their weakness, and so many to be conscious of their strength and security, renders them less disposed to employ, for this connecting chain, those invisible beings whom the fear and ignorance of their rude forefathers had engendered. (*HA*, 50)

This emergence of philosophy not only effects the transformation of religion cited earlier, it deepens society's systematic understandings of natural processes, making possible ever more complex and fruitful modes of production[2] and facilitating the transport of commodities over greater distances. This latter development encourages the finer division of labor because it opens up a broader market through which to vent the expanding surpluses that greater productive capacity can generate.

However, whereas natural philosophy has contributed to progress, moral philosophy, having started later (*WN*, 769) and having been more corrupted (*WN*, 771), has not, in Smith's view, made such a significant contribution. For most of humankind's evolution, it has been religion that has inculcated and enforced the ethical norms (the general sense of duty) that

---

[2] "All the improvements in machinery . . . have by no means been the inventions of those who had occasion to use the machines. . . . [Some have been by] those who are called philosophers or men of speculation, whose trade it is, not to do any thing, but to observe every thing; and who, upon that account are often capable of combining together the powers of the most distant and dissimilar objects" (*WN*, 21). "The invention of machines vastly increases the quantity of work which is done . . . [T]he man who first thought of applying steam of water and still more the blast of wind to turn [the mill] . . . by an outer wheel in place of a crank, was neither a millar nor a mill-wright but a philosopher, one of those men who, tho they work at nothing themselves, yet by observing all are enabled by this extended way of thinking to apply things together to produce effects to which they seem noway adapted" (*LJA*, 346–7).

complement positive law in establishing the security that is essential for the progress of opulence.

This power of religion derives from that opinion which is first impressed by nature, and afterwards confirmed by reasoning and philosophy, that those important rules of morality are the commands and laws of the Deity, who will finally reward the obedient, and punish the transgressors of their duty. (*TMS*, 163)

[Religion teaches us that w]e are always acting under the eye, and exposed to the punishment of God, the great avenger of injustice ... [This is an image that is] capable of restraining the most headstrong passions, with those at least who by constant reflection, have rendered it familiar to them.

It is in this manner that religion enforces a natural sense of duty. (*TMS*, 170)[3]

Religion and positive law play an essential, instrumental role in humankind's progress by establishing order and security in society.[4] However, while the human prospect is progress, the process of humankind's evolution is slow and discontinuous because these and other institutions do not evolve in an invariably constructive way. Smith's reading of history suggests to him that, as with the case of positive law described in Chapter Three, religious institutions can be a constructive force in the evolution of society, but they can also be an impediment to or even destructive of that end.

The Catholic Church looms large in Smith's story as an example of a religious institution that played a constructive role at one point in Europe's history, but that maintained its power long after its constructive contribution was history. His description of the Church's role in the evolution of the European university system is a case in point.

THE CHURCH AND THE UNIVERSITY SYSTEM

Smith's lengthy *WN* account of the emergence and evolution of modern European universities[5] begins with the fall of the Roman empire.

---

[3] The power of religion is further enhanced by the fact that for the great bulk of humankind "[t]he institutions for the instruction ... are chiefly those for religious instruction" (*WN*, 788).

[4] For the Scots, "the notion of a refining process, supported by the evidence of improvement in the arts and sciences, became the context for the analysis of human evolution in its entirety, including religious developments. To nearly all Scots, religious history was nothing more than an instance of the way in which civilized people had left barbarism and barbarous ideas behind. It did not provide them with an indication of the future course of events" (Spadafora, 378).

[5] In *WN*, Book I, Smith offers an interesting story of the origin of the modern use of the term university: "Seven years seem anciently to have been, all over Europe, the usual term

During the empire, "[w]hen christianity was first established by law, a corrupted Latin had become the common language of all western parts of Europe" (*WN*, 765). With the empire's collapse, "Latin gradually ceased to be the language of any part of Europe. But the reverence of the people naturally preserves the established forms and ceremonies of religion long after the circumstances which first introduced and rendered them reasonable are no more" (*WN*, 765). So even as Latin ceased to be the language of the people, it remained the language of the Church. "Two different languages were thus established in Europe . . . a language of priests, and a language of the people. . . . " (*WN*, 765) The university emerged, at least in part, to educate "priests . . . [in] that sacred and learned language in which they were to officiate. . . . " (*WN*, 765)

Because the Church decreed "the Latin translation of the Bible . . . to have been equally dictated by divine inspiration, and therefore of equal authority with the Greek and Hebrew originals" (*WN*, 766), those originals were not a part of the university training for priests. In time, however, reformers rejected the "equal authority" of the Latin translation. This issue of translation became a battleground. The Church favored its Latin translations, while reformers reached back to "the Greek text of the new testament, and even the Hebrew text of the old, [as] more favourable to their opinions than the vulgate translation, which, as might naturally be supposed, had been gradually accommodated to support the doctrines of the catholick church" (*WN*, 766). The reformers

set themselves . . . to expose the many errors of that translation, which the Roman catholick clergy were thus put under the necessity of defending or explaining. But this could not well be done without some knowledge of the original languages, of which the study was therefore gradually introduced into the greater part of universities; both of those which embraced, and of those which rejected, the doctrines of reformation. The Greek language was connected with every part of that classical

established for the duration of apprenticeships in the greater part of incorporated trades. All such incorporations were anciently called universities, which indeed is the proper Latin name for any incorporation whatever. The university of smiths, the university of tailors, etc., are expressions which we commonly meet with in the old charters of ancient towns. When those particular incorporations which are now peculiarly called universities were first established, the term of years which it was necessary to study, in order to obtain the degree of master of arts, appears evidently to have been copied from the terms of apprenticeship in common trades, of which the incorporations were much more ancient. As to have wrought seven years under a master properly qualified was necessary in order to entitle any person to become a master, and to have himself apprenticed in a common trade; so to have studied seven years under a master properly qualified was necessary to entitle him to become a master, teacher, or doctor (words anciently synonymous) in the liberal arts, and to have scholars or apprentices (words likewise originally synonymous) to study under him" (*WN*, 136–7).

learning, which . . . happened to come into fashion much about the same time as the doctrines of the reformation were set on foot. (*WN*, 766)

Each side needed to return to the Greek originals to establish the *bona fides* of its translation of the testaments. This in turn required teaching Greek, the language of the ancient classics of philosophy and, as Greek entered the curriculum, so did those classics.

Over time, the structure of that ancient philosophy became the frame for the development of the study of philosophy in the universities. Smith describes this structure as follows: "The antient Greek philosophy was divided into three great branches; physicks, or natural philosophy; ethicks, or moral philosophy; and logick. This general division seems to be agreeable to the nature of things" (*WN*, 766).

As Smith describes in his "History of Astronomy," natural philosophy emerged first as that "science which pretends to explain" "those great phenomena [that] are the first objects of human curiosity" (*WN*, 767). Then, following the systematizing model of natural philosophy, moral philosophy emerged as "the science which pretends to investigate and explain those connecting principles" (*WN*, 768–9) that weave the "rules and maxims for the conduct of human life" into a single system (*WN*, 768).[6] Finally, logic emerged as a method for resolving disputes in these realms of philosophy:

Different authors gave different systems both of natural and moral philosophy. But arrangements by which they supported those different systems, far from being always demonstrations, were frequently at best but very slender probabilities,[7] and sometimes sophisms . . . Gross sophistry has scarce ever had any influence upon the opinions of mankind, except in matters of philosophy and speculation; and in these it has frequently had the greatest. (*WN*, 769)

With alternative systems competing for the attention of and acceptance by the audience,

[t]he patrons of each system of natural and moral philosophy naturally endeavoured to expose the weakness of the arguments adduced to support the systems

---

[6] The purpose of Smith's own enterprise is to imagine "[t]he maxims of common life . . . arranged in some methodical order," and to use that foundation to represent the contours of the principles that guide the evolution of humankind. Based on his analysis of humankind's history, he offers a "systematical arrangement of different observations connected by a few common principles" (*WN*, 768–9) – a Newtonian type effort. But note the "which pretends." As with Newton's work, it is all a product of imagination. Smith uses this same image, "pretends, " when discussing natural and moral philosophy in *TMS* (*TMS*, 313–4) and in *HA* (51).

[7] As noted in Chapter One, *ceteris paribus*, the probability of a system is Smith's metric for persuasiveness.

which were opposite to their own. In examining these arguments, they were necessarily led to consider the difference between a probable and a demonstrative argument, between a fallacious and a conclusive one; and Logick, or the science of the general principles of good and bad reasoning, necessarily arose out of the observations which a scrutiny of this kind gave occasion to. (*WN*, 769–70)

These three branches of ancient philosophy became a part of the university curriculum as an unintended consequence of the debate over translation. But even as the universities evolved from their original form as "ecclesiastical corporations" (*WN*, 765) to centers of philosophical inquiry, the influence of religion continued to affect that evolution.

[The] antient division of philosophy into three parts was in the greater part of the universities of Europe, changed for another into five. [To natural philosophy, moral philosophy, and logic were added metaphysics and ontology.]

In the antient philosophy, whatever was taught concerning the nature either of the human mind or of the Deity, made a part of the system of physics. Those beings, in whatever their essence might be supposed to consist, were parts of the great system of the universe, and parts too productive of the most important effects. Whatever human reason could either conclude, or conjecture, concerning them, made, as it were, two chapters, though no doubt very important ones, of the science which pretended to give an account of the origin and revolutions of the great system of the universe. But in the universities of Europe, where philosophy was taught only as subservient to theology, it was natural to dwell longer upon these two chapters than upon any other of the science. They were gradually more and more extended, and were divided into many inferior chapters, till at last the doctrine of spirits, of which little can be known, came to take up as much room in the system of philosophy as the doctrine of bodies, of which so much can be known. The doctrines concerning these two subjects were considered as making two distinct sciences. What are called Metaphysicks or Pneumaticks were set in opposition to Physicks, and were cultivated not only as more sublime, but, for the purposes of a particular profession, as the more useful science of the two. The proper subject of experiment and observation, a subject in which a careful attention is capable of making so many useful discoveries, was almost entirely neglected. The subject in which, after a few very simple and almost obvious truths, the most careful attention can discover nothing but obscurity and uncertainty, and consequently produce nothing but subtleties and sophisms, was greatly cultivated. (*WN*, 770–1)

And, just as the debate among competing systems of natural and/or moral philosophy gave rise to the science of logic, so to the "opposition" between the sciences of metaphysics and physics "naturally gave birth to a third...called Ontology....But if subtleties and sophisms composed the greater part of the Metaphysicks...they composed the whole of this cobweb science of Ontology..." (*WN*, 771).

The Church's control over the curriculum of major universities of Europe led, in Smith's view, to a terrible distortion of the philosophical enterprise. Indicative of his disgust, he contrasts what moral philosophy, his own realm of inquiry, was and should be with what it became in these universities:

Wherein consisted the happiness and perfection of man, considered not only as an individual, but as the member of a family, of a state, and of the great society of mankind, was the object which the ancient moral philosophy proposed to investigate. In that philosophy the duties of human life were treated of as subservient to the happiness and perfection of human life. But when moral, as well as natural philosophy, came to be treated of as chiefly subservient to theology, the duties of human life were treated of as subservient to the happiness of a life to come. In the antient philosophy the perfection of virtue was represented as necessarily productive, to the person who possessed it, of the most perfect happiness in this life. In the modern philosophy it was frequently represented as generally, or rather as almost always inconsistent with any degree of happiness in this life; and heaven was to be earned only by penance and mortification, by the austerities and abasement of a monk; not by the liberal and generous, and spirited conduct of a man. Casuistry and an ascetic morality made up, in most cases, the greater part of the moral philosophy of the schools. By far the most important of all the different branches of philosophy, became in this manner by far the most corrupted. (*WN*, 771)[8]

This theological-based curriculum not only corrupted moral philosophy, it diminished the university curriculum in natural philosophy because, given the focus on metaphysics, only a "short and superficial system of Physics . . . is what still continues to be taught in the greater part of the universities of Europe. . . ."[9] (*WN*, 772)

There have been, Smith writes, "improvements" in philosophy, but these have not pierced the university "sanctuaries in which exploded

---

[8] This modern theological distortion of philosophy represented, for Smith, a step backward from the ancient philosophy. He valued the old view that places an emphasis on the human condition and conceives of virtue, not as austerity in this world or subservience to another, but as a standard of conduct vis-à-vis other humans. Smith faults theologically based philosophy for suggesting that we should manage our lives as if we *know* the intention of the deity with an eye toward some next world that the deity offers as a reward for doing its bidding in this one. For Smith, this is arrogant, useless, and even harmful. It is arrogant and useless because he did not believe we can know the mind of the deity. It is harmful because by focusing on a next world we neglect the duties we have to one another in this one, and thus diminish the human prospect – a prospect the deity offers us in this world.

[9] However, this harm was mitigated by the fact that, in many universities, nothing was taught, because of incentives that did not reward performance. Smith cites as an example his own experience at Oxford. Given a system of salaries independent of performance, "in the university of Oxford, the greater part of the publick professors have, for these many years, given up altogether even the pretence of teaching" (*WN*, 761).

systems and obsolete prejudices found shelter and protection, after they had been hunted out of every other corner of the world" (*WN*, 772).

Smith could write these words because, while "the greater part of the universities of Europe" (*WN*, 772) were trapped in a doctrinaire focused on "casuistry and an ascetic morality" (*WN*, 771), that was not the case at his own Glasgow University. At Glasgow, Smith was able to study and engage the "antient philosophy" he admired. In particular, he studied issues of virtue with Francis Hutcheson.[10]

This system ["which makes virtue consist of benevolence" (*TMS*, 300)], as it was much esteemed by many ancient fathers of the Christian church, so after the Reformation it was adopted by several divines of the most eminent piety and learning and of the most amiable manners... But of all the patrons of this system, ancient or modern, the late Dr. Hutcheson was undoubtedly, beyond all comparison, the most acute, the most distinct, the most philosophical, and what is of the greatest consequence of all, the soberest and most judicious. (*TMS*, 301)

The story Smith tells of the Church's role in the evolution of the European universities is but a part of his larger story of the evolution of institutional religion in Europe. That evolution, and the emergence of the liberal Scottish church that made possible the flowering of Glasgow University is, in turn, only one chapter in his full story of humankind's evolution. It is, however, an instructive and important chapter because it is from this chapter that Smith culls his principles concerning religion as an institution and his conception of natural religion, that form of religious belief that he sees as consistent with the liberal plan. Now we turn to that larger story, and the lessons Smith culls from it.

THE EVOLUTION OF THE CHURCH IN EUROPE: THE CHURCH AND THE REFORMATION

Smith begins his story of the evolution of the church in Europe by describing the power of an established church:[11]

The clergy of every established church constitute a great corporation. They can act in concert, and pursue their interest upon one plan and with one spirit, as much as if they were under the direction of one man; and they are frequently too

---

[10] "In Adam Smith's first period in Glasgow, students encountered at the University the 'new light' theology and moral philosophy taught by Francis Hutcheson which counteracted the 'old light' Calvinism of the bulk of the local clergy, who could be narrow and bigoted" (Ross, 33).

[11] His concern over this power that motivates the public policy he advocated toward religion is presented in the next section.

under such direction. Their interest as an incorporated body is never the same with that of the sovereign, and is sometimes directly opposite to it.... [Deference is demanded] in order to avoid eternal misery.... Should [a sovereign]... oppose any of their pretensions or usurpations [or defend a citizen who does so], the danger is equally great. (*WN*, 797)

Often, the only way for the sovereign to influence a well-established church is by "management and persuasion" and the best tool for that is "the preferment which he has to bestow upon them" (*WN*, 799). As Smith tells the story, in the case of the Catholic Church, these preferments, coming from many sovereigns, were centrally managed, and over time the power of that management became concentrated in the pope. As a consequence, "[t]he clergy of all the different countries of Europe were thus formed into a sort of spiritual army... directed by one head, and conducted upon one uniform plan... [with] detachments quartered" in every country (*WN*, 800).

The Church accumulated immense wealth from the rents of the tenants on its own estates as well as from "the tythes [that gave it] a very large portion of the rents of all the other estates in every kingdom of Europe" (*WN*, 801). This wealth became the largess that established and sustained the Church's power over retainers who were "entirely dependent... [on its] hospitality and... charity... [and were] perhaps, more numerous than those of all the lay-lords" (*WN*, 801). This army of retainers made the Church

the most formidable combination that ever was formed against the authority and security of civil government, as well as against the liberty, reason, and happiness of mankind, which can flourish only where civil government is able to protect them. (*WN*, 802–3)

The subsequent erosion of this immense power was not a product of reason. Rather it was the consequence of an evolution driven by the unintended consequences of individuals' choices as changing incentives modified particular interests.

Had this constitution [based on "private interest"] been attacked by no other enemies but the feeble efforts of human reason, it must have endured forever. But that immense well-built fabric, which all the wisdom and virtue of man could never have shaken, much less have overturned, was by the *natural course of things*, first weakened, and afterwards in part destroyed, and is now likely, in the course of a few centuries more, perhaps, to crumble into ruins altogether....

The gradual improvements of arts, manufactures, and commerce, the same causes that destroyed the power of the great barons, destroyed in the same manner, through the greater part of Europe, the whole temporal power of the clergy. (*WN*, 803, emphasis added)

As with the case of the "great barons" (described in Chapter Seven), "[t]he clergy [which] could [initially only] derive advantage from its immense surplus" (*WN*, 801) through largess, "discovered [with the emergence of an extended market] the means of spending their whole revenues upon their own persons ... " (*WN*, 803). This encouraged more production for the market in order to earn more to spend in the market. As a result, the largess that supported the army of retainers dried up and the relationship between the clergy and the tenants on Church land was transformed from custodial, sharing some of the surplus with those dependents, to legal, a lease for rent. This transformation led to tenants who were "in a great measure independent" (*WN*, 803) because their well being depended on the market rather than on this benefactor.

The corrosive effect of this change on the power of the clergy – less dependents meant less power – opened up an opportunity for temporal governors to take more power. Across much of Europe, they did so, most often by taking control of election and distributions of benefices. "The authority of the church of Rome was in this state of declension, when the disputes which gave birth to the reformation, began in Germany ... " (*WN*, 805).

The reformation came to a world fertile for change because the existing hierarchy was often resented as old and inert. The enthusiasm of those who offered these new doctrines and their greater command of the history of ideas, gave their movement energy and credibility. "The austerity of their manners [in contrast to the "vanity, luxury, and expence of the richer clergy" (*WN*, 804)] gave them authority with the common people ... " (*WN*, 805). Some sovereigns seized upon this popularity, and, seeking to eliminate the longstanding challenge of the Church, "established the reformation in their own dominions" (*WN*, 806).

As Smith tells the story, lacking a pope to resolve differences of doctrines, inevitable divisions emerged among the reformers. This "gave birth ... [to] the Lutheran and Calvinistic sects ... " (*WN*, 807). The Lutherans followed an "episcopal" model of governance, and by control of benefices "rendered ... [the sovereign] the real head of the church" (*WN*, 807). As, in effect, officers of the sovereign, the Lutheran clergy was polished and well connected to the "sovereign, to the court, and to the nobility and gentry of the country ... " (*WN*, 807). However, it was also a clergy that was out of touch with the concerns of the common people, and thus less able to persuade that public to reject the "ignorant enthusiast" (*WN*, 808).

The Calvinist model was much more individualistic and democratic. Power derived from election by the people of the parish and all clergy were of equal rank. This process invited fanaticism and conflict, and thus led to "disorder and confusion" (*WN*, 808).

The government in Scotland, the largest country to follow this sect, saw fit to manage the process so that these perverse effects did not become destabilizing. The subsequent evolution of the Scottish church is yet another example of serendipitous, unintended consequences.

State management of the elections and benefices largely diminished the fanaticism. What remained in this presbyterian model was the equality of authority and the near-equality of benefice. This meant that a clergyman had no incentive to

pay court to his patron... In all the presbyterian churches, where the rights of patronage are thoroughly established, it is by nobler and better arts that the established clergy in general endeavour to gain the favour of their superiors; by their learning, by the irreproachable regularity of their life, and by the faithful and diligent discharge of their duty.... Nothing but the most exemplary morals can give dignity to a man of small fortune. (*WN*, 809–10)

The presbyterian clergy were thus men of modest means, which allowed them to relate to and with the common people. It also necessitated that, if they sought the respect and affection of the people, they must be leaders and caregivers: noble, kind, and concerned. This, according to Smith, was precisely the character of the clergy in presbyterian countries, and above all in his own Scotland. This also is why the people of those countries were "converted, without persecution, compleatly, and almost to a man..." (*WN*, 810).

The modest benefices for the presbyterian clergy were also beneficial to the universities of the country. There was, after all, a competition between the churches and the universities for the best minds. In places where clergy were liberally rewarded – Smith cites, for example, England and France – all the best minds flowed to their best advantage, the church, to the detriment of the university. This was not the case in Scotland. There, "the mediocrity of the church benefices naturally tend[ed] to draw the greater part of men of letters ... to the employment in which they can be the most useful to the publick, and at the same time, to give them the best education, perhaps, they are capable of receiving" (*WN*, 812).[12]

---

[12] Smith notes that when a professor takes his/her work as a teacher seriously, it enhances his/her scholarship: "To impose upon any man the necessity of teaching, year after year, any particular branch of science, seems, in reality, to be the most effectual method for rendering him completely master of it himself. By being obliged to go every year over

So what lessons regarding church, state, and the liberal plan did Smith cull from this reading of history and his personal experience with religion in Scotland?

THE PRINCIPLES OF RELIGION SMITH CULLS FROM THIS HISTORY: CHURCH, STATE, AND THE LIBERAL PLAN

Smith believes, as does his dear friend David Hume, that new, independent religions are more prone to enthusiasm than established religions. This is so, according to Smith, because:

The teachers of the doctrine which contains this instruction [(religion)], in the same manner as other teachers, may either depend altogether for their subsistence upon the voluntary contributions of their hearers; or they may derive it from some other fund to which the law of the country may entitle them.... Their exertion, their zeal and industry, are likely to be much greater in the former situation than in the latter. In this respect the teachers of new religions have always a considerable advantage in attacking those antient and established systems of which the clergy, reposing themselves upon their benefices, had neglected to keep up the fervour of faith. (*WN*, 788–9)[13]

It is a market argument. The religious monopolist, fat and happy, is "indolent" and cannot match the "popular and bold, though perhaps stupid and ignorant [appeal of the] enthusiasts ... " (*WN*, 789). Smith and Hume also agree that this enthusiasm and superstition, so often associated with new religions, undermines the maturation of society.

The lesson Hume draws from this is that the best strategy to diminish the threat of religious fanaticism is for the state to finance an established religion in order to, in effect, "'bribe their indolence'" (Hume, cited in *WN*, 791). Smith disagrees. As with the Catholic Church, he fears that an established religion would become a "spiritual army ... directed by one head, and conducted upon one uniform plan" (*WN*, 800), and that it could

the same ground, if he is good for anything, he necessarily becomes, in a few years, well acquainted with every part of it: and if upon any particular point he should form too hasty an opinion one year, when he comes in the course of his lectures to reconsider the same subject the year thereafter, he is very likely to correct it. As to be a teacher of science is certainly the natural employment of a mere man of letters, so is it likewise, perhaps, the education which is most likely to render him a man of solid learning and knowledge" (*WN*, 812).

13 One of the great strengths of "the church of Rome ... [was that it maintained the] zeal of the inferior clergy" (*WN*, 789) by requiring them to generate their own income. "It is with them, as with the hussars and light infantry of some armies; no plunder, no pay" (*WN*, 790).

use its independent power base to "over-awe the chiefs and leaders" of the party in power (*WN*, 792).

Smith's reading of history suggests to him that institutional religion emerges out of political disorder when a religion's leaders align themselves with a party involved in a political power struggle. The *quid pro quo* for this support is power-sharing. If their party wins, these religious leaders:

first demand was generally, that he ["the civil magistrate"] should silence and subdue all their adversaries; and their second, that he should bestow an independent provision on themselves. As they had generally contributed a good deal to the victory, it seemed not unreasonable that they should have some share of the spoil. (*WN*, 792)

The lesson Smith draws from this is clear. However it is established, once an institutional religion becomes established, it uses all means to defend its position. When challenged, it follows the classic strategy of a monopolist under siege. The established "clergy ... call upon the civil magistrate to persecute, destroy, or drive out their adversaries, as disturbers of the peace.[14] It was thus that the Roman catholic clergy called upon the civil magistrate to persecute the protestants; and the church of England, to persecute the dissenters ... " (*WN*, 789).

In Smith's view established religions are simply particular examples of a more general political danger, the power of an established faction. Powerful factions, be they religious, mercantile, or some other sort, pursue their own interests at the expense of and thus to the detriment of the general welfare. So, in opposition to Hume, Smith argues that a more constructive model for the relationship between religion and the state is a strict separation of church and state.

Smith envisions a free competition among religious sects in a state that "dealt equally and impartially with all the different sects, and ... allowed every man to chuse his own priest and his own religion as he thought proper" (*WN*, 792).[15] He believes that this competition will lead to a

---

[14] Not unlike the mercantilists' behavior Smith describes in the *WN*.

[15] Note the parallel construction with that other ideal of the liberal plan – the freedom of resources to flow where the owner "thought proper": "The whole of the advantages and disadvantages of the different employments of labour and stock must, in the same neighbourhood, be either perfectly equal or continually tending to equality. If in the same neighbourhood, there was any employment evidently either more or less advantageous than the rest, so many people would crowd into it in the one case, and so many would desert it in the other, that its advantages would soon return to the level of other employments. This at least would be the case in a society where things were left to follow their

great many small sects, diminishing the influence of any one sect and thus the power of any one enthusiasm or superstition. It will also, he suggests, encourage:

> candor and moderation which is so seldom to be found among the teachers of those great sects whose tenets . . .[are] supported by the civil magistrate. . . . The teachers of each little sect, finding themselves almost alone, would be obliged to respect those of almost every other sect, and the concessions which they would mutually find it both convenient and agreeable to make to one another, might in time probably reduce the doctrine of the greater part of them to that pure and rational religion, free from every mixture of absurdity, imposture, or fanaticism, such as wise men have in all ages of the world wished to see established. . . . (*WN*, 793)[16]

Unlike the case of defense (*WN*, 697) or of the education of the young (*WN*, 788), both of which involve public goods (see Chapter Nine), religion is not, according to Smith, a public good. There is, therefore, no justification for government subsidization of, or in any way giving privilege to, any religion.[17] Quite to the contrary, Smith argues, such subsidies or privileges give encouragement to institutions that can become formidable to the state and destructive to the nation.

Beyond the short-term benefit of a government independent of religious influence and the long-term benefit of "reduc[ing] the doctrine of the greater part of them to that pure and rational religion, free from every mixture of absurdity, imposture, or fanaticism," Smith also believes that his many sects, market solution to the provision of religion would offer a valuable service to a liberal society.

"In a society where things were left to follow their natural course, where there was perfect liberty, and where every man was perfectly free

---

natural course, where there was perfect liberty, and where every man was perfectly free both to chuse what occupation he *thought proper*, and to change it as often as he *thought proper*. Every man's interest would prompt him to seek the advantageous, and to shun the disadvantageous employment" (*WN*, 116, emphasis added).

[16] He suggests that the Pennsylvania experiment has demonstrated the credibility of this position (*WN*, 793).

[17] Absent any justification for provision of religion at the public expense, that provision should, like most others, be determined in the market. Hume, cited in Smith, expresses it beautifully: "'[For m]ost of the arts and professions in the state . . . the constant rule of the magistrate, except, perhaps, on the first introduction of any art, is, to leave the profession to itself, and trust its encouragement to the individuals who reap the benefit of it. The artisans finding their profits to rise by the favour of their customers, increase, as much as possible, their skill and industry; and as matters are not disturbed by any injudicious tampering, the commodity is always sure to be at all times nearly proportioned to the demand'" (Hume cited in *WN*, 790).

both to chuse what occupation he thought proper, and to change it as often as he thought proper" (*WN*, 116), people move about the country in search of opportunities. As people move from the community of a "country village" to the anonymity of the "great city," they lose the moral reference point of the spectators who know them and can, through approbation and disapprobation, constructively influence their behavior. In this anonymous and lonely condition, it is easy to sink into "low profligacy and vice" (*WN*, 795). "[B]ecoming a member of a small religious sect" (*WN*, 795) can provide a new community and thus a new moral reference point. It is a morality enforced by the powerful threat that "expulsion or excommunication" (*WN*, 796) can throw one back into lonely isolation. "In little religious sects, accordingly, the morals of the common people have been always remarkably regular and orderly . . ." (*WN*, 796).

But while Smith sees his scheme of many competing sects as superior to Hume's state institutionalize religion, he is wary that even under his scheme the destructive potential of religion, enthusiasm, and superstition, could infect the citizenry. So, he offers:

two very easy and effectual remedies . . . by whose joint application the state might, without violence, correct whatever was unsocial or disagreeably rigorous in the morals of all the little sects into which the country was divided.

The first of those remedies is the study of science and philosophy, which the state might render almost universal among all people of middling or more than middling rank and fortune . . . Science is the great antidote to the poison of enthusiasm and superstition, and where the superior ranks of the people were secure from it, the inferior ranks could not be much exposed to it. (*WN*, 796)

The second remedy is insuring the "liberty" (*WN*, 796) of public diversions. Where individuals enjoy the opportunity to be entertained by the arts, they are less prone to that "melancholy and gloomy humour which is always the nurse of popular superstition and enthusiasm" (*WN*, 796). Indeed, those who seek to whip up the public frenzy are often the subject of ridicule by those in the arts, and thus freedom of the arts is a tool in extinguishing the effect of hot rhetoric.

THE MODERATE LITERATI OF SCOTLAND, NATURAL RELIGION,
AND SMITH'S OWN RELATIONSHIP TO RELIGION

Smith's competing sects scheme is his plan for creating a dynamic that would ultimately bring institutional religion toward a closer approximation of natural religion. In contrast to institutionalized religion, Smith imagines that under

the natural principles of religion...[people would not] regard frivolous observances, as more immediate duties of religion, than acts of justice and beneficence;...[or] imagine, that by sacrifices, and ceremonies, and vain supplications, they can bargain with the Deity....(*TMS*, 170)

The essence of natural religion is for Smith:

- a faith in the existence of the benevolent deity,
- a commitment to imagining and living by the principles of an ideal, impartial spectator that emphasize "acts of justice and beneficence" (*TMS*, 170), and
- a humility in one's application of those principles.

This is not the religious environment into which Smith was born, so how did Smith come to hold this view? How did his ideas regarding religion evolve?[18]

As Richard Sher describes in his (1985) *Church and University in the Scottish Enlightenment: The Moderate Literati of Edinburgh*, Smith lived during a time of significant evolution in the Church of Scotland. Central to this evolution was the emergence of the Moderate party.

This party was led by a cohort of ministers who were born within three years of 1720 (Sher, 162). Smith was born in 1723. Most of these ministers were intellectual heirs of Francis Hutcheson.[19] So, too, was Smith. "[T]he Moderate literati of Edinburgh dominated the kirk during the 1760s, 1770s, and early 1780s" (Sher, 121). These were the very years of Smith's lectures at Glasgow, the publication of the *TMS* and the *WN*, and the evolution of his ideas in the revisions of those works. In short, the Moderate literati were Smith's intellectual contemporaries. Indeed, he was a part "of the Moderate literati's circle" (Sher, 60; see also 61, 68).

The Moderate literati shared with Smith several of the central tenets of his moral philosophy:

- There is a "goodness of Providence" (Sher, 183).
- Society is evolving in a progressive way (Sher, 205, 250).

---

[18] See Raphael and Macfie, Appendix II (Raphael and Macfie, 1976) "A Passage on Atonement..." and (Bittermann, 1940) for thoughtful commentaries on this issue.

[19] Sher writes of "the Moderates' philosophical mentor Francis Hutcheson" (Sher, 16) and so, too, he served Smith.

- Religion can be a constructive force for positive change if it emphasizes "acts of justice and beneficence" (*TMS*, 170) in the context of "pure and rational religion, free from every mixture of absurdity, imposture, or fanaticism . . . " (*WN*, 793).

As Sher describes it:

Moderatism was dedicated to propagating many of the leading values of the Enlightenment, especially religious tolerance and freedom of expression, reasonableness and moderation, polite learning and literature, humanitarianism and cosmopolitanism, virtue, and happiness. (Sher, 328)

This is Smith's kind of institutional religion. Indeed, he writes that "[t]here is scarce perhaps to be found any where in Europe a more learned, decent, independent, and respectable set of men, than the greater part of the presbyterian clergy of Holland, Geneva, Switzerland, and Scotland" (*WN*, 810).

But although Smith and the Moderate literati shared mutual respect and many common values, their views diverged when it came to institutional religion itself. This divergence seems to have been due to Smith's personal evolution regarding religious orthodoxy. As Bittermann writes: Smith "may have been a tolerably orthodox, if latitudinarian, Christian in 1759 and his views may have changed subsequently. The frequent references to the Deity in the last edition of the ethical essay [*TMS* in 1790], far too numerous to constitute merely prudent camouflage, would indicate that [the older] Smith held to a natural theology. . . . " (Bittermann, 1940B, 714) In the same spirit, Raphael asserts that "[t]here is ample evidence that Smith abandoned a belief in Christian doctrine (while retaining a form of natural religion) long before 1790" (Raphael, 1992 116).

Much of the evidence to this effect comes from the successive revisions of the *Theory of Moral Sentiments*, and the most interesting of these is the evolution of Smith's words on the relationship between religion and the concept of divine judgment.

In Part II, Section II, Chapter III of the *Theory of Moral Sentiments*, entitled "Of the utility of this constitution of Nature," Smith makes the case, as described in Chapter Three of this volume, that although there is social utility in the punishment of crimes, the ultimate motivation for punishment is the natural disposition for retribution based on resentment. In the original edition of the *TMS* (1759) he notes that this desire for retribution extends beyond the grave:

For it well deserves to be taken notice of, that we are so far from imagining that injustice ought to be punished in this life, merely on account of the order of society, which cannot otherwise be maintained, that Nature teaches us to hope, and religion authorises us to expect, that it will be punished, even in a life to come. Our sense of its ill desert pursues it, if I may say so, even beyond the grave.... (*TMS*, 91, original version cited in note b–b)

He goes on in the original edition to assert that as with humankind, so, too, with the deity, virtue is rewarded or vice is punished "for its own sake":

That the Deity loves virtue and hates vice... only because it promotes the happiness of society... is not the doctrine of nature, but of an artificial, though ingenious, refinement of philosophy.... All our natural sentiments prompt us to believe, that as perfect virtue is supposed necessarily to appear to the Deity, as it does to us, for its own sake, and without any further view, the natural and proper object of love and reward, so must vice, of hatred and punishment. (*TMS*, 91–2, note c–c)

Then, given this conception of the deity's standard of judgment, in the original edition Smith turns to the fear we must naturally feel as we, such imperfect beings, prepare to stand for judgment before that perfect one:

Man, when about to appear before a being of infinite perfection, can feel but little confidence in his own merit, or in the imperfect propriety of his own conduct. In the presence of his fellow-creatures, he may often justly elevate himself, and may often have reason to think highly of his own character and conduct, compared to the still greater imperfection of theirs. But the case is quite different when about to appear before his infinite Creator. To such a being, he can scarce imagine, that his littleness and weakness should ever seem to be the proper object, either of esteem or of reward. But he can easily conceive, how the numberless violations of duty, of which he has been guilty, should render him the proper object of aversion and punishment; neither can he see any reason why the divine indignation should not be let loose without any restraint, upon so vile an insect, as he is sensible that he himself must appear to be. If he would still hope for happiness, he is conscious that he cannot demand it from the justice, but that he must entreat it from the mercy of God. Repentance, sorrow, humiliation, contrition at the thought of his past conduct, are ... the only means which he has left for appeasing the wrath which, he knows, he has justly provoked. He even distrusts the efficacy of all these.... Some other intercession, some other sacrifice, some other atonement, he imagines, must be made for him, beyond what he himself is capable of making, before the purity of the divine justice can be reconciled to his manifold offences. The doctrines of revelation coincide, in every respect, with those original anticipations of nature; and, as they teach us how little we can depend upon the imperfection of our own virtue, so they show us, at the same time, that the most powerful intercession has been made, and that the most dreadful atonement has been paid for our manifold transgressions and iniquities. (*TMS*, 91–2, note c–c)

This language ("divine indignation ... upon so vile an insect") reflects the heritage of the "straight and narrow Calvinist orthodoxy [of Smith's youth].... When Voltaire visited Britain in the late 1720s [(Smith was born in 1723)], the term 'Scotch Presbyterian' was still considered with intolerance and overbearing piety" (Sher, 152). It was this Scottish church into which Smith and the Moderate literati were born. But as the Moderate literati were transforming the church, so, too, Smith's views on religion were evolving.

As is reflected in the original passages from the *TMS* cited here, in 1759 that dimension of institutionalized religion that related to a belief in an afterlife, to judgment, and to revelation is still a part of Smith's vision. But by 1767, when Smith publishes the Third Edition of the *TMS*, he seems to be easing away from this "straight and narrow."

In a theological passage [(((*TMS*, 91, original version cited in note b–b) cited previously)] ... and the paragraph that then followed it, the categorical tone of certain phrases is softened to a problematic one: for example, 'religion authorises' becomes 'religion, we suppose, authorises', and 'neither can he [man] see any reason' becomes 'and he thinks he can see no reason'. (Raphael and Macfie, 39)

By the Sixth Edition, published in 1790, all the language about god, repentance, doctrines of revelation, and atonement cited previously (*TMS*, 91–2, note c–c) is removed and is replaced with a single sentence:

In every religion, and in every superstition that the world has ever beheld, accordingly, there has been a Tartarus as well as an Elysium; a place provided for the punishment of the wicked, as well as one for the reward of the just. (*TMS*, 91)

But even as Smith seems to abandon the institutional doctrine associated with divine judgment, he maintains his belief in its psychic utility. Recognizing that, all too often, the judgments of this life can be terribly unjust (He cites as an example the injustice perpetrated on Jean Calas in the name of religion (*TMS*, 120).), he writes in his revisions to the Sixth Edition that:

Our happiness in this life is thus, upon many occasions, dependent upon the humble hope and expectation of a life to come: a hope and expectation deeply rooted in human nature; which can alone support its lofty ideas of its own dignity.... That there is a world to come ... is a doctrine, in every respect so venerable, so comfortable to the weakness, so flattering to the grandure of human nature, that the virtuous man who has the misfortune to doubt of it, cannot possibly avoid wishing most earnestly and anxiously to believe it. (*TMS*, 132)

This leap of faith, this act of imagination, provides the virtuous man who doubts the institutional doctrine of divine judgment with the tranquility and serenity of prospective justice in the "life to come."[20] This move from institutional doctrine to deinstitutionalized faith also reflects the evolution of Smith's personal relation to religion.

For the mature Smith, the deity is not about institutional doctrine or scientific proof, the deity is about faith. As Philo, the skeptic in Hume's *Dialogues Concerning Natural Religion*, expresses it:

[T]here is no view of human life, or of the condition of mankind, from which, without the greatest violence, we can infer the moral attributes, or learn that infinite benevolence, cojoined with infinite power and infinite wisdom, which we must discover by the eyes of faith alone. (Hume, 201–2)

This faith is the source of Smith's hope for humankind and the motivation for his life as a moral philosopher, a life committed to representing the invisible connecting principles that can lead humankind toward that benevolent prospect with which the deity has endowed humankind: "the liberal plan of equality, liberty and justice" (*WN*, 664).

Smith's reading of history convinced him that if religious institutions and positive law evolve in constructive ways, they complement the natural progress of opulence; and when these three dimensions are evolving constructively together, humankind will be moving toward the human prospect. Chapters Three and Four have described Smith's analysis of two of these dimensions and the principles of progress he culls from that analysis. The next five chapters examine Smith's representation of that third dimension of humankind's evolution: the progress of opulence.

---

[20] It is a truly extraordinary being who, maintaining his virtue in the face of public rejection and disapprobation, has the internal tranquility and serenity to die at peace with himself without any expectation of an imaginary Elysium awaiting him. For Smith, David Hume was just such an extraordinary being. In his letter describing Hume's behavior in the face of impending death, Smith writes of Hume's serenity and even good humor in the face of the finality of death. Smith admired Hume, but Smith enjoyed the comfort of faith.

PART TWO

ON THE PLACE OF *THE WEALTH OF NATIONS* IN ADAM SMITH'S MORAL PHILOSOPHICAL VISION

FIVE

On the Progress of Opulence, Setting the Scene in Book I of *The Wealth of Nations*

MOVING INTO THE THIRD DIMENSION

As the name of the work implies, Smith turns his focus to an analysis of the progress of opulence in his *Inquiry into the Nature and Causes of the Wealth of Nations*. I begin my inquiry into Smith's *Inquiry* where he began, in *WN* Book I, where he sets the scene for his analysis of the progress of opulence by

- laying out the assumptions (e.g., the propensity to truck, barter, and exchange) he brings to the analysis,
- explaining the principles (e.g., the division of labor) that guide that analysis,
- defining the terms essential for presenting that analysis (e.g., wages, rent, profit, interest),
- describing the characteristics of individual markets in an exchange system through partial analysis, contrasting the natural and unnatural cases,
- anticipating some of the themes that will be developed as he moves from a partial to a general, dynamic analysis of an exchange system and the progress of opulence (the efficiency of competition, the central role of accumulation, the essential role of laws and institutions), and
- describing the process through which the commercial stage emerges in the course of the progress of opulence.

THE FOUNDATION OF THE PROGRESS OF
OPULENCE: THE DIVISION OF LABOR

The Division of Labor and Productivity

Smith believes the key to the progress of opulence is increasing the productivity of labor, so what better place to start an *Inquiry into the Nature and Causes of the Wealth of Nations* than with the words:

The greatest improvement in the productive powers of labour, and the greater part of the skill, dexterity, and judgment with which it is any where directed, or applied, seem to have been the effects of the division of labor. (*WN*, 13)

This principle of the division of labor is familiar to any introductory economics student. By dividing up the labor of society, each individual can increase his productivity. This is so because by focusing on one task, individuals enhance their "dexterity" (practice makes perfect), save time "commonly lost in passing from one species of work to another," and become more inventive (*WN*, 17). Smith suggests that the benefits of this increased productivity are obvious if we simply reflect on our own experience.

Consider, he says, "[t]he woollen coat" of "the most common artificer or day-labourer in a civilized and thriving country" (*WN*, 16). From this familiar image he develops the rich and complex idea of the division of labor by imagining all the hands involved in producing such a coat. The full quotation is long and wonderfully imaginative, but indicative of the web of connections he represents as behind the appearance of this apparently simple product, he includes the "ship-builders, sailors, sail-makers, rope-makers, [that] must have been employed in order to bring together the different drugs made use of by the dyer, which come from the remotest corners of the world!" (*WN*, 23)

It is the great multiplication of the productions of all the different arts, in consequence of the division of labour, which occasions, in a well-governed society, that universal opulence which extends itself to the lowest ranks of the people. (*WN*, 22)

"[W]ell-governed society," "that universal opulence which extends itself to the lowest ranks of the people" . . . Here, in the opening pages of the *WN*, Smith is making explicit that essential connection in his simultaneous, evolving system: the constitution of social and political institutions, the progress of opulence, and the human prospect are interdependent. As described in Chapters Three and Four, Smith believes that the fruits of the division of labor can only be reaped to the degree that the laws and institutions of a society secure justice. So a "well-governed society," governed well by its government and by the ethics of its citizens, is the *sine qua non* of the bountiful wealth of nations that begins with the division of labor and makes possible that benign prospect that "extends itself to the lowest ranks of the people."

The Source of the Division of Labor

The division of labor, from which so many advantages are derived, is not originally the effect of any human wisdom, which foresees and intends that general opulence to which it gives occasion. It is the necessary, though very slow and gradual, consequence of a certain propensity in human nature which has in view no such extensive utility – the propensity to truck, barter, and exchange one thing for another. (*WN*, 25)

Is this propensity "one of those original principles in human nature" or is it "the necessary consequence of the faculties of reason and speech"? Smith considers the former "more probable," but goes on to say that the answer to this question "belongs not to our present subject to enquire" (*WN*, 25). What matters to Smith is not the origin but the raison d'etre of this propensity.[1] It is a part of that "oeconomy of nature [which, by design,] . . . not only endowed mankind with an appetite for the end which she proposes [(in this case the progress of opulence)], but likewise with an appetite for the means by which alone this end can be brought about [(in this case the propensity to truck, barter, and exchange)]" (*TMS*, 77).[2]

---

[1] Smith's agnosticism on this point is indicative of the way he approaches moral philosophy more generally. As noted in Chapter One, beyond the basic assumption that the universe he is exploring is the design of a benevolent deity, Smith is not into metaphysics. He does not therefore get caught up in the origins of the concepts he adopts. He just imagines those concepts that make sense to tell his story. His purpose is to tell a compelling story of humankind's evolution and to imagine the principles of that process so as to inform policy. We'll see that there are several places in his story of the progress of opulence (e.g., with respect to value) when Smith briefly delves into metaphysical questions, but then moves on to the more instrumental analysis necessary to tell his story. Here he reflects on the origin of the propensity to truck, barter, and exchange but quickly moves on, noting only that whatever the origin "[i]t is common to all men" (*WN*, 25). The assumed condition in place, the metaphysics are left behind.

[2] The "oeconomy of nature" refers to an example of the elegance of the design: The deity has endowed humankind with propensities that advance the interest of the individual and that in the process, but by no intention of the individual, also advance the ends of nature. Nature also advances her ends by "deception[s]" (*TMS*, 183) that the deity plants in our nature. A classic example of such a deception is the case of "[t]he poor man's son,

Given this propensity in human nature that gives rise to the division of labor, Smith offers the following conjectural history of the emergence of the division of labor and exchange:

A savage who supports himself by hunting, having made some more arrows than he had occasion for,[3] gives them in a present to some of his companions, who in return give him some of the venison they have catched; and he at last finding that by making arrows and giving them to his neighbour, as he happens to make them better than ordinary, he can get more venison than by his own hunting, he lays it aside...and becomes an arrow-maker. In the same manner one who makes coverings for huts becomes altogether a maker of coverings, another a smith, another a tanner, etc.[4] (*LJA*, 348). ["This bartering and trucking spirit is the cause of the separation of trades and the improvements in arts" (*LJA*, 348)]...

[As the labor is divided among the people n]o human prudence is requisite to make this division...[I]f things be allowed to take their naturall course there is no danger that any branch of trade should be either over or under stocked with hands...The certainty of disposing of the su<r>plus produce of his labour in this way is what ena<b>led men to separate into different trades of ev<e>ry sort (*LJA*, 351).

This "certainty of disposing" brings us to the role of the market in Smith's analysis.

The division of labor leaves each individual with a surplus of that one item he produces and a dearth of all those other items he needs for his subsistence. The arrow-maker, for example, cannot eat his arrows. Thus, the value of the division of labor for any individual is predicated on the exchange of his surplus for other commodities from others' surpluses.

---

whom heaven in its anger has visited with ambition, when he begins to look around him, admires the condition of the rich..." (*TMS*, 181) Another is our fetish for elegance and design: "How many people ruin themselves by laying out money on trinkets of frivolous utility? What pleases these lovers of toys is not so much the utility, as the aptness of the machines which are fitted to promote it" (*TMS*, 179–80). As Winch writes: "The individual benefits associated with material goods are greatly exaggerated.... [but their pursuit is socially beneficial because] economic growth was capable of generating rising absolute living standards for the mass of society...[and with it] less 'servile dependency' in social relationships...." (Winch, 1988, 99). See also (Thompson, 227–8).

[3] "Before labour can be divided some accumulation of stock is necessary" (*LJB*, 521).

[4] According to Smith, it is this flow into different professions that gives rise to the different talents of men, not the different natural talents that gives rise to the flow: "The difference of natural talents in different men is, in reality, much less that we are aware of; and the very different genius which appears to distinguish men of different professions, when grown up to maturity, is not upon many occasions so much the cause, as the effect of the division of labour. The difference between the most dissimilar characters, between a philosopher and a common street porter, for example, seems to arise not so much from nature, as from habit, custom, and education" (*WN*, 28–9). As described in Chapter One, we may turn out very differently, but we are all molded from the same "coarse clay" (*TMS*, 162).

This, in turn, requires that what we each bring to the exchange satisfies the desires of those with whom we hope to exchange. Thus, "if we should enquire into the principle in the human mind on which this disposition of trucking is founded, it is clearly the naturall inclination of every one has to persuade" (*LJA*, 352):

It is not from the benevolence of the butcher, the brewer, or the baker, that we expect our dinner, but from their regard to their own interest. We address ourselves, not to their humanity but to their self-love, and never talk to them of our own necessities but of their advantages. (*WN*, 26–7)

This may be the most famous passage in all of Smith's work.[5] It is surely the most dangerous if it is read out of context. Smith's immediate point here is straightforward. As explained in Chapter One, self-love is the spring for human action and it can serve us. What is not on this page of the *WN* is the context. In Smith's moral philosophy, the benefits of self-love are premised on the presence of the "well-governed society." Reading this passage from *The Wealth of Nations* without that context in mind can easily lead to a significant misreading of Adam Smith.

The Limits of the Division of Labor

"The division of labour is limited by the extent of the market" (*WN*, 31). There is, after all, no reward for great productivity or very specialized production if there is not sufficient effective demand to vent one's surplus. Thus, the pursuit of greater productivity, the ever-finer division of labor, is only justified by an ever-more extensive market. This, in turn, is a function of transportation possibilities because these are a significant determinant of the transaction opportunities and costs.

Writing in the 1770s, it seems natural to Smith that, *ceteris paribus*, "water-carriage" (*WN*, 32) is by far the widest and cheapest avenue to an extended market. Thus, he argues that the natural course of development would follow those natural advantages that come with access to navigable routes through coastal ports and/or rivers. Always the empiricist, Smith makes his case by turning to history.

The nations that, according to the best authenticated history,[6] appear to have been first civilized, were those that dwelt round the coast of the Mediterranean

---

[5] The "invisible hand" is certainly the most enduring image, but this may be the most quoted passage.

[6] To his credit, Smith is consistently conscious of the credibility of his sources. To his discredit, all too often he does not cite his sources.

sea. That sea, by far the greatest inlet that is known in the world, having no tides, nor consequently any waves except such as are caused by the wind only, was, by the smoothness of its surface, as well as by the multitude of its islands, and the proximity of its neighbouring shores, extremely favourable to the infant navigation of the world; when, from their ignorance of the compass, men were afraid to quit the view of the coast, and from the imperfection of the art of ship-building, to abandon themselves to the boisterous waves of the ocean. . . .

Of all the countries on the coast of the Mediterranean sea, Egypt seems to have been the first in which either agriculture or manufactures were cultivated and improved to any considerable degree. . . . The extent and easiness of . . . inland navigation[7] was probably one of the principal causes of the early improvement of Egypt. (*WN*, 34–5)[8]

In moving from an analysis of the division of labor as an exchange between individuals to the larger issue of the refinement of the division of labor depending on the extent of the market, Smith transitions from a story about human nature and interpersonal interactions to one about human societies and their possibilities. As this broader analysis unfolds, the extent of the market becomes the tipping point that determines how societies grow within a given stage and which societies evolve from stage to stage.

To move from analyzing the simple exchange between persons to analyzing the evolution of complex exchange within and among societies,

---

[7] Always aware of the constraints of institutions, having described the natural advantages of good access to water-carriage, Smith adds a caveat regarding unnatural distortions along river routes: "The commerce . . . which any nation can carry on by means of a river which does not break itself into any great number of branches or canals, and which runs into another territory before it reaches the sea, can never be very considerable; because it is *always in the power of the nation* who possess that other territory to obstruct the communication between the upper country and the sea" (*WN*, 36, emphasis added). He cites the Danube as an example of this. In contrast, the advancement of Britain rests, according to Smith, at least in part on the good fortune that as an island it has many opportunities for unhindered coastal trade, and that the island has a large navigable river unencumbered by other national jurisdictions.

[8] He writes similarly of China and Bengal: "The improvements in agriculture and manufactures *seem* likewise to have been of very great antiquity in the provinces of Bengal, in the East Indies, and in some of the eastern provinces of China; *though the great extent of this antiquity is not authenticated by any histories of whose authority we, in this part of the world, are well assured.* In Bengal the Ganges and several other great rivers form a great number of navigable canals in the same manner as the Nile does in Egypt. In the Eastern provinces of China too, several great rivers form, by their different branches, a multitude of canals, and by communicating with one another afford an inland navigation much more extensive than that either of the Nile or the Ganges, or perhaps than both of them put together" (*WN*, 35, emphasis added). I highlight to emphasize Smith's consciousness of his own use of conjectural history.

Smith introduces the medium and measures of exchange: money, value, and prices.[9]

ON MONEY, VALUE, AND PRICES

Money. With the extension of the market and the finer division of labor, trade becomes more complex. In a complex trading environment, barter clogs the system, so general equivalents emerge. Initially cattle, salt, or the like function as a general equivalent, but eventually metals play this role because they are less perishable and more finely divisible (*WN*, 39). Raw forms of metals posed problems of assaying, however, so stamps were affixed to warrant quality. This was "the origin of coined money" (*WN*, 40). But still there was the issue of the integrity of the quantity, so to address this, full stamps "covering entirely both sides . . . and sometimes the edges" (*WN*, 41) were introduced.[10]

Having introduced the medium of exchange, money, Smith turns to the measure of exchange: value and price. He tells us, as he makes this turn, that his purpose is to:

- determine the "real measure of . . . exchangeable value; or, wherein consists the real price of all commodities,"
- identify "what are the different parts of which this real price is composed or made up," and
- understand the forces that cause the "the market, that is the actual price of commodities" to vary at any given time from their "natural or ordinary" price (*WN*, 46).

---

[9] Harpham offers a very nice summary of the structure of what Smith is doing here, and in particular the role of the piece on money, value, and prices in Smith's larger story: "Smith saw Book I as addressing two related problems: the causes of the improvement of the productive powers of labor and the natural order according to which it is distributed. The first inquiry takes up chapters 1–3. The second takes up chapters 8–11. Chapters 4–7 are transitional and provide a framework for thinking about exchange relations in a market economy based on money. Smith is not a neoclassical theorist interested in price [or value] for its own sake. He develops his theory of prices to pave the way for a discussion of the distributional shares that go to land, labor, and capital under conditions of economic growth, stagnation, and decline. His conclusions presented at the end of the chapter on rent carefully spell out how, over the long run, the general public, as well as landowners and laborers, come to benefit from the growth that proceeds from advances in social knowledge accompanying the division of labor" (Harpham, 2000, 222).

[10] Money remains problematic, however, because of government debasement – a revenue trick that Smith equates with fraud.

Before he begins this analysis, however, he addresses the distinction between value in use and value in exchange.

Ironically, he notes, "[t]he things which have the greatest value in use have frequently little or no value in exchange; and, on the contrary, those which have the greatest value in exchange have frequently little or no value in use" (*WN*, 44). For example "[n]othing is more useful than water" and yet it has very little value in exchange, while "[a] diamond . . . has scarce any value in use" but has immense exchange value (*WN*, 44–5).

This appears to be an anomaly, but as Smith goes on to explain, this diamond–water paradox is not so strange if one considers that exchange value depends on the relationship between the quantity supplied and the effective demand. Diamonds simply represent a peculiar case in which the quantity supplied cannot be continuously expanded by additional labor to meet the effective demand. This constraint on supply causes the price to be higher than the cost of production. In what he considers the normal case, such as with water, the quantity can (under undistorted circumstances and excluding the obvious case of an arid region) be expanded continuously by additional applications of labor and so the exchange value is determined in the process of production.

It sounds simple, but he warns us that "perhaps, after the fullest explication which I am capable of giving of it, . . . [the concept of value may] appear still in some degree obscure" (*WN*, 46).[11]

Value. "Labour[, according to Smith,] . . . is the real measure of the exchangable value of all commodities" (*WN*, 47). Because it represents the "toil and trouble of acquiring" a commodity, it reflects its real worth to the individual (*WN*, 47). But labor is rarely embodied in a pure, unaided form in the production process (it is generally used in concert with capital) and the requirements of various kinds of labor (the physical or mental demands, the preparation, the maturity) are different, so labor embodied becomes a muddled image. Smith turns, therefore, to the concept of labor commanded: for how much "labor" can a commodity be exchanged? He recognizes that this is "an abstract notion" (*WN*, 49), but he believes that it represents the purest image of the labor value of a commodity.[12]

---

[11] His next words reemphasize this caveat: "I am always willing to run some hazard of being tedious in order to be sure that I am perspicuous; and after taking the utmost pains that I can to be perspicuous, some obscurity may still appear to remain upon a subject in its own nature extremely abstracted" (*WN*, 46).

[12] Subsequently, when he discusses the value of a commodity in the abstract, he consistently uses the labor command notion as his measure. See (*WN*, 162, 176, 185, 191–2, 194, 205,

Smith's caveat on his presentation of value – that, "perhaps, after the fullest explication which I am capable of giving of it, [it may] appear still in some degree obscure" – is well taken. After two centuries of examination, dissection, and debate, his conception of value is still "obscure."[13] So if Smith does not feel his analysis has done the subject of value justice, why does he leave it in this form? In 1784, he returns to *The Wealth of Nations* and makes very significant additions and corrections, but the only significant change in the chapter that addresses value is an additional paragraph (after the original second paragraph) in which he distinguishes wealth from direct "political power" (*WN*, 48). In 1790, he publishes very significant changes to the *Theory of Moral Sentiments*, but still his "obscure" value theory in the *WN* remains untouched.[14]

I believe the reason Smith does not return to his analysis of value theory is that, with regard to value, he has accomplished all that mattered to his subsequent analysis. His objective is not metaphysical, to reveal the source of value.[15] His purpose is immensely practical. He needs an intertemporal metric or index of value to make price comparisons as he tells his evolutionary story of change in humankind's material condition, his story of the progress of opulence.[16]

Early in the *WN*, Smith writes that "[i]n such a work as this … it may sometimes be of use to compare the different real values of a particular commodity at different times and places. … " (*WN*, 55) For this purpose, the measure he settles on as the best available, consistent metric of value over the long term is corn.

207, 210, 224, 229, 236, 237, 255, 262, 264, 355, 356, 535) for some of the occasions on which he cites labor command as his metric.

[13] See Hueckel (2000) for an excellent piece on Smith's value analysis.

[14] Griswold describes Smith as "a careful writer, who went to some pains … to 'comb and curl' his works through several editions. He had many opportunities to straighten out infelicities or errors in his formulations, and he did so" (Griswold, 1999, 29). Yet, Smith never addressed the value muddle in a revision.

[15] He does offer a metaphysical perspective about value. He believed it is based on labor. However, as in that earlier propensity to truck, barter and exchange case, here, too, he is not concerned about the metaphysics. Indicative of this, it seems that Smith altered his language to distance himself from any metaphysical connotations. In Chapter Six, in two places he replaces the phrase "source of value" with the term "component part." See editors' notes d-d and j-j (*WN*, 67). There is much value in exploring Smith on value. This issue becomes paramount beginning with Ricardo, and Smith offers an important frame for understanding the subsequent focus on value. However, to attribute Ricardo's concern about value to Smith is, I believe, a mistake.

[16] As he puts it: "[T]he distinction between the real and the nominal price of commodities and labour, is not a matter of pure speculation, but may sometimes be of considerable use in practice" (*WN*, 51).

Upon all... accounts... we may rest assured, that equal quantities of corn will, in every state of society, in every stage of improvement, most nearly represent, or be equivalent to, equal quantities of labour, than equal quantities of any other part of the rude produce of land. Corn accordingly... is, in all the different stages of wealth and improvement, a more accurate measure of value than any other commodity or sett of commodities. (*WN*, 206)[17]

Here, Smith not only explains his choice of corn as a consistent intertemporal measure of value, he also makes it clear why his concern is not with value theory but with value measurement. He is going to be telling a story of humankind's evolution "in every state of society, in every stage of improvement." If he is to make comparisons of human material improvement across the four stages of humankind's history, he needs an index with which to transform nominal values into real values for direct intertemporal comparison. Corn works. Enough said.

Prices. The natural level of a commodity's price is that which is "ordinary and average" for that society in the given "neighborhood." (*WN*, 72) That, in turn, is the cost of production if the cost is based on the ordinary and average wages, profits, and rent in that neighborhood.

Smith uses the term "neighborhood" to represent the extent of the market, the relevant trading area for a commodity. What is natural is determined by the "general circumstances" in a given neighborhood (*WN*, 72). The natural price of a commodity reflects "what it really costs the person who brings it to market [(the real cost of production)]... where there is perfect liberty" (*WN*, 72–3).

Consistent with his general method of establishing the norm and then analyzing the real case in that context, Smith's purpose in defining the natural price is to establish a conceptual, normative frame of reference for further price analysis. The key to the frame he is constructing here is the phrase, "where there is perfect liberty." This is Smith's shorthand for the freedom and thus the fluidity of movement of people and resources that exists in a liberal society – his ultimate norm.

Having established the concept of natural price, Smith introduces market price. Market price is the actual price at which a commodity is

---

[17] Again and again throughout the story, Smith reminds us that corn is his index, his metric of value (*WN*, 206, 217, 248). More than half way through the work, he is still reminding us that "[w]oollen or linen cloth are not the regulating commodities by which the real value of all other commodities must be finally measured and determined. Corn is.... [It plays its role as intertemporal metric well because t]he real value of corn does not vary with those variations in its average money price, which sometimes occur from one century to another" (*WN*, 516).

exchanged in a given neighborhood. This market price is determined by the relationship between the "effectual demand" (*WN*, 73), the quantity demanded at the natural price, and the quantity actually supplied in the market. If the effectual or effective demand is equaled by the quantity supplied, the market price will equal the natural price. If the quantity supplied is less (greater) than the effective demand, the market price will be higher (lower) than the natural price. If there is perfect liberty, the market price will oscillate around the natural price, the degree of oscillation depending on the volatility of the quantity supplied.

"[Y]et sometimes particular accidents, sometimes natural causes, and sometimes particular regulations of police, may, in many commodities, keep up the market price, for a long time together, a good deal above the natural price"[18] (*WN*, 77). Smith cites as examples: trade or manufacturing secrets, singularly productive land (e.g., uniquely fine vineyards (*WN*, 78)), or "exclusive privileges of corporations, statutes of apprenticeship, and all those laws which restrain, in particular employments, the competition.... " (*WN*, 79)

As he develops his analysis of price, Smith is both building a normative framework for his subsequent analysis and framing our minds by anticipating some central issues in that analysis. For example, government regulations that serve the interests of a particular faction in violation of "perfect liberty" become his central theme when, in *WN* Book IV, he turns to the mercantile system (Chapter Eight).

Events in humankind are never as simple as the conjectural or theoretical case because there are, invariably, disturbing forces, distortions, that affect the dynamics. Here, as always, Smith's method is to represent the connecting principles that guide the theoretical case, and with this as a frame of reference, to then represent the actual twists and turns of real human events in light of the inevitable disturbing forces.

ON DISTRIBUTION

As individuals move from autonomous production to that more fruitful production based on the division of labor, the distribution of the growing product becomes an issue. In order to explain how this distribution is determined, Smith begins by taking us back to the rude state: "In the

---

[18] He suggests that, absent institutional constraints, the opposite case of a long-term depressed price is very unlikely because producers will abandon a market in which they cannot cover costs (*WN*, 79).

early and rude state of society which precedes both the accumulation of stock and the appropriation of land" (*WN*, 65), the entire product goes to labor because all production is from unaided labor.

Humankind escapes from this hand-to-mouth bare subsistence by the division of labor, an escape that is predicated on individuals accumulating capital to support the division of labor. However, although this accumulation is liberating, it is also a complicating factor in Smith's analysis. It is liberating because, by providing the resources to support an ever-finer division of labor, it takes humankind from the world of bare subsistence to a world of much richer possibilities. It is complicating because it makes the distribution of the fruits of production an issue.

The worker must receive a wage in order to survive and as an incentive to work, and so, too, "something must be given for the profits of the undertaker of the work who hazards his [accumulated] stock in this adventure" (*WN*, 66). Similarly, "[a]s soon as the land of any country has all become private property, the landlords, like all other men, love to reap where they never sowed, and demand a rent even for its natural produce" (*WN*, 67). Thus, with "the accumulation of stock and the appropriation of land" the component parts of price must encompass a return to the worker (wage), to the undertaker (profit), and to the landlord (rent). "[I]n every improved society, all the three enter more or less, as component parts, into the price of the far greater part of commodities" (*WN*, 68).

In specifying these component parts of commodities' prices, Smith sets out a language of functional distribution that becomes an essential tool for his analysis of nations' growth, stagnation, and decline ... the heart of his *Inquiry into the Nature and Causes of the Wealth of Nations* that is to follow. Indicative of their importance, having laid out the general principles of distribution Smith proceeds to examine these functional shares in more detail. In the process, he begins to tell his story of the progress of opulence.

ON THE WAGES OF LABOUR

As we've seen, in the rude state of society "the whole produce of labour belongs to the labourer" (*WN*, 82). But where accumulation is significant, the laborer works for "the owner of stock ... [In that case w]hat are the common wages of labour depends ... upon the contract usually made between those two parties, whose interests are by no means the same" (*WN*, 83).

The workers want a wage that provides a tolerable subsistence or better, while the least that a sustainable labor market can bear is that "bare subsistence" (*WN*, 113) sufficient to maintain and sustain the labor force by reproducing it (*WN*, 85). The merchants approach these negotiations with that classic mercantile zero-sum game mentality: If I give higher wages, I suffer lower profits. So they seek to pay nothing more than the bare subsistence.

Smith is acutely aware that in these negotiations there is an asymmetry of power in favor of the merchants, an asymmetry exacerbated by the fact that the political power structure and thus the legal system are often stacked against the workers:[19]

It is not . . . difficult to foresee which of the two parties [in wage bargaining] must, upon all ordinary occasions, have the advantage in the dispute, and force the other into a compliance with their terms. The masters, being fewer in number, can combine much more easily; and the law, besides, authorises, or at least does not prohibit their combinations, while it prohibits those of the workmen. (*WN*, 84)

Smith's metric of a good society is how the least among the working class are doing, so where this asymmetry of power leads to artificially low wages, he considers it a distortion that undermines the distributive justice he envisions for the ideal case. Not only is this a distributive injustice, it is also economically inefficient.

The liberal reward of labour, as it encourages the propagation, so it increases the industry of the common people. The wages of labour are the encouragement of industry, which, like ever other human quality, improves in proportion to the encouragement it receives. A plentiful subsistence increases the bodily strength of the labourer, and the comfortable hope of bettering his condition, and of ending his days perhaps in ease and plenty, animates him to exert that strength to the utmost. Where wages are high, accordingly, we shall always find the workmen more active, diligent, and expeditious, than where they are low. . . . (*WN*, 99)

In contrast, poverty animates no one, diminishes the health of all who suffer it, and "is extremely unfavourable to the rearing of children" (*WN*, 97).

Echoing his criticism of that nexus of power and narrow perspective with which the merchants run Bengal (Chapter Three), Smith's case here is that the low-wage economy pursued by the merchants generates a small short-term gain for the mercantile interests purchased at an expense of a large long-term loss to society as a whole.

---

[19] See (*WN*, 643–4) for a classic example of how "[t]he avidity of our great manufacturers" has led to severe oppression of workers and, in particular, women.

He believes that the best way to ameliorate this injustice and the associated inefficiency is to pursue policies that encourage the progress of opulence, for in an advancing state, accumulation outstrips population growth and under that condition there is a competition for the available workers that raises wages.[20] "It is not the actual greatness of national wealth, but its continual increase, which occasions a rise in the wages of labour.... [Since high wages encourage population growth, t]he most decisive mark of the prosperity of any country is the increase in the number of inhabitants" (*WN*, 87–8). And what, according to Smith, is the best predictor of how any given state will fare given this metric of success?: The "nature of its laws and institutions" (*WN*, 89).

Again we see the duality of limits in Smith's analysis of humankind's evolution. There is the ultimate limit set by the deity – that ideal liberal society of independent beings enjoying perfect liberty, making the most for all, and doing tolerably well for the least. This is the norm against which all societies can be compared to determine their level of advancement. Then there are the artificial limits a society imposes on itself by "the nature of its laws and institutions." As we saw in Chapter Three, the stagnation and decline of China and Bengal, respectively, are classic cases of the perverse effects of bad laws and institutions. In those places, workers live in poverty or, worse, they suffer "[w]ant, famine, and mortality" (*WN*, 91). Those sad cases make a particularly stark comparison with conditions in the British American colonies, where workers who benefit from the "the genius of the British constitution which protects and governs North America" (*WN*, 91) are doing as well or better than any other workers in the world (*WN*, 87–8).

ON THE PROFITS OF STOCK

Smith is very careful in his analysis of the profits of stock to distinguish between profit and interest.

[Profit is the return] derived from stock, by the person who manages or employs it. That [return] derived from it by the person who does not employ it himself, but lends it to another, is called the interest or the use of money. It is the compensation which the borrower pays to the lender, for the profit which he has an opportunity of making by the use of the money. Part of that profit naturally belongs to the

---

[20] In contrast, in the stationary state, as population grows, it outstrips the level of accumulation. In such a world "the competition of the labourers and the interests of the masters would soon reduce them [the workers] to this lowest rate which is consistent with common humanity" (*WN*, 89).

borrower, who runs the risk and takes the trouble of employing it; and part [the interest] to the lender, who affords him the opportunity of making this profit.... (*WN*, 69)

Smith clarifies his use of profit and interest further, distinguishing between "neat or clear profit" and "gross profit" (*WN*, 113). Gross profit includes net profit and interest. The net profit is the "lowest ordinary rate of profit... sufficient to compensate... the risk... [and to provide] a sufficient recompence for the trouble of employing the stock" (*WN*, 113–14). The "interest on money... [l]ike rent on land,... is a neat produce which remains after completely compensating the whole risk and trouble of employing the stock" (*WN*, 847–8). Thus, for Smith, "neat or clear profit" is a return to productive activity, but interest, "[l]ike rent on land," is not.

Profit plays an important, instrumental role in Smith's evolutionary analysis.

The division of labor increases productivity. This greater productivity means that the aggregate wealth increases. This increase in wealth represents a deeper pool of accumulated stock available for use as capital. In an ideal liberal society where there is perfect liberty, this accumulated stock will flow to its best advantage. Higher rates of profit, *ceteris paribus*, signal better opportunities, so when the accumulated returns from one circuit of production are thrown back into the production system,[21] that capital flows to those advantageous opportunities that offer the higher rates of profit. But as more capital flows into these attractive opportunities, the rates of profit in those pursuits are driven down until, at some point, the returns from all opportunities are equalized.

The whole of the advantages and disadvantages of the different employments of labour and stock must, in the same neighbourhood, be either perfectly equal or continually tending to equality.... This at least would be the case in a society... where there was perfect liberty.... Every man's interest would prompt him to seek the advantageous, and to shun the disadvantageous employment. (*WN*, 116)

As more capital accumulates with each new circuit of production, the rate of profit on existing investments falls and previously unattractive opportunities become attractive. Thus, the diffusion of the available capital stock across the entire economy continually drives down the rate of profit and extends the margins of investment. The degree of this effect on the

---

[21] Chapter Six will present Smith's story of capital flowing through cycles of production in detail.

rate of profit and on the extent of the margin is determined by the quantity of stock available and the set of available opportunities.

Based on his distinction between profit and interest, Smith lays out the normative case that is so important to his evolutionary analysis. As a consequence of the dynamic just described, in a "well governed society"

which had acquired its full complement of riches, where in every particular branch of business there was the greatest quantity of stock that could be employed in it, as the ordinary rate of clear profit would be very small, so that usual market rate of interest which could be afforded out of it, would be so low as to render it impossible for any but the very wealthiest people to live upon the interest of their money. (*WN*, 113)[22]

In Smith's evolutionary analysis, the limiting case would be "[a] country fully stocked in proportion to all the business it had to transact.... The competition, therefore, would everywhere be as great, and consequently the ordinary profit as low as possible.... ["Holland [which "in proportion to the extent of its territory and number of people, is a richer country than England" (*WN*, 108)] seems to be approaching near to this state" (*WN*, 113).[23]] But perhaps no country has ever yet arrived at this degree of opulence" (*WN*, 111).

One reason why no country has reached this condition is that, as Smith understands very well, "[t]he proprietor of stock is properly a citizen of the world, and is not necessarily attached to any particular country" (*WN*, 848–49). Given this global range, as the opportunities for the domestic employment of stock fill up and the domestic rate of profit falls, stock will spill out into the larger international arena as holders of stock search the world for attractive risk adjusted rates of return. This analysis of capital deepening and its spilling into ever-wider spheres of opportunity is central to Smith's story of the progress of opulence as it unfolds in the fourth stage, commercial society. This dynamic is the subject of the next chapter.

---

[22] Smith refers to these "very wealthiest people to live upon the interest of their money" as the "monied interest" (*WN*, 351). These are the folks Keynes refers to as the "rentier" class (Keynes, 1964, 376). We'll visit with them again in Chapter Twelve.

[23] In contrast, in "China [which] seems to have been long stationary...[t]welve percent.... is said to be the common interest of money...and the ordinary profits of stock must be sufficient to afford this large interest" (*WN*, 111–12). As we saw in Chapter Three, Smith ascribes this high interest rate in China to the "laws and institutions...[that] establish the monopoly of the rich" (*WN*, 112).

CONTRASTING CONDITIONS, AND THE LEVELS
OF WAGES AND PROFITS

The Natural Condition Under Perfect Liberty

As cited before, Smith describes the natural dynamics of flows of labor and stock under perfect liberty as follows:

The whole of the advantages and disadvantages of the different employments of labour and stock must, in the same neighbourhood, be either perfectly equal or continually tending to equality. If in the same neighbourhood, there was any employment evidently either more or less advantageous than the rest, so many people would crowd into it in the one case, and so many would desert it in the other, that its advantages would soon return to the level of other employments. This at least would be the case in a society where things were left to follow their natural course, where there was perfect liberty, and where every man was perfectly free both to chuse what occupation he thought proper, and to change it as often as he thought proper. Every man's interest would prompt him to seek the advantageous, and to shun the disadvantageous employment. (*WN*, 116)

This is a beautiful capsule image of the dynamics of competition and of the effect of such competition on the allocation of resources and the distribution of returns in the ideal liberal order where there is "perfect liberty." In such a society, all resources are used to their best advantage (most efficiently) and the returns to those resources are driven to the level of "ordinary" (*WN*, 118) or natural returns.

This is not to suggest, however, that under perfect liberty every allocation of a resource will receive the same return. "Pecuniary wages and profit, indeed, are every-where in Europe extremely different according to the different employments of labour and stock" (*WN*, 116), and some of this difference can be attributed to natural differences among employments. Smith cites five basic sources of natural variation:

1. Differences in psychic benefits, "agreeableness or disagreeableness" (*WN*, 116).
2. Differences in the psychic and pecuniary cost of acquiring the human capital necessary for the employment.
3. "[T]he constancy or inconstancy of employment" (*WN*, 116).
4. The degree of trust required.
5. "[T]he probability or improbability of success," (*WN*, 116–17) the risk factor.[24]

---

[24] When discussing risk as it relates to investments in human capital, Smith writes that "in the liberal professions," the "probability that any particular person shall ever be qualified

According to Smith, all five of these affect wages, whereas only the first and last affect profits.

The UnNatural Condition

The factors just cited are the sources of natural variations in the normative case, but they are not the only sources of observed variations. Private collusion and/or public institutional power can create and sustain artificial market advantages that, in turn, generate and sustain unnatural distributive advantages/disadvantages. Indeed, these public and private sources of power are often complements to one another.

Recall, for example, the "[m]asters [who] are always and every where in a sort of tacit, but constant uniform combination . . . sometimes . . . to sink the wages of labour below this [their natural] rate" (*WN*, 84). When the workers form a "defensive combination" and "clamour" for higher wages, "[t]he masters upon these occasions are just as clamorous upon the other side, and never cease to call aloud for the assistance of the civil magistrate, and the rigorous execution of those laws which have been enacted with so much severity against the combinations of servants, labourers, and journeymen" (*WN*, 84–5). This reflects a constant theme in *The Wealth of Nations*: Particular interests can and do exert powerful self-serving and distorting influences on government policy for distributive advantages.

Another example of such influence is the "policy of Europe, [which] by not leaving things to perfect liberty, occasions other inequalities [beyond the natural ones] of much greater importance" (*WN*, 135). These policies create distributive distortions in three ways. They artificially reduce the amount of labor or stock in a market by limiting access. They

---

for the employment to which he is educated . . . [is] very uncertain" (*WN*, 122). So given the great expense of the investment and the great risk of failure, one would expect the return to be very high in the liberal professions. But it is not as high as the theory predicts. The reason is twofold. First, "the chance of gain is naturally overvalued" (*WN*, 125), and, second, a great deal of the benefits are psychic:

To excel in any profession, in which but few arrive at mediocrity, is the most decisive mark of what is called genius or superior talents. The public admiration which attends upon such distinguished abilities, makes always a part of their reward; a greater or smaller in proportion as it is higher or lower in degree. It makes a considerable part of the reward in the profession of physick; a still greater perhaps in that of law; in poetry and philosophy it makes almost the whole. (*WN*, 123)

This from a professor of moral philosophy.

artificially increase the amount of labor or stock in a market by forcing allocations there. They obstruct "the free circulation of labour and
stock, both from employment to employment and from place to place"
(*WN*, 135).

Smith points to laws of apprenticeship in incorporated trades as a classic case of "[t]he exclusive privileges of corporations"[25] that artificially
reduce the amount of labor or stock in a market by limiting access (*WN*,
135). He traces these incorporations to the "Statute of Apprenticeship"
in England in 1562.[26] In order to explain the source of the power that enables traders and artificers to enjoy these protections, he returns to that
theme he presented in his analysis of the relationship between masters
and workmen: collusion.[27]

According to Smith, the ability of traders and artificers to collude, and
thus to generate power and in turn artificial market advantages with attendant distributive benefits, grew out of their location together in towns.
Historically, "[t]he government of the towns corporate was altogether in
the hands of the traders and artificers" (*WN*, 141). Given this shared
power, the various trades allowed each other to form corporate constraints limiting entry into their trades and thereby making it possible
for all of them to exploit the unorganized people in the country.

The consequence of this asymmetric power was a distributive benefit.
Towns got a disproportionate share of the social product and thus were
able to accumulate much more than the country. However, as always,
to the degree there is liberty, the design imposes itself on the flow of
events. In this case, the engrossment of accumulation in the towns led to
an engorgement of accumulation. This meant falling profit rates. Smith
describes the ensuing dynamic as follows:

It [the accumulated stock] then spreads itself, if I may say so, over the face of
the land, and by being employed in agriculture is in part restored to the country, at the expence of which, in a great measure, it had originally been accumulated in the town. That everywhere in Europe the greatest improvements of the
country have been owing to such overflowings of stock originally accumulated

---

[25] Smith also cites distortions such as subsidies for training that artificially glut a market
(*WN*, 148), and those "absurd laws" (*WN*, 151) that limit the mobility of labor (e.g., poor
laws) and stock.

[26] He presents an extensive analysis of the history, the twists and turns, of this law (*WN*,
135–147).

[27] "People of the same trade seldom meet together, even for merriment and diversion, but
the conversation ends in a conspiracy against the publick, or some contrivance to raise
prices" (*WN*, 145).

in towns, I shall endeavour to show hereafter; and at the same time to demonstrate, that though some countries have by this course attained to a considerable degree of opulence, it is in itself necessarily slow, uncertain, and in every respect contrary to the order of nature and of reason. The interests, prejudices, and laws and customs which have given occasion to it, I shall endeavour to explain as fully and distinctly as I can in the third and fourth books of this enquiry. (*WN*, 145)[28]

As Smith makes clear, this brief summary is a rich representation and anticipation of significant themes that are still to unfold in his *Inquiry into the Nature and Causes of the Wealth of Nations*. Let's take a moment to reflect on these themes.

Consider the premise of the paragraph just cited. Private and public power, respectively the collusion among tradesmen and the towns' political prerogative to create corporations, were used to establish advantages for the sake of a distributive benefit. This, in turn, skewed opportunities for accumulation toward the towns. *Ceteris paribus*, increasing accumulation means lower profit rates, and where capital stock enjoys the liberty to do so, it will spill out in search of better returns. In the case of England and, as we will see in Chapter Seven in the case of Europe more generally, this very unnatural course of events did not lead to stagnation or decline, but it did result in a "necessarily slow, uncertain" progress of opulence. This slow, uncertain progress, "in every respect contrary to the order of nature and of reason," was in part the consequence of political structures that existed for the purposes of "extorting money ... [rather] than for the defence of the common liberty against ... oppressive monopolies" (*WN*, 140).

As Smith lays out his analysis of distribution, his purpose is practical, not metaphysical.[29] He is building the analytical tool kit he will employ in *WN* Book II, where he presents his dynamic growth theory (examined in Chapter Six here); in *WN* Book III, where he demonstrates the power of that theory in the context of European history (the story just previewed, and presented here in Chapter Seven); in *WN* Book IV, where he critiques the power of those partial, mercantile interests that distort the market system and impede the progress of society (analyzed in Chapter Eight here); and in *WN* Book V, where he describes the proper and improper roles of government (described here in Chapter Nine).

---

[28] The subjects here are those of Chapters Seven and Eight, respectively.

[29] Does his faith in a design make it metaphysical? No. As I noted in Chapters One and Four, the design is a source of faith, but it has no real bearing on what is a very empirically based moral philosophy with a very practical purpose – contributing to humankind's progress.

ON THE RENT OF LAND

The Concept

The concept of rent on land is the last tool Smith adds to his analytical tool kit in *WN* Book I. As always, his purpose is practical. Rent is an important concept because of the role it plays in the progress of opulence and because it provides a very clear signal by which to follow that progress.[30]

Unlike wages or profits (net of interest), rent is not a return to productive activity. "The rent of land . . . is naturally a monopoly price" (*WN*, 161).[31] The ordinary level of rent is, along with the ordinary wages and profits, a component of the natural price of a commodity. But rent enters into that price in a different way than wages and profits. The latter two are built into the price because together they constitute the cost of production, the supply cost that must be covered if a product is to be brought to market. Rent, on the other hand, "depends upon the demand" (*WN*, 162). If demand is sufficient to raise price above the cost of production, then "the surplus part of it will naturally go to the rent of the land" (*WN*, 161). This is so because in a competitive environment, the landlord is able to extract "the highest [rent] the tenant can afford to pay [(all the surplus above cost of production)] in the actual circumstances of the land" (WN, 160).

Those "circumstances" that determine the level of rent are the "fertility" and the "situation" of the land (*WN*, 163). By situation Smith means the extent of the market for the product of that land. *Ceteris paribus*, the larger the market, the higher the rent will be. As explained previously, the extent of the market is largely a function of transportation costs. "Good roads, canals, and navigable rivers, by diminishing the expense of carriage, put the remotest parts of the country more nearly upon a level with those in the neighbourhood of towns. They are upon that account the greatest

---

[30] In the course of his rent analysis, Smith presents a long digression on the value of silver. There, he offers an analysis of the variations of that value as a vehicle to critique the standard, mercantilist logic of his time and to demonstrate that when accounting for "particular accidents" (*WN*, 193) (e.g., the English civil war [*WN*, 212] or the discoveries in America [*WN*, 220]), his analysis explains the variations in value very nicely, thank you.

[31] Rent is a monopoly price, yet it has a natural level – the ordinary level that equally well-cultivated and fertile land in a given neighborhood can command. It also has an unnatural level. An unnatural rent would be "the rent of some vineyards in France" – a rent above the level of "equally fertile and equally well-cultivated land in its neighbourhood" (*WN*, 78). Smith's adoption of natural rent is a reflection of his usage of natural here as meaning "ordinary." Because even where there is perfect liberty much of the land receives a rent, the ordinary level of that rent is the natural level for that neighborhood.

of all improvements" (*WN*, 163). These improvements extend the market, making possible an increasing division of labor and, *ceteris paribus*, increasing rents. Thus, in Smith's analysis, higher rents are, *ceteris paribus*, a sign of greater improvements and progress.[32]

Rent as Instrumental in Smith's Analysis of Progress

Rents do not emerge until land is divided as private property and this occurs with the emergence of agriculture. Smith describes the process that leads to that point in humankind's evolution as follows:

[T]he first method [individuals] would fall upon for their sustenance would be to support themselves by the wild fruits and wild animalls which the country afforded.... [But as their numbers increased] they would find the chase too precarious for their support.... [They might try to store food, but this would not be sufficient for their needs.] The most naturally contrivance they would think of, would be to tame some of those wild animals they caught... [and] enduce them... [to] multiply their kind. Hence would arise the age of shepherds. They would more probably begin first by multiplying animalls than vegetables, as less skill and observation would be required.... But when a society became so numerous they would find a difficulty in supporting themselves by herds or flocks. Then they would naturally turn themselves to the cultivation of the land... [Having observed seeds falling and sprouting, and the conditions that were most fruitful for this, t]hese observations they would extend to the different plants and trees they found produced agreable and nourishing food. And by this means they would gradually advance in to the age of agriculture. (*LJA*, 14–15)

Early in this transition from pasturage to agriculture, the vast majority of land is still uncultivated, the domain of free grazing cattle,[33] so butcher's

---

[32] He observes that "not more than fifty years ago... some of the counties in the neighbourhood of London, petitioned the parliament against the extension of the turnpike roads into the remoter counties" (*WN*, 164). Those in the proximity of London feared that the outlying areas, having cheaper labor, would undercut their position in the London market and thereby reduce rents in the local area. In fact, however, "[t]heir rents have risen, and their cultivation has been improved since that time" (*WN*, 164).

[33] A note on this reference to cattle and, more generally, the importance of this transition from pasturage to agriculture in Smith's story: J.G.A. Pocock writes that:

Smith's most remarkable contribution to the natural history of society was his insistence that the shepherd stage was dynamic, a decisive breach with the hunting and food-gathering condition of the 'savage'.... In most previous systems of this kind, the shepherd was little distinguished from the hunter.... (Pocock, 1999, 315–16)

Pocock goes on to point out that Smith's "dialectic of shepherd and ploughman... was imaginable only in Eurasia... [and] did not apply in the Americas or in Polynesia," suggesting that Smith's intention may have been to assert "European uniqueness"

meat is cheap relative to corn.[34] Agriculture offers a ripe opportunity for productivity gains, however, because "[n]o equal capital puts into motion a greater quantity of productive labour than that of the farmer...[for i]n agriculture...nature labours along with man....[Farmers laboring at] planting and tillage frequently regulate more than they animate the active fertility of nature; after all their labour, a great part of the work always remains to be done by her"[35] (*WN*, 363).

Thanks to this beneficent labor of nature, the productivity of agriculture is greater than that of pasturage...

A corn field of moderate fertility produces a much greater quantity of food for man, than the best pasture of equal extent. Though its cultivation requires much more labour, yet [thanks to the labor of nature] the surplus which remains after replacing the seed and maintaining all that labour, is likewise much greater. (*WN*, 164)

...But, agriculture will not progress until the extent of the market is sufficient to provide a vent for this surplus. This extended market emerges by "design."

Where nature chooses to be beneficent (e.g., where the land is fruitful and there are natural avenues to market) and where institutions do not impede the process, the expanding market necessary to encourage agriculture will emerge naturally: As farmers begin to exploit the natural productivity of agriculture this lowers the price of corn. Cheaper subsistence encourages population growth. Thus, the productivity of agriculture naturally produces more stomachs to feed and, in turn, a growing market, and so the agricultural stage takes off.

As population grows, the margins of agriculture are extended to accommodate the expanding demand. As cultivation is extended, the range

(Pocock, 1999, 316). Clearly, the story Smith is telling is drawn from his Scottish experience. Certainly, that story is unique. But if "assert[ing]...uniqueness" implies superiority, I don't think this is Smith. He would say Britain has advanced most among nations, and certainly some individuals made intended choices that facilitated that progress (recall Henry 2nd and Edward 1st in Chapter Three). But he largely ascribes Britain's progress to chance, circumstance, and the unintended consequences of individuals' choices. The Brits are made of the same coarse clay as all of the rest of us. My thanks to Leon Montes for directing me to this work by Pocock.

[34] Smith cites evidence from "Byenos Ayres,...[as] told by Ulloa," (*WN*, 164) to support this image.

[35] Even "his labouring cattle, are productive labourers" (*WN*, 363). This role of nature and cattle in generating value suggests, as I have argued previously, that Smith was not wedded to or even interested in making a case (unlike his successors Ricardo and Marx) for a metaphysical "source of value" in labor.

for free grazing cattle becomes constrained and more distant from centers of population relative to the land under cultivation. The effect of this is that the cost of production and transport of butcher's-meat goes up, its supply lags behind the demand, and thus "the price of butcher's-meat becomes greater than the price of bread" (*WN*, 164).

As the price of butcher's meat rises, those farms that are most productive and thus have the lowest cost of production for corn find it profitable to raise cattle on feed-corn in a stable rather than by grazing. This, in turn, produces large concentrations of manure at the stable. Manure is the best fertilizer,[36] so these cattle concentrations become a convenient resource for greatly enhancing agricultural productivity. Greater productivity reduces the price of corn, making it possible for more farmers to raise cattle in this manner, thereby expanding the number of farms that can benefit from the productivity of fertilizing with manure . . . and so productivity is enhanced further.[37]

In Smith's analysis, the emergence of agriculture has a profound impact on the progress of opulence: The increased improvement of agriculture is the foundation for larger population. This gives rise to a growth in demand for nonagricultural products and this ready market for those products encourages the ever-finer division of labor. Indicative of the key role of agriculture in setting this dynamic in motion, Smith writes that "the compleat improvement and cultivation of the country . . . most certainly is, the greatest of all publick advantages. . . . " (*WN*, 245).

The thread Smith follows as he tells his story of the transition from the stage of pasturage to that of agriculture is his analysis of rents. As his story moves to the transition from the stage of agriculture to the emergence of the commercial stage, he continues to follow that thread.

Rent and the Emergence of Commercial Society

Human food seems to be the only produce of land which always and necessarily affords some rent to the landlord. Other sorts of produce

---

[36] My sincere thanks to Erick Jank, an experienced farmer and philosopher, who confirmed Smith's view that cow manure is indeed an especially good fertilizer.

[37] This story of the benefits of cattle and manure in the transition from pasturage to agriculture leads Smith to observe that "[o]f all the commercial advantages . . . which Scotland has derived from the union with England . . . [the] rise in the price of cattle is, perhaps, the greatest" (*WN*, 239–40). However, he goes on to observe, the benefits of Union did not spread quickly over the face of the country because the "obstructions to the establishment of a better system [such as endemic poverty that precludes accumulation], cannot be removed but by a long course of frugality and industry. . . . " (*WN*, 239)

sometimes may and sometimes may not, according to different circumstances.

After food, cloathing and lodging are the two great wants of mankind (*WN*, 178).

In the rude state, with land plentiful relative to population, clothing and lodging are available in "super-abundance" (*WN*, 178) relative to the demand, but not so, food. Thus, in the rude state, "ninety-nine parts" "of the labour of the whole year" (*WN*, 180) must be spent on getting sufficient food.

But when by the improvement and cultivation of land the labour of one family can provide food for two, the labour of half the society becomes sufficient to provide food for the whole. The other half, therefore, or at least the greater part of them, can be employed in producing other things or in satisfying the other wants and fancies of mankind. (*WN*, 180)

So, with the advancement of agriculture comes the surplus necessary to support the extension of the division of labor into the realm of manufacturing. This transition unleashes a powerful force in the progress of opulence because the possibilities for the division of labor are much greater in the manufacturing realm: "The nature of agriculture . . . does not admit of so many subdivisions of labour, nor of so complete a separation of one business from another, as manufactures" (*WN*, 16). Furthermore, manufacturing and its immense productivity are greatly encouraged by the fact that unlike

[t]he desire of food [which] is limited in every man by the narrow capacity of his stomach . . . the desire of the conveniencies and ornaments of building, dress, equipage, and household furniture, seems to have no limit or certain boundary. (*WN*, 181)

With this turn in Smith's analysis, the advancement of agriculture becomes the natural foundation for the emergence of the commercial stage.[38] The evidence that a nation has made this turn can be found in the rent structure. Given that our desire for all the "conveniencies and ornaments" of life seem to have no limit, as society advances, nonagricultural

---

[38] In *WN* Book III, Smith presents a classic inversion of this natural process of progress, beginning in agriculture and then extending to manufacturing, in order to demonstrate the power of his analysis to represent large peculiar conditions, and also to demonstrate the long-term power of the design to guide events in spite of these peculiar distortions. This is the subject of Chapter Seven in this book.

rents emerge and eventually surpass agricultural rents as rents in general rise.[39]

This emerging commercial stage brings progress not only to society in general but also, and more significantly for Smith, to the working class in particular. Food is a man's most essential need and although the extension and improvement of cultivation causes animal food prices to rise, its lowers the prices of vegetable foods. "The circumstances of the poor through a great part of England cannot surely be so much distressed by any rise in the price of poultry, fish, wild-fowl, or venison, as they must be relieved by the fall in that of potatoes" (*WN*, 259).

Indeed, with progress comes not only lower vegetable prices, but also, *ceteris paribus*, lower prices for manufactures because the division of labor increases the productivity of workers. Smith believes that this productivity is even further enhanced by the encouragement that the division of labor gives to technological innovation.[40] His only caveats regarding this progress into manufacturing are its effect on the minds of workers[41] and the possibility of upward pressure on raw commodity prices for manufacture (e.g., "barren timber [*WN*, 260]). His concern about and his policies for ameliorating the effect on the minds of workers will be examined in Chapter Nine. With respect to input prices, he believes that this effect is, *ceteris paribus*, more than offset by the effect of increased productivity on the cost of production. Furthermore, he believes that, *ceteris paribus*, with increased productivity, workers' incomes rise.

In sum, the net effect of higher incomes and the lower costs of vegetable foods and manufactures is, *ceteris paribus*, to increase the standard of living among the workers. This is precisely what Smith would expect

---

[39] As always, there are particular exceptions, but these can be understood as consistent with his general analysis if we appreciate the effects that make them peculiar. For example, Smith notes that mining rents behave differently than the general case. The level of mining rents is relative to the fertility of the best mine, because prices for the mined materials are generally determined by scarcity. This is in contrast to the more general case of surface rents, wherein the rents generally move to a natural level because the quantity can expand to meet the effective demand.

[40] As noted previously, the division of labor is the mother of invention, be it in agriculture, trade, or manufacturing: "That the originall invention of machines is owing to the division of labour is not to be doubted" (*LJA*, 351).

[41] "In the progress of the division of labour, the employment of the far greater part of those who live by labour . . . comes to be confined to a few very simple operations . . . The man whose whole life is spent in performing a few simple operations . . . has no occasion to exert his understanding, or to exercise his invention. . . . He naturally looses, therefore, the habit of such exertion, and generally becomes as stupid and ignorant as it is possible for a human creature to become" (*WN*, 781–2).

and hope for as humankind more closely approximates the ideal human prospect.

In his "Introduction and Plan of the Work" of the *WN*, Smith writes:

The causes of ... [the] improvement, in the productive power of labour, and the order, according to which its produce is naturally distributed among the different ranks and conditions of men in society, make the subject of the First Book of this Inquiry. (*WN*, 10)

We can see now why he laid such an emphasis on production and distribution at the outset of his *Inquiry*. These two concepts are the foundation of his story of the progress of opulence.

The "Introduction and Plan" goes on to inform the reader that:

The Second Book ... treats of the nature of capital stock, of the manner in which it is gradually accumulated, and of the different quantities of labour which it puts into motion, according to the ways in which it is employed. (*WN*, 10–11)

It is in the commercial stage that the role of capital comes to the fore. While capital accumulation is essential from the earliest ages for the division of labor, it is in the age of commerce, with its complex transactions, extended markets, and time lags from production to exchange to return, that capital deepening and fluidity take center stage in Smith's analysis. A deep and fluid capital stock unleashes the dynamic of global markets in the commercial stage. But the depth and fluidity of capital depends on individuals enjoying security and full market access. In other words, the realization of the possibilities of the commercial stage go hand-in-hand with the realization of liberty and justice for all. Capital ... its security, its freedom, its flows, and its instrumental role in the progress of opulence ... these are the subjects of *WN* Book II. We now turn to that piece in Smith's analysis.

SIX

On The Role of Capital in the Progress of Opulence

The Analysis of Book II of *The Wealth of Nations*

ON THE CENTRALITY OF CAPITAL TO THE
PROGRESS OF OPULENCE

Capital is a central concept, maybe the central concept, in Adam Smith's *Inquiry into the Nature and Causes of the Wealth of Nations.*

- "[T]he whole annual produce [of a nation], if we except the spontaneous productions of the earth . . . [is] the effect of productive labour"[1] (*WN*, 332).
- The share of a nation's accumulation that is used as capital is directly related to the proportion of its labor that is productive and to the productivity of that labor.
- An increase in accumulation allocated to capital expands the productive labor of a nation and/or increases its productivity.
- Thus, it is the growth of capital that fuels the progress of opulence in Smith's representation of *The Nature and Causes of the Wealth of Nations.*

Now we turn our attention directly to capital and the role it plays in the progress of opulence, the analysis Smith presents in Book II of his *Wealth of Nations.*

HOW CAPITAL FUELS THE PROGRESS OF OPULENCE

In the early days of the rude state of society, an individual accumulates to smooth the pattern of his own consumption. "He seldom thinks of

---

[1] Smith's distinction between "productive" and "unproductive" labor will be explained later.

deriving any revenue from it" (*WN*, 279). With time, however, a person's stock can grow beyond the level necessary to cover any contingencies in life. When that occurs, "he naturally endeavours to derive a revenue from the greater part of it...." (*WN*, 279). At that point,

[h]is whole stock ... is distinguished into two parts. That part which, he expects, is to afford him ... revenue, is called his capital. The other is that which supplies his immediate consumption.... (*WN*, 279)

If, having employed some stock as capital, the entire revenue from that capital is then used to supply his immediate consumption, the individual has no more capital and thus no resource for generating more revenue.

If, on the other hand, the revenue from the employment of stock as capital is continually thrown back into production to support further production, then, *ceteris paribus*, a circuit is formed in which the capital thrown in expands with every circuit. It is the continuous circulation of a growing capital stock that fuels a nation's progress of opulence. Smith represents the emergence and the potentially self-sustaining dynamic of this circuit as follows:

As described in Chapter Five, in the transition from agriculture to the early stages of commerce, it is the net revenue of agriculture, the surplus in agriculture derived from "nature['s] labours" (*WN*, 363), which generates the initial capital stock that finances the emergence and the early refinement of the division of labor in manufacturing.[2] With this refinement comes increased manufacturing productivity, and this, in turn, generates increasing revenue from manufacturing activity. This increasing revenue means that manufacturing is generating a gross revenue that is sufficient to both replenish the capital stock initially invested and yield a net revenue beyond replacement cost.[3]

If this growing revenue is thrown back into that circuit of production, it can finance an even finer division of labor in the next circuit.[4] This finer division of labor leads to even greater manufacturing productivity

---

[2] Smith offers a nice, brief description of some of this dynamic in *WN* Book III (*WN*, 408–10).

[3] "[A]s the fertility of the land had given birth to the manufacture, so the progress of the manufacture re-acts upon the land, and increases still further its fertility" (*WN*, 409). This because as the cities grow, the increased population increases demand and in turn the returns to agriculture encouraging competition that drives improvements in production.

[4] "Smith asserts that the accumulation of capital is a necessary precondition to the division of labor. As the division of labor advances, an increasing amount of capital must be accumulated beforehand in order to provide workers with the equipment and materials necessary for production" (Harpham, 1984, 766).

and a yet-again larger gross revenue that both replenishes the original capital stock and produces a net revenue that can add to that stock. At this point, with manufacturing generating its own net revenue, the growth in manufacturing and thus the progress of opulence is potentially self-sustaining: If the expanded revenue from each circuit is consistently thrown into the subsequent circuit, in each successive circuit there will be an increasing division of labor ... increasing productivity ... increasing revenue ... increasing capital for the next circuit ... and, in turn, an even finer division of labor ... even greater productivity ... even more revenue ... even more capital ... and so it can go with capital and wealth expanding in each round of this circuit.

Or so it goes where laws and institutions make capital secure, and where an ethic of parsimony encourages personal accumulation. Smith describes this case of growth and the alternative case of contraction as follows:

If the exchangeable value of the annual produce ... exceeds that of the annual consumption, the capital of the society must annually increase in proportion to this excess. The society in this case lives within its revenue, and what is annually saved out of its revenue is naturally added to its capital, and employed so as to increase still further the annual produce.[5] If the exchangeable value of the annual produce, on the contrary, fall short of the annual consumption, the capital of the society must annually decay in proportion to this deficiency. The expense of the society in this case exceeds its revenue, and necessarily encroaches upon its capital. Its capital, therefore, must necessarily decay, and together with it the exchangeable value of the annual produce of its industry. (*WN*, 497)

In his analysis of capital and the progress of opulence, Smith distinguishes between two kinds of capital:

- fixed capital, and
- circulating capital.

Fixed capital refers to those "useful machines and instruments of trade which facilitate and abridge labour" (*WN*, 282), as well as improvements on land and also buildings "such as shops, warehouses, workhouses, farmhouses" (*WN*, 282), which, like improvements on land, produce revenue above and beyond the net rent. Fixed capital is "fixed" because it does not travel the circuit of production; rather it "yield[s] a revenue or profit without changing masters, or circulating any further" (*WN*, 279).

---

[5] "Every increase ... of capital ... naturally tends to increase ... the real quantity of industry, the number of productive hands, and consequently the exchangeable value of the annual produce of the land and labour of the country, the real wealth and revenue of all its inhabitants" (*WN*, 337).

Circulating capital "is composed . . . of four parts: First, of money by means of which all the other three are circulated and distributed to their proper consumers" (*WN*, 282). The "other three" are different forms of inventory: provisions for the support of labor; the materials of production, both raw and intermediate; and the finished products waiting for sale. In contrast to fixed capital, circulating capital leaves the hand of its owner and, except for money, it changes shape as it passes through the circuit of production. But even as it transforms shape in this circuit, so long as it is in the circuit of production, it is always and everywhere capital.[6]

Capital is not an end in itself; it is a means to an end: "To maintain and augment the stock which may be reserved for immediate consumption, is the sole end and purpose of both the fixed and circulating capital" (*WN*, 283).[7] However, in order to accomplish this end, the capital stock must be maintained and augmented, and the various parts of the capital stock, invariably owned by different individuals, must be put to work in concert. Markets make it possible for the independent owners of these interdependent parts of the capital stock to make the exchanges necessary to put their resources to work in concert. The smooth and efficient functioning of this market nexus depends, however, on the presence of "tolerable security."

In all countries where there is tolerable security, every man of common understanding will endeavour to employ whatever stock he can command in procuring either present enjoyment or future profit. . . . A man must be perfectly crazy who, where there is tolerable security, does not employ all the stock which he commands. . . . (*WN*, 284–5)

Absent the "tolerable security" that comes with justice, what could be active, productive capital stock becomes dead stock:

In those unfortunate countries, indeed, where men are continually afraid of the violence of their superiors, they frequently bury and conceal a great part of their stock in order to have it always at hand to carry with them to some place of safety, in case of their being threatened with any of those disasters to which they consider themselves as at all times exposed. (*WN*, 285)

---

[6] In Smith's analysis, except for money, circulating capital is not a specific physical form; it is value committed to this circuit. Whether or not it was from Smith that Marx developed his notion of capital as self-expanding value, the outlines of that conception were certainly available to him in Smith.

[7] "The production of the necessaries of life is the sole benefit of industry. . . . The whole benefit of wea<l>th and industry is that you either employ a greater number or give those already employed a more comfortable subsistence. . . . " (*LJA*, 390–1)

Smith cites the period of feudal government in Europe as such a time and place. Insecurity in those days led so many people to bury treasure that the laws of the time explicitly granted to the sovereign the rights to any treasure-trove discovered. Buried stock cannot function as capital and so, as we'll see in Chapter Seven, that feudal period was one of stagnation or, at best, retarded growth.

Smith's reference to "tolerable security" is a thread that weaves his economic analysis into his larger analysis of the evolution of humankind. The economic system can only produce those fruits that come with the progress of opulence to the degree that the social and political dimensions of society provide "laws and institutions" (*WN*, 89) that insure justice and, thereby, "tolerable security."

Laws and institutions are instrumental in Smith's story of the progress of opulence. So, too, are fixed and money capital. Neither money nor fixed capital changes shape as it plays its role in the circuit of production, nor does either become a component part of the revenue of the nation. Both, however, are instrumentally essential if the rest of the circulating capital thrown into each circuit is to emerge from successive circuits as an ever-expanding stock of capital. This is so because the quality of these instruments – fixed and money capital – determines the productivity of every circuit. Smith describes the instrumental role of money at length, beginning with the analogy to fixed capital.

MONEY AS CAPITAL: PAPER MONEY, BANKS, AND THE CAPITAL MARKET

Smith's description of the effect of improvements in fixed capital reflects the instrumental nature of fixed capital:

In manufacturers the same number of hands, assisted with the best machinery, will work up a much greater quantity of goods than with more imperfect instruments of trade.... It is upon this account that all such improvements in mechanicks... are always regarded as advantageous to every society. (*WN*, 287)

However, precisely because it is *fixed* capital, it does not become a part of the revenue from the circuit of production because it does not *flow* into the pool of accumulation available to support productive labor in the next circuit.[8] In this respect, fixed capital is different from three

---

[8] "The whole expense of maintaining the fixed capital must evidently be excluded from the net revenue of the society.... [A]s the workmen so employed may place the whole value of

parts of circulating capital (provisions, materials, and finished work), but it is very similar to the fourth: money.

"The fixed capital, and that part of the circulating capital which consists of money . . . bear a very great resemblance to one another" (*WN*, 288). As with fixed capital, money is instrumental in producing the revenue of society, but it is not part of that revenue:[9]

> The great wheel of circulation is altogether different from the goods which are circulated by means of it. The revenue of the society consists altogether in those goods, and not in the wheel which circulates them. In computing either the gross or neat revenue of any society, we must always, from their whole annual circulation of money and goods, deduct the whole value of the money, of which not a single farthing can ever make any part of either. . . .
>
> Money, therefore, the great wheel of circulation, the great instrument of commerce, like all other *instruments* of trade [(fixed capital)], though it makes a part and a very valuable part of the capital, makes no part of the revenue of the society to which it belongs; and though the metal pieces of which it is composed, in the course of their annual circulation, distribute to every man the revenue which properly belongs to him, they make themselves no part of that revenue.[10] (*WN*, 289, 291, emphasis added)

As money is like fixed capital in that it is instrumental in the production of revenue but is not a part of that revenue, so, too, it is like fixed capital in that, to the degree it can function more efficiently, it can increase the productivity of the circuits of production. This point brings Smith to an analysis of paper money because he believes that, properly managed, paper money can, as "with the best machinery . . . [allow "the same number of hands" (*WN*, 290) to] work up a much greater quantity of goods than with more imperfect instruments of trade" (*WN*, 287).

---

their wages in their stock reserved for immediate consumption . . . in other sorts of labour, both the price and the produce go to this stock, the price to that of the workmen, the produce to that of other people. . . . " (*WN*, 287) In other words, the cost of labor expended on fixed capital gets eaten up without generating any produce that will sustain subsequent labor, while labor expended on other forms of circulating capital generates production that sustains subsequent workers in the circuit of production. Thus fixed capital is like a catalyst, essential for the operation but not embodied in the product, the revenue, of the operation.

[9] "[A]s the machines and instruments of a trade, etc., which compose the fixed capital either of an individual or of a society, make no part either of the gross or of the net revenue of either; so money, by means of which the whole revenue of the society is regularly distributed among all its different members, makes itself no part of that revenue" (*WN*, 289).

[10] Here he anticipates his case that the mercantilists confuse money with wealth (*WN*, 429).

Smith cites "circulating notes of banks and bankers...[as the] best known" form of paper. He describes how, where there is full "confidence in the fortune, probity, and prudence" (*WN*, 292) of those issuing the notes, those notes can become the basis for a fractional reserve system. For example, he suggests that if "twenty thousand pounds of gold and silver [are sufficient reserves "for answering occasional demands" of a fractional reserve system, then that twenty thousand can] perform all the functions which a hundred thousand could otherwise have performed" (*WN*, 293).

Scaling up his case, Smith supposes a nation with a million pounds sterling: an amount just sufficient for domestic circulation needs, just sufficient to service what he refers to as the domestic "channel of circulation" (*WN*, 293). If two hundred thousand of this sterling is used as reserves to support a million pounds paper, the full circulating money of the nation would be one million eight hundred thousand. He continues:

One million we have supposed sufficient to fill that [domestic] channel. Whatever, therefore, is poured into it beyond this sum, cannot run in it, but must overflow....Eight hundred thousand pounds...must overflow, that sum being over and above what can be employed at home, it is too valuable to be allowed to be idle. It will, therefore, be sent abroad, in order to seek that profitable employment which it cannot find at home. (*WN*, 293–4)

It is not the paper that will travel, because paper would be discounted so far from home. It is the gold and silver that will flow out. Is this a bad thing? Only if the money brings home "goods as are likely to be consumed by idle people who produce nothing. . . . " (*WN*, 294). It seems more likely to Smith, however, that this overflow will pour into more productive channels: Either purchasing goods in one country for sale in another, the carrying trade – a revenue-generating venture; or purchasing goods "destined for the employment of [domestic] industry" (*WN*, 295) – also a revenue-generating enterprise.

Money as an instrumental form of capital is central to Smith's analysis in *The Nature and Causes of the Wealth of Nations*. Employing paper money for domestic commerce allows the specie money from the nation's capital stock to spill from domestic channels like a liquid, an image Smith likes very much and uses often, into the larger circuits of international trade. By channeling the flow of their capital into the most productive circuit available, the holders of capital are simply pursuing their best advantage. However, in doing so, by no intention of their own, they are generating the greatest revenue for the nation and thus contributing to the progress of opulence, the increasing wealth of the nation.[11]

As evidence of the benefits of paper money, Smith cites "[t]he effects [of the "erection of new banking companies" in Scotland during the preceding twenty-five to thirty years, suggesting that the benefits] . . . have been precisely those above described" (*WN*, 297).[12] However, although he sees great virtue in paper currency, Smith also appreciates the dangers. In particular, he warns that "[s]hould the circulating paper exceed . . . the value of the gold and silver, of which it supplies the place, or which . . . would circulate there, if there were no paper money" (*WN*, 300), this could ultimately lead to "a run upon the banks" (*WN*, 301). Or, short of a run, such behavior by banks (holding inadequate reserves for the notes issued) increases the cost of maintaining the paper and decreases the benefit of doing so. This inefficiency occurs because if adequate reserves are not in the coffers of the bank, repayment demands must be covered by buying reserves at a premium. Unfortunately, according to Smith, banks are far too often guilty of issuing more paper than is warranted by their assets.[13]

He traces the source of this problem to bank dealings with "bold projectors" (*WN*, 304) who, unlike sober businessmen, are constantly drawing more out of the bank than they are paying back. When dealing with the sober businessmen "[t]he coffers of the bank . . . resemble a water pond, from which, though a stream is continually running out, yet another is continually running in, fully equal to that which runs out; so that, without any further care or attention, the pond keeps always equally, or very near equally full. Little or no expense can ever be necessary for replenishing the coffers of such a bank" (*WN*, 304). The projectors, on the other hand, drain the bank and force it to purchase reserves at a premium in order to cover the demand that comes when the paper issue is out of balance.

The problem gets worse when unscrupulous projectors tap into banks and create problems for the banks by scamming them. Smith cites, as a classic example, "[t]he practice of drawing and re-drawing" (*WN*, 308) bills of exchange. Drawing and re-drawing is, in effect, a process of rolling

---

[11] As we will see subsequently, it is in describing precisely this unintended, but optimal capital flow that Smith uses the "invisible hand" image.

[12] He reviews the Scottish experience in detail, explaining how "discounting bills of exchange" work (*WN*, 298), describing the path of circulation (*WN*, 299), and contrasting the benefits of the flexible Scotch system to that with which the London merchant must deal (*WN*, 300).

[13] Smith cites examples of this behavior. (*WN*, 304)

over notes to cover previous debts. Two people can dupe banks into valuing otherwise valueless paper by "drawing and re-drawing upon one another ... [and] discount[ing] their bills sometimes with one banker, and sometimes with another" (*WN*, 311). A "great circle of projectors" can dupe banks even more effectively by making it seem that there are real exchanges going on between any two, when, in fact, the same paper just circulates among the many. In such a scheme, it is "as difficult as possible to distinguish between a real or fictitious bill of exchange; between a bill drawn by a real creditor upon a real debtor, and a bill for which there was properly no real creditor but the bank which discounted it; nor any real debtor but the projector who made use of the money" (*WN*, 312). Once a bank is drawn into such a scheme, it is very difficult for the bank to get out because refusing to loan more can bring the scheme crashing down and such a crash can bring the bank down with it.

Smith offers examples of banking gone awry[14] in order to make a point about banks and the capital market. The private capital market is more efficient where it is less concentrated. This is so, he asserts, because large lending enterprises cannot know their borrowers as well as small lenders who serve people they know. The "bank which lends money, perhaps, to five hundred different people, the greater part of whom its directors can know very little about, is not as likely to be more judicious in the choice of its debtors, than a private person who lends out his money among a few people whom he knows, and in whose sober and frugal conduct he thinks he has good reason to confide" (*WN*, 316). Banking is based on trust, and trust has a richer foundation in private markets when the banker and the borrower are each more directly visible to those whose interest they hold.

Smith distinguishes this role and therefore the size of banks in the private banking system from the role and size of The Bank of England. The

---

[14] Smith describes, for example, the "solution" that emerged in Scotland to address such schemes as follows: "In the midst of this clamour and distress, a new bank was established in Scotland [the Ayr Bank] for the express purpose of relieving the distress of the country.... This bank was more liberal than any other had ever been...." (*WN*, 313). What unfolded was ironic and tragic. Because the new bank was liberal with its funds, the projectors were able to get the capital they needed. This, in turn, allowed the rival banks that had been caught up in the scheme to get their money out. This fresh line of credit from this new bank "enabled them [(the projectors)] to carry on their projects for about two years longer than they could otherwise have done.... so that when ruin came, it fell so much the heavier both upon them and upon their creditors" (*WN*, 315). This Ayr Bank mess was only the most recent example of the dangers of excess paper. Smith cites John Law's "Mississippi scheme [as the classic example of capital market folly, calling it] the most extravagant project both of banking and stock-jobbing that, perhaps, the world ever saw" (*WN*, 317).

Bank of England "acts, not only as an ordinary bank, but as a great engine of state" (*WN*, 320). The public trust in the bank is based on the warrant of the British government so "[t]he stability of the bank of England is equal to that of the British government" (*WN*, 320). But whether it be the Bank of England or a private bank, according to Smith, one principle underlies the contribution of a banking system to enhancing the wealth of the nation – it facilitates the instrumental role of money in the progress of opulence:

It is not by augmenting the capital of the country, but by rendering a greater part of that capital active and productive than would otherwise be so, that the most judicious operations of banking can increase the industry of a country.... The judicious operations of banking, by substituting paper in the room of a great part of ... [the nations stock of] gold and silver, enables the country to convert a great part of this dead stock into active and productive stock; into stock that produces something for the country. The gold and silver money which circulates in any country may very properly be compared to a highway, which, while it circulates and carries to market all the grass and corn of the country, produces itself not a single pile of either. The judicious operations of banking, by providing, if I may be allowed so violent a metaphor, a sort of wagon-way through the air; enable the country to convert, as it were, a great part of its highways into green pastures and corn fields, and thereby to increase very considerably the annual produce of its land and labour. The commerce and industry of the country, however, it must be acknowledged, though they may be somewhat augmented, cannot be altogether so secure, when they are as thus, as it were, suspended upon the Daedalian wings of paper money, as when they travel about upon the solid ground of gold and silver. (*WN*, 320, 321)

Lack of judiciousness is only one of the problems with paper money that makes its Daedalian wings a less secure carrier of commerce than the solid ground of gold and silver. Smith cites two other concerns.

One is the vulnerability of such a system in time of war: If an enemy captures the reserves that underlie the circulating paper, then the confidence in the system is destroyed and the nation's ability to carry on public and private exchanges is undermined with the collapse of its currency.

Another concern is the appropriate denominations of paper currency: The wholesale trade can be transacted with bills of large denomination since the transactions are themselves large. Retail, being generally small transactions, requires smaller denominations that move at a faster velocity. Smith believes that such small denominations are problematic because they can be issued by small, unscrupulous banks that do not hold adequate reserves. A collapse of these small bills can lead to "a very great calamity to many poor people...." (*WN*, 323). Noting that "[p]aper money may be so regulated, as . . . to confine itself very much to the circulation between the different dealers" (*WN*, 322), he asserts that this is precisely what should be done.

This is government intervention in the liberal system, so Smith feels compelled to explain further:

Such regulations may, no doubt, be considered as in some respect a violation of natural liberty. But those exertions of the natural liberty of a few individuals, which might endanger the security of the whole society, are, and ought to be, restrained by the laws of all governments; of the most free, as well as of the most despotical. The obligation of building party walls, in order to prevent the communication of fire, is a violation of natural liberty, exactly of the same kind with the regulations of the banking trade which are here proposed. (*WN*, 324)

Smith's need to explain his position and the explanation itself are worthy of note.

As described in Chapter One, natural liberty is among Smith's dearest values. Indeed, the raison d'etre of his moral philosophy is to describe the hope of the human prospect: an evolution of humankind toward the ideal "liberal plan of equality, liberty and justice" (*WN*, 664). However, also central to his moral philosophy is the view that humankind is only in the course of that evolution, and that the ideal is a limit, not an achievable end. Along the way, human frailty can distort or even destroy progress. In Smith's analysis, institutions are instrumental, and those instruments function constructively to the degree that they establish conditions that offset the negative effects of human frailty. In the domain of positive law, this implies that laws are sometimes required that are not entirely consistent with that system of natural jurisprudence which would prevail in an ideal world. Smith believes this paper money issue is just such a case.[15] The possibility of unscrupulous banking behavior makes restricting the denominations a good policy.

All these dangers of the Daedalian wings notwithstanding, Smith believes that a properly regulated paper money is good for an economy. To those who argue that expanding the money supply with paper is invariably inflationary, Smith says it need not be so. He cites the Scottish experience to support his contention. Prices have not risen, he asserts, with the expansion of paper in Scotland. Indeed, they have fallen. The only exception being in "1751 and in 1752, when . . . there was a very sensible rise in the price of provisions, owing, probably, to the badness of the seasons, and not to the multiplication of paper money" (*WN*, 325).

---

[15] As we'll see shortly, a limitation on the rate of interest is another.

The perverse effect of paper money on prices is not, according to Smith, inherent in the concept. It is a function of a corrupt execution of the issue. He cites the American colonies as an example of such a corruption. There, the corruption involved "government paper, of which the payment was not exigible till several years after it was issued [(so it is inherently discounted)]...[but which was, by law] a legal tender of payment for the full value for which it was issued" (*WN*, 326). This abuse of paper money was, according to Smith, "an act of such violent injustice, as has scarce, perhaps, been attempted by the government of any other country which pretended to be free" (*WN*, 326). He agrees with the "honest and downright Doctor Douglas...[that] it was, a scheme of fraudulent debtors to cheat their creditors" (*WN*, 326).

Here, again, we hear a theme that weaves its way through Smith's moral philosophy. Factions can and do use government to implement schemes to defraud and cheat the public. Thus government can be a destructive instrument, as in this case of using paper money to cheat creditors...or it can be a tool for constructive policy such as when, in response to this abuse by colonial governments, the British parliament removed the colonies' right to issue legal tender.[16]

Smith spends a good deal of ink on paper money because he believes it is an essential instrument for capital mobilization. He establishes two basic principles that a private banking system should follow in order to constructively issue and administer such paper. First, the paper issued by banks should be of large denominations payable immediately and unconditionally in full upon demand. This will insure the security of the public. Second, competition among banks is desirable, so small is beautiful. A system of small, competitive banks is at one and the same time more informed of risks, more agile, and more responsive to customers. It is also less vulnerable to catastrophic consequences of a single bank's imprudence. "In general, if any branch of trade, or any division of labour, be advantageous to the publick, the freer and more general the competition, it will always be the more so" (*WN*, 329). Keen competition directs stock to the employment of productive labor, and that is good for society.

Productive labor...unproductive labor...we now examine this distinction that is central to Smith's analysis of capital and the progress of opulence.

---

[16] While Smith is wary of government, he believes that good government is essential for humankind's progress. He comes to believe as he grows older, however, that realizing such a government requires noble, civic humanist leadership. More on this in Chapter Eight.

CAPITAL AND PRODUCTIVE VERSUS UNPRODUCTIVE LABOR

There is one sort of labour which adds to the value of the subject upon which it is bestowed: There is another which has no such effect. The former, as it produces value, may be called productive; the latter, unproductive labour. (*WN*, 330)

To understand this distinction between productive and unproductive labor, a distinction that underlies Smith's analysis in the *WN*, it is useful to reflect on another of Smith's distinctions, that between

- stock that is capital to the individual and
- stock that is capital for the nation.

Smith is careful to note that what functions as capital – i.e., yields revenue – for the individual may not be capital for the nation. For example: "Though a house ... may yield a revenue to its proprietor, and thereby serve in the function of capital to him, it cannot yield any to the publick, nor serve in the function of a capital to it, and the revenue of the whole body of people can never be in the smallest degree increased by it" (*WN*, 281).

This distinction between what is capital to the individual and what is capital to the nation does not turn on whether the stock is useful. A house is useful. It is not, however, capital to the nation because it is not one of the *Causes of the Wealth of Nations*. The machinery of a workhouse is also useful and, unlike the house, it is capital to the nation because through its application in the process of production it is instrumental in generating the national product. In Smith's analysis, in order for stock to count as capital in the larger, national frame it has to be engaged in the circuit of production ... reproducing and expanding the wealth of the nation with each new circuit.

Similarly, the distinction between productive and unproductive labor is not based on whether the labor is useful, but on how it is useful.

Productive labor is labor engaged in the circuit of production. It is "productive" because its activity both replaces the stock required to produce itself and adds to the stock that can be used for further production in the next circuit. It "promotes industry; and though it increases the consumption of the society, it provides a permanent fund for supporting that consumption, the people who consume reproducing, with a profit, the whole value of their annual consumption" (*WN*, 295).

Unproductive labor can be useful labor. Indeed, in some cases it is essential for society. But it does not contribute to *The Wealth of*

Nations because it is not labor engaged in the expanding circuit of production:

The sovereign, for example, with all the officers both of justice and war who serve under him, the whole army and navy, are unproductive labour.... In the same class must be ranked, some both of the gravest and most important, and some of the most frivolous professions: churchmen, lawyers, physicians, men of letters of all kinds; players, buffoons, musicians, opera-singers, opera-dancers, &c. (*WN*, 330–1)

These labors do not replace the stock used to cover their own cost, much less add to the nation's stock for production in the subsequent circuit.[17] Thus, unlike productive labor, which sustains or expands the capital stock as it flows through the circuit of production, unproductive labor diminishes that stock by diverting resources from that circuit.[18]

The current level of opulence is maintained by employing productive labor that constantly replenishes the capital stock. The progress of opulence is fueled when that stock is augmented from the net product to employ even more productive labor or to enhance the productivity of that labor in each successive circuit of production by improving the fixed capital.

To illustrate this point, Smith contrasts the current state of the "opulent countries of Europe" with their condition in feudal times. In those earlier times, given the predilection of men for consumption, the insecurity of the times, and the lack of opportunities for productive applications, the

---

[17] Clearly human capital investments fit into Smith's conception of capital, but here he cites, among the professions that are unproductive labor and thus outside the circuit of production "physicians [and] men of letters of all kinds" (*WN*, 331). Why isn't this productive labor? I think his categorization here turns on the notion that the return from the investment in these skills is too lagged to be available in the next circuit of production. It does not replenish and augment itself for the next circuit and thus it is outside of his 'circuits of capital' frame. I find this distinction problematic at best.

[18] A reviewer questioned the fact that I don't make use of the "tangible" versus "intangible" distinction as I present my analysis of productive and unproductive labor in Smith. I appreciate the reviewer's point that this is a common distinction in the literature. My decision to avoid this tangible/intangible distinction is primarily stylistic. I do not think it is a sufficiently sharp distinction to capture Smith's meaning.

It is certainly true that the production of intangibles is unproductive labor because these intangibles cannot be accumulated and thus cannot contribute to the circuit of production. It does not follow, however, that labor expended on tangible items is invariably productive labor. Although the tangible can be accumulated and thus can contribute to the circuit of production – making the labor spent on it productive labor – there can be tangible production that does not represent the output of productive labor because that output is not thrown back into the circuit of production as capital. As we will see in the next Chapter, Smith cites the labor expended on the feudal manors as a case in point.

net product was largely expended on unproductive labor: retainers and tenants, individuals dependent on the lord for their livelihood. The stagnation of those times was further exacerbated by the fact those dependents, lacking incentive, were indeed very unproductive. In feudal society, those many who were dependent upon the lord were "in general idle, dissolute, and poor...." "It is better, says the proverb, to play for nothing, than to work for nothing" (*WN*, 335). The only engaged working class of those days was found in the "mercantile and manufacturing towns" where men were employed by capital – that is, employed in an expanding circuit of production, augmenting capital rather consuming all of the fruits of their production (*WN*, 335).[19]

CAPITAL ACCUMULATION AND INCENTIVES: ETHICS AND "BETTERING ONE'S CONDITION"

Clearly, the key to the progress of opulence lies in expanding the capital stock of the nation. So how, according to Smith, is that accomplished?

Capitals are increased by parsimony, and diminished by prodigality and misconduct.... Parsimony, and not industry, is the immediate cause of the increase of capital. Industry, indeed, provides the subject which parsimony accumulates. But whatever industry might acquire, if parsimony did not save and store it up, the capital would never be the greater. (*WN*, 337)[20]

Here, again, in the context of his analysis of capital, we are reminded that Smith is a moral philosopher. The key to expanding *The Wealth of Nations* is ethics, in this case parsimony. Parsimony is an expression of prudence, and prudence is a mature manifestation of self-love, one of Smith's sentiments. In his *Theory of Moral Sentiments*, Smith writes that the prudent man demonstrates a "steadfastness of... industry and frugality, in his steadily sacrificing the ease and enjoyment of the present moment for the probable expectation of the still greater ease and enjoyment of a more distant but more lasting period of time...." (*TMS*, 215).

---

[19] "The proportion between capital and revenue [supporting workers]...seems every where to regulate the proportion between industry and idleness. Wherever capital predominates, industry prevails: wherever revenue, idleness" (*WN*, 337).

[20] Smith attributes the confusion of the Physiocrats to the fact that agriculture is an exception to this general principle. Thanks to the natural productivity of agriculture, while "[a]rtificers, manufacturers, and merchants can augment the revenue and wealth of their society by parsimony only... Farmers and country labourers, on the contrary, may enjoy completely the whole funds destined for their own subsistence, and yet augment at the same time the revenue and wealth of their society" (*WN*, 668).

At the heart of Smith's representation of *The Nature and Causes of The Wealth of Nations* is his analysis of how independent, productive labor financed by a growing accumulation of capital expands the wealth of a nation. Now we see how that heart is guided by a moral philosophical soul. The wealth of a nation is ultimately a function of the character and condition of its citizens: Only a free, secure, independent people have the incentive to work hard and the confidence to accumulate capital and to seize opportunities presented by markets. Only an ethically mature citizenry embodies the justice necessary to insure security, the prudence necessary to be parsimonious, and thus the ethics that are essential to grow the capital stock of the nation.[21] One can hear the moral standing of parsimony in Smith's words on frugality and prodigality:

By what the frugal man annually saves, he not only affords maintenance to an additional number of productive hands, for the ensuing year, but ... he establishes as it were a perpetual fund for the maintenance of an equal number in all times to come....

The prodigal ... [b]y not confining his expense within his income ... encroaches upon his capital.... [H]e pays the wages of idleness with those funds which the frugality of his forefathers had, as it were, consecrated to the maintenance of industry. By diminishing the funds destined for the employment of productive labour, he necessarily diminishes, so far as it depends upon him, the quantity of that labour which adds a value to the subject upon which it is bestowed, and consequently, the value of the annual produce of the land and labour of the whole country, the real wealth and revenue of its inhabitants. (*WN*, 338, 339)

The prodigal who spends the gold and silver generated by the productive enterprises of his predecessors on the consumption of domestic products does keep that specie in his nation, but he is not doing his nation a favor. With each such cycle, the capital stock and thus the real productive capacity of the nation is diminished. With less to buy domestically, specie "will, in spite of all laws and prohibitions, be sent abroad, and employed in purchasing consumable goods which may be of some use at home" (*WN*, 340). Thus, prodigality brings decline and, contrary to early mercantile thought, "[t]he exportation of gold and silver is, in this case, not the cause, but the effect of ... [this] declension...." (*WN*, 340). In contrast, where parsimony expands the capital stock and thus the production of the economy, this increase in goods "will require a greater quantity of money to circulate them.... The increase of those metals will,

---

[21] "The laws of justice would encourage the extension of a complex web of trade and production, while the other virtues [prudence] would help augment the capital stock and put the economy into rapid motion" (Fitzgibbons, 125).

in this case, be the effect, not [as mercantilists argue] the cause, of the publick prosperity" (*WN*, 340).[22]

Smith does not believe that such saving by the parsimonious person diminishes demand. Rather, this saving becomes capital stock that flows into the hands of productive laborers who use that stock to support themselves.

> What is annually saved is as regularly consumed as what is annually spent, and nearly at the same time too; but it is consumed by a different set of people. (*WN*, 337–8)

Ultimately, "[t]he consumption is the same ["food, cloathing, and lodging"], but the consumers are different" (*WN*, 338). When the circuits of production are filled with capital, the production of that "food, cloathing, and lodging" is greatest, and the condition of the working class, those who do most of the producing in any society, is best.

Prudence is essential if this desirable end is to be realized and, as is so often the case in Smith's moral philosophy, the benevolent deity does not leave the human prospect that requires such prudence to the vagaries of human wisdom. Rather, the deity has designed propensities and desires into human nature that encourage and reinforce such constructive behaviors (recall the "oeconomy of nature" (*TMS*, 77)). In the case of frugality, it is not only moral to be prudent, it is encouraged by our natural desire for "bettering our condition...[For a]n augmentation of fortune is the means by which the greater part of men propose and wish to better their condition" (*WN*, 341). This desire and the ethic it nurtures make Smith sanguine with respect to private accumulation and the capital stock.

Prodigality certainly exists and projectors will always be sinking capital into "injudicious and unsuccessful project[s]" (*WN*, 341), so there will always be forces reducing the capital stock. But private individuals have the incentive and the imagination to accumulate and, as society matures, so too do individuals' ethics, including prudence. Given this incentive and this ethic, Smith envisions the net effect of private behavior on the capital stock as progressively more positive. The real danger to the capital stock and thus to the progress of opulence of a nation is, according to Smith, not individual prodigality. It is government prodigality.

> Great nations are never impoverished by private, though they sometimes are by publick prodigality and misconduct. The whole, or almost the whole publick

---

[22] Here, Smith is anticipating the attack he makes on mercantile logic in *WN*, Book IV, presented here in Chapter Eight.

revenue, is in most countries employed in maintaining unproductive hands. Such are the people who compose a numerous and splendid court, a great ecclesiastical establishment, great fleets and armies, who in time of peace produce nothing, and in time of war acquire nothing which can compensate the expense of maintaining them, even while the war lasts. (*WN*, 342)[23]

Here, again, we see a theme of Smith's moral philosophy: A society's progress ultimately depends not on institutional government but on individual citizens' self-government; on their civic ethics. He passionately asserts that the progress of great nations is attributable to the "frugality and good conduct of individuals" (*WN*, 342) who, given their parsimony and their desire to better their condition, accumulate capital at a rate sufficient to offset the perverse effects of other individuals. Government is instrumental and that instrument can either be constructive or destructive. Thanks to the "oeconomy of nature," government need not be perfect, it need only be constructive for progress to be possible:

[T]he natural effort which every man is continually making to better his own condition is a principle of preservation capable of preventing and correcting, in many respects, the bad effects of [bad policy]... If a nation could not prosper without the enjoyment of perfect liberty and perfect justice, there is not in the world a nation which could ever have prospered. In the political body, however, the wisdom of nature has fortunately made ample provision for remedying many of the bad effects of the folly and injustice of man, in the same manner as it has done in the natural body for remedying those of his sloth and intemperance. (*WN*, 674)

However, sometimes governments do destroy progress. In those cases, such nations will be left behind in the course of humankind's evolution by natural selection. In Chapter Three, we saw Smith's story of China and Bengal as examples of artificial limits imposed on a nation's progress by perverse laws and institutions. In Chapter Eight, we'll see that Smith's growing concern that mercantile policies might have just such an effect in Britain drives the evolution of his work from 1775 on.

Smith summarizes his analysis of accumulation, capital stock and productive labor as follows:

The annual produce of the land and labour of any nation can be increased in its value by no other means, but by increasing either the number of its productive labourers, or the productive power of those labourers who had before been employed. The number of its productive labourers, it is evident, can never be much

---

[23] As Chapter Eight demonstrates, the effect of mercantile-inspired wars on public debt is central to Smith's *WN*, Book IV attack on the mercantile system in Britain.

increased, but in consequence of an increase of capital, or of the funds destined for maintaining them. The productive powers of the same number of labourers cannot be increased, but in consequence either of some addition and improvement to those machines and instruments which facilitate and abridge labour; or of a more proper division and distribution of employment. In either case an additional capital is almost always required. (*WN*, 343)

To establish the credibility of his analysis of the role of capital in the progress of opulence, Smith offers a brief description of how this progress unfolded in England. He begins, however, with a caveat. Because the progress of opulence made possible by accumulation, increasing capital stock, and an increase in productive labor "is frequently so gradual, that, at near periods, the improvement is not...sensible" (*WN*, 343) or may even be overshadowed by short-term declines, it is necessary to "compare the state of the country at periods somewhat distant from one another" (*WN*, 343).

This point is relevant not only to the example at hand, but also to Smith's larger moral philosophical vision. When representing the power of his general principles, he focuses on long rather than short historical intervals because his vision, and thus his moral philosophical analysis, encompasses the long flow of humankind's evolution. Short periods are no test of the persuasiveness of such an analysis except to demonstrate its ability to deal with distortions, because in such a frame, the larger patterns may not be observable due to such distortions. Indeed, as we will see in Chapter Seven, in "shorter" frames, the larger patterns may even be so distorted as to be inverted.

Returning to the case in point, Smith asserts that the "annual produce of the land and labour of England" (*WN*, 344) is certainly more than it was a century ago, a century ago it was greater than it had been a century before that, and even then it was greater than at the time of the Norman conquest. In sum, the general trend of England's wealth over the long term has been growth. This in spite of public and private prodigality, wars, and civil unrest, all of which are impediments to the growth of capital and much of which has been attributable to the government.[24]

But though the profusion of government must, undoubtedly, have retarded the natural progress of England toward wealth and improvement, it has not been able

[24] He is particularly keen to point out the immense cost of "four French wars" (1688, 1702, 1742, 1756) for which "the nation has contracted more than a hundred and forty-five million of debt...." (*WN*, 345). This particular example anticipates his scathing attack on the mercantile system, for he blames this public profligacy on the political power of those private interests...more on this in Chapter Eight.

to stop it.... In the midst of all the exactions of government...capital has been silently and gradually accumulated by the private frugality and good conduct of individuals, by their universal, continual, and uninterrupted effort to better their condition. It is this effort, protected by law and allowed by liberty to exert itself in the manner that is most advantageous, which has maintained the progress of England towards opulence and improvement in almost all former times, and which, it is to be hoped, will do so in all future times. (*WN*, 345)

It is valuable to pause here and consider again Smith's conception of government. In the quotation just cited he clearly blames government for retarding natural progress. Yet, in the same quotation, he attributes the private accumulation to the fact that it is "protected by law and allowed by liberty." This law and this liberty are also a function of government.

Not all governments afford such security. As we've seen in Chapter Three, Smith believes that among the nations of his day, Great Britain enjoys the greatest progress because, all of its foolish wars and regulations notwithstanding, it enjoys the best government humankind has produced. Smith's views on government are not simply summed up by the Physiocratic term "laissez-faire." Government can be a destructive instrument, but progress is only possible where government functions as a constructive instrument.

We'll return to Smith's views on the role of government in Chapter Nine, but at this point one thing is clear about the relationship Smith envisions between government and the economy. The government should never try to micromanage the economy: "It is the highest impertinence and presumption...in kings and ministers, to pretend to watch over the economy of private people" (*WN*, 346). For example, lenders and borrowers should be generally free to interact in a competitive market so that capital flows to its best advantage.

CAPITAL AND INTEREST

A lender always sees that "stock...lent at interest...as a capital" (*WN*, 350), but the borrower may actually use that stock as capital or for immediate consumption. Here, again, we see the distinction Smith makes between what is capital to the individual and what is capital to the nation. If stock lent at interest is used for consumption, it may pay interest but it is not capital in Smith's analysis. Fortunately for the economy, according to Smith, such lending is not the norm.

Smith refers to those who lend stock at interest as "the monied interest" (*WN*, 351). He is careful to note that although it is money that exchanges hands, "what the borrower really wants, and what the lender really supplies him with, is, not the money, but the money's worth...." (*WN*, 351). The terms of such a loan require that the borrower return the full portion borrowed; Smith refers to this as "the repayment" and, in addition, "a smaller portion, called the interest" (*WN*, 352).

With the progress of opulence, the general stock of capital in a nation grows and so does the stock of capital available for loan by the monied interest. As the liquid capital of a nation deepens, "[i]t becomes gradually more and more difficult to find within the country a profitable method of employing any new capital" (*WN*, 352–3). This gives rise to an increasingly fierce "competition between different capitals" (*WN*, 353), a competition that unfolds in both the product and the factor markets. On the product side, the competition is over market share and the only way to succeed, or even survive, is "by dealing on more reasonable terms" (*WN*, 353). This becomes one jaw of a vise that squeezes profits and, in turn, interest.

The other jaw of this vise is in the factor market for "[h]e must not only sell what he deals in somewhat cheaper, but in order to get it to sell, he must sometimes buy it somewhat dearer" (*WN*, 353). For example, capitals must compete with one another for the available labor. "Their competition raises the wages of labour, and sinks the profits of stock. But when the profits which can be made by the use of capital are in this manner diminished, as it were, at both ends [(in the product and factor markets)], the price which can be paid for the use of it, that is, the rate of interest, must necessarily be diminished with them" (*WN*, 353).

Thus, "[a]s the quantity of stock to be lent at interest increases, the interest, or the price which must be paid for the use of that stock necessarily diminishes...." (*WN*, 352). This is the natural course of events when markets are functioning in a constructive environment. And, as Smith sees it, this natural course is a good course because, like rent, interest is "a monopoly price" (*WN*, 161). Thus its diminution reduces an unearned return without reducing the incentive for industry.[25]

His analysis of interest brings Smith to the issue of usury laws.[26] Such laws are, according to Smith, perverse. They do not eliminate lending, they simply add a risk premium to the rate of interest. But although he is against usury laws that totally outlaw interest, he is not against fixing a

---

[25] This point is central to Smith's presentation in Book V, covered in Chapter Nine here, on the "Taxes on Profit" (*WN*, 847).

[26] Maria Pia Paganelli (2003) makes a very nice contribution on this issue.

legal ceiling on the rate of interest so long as that ceiling is "not too much above the lowest market rate" (*WN*, 357).

Smith advocates this ceiling because he is concerned about the effect of projectors who, with an unrealistic estimation of their probability of success ("their golden dreams" (*WN*, 310)), seek capital for fruitless schemes from banks that are too big to accurately assess their worthiness. This combination leads to perversely high interest rates as the projectors outbid the more sober investors for a share of the available capital.

If the legal rate of interest in Great Britain, for example, was fixed so high as eight or ten per cent., the greater part of the money which was to be lent, would be lent to prodigals and projectors, who alone would be willing to give this high interest. Sober people, who will give for the use of money no more than a part of what they are likely to make by the use of it, would not venture into the competition. (*WN*, 357)

Having described the case of banks being duped by schemes for drawing and re-drawing bills of exchange, he has established the fact that banks are not always wise in their lending. He argues, therefore, for limiting the rate of interest because, in his view, "[w]here the legal rate of interest . . . is fixed but a very little above the lowest market rate, sober people are universally preferred, as borrowers, to prodigals and projectors" (*WN*, 357).[27] Again, we see prudent government intervention as a break on the effect of human frailty, in this case the human inclination to overestimate one's own prospects.

CAPITAL DEEPENING, OVERFLOWS, EXPANDING CIRCUITS, AND THE NATURAL PROGRESS OF OPULENCE: THE GLOBALIZATION OF CAPITAL FLOWS AND TRADE

As we've seen, in an undistorted, secure environment, capital is accumulated and flows to its best advantage. This secure accumulation and free flow provide the fuel for the natural progress of opulence. Thus, a logical way to trace and analyze the natural progress of *The Wealth of Nations* is to describe and explain the succession of circuits into which capital flows in an undistorted, secure environment. This is precisely how Smith proceeds.

---

[27] Again, as with the denomination of bills (*WN*, 324), we hear Smith calling for regulation. In this case, his advocacy of the regulation of interest rates is, no doubt, also a function of his view that interest is, like rent, a monopoly price. (*WN*, 847–8).

He begins by citing three applications of a nation's capital. It can be used to:

- "improve and cultivate all its lands,"
- "manufacture and prepare their whole rude produce for immediate use and consumption,"
- "transport the surplus part either of the rude or manufactured produce to those distant markets where it can be exchanged for something for which there is a demand at home" (*WN*, 365). He refers to this last as the "wholesale trade" (*WN*, 368).

According to Smith, capital naturally flows first into agriculture because, thanks to the labor of nature, agriculture is initially the most productive application of capital.[28] Then, as the capital stock in agriculture grows deeper, the rate of return in agriculture falls and, at some point, the capital spills out of agriculture and into manufacturing, where it grows with each successive circuit of production.

This much is a review of the analysis Smith has presented earlier, in *WN* Book II. Now, with his analysis of money and particularly the role of paper money in place, Smith opens up his analysis to explore the globalization of capital flows and trade in his *Inquiry into the Nature and Causes of the Wealth of Nations*.

With successive circuits of production in the manufacturing sector, the capital stock continues to deepen and, at some point, it begins to spill out into the wholesale trade. *Ceteris paribus*, capital flows there last because this application "has the least effect [is least productive] of any of the three" (*WN*, 366).

Smith subdivides this wholesale trade into three categories:

- "the home trade,
- the foreign trade of consumption, and
- the carrying trade" (*WN*, 368).

He distinguishes these three categories of trade along two dimensions: the quantity of domestic productive labor each engages and the velocity with which capital makes the circuit. (He introduces risk later. See Chapter Seven in this volume.[29]) In comparing the home and the foreign

---

[28] He cites the American colonies as evidence of this writing: "It has been the principal cause of the rapid progress of our American colonies towards wealth and greatness, that almost their whole capitals have hitherto been employed in agriculture" (*WN*, 366).

[29] Smith introduces and develops one more consideration that reinforces the order of priority, the risk of capital loss, in Books III (see *WN*, 377–9) and IV (see *WN*, 628–9). He

trade of consumption with regard to the quantity of domestic productive labor each respectively engages, Smith says that the former is more advantageous to the nation because all of the capital is engaged in employing domestic productive labor, whereas in the latter case, only half is so employed. With respect to velocity, the speed of a circuit, he writes:

[T]he returns of the foreign trade of consumption are very seldom so quick as those of the home-trade. The returns of the home-trade generally come in before the end of the year, and sometimes three or four times in the year. The returns of the foreign trade of consumption seldom come in before the end of the year, and sometimes not till after two or three years. A capital, therefore, employed in the home-trade will sometimes make twelve operations, or be sent out and returned twelve times, before a capital employed in the foreign trade of consumption has made one. If capitals are equal, therefore, the one will give four and twenty times more encouragement and support to the industry of the country than the other. (*WN*, 368–9)[30]

Extending the comparison, the carrying trade is least advantageous to the nation because it uses capital to support the least domestic productive labor (the products beings transported are all being produced by foreign workers), and it has the slowest velocity because it involves the longest circuit.

Given that the greatest velocity of trade is in the inner, domestic circuit, from the perspective of the holder of capital the best returns are to be had, at least initially, in the home trade ... so, *ceteris paribus*, capital will initially stay home. This is good for the wealth of the nation: "The capital ... employed in the home-trade of any country will generally give encouragement and support to a greater quantity of productive labour in that country, and increase the value of its annual produce more than an equal capital employed in the foreign trade.... " (*WN*, 371).

However, as the stock of the capital in the domestic economy deepens, the rate of return on that capital falls. At some point, this fall will make the returns from the foreign trade in consumption attractive. Capital will spill into this wider circuit as the interests of the merchant holders of liquid, mobile capital induce them to seek these now-attractive returns.

asserts there that it is most commonly the case that the closer capital stays to home, the less risky, so, *ceteris paribus*, home is less risky than foreign trade in consumption, is less risky than carrying trade. This analysis will be presented in Chapter Seven.

[30] He goes on to note that "round-about foreign trade of consumption" (*WN*, 602), like the famous triangle trade with the American colonies, is even slower than normal foreign trade. This reference anticipates the argument he will make (*WN* Book IV; Chapter Eight here) about the foolishness of mercantile policies that force British capital into that "one great channel" that serves their private interest (*WN*, 604).

"[T]he capital employed in this latter [foreign] trade [of consumption] has...[an] advantage over equal capital employed in the carrying trade...." (*WN*, 371–2), but this advantage diminishes with progress. Each new circuit of capital deepens the stock, and as the stock of capital deepens in these first two circuits of trade – home and foreign trade in consumption – the rate of return falls. At some point, the capital in these first two circuits becomes so deep and the rate of return so low, that "the surplus part of it naturally disgorges itself into the carrying trade...." (*WN*, 373).

In sum, as capital stock of a country deepens, it successively fills each of these circuits and then spills into the next. This is good for the nation according to Smith:

Each of these different branches of trade...is not only advantageous, but necessary and unavoidable, when the course of things without constraint or violence, naturally introduces it. (*WN*, 372)

As always in Smith, the good ultimately follows from the natural. In this case, it comes "when the course of things without constraint or violence, naturally introduces it."

ON THE CAPITAL MARKET, THE IDEAL AND ITS DISTORTION

Smith's analysis of capital can be summarized briefly as follows. Productive labor is the source of the wealth of a nation. The share of the accumulation that is allocated to the capital stock determines the resources available to employ productive labor and to buy the tools, etc. that determine the productivity of that labor. Given laws and institutions that insure liberty and justice for all, secure, independent, ethically mature (prudent) citizens will accumulate capital stock and allocate it to their best advantage. Capital will naturally flow first into agriculture, then into manufacturing, then into subsequent circuits of trade: home, foreign consumption, carrying. This dynamic is consistent with the production of the greatest wealth for the nation because this flow, motivated by the self-interest of the participants, always takes capital to its most productive allocation.

In *WN* Book IV, as he analyzes the perverse consequences of mercantile policies that distort capital flows, Smith refers back to his analysis of natural, unimpeded capital flows[31] and concludes with that most

---

[31] Complemented in *WN* Book IV by risk considerations.

famous of Smithian images:

As every individual ... endeavours as much as he can both to employ his capital in the support of domestick industry, and so to direct that industry that its produce may be of the greatest value; every individual necessarily labours to render the annual revenue of society as great as he can. He generally, indeed, neither intends to promote the publick interest, nor knows how he is promoting it. By preferring the support of domestick to that of foreign industry, he intends only his own security; and by directing that industry in such a manner as its produce may be of the greatest value, he intends only his own gain,[32] and he is in this, as in many other cases, led by an invisible hand to promote an end which was no part of his intention. (*WN*, 456)

This invisible hand is not, as the modern discourse generally suggests, the magic of a market economy at work. That is but one of its handiworks. This invisible hand is for Smith the hand of the deity that designed the "oeconomy of nature" (*TMS*, 77) and those invisible "connecting principles" (*HA*, 45) that guide humankind's evolution.[33] Where that design is least distorted by human frailty, the progress of opulence proceeds most successfully.

In the course of this progress, distribution becomes more just: With each circuit, as the stock of capital deepens, more capital competes for the available labor. As a consequence, wages rise and the rate of profit falls. Thus, the natural progress of opulence brings workers a better life[34] and, in a nation that has "acquired its full complement of riches ... the ordinary rate of clear profit ... is very small, so that usual market rate of interest which could be afforded out if it, would be so low as to render it impossible for any but the very wealthiest people [among "the monied interest" (*WN*, 351)] to live upon the interest of their money" (*WN*, 113).

Progress also extends the nexus of trade and, in the process, capital flows from nations with more capital resources to nations with less of those resources. This, in turn, means that the benefits of accumulation are extended globally. This expanding nexus of trade makes all nations in this

---

[32] "The consideration of his own private profit, is the sole motive which determines the owner of any capital to employ it either in agriculture, in manufactures, or in some particular branch of the wholesale or retail trade. The different quantities of productive labour which it may put into motion, and the different values which it may add to the annual produce of the land and labour of the society, according as it is employed in one or other of those different ways, never enter into his thoughts" (*WN*, 373–4).

[33] I do not think Smith's "image of the invisible hand is best interpreted as a mildly ironic joke" (Rothschild, 116).

[34] As I explained in Chapter One and as Muller writes: "Their welfare [that of the working class] is the prime concern of economic policy, as Smith conceived it" (Muller, 1993, 75).

net interdependent. This interdependence can, in turn, ameliorate the asymmetries in international power.[35] As Smith writes when describing the forces that might reduce the colonial hegemony Europe enjoyed over much of the world in his day:

Hereafter, perhaps, the natives of those countries may grow stronger, or those of Europe may grow weaker, and the inhabitants of all the different quarters of the world may arrive at that equality of courage and force which, by inspiring mutual fear, can alone overawe the injustice of independent nations into some sort of respect for the rights of one another. But nothing seems more likely to establish this equality of force than that mutual communication of knowledge and of all sorts of improvements which an extensive commerce from all countries to all countries naturally, or rather necessarily, carries along with it. (*WN*, 626–7)

This, in turn, might lead to a system of international relations that requires much less expenditure on what Smith considered very expensive unproductive labor – the military. As Haakonssen writes, Smith believes that:

free trade is more likely than anything else to further that integration between nations which tends to make their relations more a matter for diplomacy than for the military. (Haakonssen, 1981, 180)

These images represent for Smith the human prospect: The liberal plan, the progress of opulence, a more just distribution, and, with the globalization of this process, more wealth and less war. But Smith is not Pollyanna. He fully appreciated that:

- This is an ideal vision.
- Reality is a long way from this ideal.
- The ideal is a limit we can approximate but never achieve.
- We will always have to deal with the reality of human frailty.

At the end of *WN* Book II, having laid out the role of capital and the natural path that the progress of opulence would follow if capital were secure and free, Smith observes that events in Europe have not, in fact, followed this natural path. Book II closes with the following words:

What circumstances in the policy of Europe have given the trades which are carried on in towns so great an advantage over that which is carried on in the country,

---

[35] It should be noted that whereas Smith would reject Marx's view that concentrations of capital are an inevitable product of the capitalist mode of production, Smith did share concern with Marx (nascent in Smith) that concentrated control over and the associated constrained access to capital is problematic for a liberal system and can occur if the laws and institutions allow. I return to this issue in Chapter Twelve.

that private persons frequently find it more for their advantage to employ their capitals in the most distant carrying trades of Asia and America, than in the improvement and cultivation of the most fertile fields in their own neighborhood, I shall endeavour to explain at full length in the following two books. (*WN*, 374–5)

This transition from Books I and II to Books III and IV of *The Wealth of Nations* represents Smith's approach to moral philosophy beautifully. Having, in *WN* Books I and II, laid out the general principles and the conjectural history, the natural progress, they imply; with this frame of reference in place, in *WN* Book III Smith moves from conjectural history to a narrative history of unnatural progress of Europe, and in *WN* Book IV he presents a narrative history of the evolution of commercial policy in England. Pocock writes of this same transition when it appears in Smith's *Lectures on Jurisprudence*:

[I]n his Glasgow lectures [Smith] may be found speaking of 'the history of Europe' and offering to give an account of it; and from the moment he does so, the problem of the relation of natural to civil history, of philosophy to historiography, is before us.... Smith ... was not content to remain a theoretical historian; ... [he] offered to narrate, if not necessarily to unify, the histories of Europe and mankind. (Pocock, 1999, 315)

Absolutely so. Recall Smith's two history strategy described in Chapter One.[36] His conjectural history demonstrates the power of his principles to explain the broad flow of humankind's history, while his narrative of the particular, unnatural events in recorded history demonstrates the power of those same principles when the analysis is adjusted for the presence of distortions.[37]

Having laid out the general principles that guide the progress of opulence in *WN* Books I and II, including the general principle that progress begins in agriculture and proceeds from there to the cities, in *WN* Book III Smith turns to the sources of distortions of "the natural Progress of Opulence" (*WN*, 376). To tell that story he narrates a history of Europe

---

[36] Pocock writes that although Gibbon "names Hume and Robertson alongside Smith [as noteworthy contributors to that "'strong ray of philosophic light [that] has broke from Scotland'" "'[o]n this interesting subject, the progress of society in Europe'" (Gibbon cited in Pocock, 1999, 309)] ... he [Gibbon] names them first, because they are historians in the same sense that he is. Smith claimed no authority over civil history...." (Pocock, 1999, 317). Smith is not an historian. History is instrumental in his work as a moral philosopher.

[37] With respect to those who "dismiss ["'irregularities' and 'corruptions'"" (Campbell, 1971, 55)] ... as interesting irrelevances ... [I agree with Campbell that f]ar from being irrelevant, these irregularities are, for Smith, crucial tests for his theory, and the more of them he can explain the more secure he regards its empirical basis" (Campbell, 1971, 55).

from the fall of Rome. In the process, he demonstrates how laws and institutions became severe impediments to the natural course of capital accumulation and thus to the natural progress of opulence, and he describes the very unnatural turn of events that, nevertheless, made progress possible. We now turn to that narrative.

SEVEN

An Unnatural Path to Natural Progress

Smith Represents the Power of His Principles in Book III of *The Wealth of Nations*

REVIEWING "THE NATURAL PROGRESS OF OPULENCE"

Smith titles Chapter 1 of *WN* Book III "Of the natural progress of opulence" because therein he reviews the "general rule" (*WN*, 377) of "the progress of opulence" that he has established in *WN* Book II: the progress of opulence begins where the essentials of human life ("subsistence" (*WN*, 377)) are produced, in agriculture. It is from that foundation and with that support that the production of commodities for "conveniency and luxury" (*WN*, 377) follows.

Using Smith's country/town dichotomy, progress begins in the country and proceeds to the towns, where concentrations of people allow for the finer division of labor and thus the production of more complex and elegant goods. Variations on this pattern are feasible since towns can reach beyond their immediate locale for sources of subsistence, but although there are "considerable variations," (*WN*, 377) these form "no exception to the general rule" (*WN*, 377).

Here, as he reviews his representation of the "natural progress of opulence" (*WN*, 376), Smith introduces the issue of risk. His risk analysis complements those general principles he developed in *WN* Book II, and it provides a segue to the narrative history he is about to tell.

Human beings are, according to Smith, naturally risk averse.[1] As a consequence,

[u]pon equal, or nearly equal profits, most men will chuse to employ their capitals rather in improvement and cultivation of land, than either in the manufactures

---

[1] It is an "order of things...promoted by the natural inclinations of man" (*WN*, 377) to, *ceteribus paribus*, place one's capital in the least risky position.

167

or in foreign trade. The man who employs his capital in land, has it more under his view and command, and his fortune is much less liable to accidents than that of the trader, who is obliged frequently to commit it, not only to the wind and the waves, but to the more uncertain elements of human folly and injustice, by giving great credits in distant countries to men with whose character and situation he can seldom be thoroughly acquainted. The capital of the landlord, on the contrary, which is fixed in the improvement of land, seems to be as well secured as the nature of human affairs can admit of.[2] ... In seeking for employment to a capital, manufactures are, upon equal or nearly equal profits, naturally preferred to foreign commerce, for the same reason that agriculture is naturally preferred to manufactures. (*WN*, 377–8, 379)

Thus, risk aversion reinforces the general principle that the natural progress of opulence begins with investments in agriculture and proceeds to manufacturing and then to ever-expanding circuits of trade as capital deepens and successively spills into each of these broader circuits. Or so it would be,

[h]ad human institutions ... never disturbed the natural course of things. ... But though this natural order of things must have taken place in some degree in every ... society, it has, in all the modern states of Europe been, in many respects, entirely inverted. (*WN*, 378, 380)

With this turn, Smith moves from conjectural or theoretical to narrative history. As he does so, he highlights the source of the distortions that disturb "the natural course of things" and thus necessitate the turn: "human institutions." *WN* Books I and II lay out the general principles of natural progress. *WN* Book III presents a narrative history of the particular unnatural process that led to progress in Europe.

All narrative history is particular. Every story is unique, driven by the peculiarities of chance, circumstance, and intended and unintended consequences of individuals' choices at the time and place covered by the narrative. Smith's purpose in moving from theoretical to narrative history is to demonstrate that his general principles regarding the natural progress of opulence are applicable to particular cases, even those that seem, on the face of it, to be entirely inconsistent with those principles, if one adapts those general principles to the particular conditions prevailing in that time and place.

In *WN* Book III, Smith traces the evolution of laws and institutions in feudal Europe that led to unnatural progress. In this story, distorting

---

[2] Smith also notes the "pleasures of country life": "The beauty of the country, ... the tranquility of the mind which it promises, and wherever the injustice of human laws do not disturb it, the independency which it really affords. ..." (*WN*, 378).

laws and institutions caused the towns to progress before the country, but those laws and institutions ultimately evolved such that the country followed the towns in making progress. This progress is an inversion of the natural course but it is progress, and the principles that give rise to this progress are those general principles that always lie behind progress in Smith's moral philosophy: laws and institutions maturing to bring justice, independence, and security.

Smith's goal in *WN* Book III is to persuade his reader of the power of the analysis he has developed in *WN* Books I and II by demonstrating that:

- His general principles are operative even in cases where the course of actual events – the narrative history – seems so unnatural.
- The economy of nature and the deceptions of nature, those handiworks of the designer, can guide humankind toward progress, albeit along a convoluted path, even in the face of distortions.

"OF THE DISCOURAGEMENT OF AGRICULTURE IN THE ANTIENT STATE OF EUROPE AFTER THE FALL OF THE ROMAN EMPIRE"

Smith describes the initial condition of Europe after the fall of Rome as follows: "[T]owns were deserted" (*WN*, 381) because invaders choked off connections to the countryside, the source of their subsistence.[3] In the countryside chaos led to a lack of cultivation. As a consequence of this chaos and insecurity "the western provinces of Europe, which had enjoyed a considerable degree of opulence under the Roman empire, sunk into the lowest state of poverty and barbarism" (*WN*, 381–2).

Into this vacuum stepped "a few great proprietors" who "engrossed" the land and established "[t]he law of primogeniture ... [and] of entails" which precluded the subdivision of these large parcels and insured that succession was the right of the oldest male.[4] Smith is quite clear in asserting that these laws violate the "natural law of succession [which, as was the rule under Roman law,] divides it ... [with] no ... distinction between elder and younger, between male and female" (*WN*, 382). But in this particular circumstance, the power vacuum left by the fall of Rome, Smith

---

[3] This conception of towns as dependent on the country is entirely consistent with Smith's principles.

[4] He writes that "[t]he male sex is universally preferred to the female," so it was the men who held the power (WN, 383).

sees these laws as constructive. In a world of chaos, any source of order is to be desired.[5] If there were no such estates, there would be no landlord with the power to enforce local order or to protect the locals from being preyed upon by neighbors.

"In those disorderly times, every great landlord was a sort of petty prince. His tenants were his subjects. He was their judge, and in some respects their legislator in peace, and their leader in war" (*WN*, 383). Order was maintained by the lord, and order was maintained intergenerationally by entail and primogeniture, which made succession straightforward, so order could be seamlessly passed on from generation to generation.

However, although the great lords did provide law and order, neither their abilities nor their inclinations (immediate gratification) made them "great improvers" (*WN*, 385). And "if great improvements are seldom to be expected from great proprietors, they are least of all to be expected when they employ slaves for their workmen" (*WN*, 387). The work of a slave – and the "tenants at will . . . [of this feudal world] were all or almost all slaves" (*WN*, 386) – is, according to Smith, the least productive of all labor.[6] "Whatever work he [the slave] does beyond what is sufficient to purchase his own maintenance, can be squeezed out of him by violence only, and by no interest of his own" (*WN*, 387–8). Dependence is inherently insecure and it breeds ignorance and indolence. Thus, this feudal world was miserably unproductive.

Smith's perspective on these instrumental institutions – entail and primogeniture – is indicative of his view that the laws and institutions of a given time and place must be consistent with the circumstances and requirements of that time and place if that society is to function. In this period after the fall of Rome, security was the first priority and the lords provided that security.

---

[5] This is a classic example of a law that is reasonable in the peculiar context of its initial implementation but in time becomes an impediment to progress. Another is the exclusive rights of corporations: "To bring about . . . the separation of trades sooner than the progress of society would naturally effect, and prevent the uncertainty of all those who had taken themselves to one trade, it was found necessary to given them a certainty of a comfortable subsistence. – And for this purpose the legislature determined that they should have the priviledge of exercising their separate trades without fear of being cut out of the lively hood by the increase of their rivalls. That this was necessary . . . in the 1st stages of the arts to bring them to their proper perfection, appears very reasonable . . . But as this end is now fully answered, it were much to <be> wished that these as well as many other remains of the old jurisprudence should be removed" (*LJA*, 86).

[6] Smith notes that in his day only the incredibly high-profit production of sugar and tobacco in the colonies returns enough to support "the expence of slave-cultivation" (*WN*, 389).

For Smith the evolutionist, the problem with such laws is that while they may be appropriate for the particular time and place in which they emerge, these "[l]aws frequently continue in force long after the circumstances, which first gave occasion to them, and which could alone render them reasonable are no more" (*WN*, 383). Such inert institutional structures impede evolutionary change and, thus, progress. Constructive change requires breaking down these barriers.

In Smith's analysis, humankind's evolution is a very tedious and unpredictable process precisely because:

- Laws and institutions do tend to ossify as advantaged particular interests exert themselves to protect extant social constructions.
- Where such obstacles are eliminated, it is not primarily as a consequence of human reason; rather, it is the cumulative effect of chance, circumstance, and the unintended consequences of individuals' choices.

Smith's *WN* Book III narrative history presents a complex example of just such an evolutionary process as the inert institutions of feudal Europe slowly gave way to new institutional arrangements that made progress possible. It is a story of convoluted change because, contrary to the natural course of events, the advancements in the countryside followed from the progress of the towns. To explain why events unfolded in this unnatural, inverted way, Smith's narrative begins with the evolution of events that gave the towns the lead in the progress of opulence.

"OF THE RISE AND PROGRESS OF CITIES AND TOWNS, AFTER THE FALL OF THE ROMAN EMPIRE"

Immediately after the fall of Rome, the town people, largely "tradesmen and mechanicks" (*WN*, 397), were "very nearly in the same state of villanage with the occupiers of land in the country" (*WN*, 397). Their livelihood depended on peddling goods for sale and these goods were liable to taxes at every turn. Taxes were "levied upon the persons and goods of travelers, when they passed through certain manors, when they went over certain bridges, when they carried about their goods from place to place in a fair, when they erected in it a booth or stall to sell them in" (*WN*, 397). Obviously "these different taxes" (*WN*, 397) were a severe burden.

Sometimes the king, sometimes a great lord who had, it seems, upon some occasions, authority to do this, would grant to particular traders . . . a general exemption from such taxes. Such traders, though in other respects of servile, or very nearly of servile condition, were upon this account called Free-traders. They in return usually paid to their protector a sort of annual poll-tax[7]. (*WN*, 398)

This free-trader status relieved some of the onerous burden of the tax structure, but it did not increase the security of those in the towns and, as we've seen, security is the *sine qua non* of progress. There was, however, a political dynamic in play among the king, the lords, and the towns that ultimately allowed the towns to establish a significant degree of security and independence.

The payments from a town's people to the king were initially fixed lease payments from the individuals to the king. Over time, however, the burghers of the town became "jointly and severally answerable for the whole rent; but in return being allowed to collect it in their own way, and to pay it into the king's exchequer by the hands of their own bailiff, and being altogether freed from the insolence of the king's officers; a circumstance in those days regarded as of the greatest importance" (*WN*, 400).

This payment from the towns to the king evolved from an intermittently recontracted term payment into a perpetual fixed payment for a perpetual set of privileges. "Those exemptions ... could not afterwards be considered as belonging to individuals as individuals, but as burghers of a particular burgh[8] ... Along with this grant, ... [privileges] that they might give away their own daughters in marriage, that their children should succeed them, and that they might dispose of their own effects by will, were generally bestowed upon the burghers of the town to whom it was given. ... [In this process] they now, at least, became really free in our present sense of the word Freedom"[9] (*WN*, 400, Smith's capital "F").

"Nor was this all" (*WN*, 400). Smith goes on to describe more elements of self-governance that emerged, including the "authority to compel their inhabitants to act according to some certain plan or system" that made possible "regular government ... [and] voluntary league of mutual defence" (*WN*, 402) among towns. "[I]n this manner [kings] voluntarily

---

[7] Smith cites "the very imperfect accounts ... from Domesday-book" to support this story (*WN*, 398).

[8] [W]hich, upon this account was called a Free-burgh. ..." (*WN*, 400).

[9] Smith writes in this context: "Whether such privileges had before been usually granted along with the freedom of trade, to particular burghers, as individuals, I know not. I reckon it not improbable that they were, though I cannot produce any direct evidence of it" (*WN*, 400). This caveat reflects Smith's respect for empirical evidence, and also his style as a moral philosopher telling an historical story as opposed to an historian. He cites the gap, and moves on with the story.

erected a sort of independent republicks in the heart of their own dominions" (*WN*, 401).

But why, Smith poses the question, would a king make all these con-
cessions to the towns? The answer lies, according to Smith, in a political
struggle between the king and the lords.

In this age, the king did not have sufficient power to control the lords,
so the towns were at the mercy of the great lords. The lords looked down
upon the burghers as lesser beings, were galled by any wealth the burghers
accumulated, and preyed upon them whenever they could.

> The lords despised the burghers . . . The burghers naturally hated and feared the
> lords. The king hated and feared them too; but though he perhaps might despise,
> he had no reason either to hate or fear the burghers. Mutual interest, therefore,
> disposed them to support the king, and the king to support them against the lords.
> They were the enemies of his enemies, and it was his interest to render them as
> *secure and independent* of those enemies as he could. (*WN*, 402, emphasis added)

Only in league with one another could towns muster enough power to
be formidable to a great lord. By offering the towns the opportunity to
establish independent, regular government under a magistrate, the king
empowered the towns to form such alliances for their own security and for
his benefit. As empirical evidence of the power of this incentive for coali-
tion building between king and towns, Smith cites evidence that "[t]he
princes who lived upon the worst terms with their barons, seem accordingly to have been the most liberal in grants of this kind to their burghs"[10]
(*WN*, 402). The consequence of these alliances was the independence and
security that nurtures the progress of opulence:

> Order and good government, and along with them the liberty and security of
> individuals, were, in this manner, established in cities at a time when the occupiers
> of land in the country were exposed to every sort of violence. But men in this
> defenceless state naturally content themselves with their necessary subsistence;
> because to acquire more might only tempt the injustice of their oppressors. On
> the contrary, when they are secure of enjoying the fruits of their industry, they
> naturally exert it to better their condition, and to acquire not only the necessaries,
> but the conveniencies and elegancies of life. That industry, therefore, which aims at
> something more than necessary subsistence, was established in cities long before
> it was commonly practised by the occupiers of land in the country. (*WN*, 405)

---

[10] He explores some of the European examples, noting that where kings were especially weak, "as in Italy and Switzerland, . . . the towns became independent republicks,"
whereas in England and France, "the representation of the burghs in the states general"
can be traced to this alliance with the king against the lords (*WN*, 403, 404).

This narrative history represents a distortion – indeed an inversion – of the natural course that Smith describes in his theoretical or conjectural history, and that is precisely Smith's point. His case for the persuasiveness of those general principles that he imagines guide the natural course of humankind's evolution, principles presented in *WN* Books I and II, lies in his ability to explain why particular distortions occur in that natural course, and how, even in the face of such distortions, the general course of humankind's history follows his principles and represents progress.

The story Smith tells in *WN* Book III of the evolution of Europe after the fall of Rome is not presented as a proof of the truth of his vision. Smith is not so arrogant as to think he knows "Truth." He narrates and analyzes this history because he believes its story is consistent with the principles he has presented and thus enhances the persuasiveness of his moral philosophical vision.

It was the self-interests of the king and of the burghers, not any intent on their parts to bring progress to humankind, that led to an alliance that gave the towns independence, security, and good government. This, in turn, encouraged accumulation and growth. In contrast, the power of the great lords over the countryside resulted in dependence, insecurity, and oppressive government. This destroyed any incentive to work hard or accumulate. Indeed, "[w]hatever stock . . . accumulated in the hands of the industrious part of the inhabitants of the country, naturally took refuge in cities, as the only sanctuaries in which it could be secure to the person who acquired it" (*WN*, 405). So instead of the natural course, in which progress begins in the country and only later contributes capital to the nascent commerce of the town, in feudal Europe any capital accumulated in the country flowed immediately into the towns as a safe haven.

The towns were able to absorb this capital and to grow independent of the countryside to the degree that they were able to reach markets beyond their neighborhood.

The inhabitants of a city, it is true, must always ultimately derive their subsistence, and the whole materials and means of their industry from the country. But those of a city, situated near either the sea-coast or the banks of a navigable river, are not necessarily confined to derive them from the country of their neighborhood. They have a much wider range, and may draw them from the most remote corners of the world, either in exchange for manufactured produce of their own industry, or by performing the office of carriers between distant countries, and exchanging the produce of one for that of another. A city might in this manner grow up to great wealth and splendor, while not only the country in its neighbourhood, but all those to which it traded, were in poverty and wretchedness. (*WN*, 405)

The narrative Smith presents so far is of towns progressing and the country mired in the oppression of the lord. How then did progress come to the country?

"HOW THE COMMERCE OF THE TOWNS CONTRIBUTED
TO THE IMPROVEMENT OF THE COUNTRY"

The country benefited from the success of the towns first and foremost because the towns provided an expanding market for the produce of the country. This "gave some encouragement to industry and improvement" in the country (*WN*, 411). The country also benefited from the movement of some merchants into the country. "Merchants are commonly ambitious of becoming country gentlemen, and when they do, they are generally the best of all improvers" (*WN*, 411). Unlike the lords, the merchants see accumulated stock as capital that should return a profit, so they invest in the land and improve it.

Thirdly, and lastly, commerce and manufactures gradually introduce order and good government, and with them, the liberty and security of individuals, among the inhabitants of the country, who had before lived almost in a continual state of war with their neighbours, and of servile dependency upon their superiors. This, though it has been the least observed, is by far the most important of all their effects. Mr. Hume is the only writer, who, so far as I know, has hitherto taken notice of it. (*WN*, 412)

This is a classic expression of what Smith values in his own vision.

He is very proud of his analysis of the natural progress of opulence: the division of labor and exchange of surpluses through markets, the importance of the extent of the market in limiting this division of labor, the role of capital accumulation in determining how extensively this division of labor can be financed, the flows of capital that extend markets and thus the division of labor, and the natural inclinations and propensities in humans that drive this process and thus the progress of opulence with no need for anyone to be in charge.

But he is equally proud that his analysis is consistent with the unnatural course of humankind's actual history, and that it can offer plausible, persuasive explanations of the peculiar paths of particular societies based on an analysis of the evolution of the laws and institutions of those societies. Aside from his dearest friend David Hume, he alone highlights this "most important" relationship between the progress of opulence and the evolution of laws and institutions as he inquires into the nature and causes of the wealth of nations.

The three factors cited previously carried the progress of the town into the country, but this process and, in particular, the emergence of "order and good government" in the countryside, did not happen overnight. It was an evolutionary process that followed a path peculiar to the conditions of the times. Having identified these factors, Smith proceeds to represent why this particular path of evolution occurred in this time and place. In his narrative, the movement of European progress from town to country was propelled most of all by the unintended consequences of the greed and material fetishes of the lords.

In wake of Rome's fall, when lords lorded over both town and country, there was "neither foreign commerce, nor any of the finer manufactures, [so] a great proprietor, having nothing for which he can exchange the greater part of the produce of his lands which is over and above the maintenance of the cultivators, consumes the whole in rustick hospitality at home" (*WN*, 412–13). In Smith's terms, all of the accumulation went to the maintenance of unproductive, dependent labor. He offers as an example of the reported extravagances of that age "[t]he great earl of Warwick [who] is said to have entertained every day at his different manors, thirty thousand people; and though the number here may have been exaggerated, it must, however, have been very great to admit of such exaggeration" (*WN*, 413).

Again we see an example of Smith's use of history. He regularly cites evidence from history with caveats about its absolute accuracy, but as indicative of what he believes was the spirit of the occasion. He considers this sufficient for his purposes because he is not writing as an historian. He is a moral philosopher examining the flow of history in order to establish the persuasiveness of the principles that he believes guide the course of history.[11] His story is about that general course, not the absolute accuracy of the details. By the standards of an historian, this is sloppy work. This is, nevertheless, how Smith, the moral philosopher, uses history.

However accurate, the point of Smith's story of the conspicuous consumption of the lords in these early days is clear. There was stagnation then because all accumulation went into immediate consumption rather than a growing capital stock, and because dependence eliminated any

---

[11] "If the overall account convincingly [persuasion is the key] shows us how the phenomena can be brought into a satisfying explanatory system when certain stable principles are posited, then of course we have good reason to accept those principles" (Griswold, 1999, 352). This is precisely what Smith is doing in *WN* Book III.

incentive for workers to exert themselves beyond the acquisition of necessities and/or the avoidance of punishment. The lords determined what was law, enforced that law, and judged any question of law for all who lived under them. Based on this power, the lords had an army of dependents to make up a militia. Thus, the lords had real power and the king was "in those ancient times ... little more than the greatest proprietor in his dominions. ... " (*WN*, 415).

The authority of the lords in these early days was not based on feudal law. "That authority and those jurisdictions all necessarily flowed from the state of property and manners [of the age.] ... The introduction of the feudal law, so far from extending, may be regarded as an attempt to moderate the authority of the great allodial lords" (*WN*, 416–17), to reduce the power of the lords vis-à-vis the king, and to bring some regularity and, with it, some semblance of order and good government. But it was too weak a system to undermine the power of the lords. Ironically, only their own greed and their fetishes for the material, in the context of an expanding market system through the towns, could accomplish that.

[W]hat all the violence of the feudal institutions could never have effected, the silent and insensible operation of foreign commerce and manufactures gradually brought about. These gradually furnished the great proprietors with something for which they could exchange the whole of their surplus produce of their lands, and which they could consume themselves without sharing it wither with tenants or retainers. All for ourselves, and nothing for the other people, seems, in every age of the world, to have been the vile maxim of the masters of mankind. ... For a pair of diamond buckles perhaps, or for something as frivolous and useless, they exchanged the maintenance, or what it the same thing, the price of the maintenance of a thousand men for a year, and with it the whole weight and authority which it could give them. ... [A]nd thus, for the gratification of the most childish, the meanest and the most sordid of all vanities, they gradually bartered their whole power and authority.[12] (*WN*, 418)

The invasion of markets and of those fineries that markets can bring was made possible by a development that, as Smith has already explained, was unfolding in the towns.

Markets are very opportunistic. The town merchants who were selling fineries found a ready market in the vain, rich, and selfish lords of the country. The more the lords engaged in this market exchange, the less of their produce went to supporting their army of dependents. The fewer dependents they had, the smaller the following that made up their power

---

[12] This parallels the story (see Chapter Four in this book), that Smith tells about the decline of the Roman clergy (*WN*, 803).

base. As Smith describes it, the lord who once supported the whole subsistence of a thousand dependents with the surplus of his estate, came, through the market, to support a fraction of the subsistence of a much larger number of workers, but none of them was dependent upon him.

In the market nexus, many workers contributed to supplying the fineries that the lords purchased, but no one of these workers was dependent on any one lord because each worker was producing not for a single lord but for the market in which that lord was but one customer. "Though he [the lord] contributes, therefore, to the maintenance of them all, they are all more or less independent of him, because generally they can all be maintained without him" (*WN*, 420). This process led not only to the lord supporting more independent workers in the larger market nexus, but also more independence for the workers in the lord's own country domain.

In order buy in the market, the lords needed to produce for the market and to exchange in the market. This transformed the relationship between the lords and the workers on their land. Redirecting the surplus from feeding tenants to buying baubles dictated that there must be fewer tenants working larger plots, so the size of the "[f]arms were enlarged" (*WN*, 420). The landlord desired greater rents from these larger farms so that he could buy more baubles. "His tenants could agree to this upon one condition only, that they should be secured in their possessions, for such a term of years as might give them time to recover with profit whatever they should lay out in the further improvement of the land. The expensive vanity of the landlord made him willing to accept of this condition; and hence the origin of long leases" (*WN*, 421).[13] With long leases came independence and security for the workers of the land. As Smith has already explained, with independence and security comes the real opportunity to better one's condition.

Smith concludes his story of how "the Commerce of the Towns contributed to the Improvement of the Country" (*WN*, 411):

A revolution of the greatest importance to the publick happiness, was in this manner brought about by two different orders of people, who had not the least intention to serve the publick. To gratify the most childish vanity was the sole motive of the great proprietors. The merchants and artificers, much less ridiculous, acted merely from a view to their own interest, and in pursuit of their own pedlar

---

[13] "The relationship evolved from serfdom, to tenancy, to rental tenancy with long leases. Each step encouraged the tenant to invest more heavily in improving the land, and each step made the tenant's relationship with the landlord more contractual and less arbitrary" (Muller, 1993, 122).

principle of turning a penny wherever a penny was to be got. Neither of them had either knowledge or foresight of that great revolution which the folly of the one, and the industry of the other, was gradually bringing about.... [This revolution] being contrary to the natural course of things ... [was] necessarily both slow and uncertain. (*WN*, 422)

Again and again and again, we hear this theme from Smith: The oeconomy of nature ... the deceptions of nature ... the invisible hand of the deity as designer is at work.

If the laws and institutions of society evolve such that human beings have the increasing independence and security necessary to pursue a better life, they will do so, and the progress of opulence will flow from that pursuit. But the big issue in human history (and, as we will see in Chapter Eight, in Smith's contemporary British society as well) is the "*if.*" In Smith's moral philosophy, social and political institutions evolve as part of a simultaneous system with economic institutions. This process is, as Smith puts it, "necessarily both slow and uncertain" (*WN*, 422) and progress is not a given for any particular society. The very fact that over the course of humankind's history so many societies have come and gone and that no society has advanced to a condition even close to the limit makes this clear.

Smith's story of the progress of opulence in Europe after the fall of Rome is a particular story of unnatural progress because it represents a course of events that inverts the natural course. However, at the same time, it is a part of his general story of natural progress because it reflects the power of the design. Thanks to the serendipitous convergence of chance, circumstance, and the oeconomy and deceptions of nature, progress did come to Europe. Among the nations of Europe, this dynamic was most kind to England.

England, upon account of the natural fertility of the soil, of the great extent of the sea-coast in proportion to that of the whole country, and of the many navigable rivers which run through it, and afford the conveniency of water carriage to some of the most inland parts of it, is perhaps as well fitted by nature as any large country in Europe, to be the seat of foreign commerce, of manufactures for distant sale, and of all the improvements which these can occasion. From the beginning of the reign of Elizabeth too, the English legislature has been particularly attentive to the interests of commerce and manufactures.... (*WN*, 424)

English agriculture was also favored by the legislature, with protections such as the corn laws.

However, it was not, according to Smith, these artificial advantages (a "monopoly against their countrymen" (*WN*, 425)) that account for

England's progress. If anything, they were impediments. As described at length in Chapter Three, it was the evolution of the laws and institutions of England toward a mature system of justice that was instrumental in England's progress. Thanks to these laws and institutions, "the yeomanry of England are rendered as secure, as independent, and as respectable as law can make them" (*WN*, 425), and "[t]hose laws and customs so favourable to the yeomanry, have perhaps contributed more to the present grandeur of England than all their boasted regulations of commerce taken together" (*WN*, 392).

The inverted development of Europe that began with trade favored France, Spain, and Portugal with great wealth long before England. But wealth based on trade is a fickle foundation for long-term progress. This is so, in part, because "[a] merchant, it has been said very properly, is not necessarily the citizen of any particular country" (*WN*, 426) so his circulating capital can abandon a nation quickly. Furthermore, the kind of fixed capital a merchant invests in is very vulnerable to wartime destruction. In contrast, agricultural capital is fixed on the land, so it cannot leave and those investments are much less vulnerable to the destruction of war. For these reasons, according to Smith, "the more solid improvements of agriculture . . . [are a] much more durable" foundation for progress (*WN*, 427). Thus, although the origins of Europe's progress came from trade, that initial progress became a foundation for long-term success where, as in England, agriculture was nurtured through laws and institutions that protected the independence and security of those in the countryside – e.g., "the yeomanry of England."

As always, Smith's story returns to his natural principles. Agriculture is the bedrock of production and mature laws and institutions are essential if the progress of opulence is to be sustained. The independence and security provided by the mature laws and institutions of England nurtured its agriculture and facilitated its trade, and so England became the most advanced nation in the most advanced continent of the world. As English laws and institutions continued to mature, that progress was sustained. Smith writes in 1776: "It is now more than two hundred years since the beginning of the reign of Elizabeth, a period as long as the course of human prosperity usually endures" (*WN*, 425).[14]

---

[14] Haakonssen offers a long story of Smith's four stages and the history of Europe (Haakonssen, 1981, 155–70), but he doesn't give it Smith's full treatment by demonstrating how this dynamic is full of unnatural twists and turns. "Smith naturally paid very great attention to the special case of Britain but it is of importance to notice that

FROM THE ENGLISH PAST TO THE ENGLISH PRESENT

Smith is clearly proud of this success but, at the same time, he is deeply concerned that this period of prosperity in England is at risk due to the misguided and self-serving principles of the mercantile system; principles that are currently directing much of English policy.

In *WN* Book IV, Smith turns from the past to his present. The title of *WN* Book IV is "Of Systems of political Oeconomy" suggesting that he will take on all comers in contrasting his principles with those of other systems. Smith does address the agricultural system of the Physiocrats, but only briefly. The vast majority of his effort in *WN* Book IV is dedicated to a critique of the mercantile system, and in successive editions this critique becomes an ever more virulent attack. He believes that the mercantile system, always flawed, has, since the 1760s, been appropriated and revised to serve the mercantile interests. Thus, according to Smith, the mercantile system of his day is not only wrong, it is a gross and dangerous misuse of philosophy.

he sets his discussion in a total European framework and makes it largely comparative" (Haakonssen, 170). Haakonssen doesn't develop the dynamic dimensions of this comparative analysis. The dynamic, intertemporal, comparative analysis Smith offers is essential to his story because that story is presented in order to cull from this dynamic the characteristics of a society that seem to contribute to its progress and, ultimately, the contours of a successful liberal order so that he can imagine the invisible connecting principles that make progress toward that ideal order possible. It is the contours he believes he sees in history that inform the critiques Haakonssen describes (Haakonssen, 155–70).

EIGHT

Smith on the Mercantile System and the Evolution of His Voice

Book IV of *The Wealth of Nations* and Part VI of *The Theory of Moral Sentiments*

By the close of *WN* Book III, Smith has completed his system and his empirical (historical) case for his system's persuasiveness. However, there were alternative systems available, and in *WN* Book IV, "Of Systems of political Oeconomy," Smith addresses his competition.

The competitors he identifies are the "agricultural systems" (*WN*, 663) of the Physiocrats and the "mercantile System" (*WN*, 429). Smith makes the case that both of these are less persuasive than his model, but in one very important respect, he sees these two systems very differently. Although he disagrees with the Physiocrats, he admires and respects them as noble philosophers. In contrast, he sees the contemporary advocates of the mercantile system as selfish rogues who have captured and reshaped a philosophical enterprise in order to advocate policies that line their own pockets under the guise of philosophy.

This misuse of philosophy galls Smith doubly. First, having prevailed in the Parliament, the mercantile interests have led Britain down a path that he fears is very self-destructive. This concerns Smith, the policy person, deeply. Second, by presenting themselves as bearing the mantle of a philosophy concerned only for the well-being of the state, the mercantile interests have invaded and sullied Smith's own beloved realm: philosophy.

There are nine chapters in the final version of *WN* Book IV.[1] Eight cover the mercantile system. Only one is dedicated to the agricultural system. Smith respects the philosophers who have designed and advocate for the agriculture system, referring to them as "a few men of great

---

[1] There were initially eight, but Smith inserted a new chapter titled "Conclusion of the Mercantile System" in the third edition – more on this later in this Chapter.

learning and ingenuity in France" (*WN*, 663). However, for all of their zeal, they have no prospect, Smith believes, of affecting policy, so all he offers the reader is "the great outlines of this very ingenious system" (*WN*, 663). Not so mercantilism. As reflected in his allocation of space, this doctrine is his primary concern because he believes that it is driving British policy in a very destructive direction.

"OF THE AGRICULTURAL SYSTEMS"

As was Smith, the Physiocrats were philosophers who were concerned about the course of contemporary policy, in their case the policy of France. France was a leader in mercantilist protectionism because "Mr. Colbert, the famous minister of Lewis XIV" (*WN*, 662), "notwithstanding his great abilities, seems ... to have been imposed upon by the sophistry of the merchants and manufacturers, who are always demanding a monopoly against their countrymen" (*WN*, 467) and "so he had embraced all the prejudices of the mercantile system...." (*WN*, 663).

Colbert's policy was designed to support the manufacturing interests of the towns, a classic mercantile position. Under his system, the agricultural sector was treated as merely instrumental, a source of commodities needed for workers in the towns. The Physiocrats' "agriculture system" was a response to what they perceived as the perverse oppression of agriculture interests under Colbert. However, Smith writes, "[i]f the rod be bent too much one way, says the proverb, in order to make it straight you must bend it as much the other" (*WN*, 664). In this case, just as Colbert over-valued manufactures, so, too, the "French philosophers, who have proposed the system which represents agriculture as the sole source of revenue and wealth of every country ... [over-valued agriculture and] certainly under-valued" manufacturing (*WN*, 664).

According to the Physiocrats, as Smith tells it, all net product comes from agriculture, and so only those who improve or work the land, the proprietors and the cultivators, are "honor[ed] with the peculiar appellation of the productive class" (*WN*, 664). The "artificers, manufacturers and merchants ... [are] degrade[d] by the humiliating appellation of the barren or unproductive class" (*WN*, 664). The Physiocrats based their judgment that only agriculture produces a net product on the observation that only land yields a rent.

As we've seen, Smith appreciates the unique character of agricultural production: "No equal capital puts into motion a greater quantity of productive labour than that of the farmer ... [because i]n agriculture ... nature labours along with man" (*WN*, 363), whereas in manufacturing, "nature does nothing; man does all...." (*WN*, 364). Furthermore, Smith agrees with the Physiocrats that it is this labor of nature that occasions a return in agriculture that is beyond the profits of stock – the return to the landlord, a rent (*WN*, 364).

However, in Smith's analysis, although agriculture is, thanks to the generosity of nature, the foundation of economic growth, the vast possibilities of the wealth of nations are thanks to artificers and manufacturers. This is so because the productive power of labor is determined by the extent of the division of labor, and the labor of the "artificers and manufacturers ... is capable of being more subdivided ... than that of farmers and country labourers, so it is likewise capable of ... improvement in a much higher degree" (*WN*, 676). Thus the artificers and manufacturers are a very productive class over the long haul. To suggest that their labor is sterile is, according to Smith, simply wrong.

Although Smith does not agree with these "Oeconomists" (*WN*, 678), he admires and respects them:

> This [agricultural] system, however, with all its imperfections is, perhaps, the nearest approximation to the truth that has yet been published upon the subject of political oeconomy ... [T]he notions which it inculcates are perhaps too narrow and confined; yet in representing the wealth of nations as consisting, not in unconsumable riches of money [as does the mercantile system], but in the consumable goods annually reproduced by the labour of the society; and in representing perfect liberty as the only effectual expedient for rendering this annual reproduction the greatest possible, its doctrine seems to be in every respect as just as it is generous and liberal. (*WN*, 678)

As with his own, the scope of their work includes "not only what is properly called Political Oeconomy, or of the nature and causes of the wealth of nations, but ... every other branch of the system of government...." (*WN*, 678–9). And, as he does, so, too, they value the principles of and seek to enhance the realization of a "liberal plan of equality, liberty and justice" (*WN*, 664). Indeed, he believes that the Oeconomists have achieved some good for their nation: The limitations of their system notwithstanding, "by influencing in some measure the publick administration ... the agriculture of France has been delivered from several of the oppressions which it before laboured under" (*WN*, 678).

Respect notwithstanding, Smith is brief in his analysis of the Physiocrats because that system "has, so far as I know, never been adopted by any nation ... It would not, surely, be worthwhile to examine at great length the errors of a system which never has done, and probably never will do any harm in any part of the world" (*WN*, 663).

Note the words "do any harm." Harm is the last thing a system of philosophy should do. In contrast to the Physiocrats' system, Smith believes that the mercantile system of his day is not only wrong, it is doing immense harm.

SMITH ON THE MERCANTILE SYSTEM – BACKGROUND

According to Smith, the logic that underlies the mercantile system reflects the fetishism of money in society: the "popular notion" that "[t]o grow rich is to get money; and wealth and money ... are, in common language, considered as in every respect synonymous" (*WN*, 429). The mercantilist view of the wealth of a nation is a simple extrapolation of this popular usage: "A rich country, in the same manner as a rich man, is supposed to be a country abounding in money. . . . " (*WN*, 429).

As a system of political economy, mercantilism was a natural response to the times in which it was first proposed.[2] In an age of emerging nation states, when the popular view was that the progress of opulence is driven by the accumulation of money, the common national policy question at hand seemed to be: How can our nation advance its interest in a world in which other nations are pursuing the same end – more money?[3] The world appeared to most to be a zero-sum game, and the mercantile system seemed to offer a winning strategy.

In his *Lectures on Jurisprudence* Smith suggests that the mercantile system, advocated by many, gained the imprimatur of philosophical legitimacy when:

Mr. Locke ... published a treatise to show the pernicious consequences of allowing the nation to be drained of money. His notions were likewise founded upon the idea that public opulence consists in money, tho' he treats the matter in a more philosophical light than the rest. (*LJB*, 508)[4]

---

[2] Smith traces the history of the mercantile system in *WN* Book V (*WN*, 879).

[3] Smith notes that mercantilism only makes sense in a multinational context. Even those who held mercantile views recognized that a nation in isolation had no need for more money if there were no other nations with which to trade. (WN, 430–1).

[4] In his earlier *Lectures* (*LJA*), Smith told his students that "Mr. Locke ... made it indeed have somewhat more of a philosophicall air and the appearance of probability by some amendments" (*LJA*, 381). In a letter from William Robertson to Smith (8 April 1776) complementing him on the "uncommon and meritorious" "Inquiry," Robertson expresses the

But what in the hands of Locke was a philosophical approach to political economy became in time a political tool used by the mercantilists to advance their interests. From Locke's day to Smith's day the visible hand of those interests slowly but surely reached ever more deeply into the structures of political power in order to guide policy.

We pick up the story of the growing influence of these mercantile interests in the last decade of the seventeenth century, the age of Locke. Telling this story is essential if we are to appreciate the momentum and the power of mercantile interests that Smith increasingly saw as a threat to the British experiment in liberal society.

In the last decade of the seventheenth century,

prolonged and still deepening crisis over the balance of payments and the appalling state of the coinage... brought the politicians to the necessity of a new board of trade... [But with that necessity came] another crisis, a constitutional crisis over who should create and control that board – Parliament or the King. (Laslett, 374)

Having lost influence in earlier transformations of the councils responsible for trade,[5] the merchants "were busy in the House of Commons...determined to get a board of trade appointed by Parliament and responsible to it, a committee which knew what it was doing and which would listen to them" (Laslett, 375). This would have represented a dramatic shift of power "from the executive to the legislature" (Laslett, 375). Their proposal failed, however, and the board was established by the King.

The purpose of this new board was to propose policies that would serve, not the narrow interests of the merchants, but the broader needs of the commonwealth. Who better to serve on such a board than the leading philosopher of the day and a man who had served on similar boards before: Locke.[6] Locke was "implored by an almost abject Secretary of State to give his services" to this body (Laslett, 377). He accepted the position and

---

hope that "the English be capable of extending their ideas beyond the narrow and illiberal arrangements introduced by the mercantile supporters of Revolution principles, and countenanced by Locke...." (Correspondence, 192). That countenance gave the position the imprimatur of philosophy, of integrity.

[5] When the Council of Trade was established in 1670, "one group that had been heavily represented, and indeed dominant, in the past was now conspicuously absent – the merchant magnates, excluded perhaps... [because they were] too partial to attend to the public good...." (Letwin, 1964, 174–5).

[6] See Karen Vaughn's *John Locke: Economics and Social Scientist* for a very nice survey of Locke's service.

served the board[7] as a "'practical philosopher'" (Laslett, 397–8), one who used "the opportunity to demonstrate to the world what was meant . . . by the social and political responsibilities of an intellectual" (Laslett, 402).[8]

Locke took his position on the Board of Trade at the beginning of what Kammen refers to as the "Age of Walpole 1696–1748" (Kammen, 45). During this period the colonies expanded and came to be "regarded as important in contributing to a self-sufficient empire" (Kammen, 46). The contemporary mercantilist writing focused on "the needs of the realm" and gave rise to "a complete body of regulations . . . raised almost to the level of principles" (Kammen, 46–7). However, while

mercantilist doctrine stressed the importance of national economic interests, it also contained implicitly the potential disharmony between particular commercial groups, individual merchants, and classes on one hand, and the welfare of the commonwealth as a whole, on the other. (Kammen, 41)

By the 1730s, these "particular" interests were beginning to exert themselves as merchants became more organized and hired lobbyists to handle their interests in London (Kammen, 64, 66).

Once the relative stability of the age of Walpole and Pelham ended in 1754, opportunities for interests increased even more. . . .
[Starting in] 1763 . . . interests . . . so dominated politics that men observed that mercantilism had changed from the control of trade in the interest of national policy, to the control of national policy in the interest of trade . . . The increasing importance of Parliament [and its "factionalized and undisciplined party system" (Kammen, 97)] seemed to encourage efforts by powerful groups seeking to influence regulation by political pressure. (Kammen, 75, 95)

In his classic study of *The structure of politics at the accession of George III*, Sir Lewis Namier surveys the parliamentary history of the first half of the eighteenth century and concludes that "in 1706 it [the purpose of the Commons] was 'faithful service to your country'; in 1760 'service to one's friends'" (Namier, 18). Kammen describes Namier's conception of interests as a "fragmented view of the essential units competing for favor and power" emphasizing "family connections and parliamentary

---

[7] Indeed, Laslett writes that "the evidence goes to show that Locke helped to bring it into being and that he dominated its earlier history" (Laslett, 372).

[8] Letwin (1964) and Vaughn (1980) also represent Locke as having a larger public purpose. Vaughn distinguishes "scientists-theorists," like Locke, who advocated mercantilist policies based on philosophical perspectives from the "mercantilist-practitioners," "usually businessmen who understood how national policy affected their private interests and tried to defend those interests in their tracts" (Vaughn, 49, 47).

interests," thus "reducing the dynamic elements in public life to individuals, families and 'circles which are primarily concerned with the nation's political business'" (Kammen, 9). This Namierian conception of interests is consistent with that found in much of the eighteenth-century political literature on corruption into the 1760s,[9] and it is this conception of interests, therefore, that dominated the discourse on interests and corruption during Smith's formative years.[10]

However, by the 1760s the nature of the interests surrounding and in parliament was beginning to change. A new form of interests was emerging, best described by "Robert MacIvers['s] . . . general definition of interests: 'When a number of men unite for the defense, maintenance, or enhancement of any more or less enduring position or advantage which they possess alike or in common, the term interest is applied both to the group so united and to the cause which unites them'" (Kammen, 10–11). These are the interests Kammen refers to when he dates the "Age of Interests" from 1763 (Kammen, 95).[11] And these are the interests that become the focal point of Smith's concerns when he arrives in London to publish *The Wealth of Nations*.

On 8 November 1763, Smith resigned his Chair of Moral Philosophy at Glasgow in order to accept Charles Townshend's offer to tour Europe as the tutor to the Duke of Buccleuch (Ross, 196). Smith spent most of the following three years on the Continent with the Duke. Then, after a brief stay in London over the winter of 1766–67, with "[w]riting *WN* . . . on his mind" (Ross, 227) he returned "to be with his mother and cousin in Krikcaldy" (Ross, 227). From early 1767 to 1772, Smith was in Kirkcaldy working on *The Wealth of Nations*. On 3 September 1772, he writes to Sir William Pulteny that "[m]y book would have been ready for the Press by the beginning of this winter; but for interruptions . . . [that] will oblige me to retard its publication for a few months longer" (*Correspondence*, 164).

---

[9] For instance, Bolingbroke's criticisms of the Walpole ministry. See Pocock (1975, 423–61).

[10] On 21 Feb. 1759, Smith writes to Lord Fitzmaurice: "I hear there is no faction in parliament, which I am glad of" (*Correspondence*, 28).

[11] These "modern" interests certainly existed before 1763. Ralph Davis notes that in the late seventeenth century, when fiscal concerns raised tariffs significantly, English merchants recognized the protectionist potential of tariffs (Davis, 306–13), and after the Walpolean custom reform of 1722 "industrial protection . . . [had] plainly arrived" (Davis, 313). However, Kammen argues, these interests reached their full maturity between 1763 and 1783, that "Age of Interests," because they were able to exploit the "search for stability" (Kammen, 96). Although the Lord North ministry maintained its position through much of this period, that apparent stability was attributable more to a lack of alternative than to North's strength. Indeed, when the American situation began to unravel, North "begged to resign," but George III, seeing no alternatives, rejected the idea (Watson, 211).

In fact, it took not a few months longer but a few years longer. The world was changing, and Smith's perspective on the world was about to change.

When Smith arrives in London in 1773, he integrates into the intellectual and political society of the city very quickly. "He was admitted to the Royal Society in May 1773, attended Lord Wedderburn's weekly dining club, and was admitted to Johnson's Literary Club" (Stevens, 202). Smith's new, London perspective offers him insights into the changing world of interests. This transformation of his understanding of the nature of interests goes hand-in-hand with the transformation of his literary voice. He arrives in 1773 ready to publish the *WN*, but it is not finally published until 9 March 1776 (Todd, "The Text and Apparatus," *WN*, 61). Much of that lag is attributable to time spent on our present subject: the mercantile system.

SMITH ON THE ERRORS AND DISTORTIONS OF THE MERCANTILE SYSTEM

In the *WN*, Smith traces the evolution of the mercantile system from the days of Locke, when it represented an advocacy for the accumulation of bullion, to the contemporary mercantile case for a positive trade balance. He attributes this transformation of the mercantile system not to philosophical reflection but to self-serving revisions by merchants pursuing their interests.

When those countries became commercial, the merchants found this prohibition [of exporting bullion], upon many occasions, extremely inconvenient. They remonstrated, therefore, against this prohibition as hurtful to trade. (*WN*, 431)

Rejecting the earlier mercantile view that hoarding bullion was the proper policy to enhance the wealth of the nation, the merchants made the case that using domestic stocks of bullion to buy raw materials to be worked up for re-export "and [then these finished products] being . . . sold at a large profit, might bring back much more treasure than was originally sent out to purchase them" (*WN*, 431). Furthermore, they argued that the prohibition of bullion exports put domestic traders at a disadvantage in the international marketplace because "the merchant who purchased a bill upon the foreign country [was] . . . obliged to pay the banker who sold it, not only for the natural risk, trouble and expense of sending the money thither, but for the extraordinary risk arising from [evading] the prohibition" (*WN*, 432). This additional risk premium hurt the trade balance and caused bullion to leave the country as a consequence of the policy meant to protect the nation's stock of bullion. Ironically, according to the merchants, the prohibition of bullion export undermined the very objective of the mercantile system: accumulating monetary wealth.[12]

Thus, in the hands of the merchants, the mercantile system was transformed: According to the merchants, it is not hording bullion but, rather, a positive trade balance that makes a nation rich. They made the case for policies accordingly.

"Those arguments were partly solid and partly sophistical," according to Smith (*WN*, 433). The mercantilists were correct in saying that using bullion in trade "might frequently be advantageous to the country" (*WN*, 433) and that a prohibition is impossible to enforce completely given the incentive of profits to be made in trade. "But they were sophistical in supposing, that either to preserve or to augment the quantity of those metals required more the attention of government, than to preserve or to augment the quantity of any other such useful commodities, which the freedom of trade, without any such attention, never fails to supply in the proper quantity" (*WN*, 433).

According to Smith, the mercantilists' sophistry was successful because they took advantage of an asymmetry of information. The case about trade was:

by merchants to parliaments, and to the councils of princes, to nobles, and to country gentlemen; by those who were supposed to understand trade, to those who were conscious to themselves that they knew nothing about the matter. That foreign trade enriched the country, experience demonstrated to the nobles and country gentlemen, as well as to the merchants; but how, or in what manner, none of them knew well. The merchants knew perfectly in what manner it enriched themselves. It was their business to know it. But to know in what manner it enriched the country, was no part of their business. This subject never came into their consideration, but when they had occasion to apply to their country for some change in the laws relating to foreign trade. It then became necessary to say something about the beneficial effects of foreign trade, and the manner in which those effects were obstructed by the laws as they then stood. To the judges who were to decide the business, it appeared a most satisfactory account of the matter.... (*WN*, 434)[13]

---

[12] Smith offers an extended analysis of the absurdity of bullion prohibitions in his analysis of Spain's and Portugal's policies in *WN* Book IV Chapter v: Of Bounties (WN, 505). See (*WN*, 512–3) for a summary of his point.

[13] Smith makes this point at length at the very end of Book I of *WN*: "Merchants and master manufacturers are, in this order, the two classes of people who commonly employ the largest capitals, and who by their wealth draw to themselves the greatest share of the public consideration. As during their whole lives they are engaged in plans and projects,

Thus the merchants adopted and adapted a philosophical system with respect to political economy that they had inherited from Locke and others, but their purpose was not philosophical – it was profit.

Smith laments that, given the success of their sophistry, "in our own country and in our own times" the economic policies of the nation are being guided by the merchants of the nation. Smith was not alone in this assessment. In 1769, as Smith is writing the *WN*, Benjamin Franklin writes to Lord Kames: "'Most of our acts of Parliament for regulating [trade, manufacturers, and taxes] are, in my opinion, little better than political blunders, owing to ignorance of the science, or to the designs of crafty men, who mislead the legislature, proposing something under the specious appearance of public good, while the real aim is, to sacrifice that to their own private interest'" (Quoted in Kammen, 126).

In pursuit of the positive trade balance advocated by Smith's mercantilist contemporaries,

it necessarily became the great object of political oeconomy to diminish as much as possible the importation of foreign goods for home-consumption, and to increase as much as possible the exportation of the produce of domestick industry. Its two great engines for enriching the country, therefore, were restraints upon importation, and encouragements to exportation. (*WN*, 450)

they have frequently more acuteness of understanding than the greater part of country gentlemen. As their thoughts, however, are commonly exercised rather about the interest of their own particular branch of business, than about that of the society, their judgment, even when given with the greatest candour (which it has not been upon every occasion) is much more to be depended upon with regard to the former of those two objects than with regard to the latter. Their superiority over the country gentleman is not so much in their knowledge of the public interest, as in their having a better knowledge of their own interest than he has of his. It is by this superior knowledge of their own interest that they have frequently imposed upon his generosity, and persuaded him to give up both his own interest and that of the public, from a very simple but honest conviction that their interest, and not his, was the interest of the public. The interest of the dealers, however, in any particular branch of trade or manufactures, is always in some respects different from, and even opposite to, that of the public. To widen the market and to narrow the competition, is always the interest of the dealers. To widen the market may frequently be agreeable enough to the interest of the public; but to narrow the competition must always be against it, and can serve only to enable the dealers, by raising their profits above what they naturally would be, to levy, for their own benefit, an absurd tax upon the rest of their fellow-citizens. The proposal of any new law or regulation of commerce which comes from this order ought always to be listened to with great precaution, and ought never to be adopted till after having been long and carefully examined, not only with the most scrupulous, but with the most suspicious attention. It comes from an order of men whose interest is never exactly the same with that of the public, who have generally an interest to deceive and even to oppress the public, and who accordingly have, upon many occasions, both deceived and oppressed it" (*WN*, 266–7).

High duties and prohibitions became the tools to limit importation, whereas "[e]xportation was encouraged sometimes by drawbacks, sometimes by bounties, sometimes by advantageous treaties of commerce with foreign states, and sometimes by the establishment of colonies in distant countries" (*WN*, 450).

Given the restraints on importation, "the monopoly of the home-market is more or less secured to the domestic industry" (*WN*, 452). The effect of this was to channel capital into these advantaged industries and, in turn, to increase production in them. But, Smith asks: Is this good? During any given circuit of trade there is only so much capital to allocate; "[n]o regulation of commerce" (*WN*, 453) can change that.

> It can only divert a part of it into a direction into which it might not otherwise have gone; and it is by no means certain that this artificial direction is likely to be more advantageous to the society than that into which it would have gone of its own accord.

> Every individual is continually exerting himself to find out the most advantageous employment for whatever capital he can command. It is his own advantage, indeed, and not that of the society, which he has in view. But the study of his own advantage naturally, or rather necessarily leads him to prefer that employment which is most advantageous to the society. (*WN*, 453–4)

Or at least so it would be where there is "perfect liberty" (*WN*, 606).

As we've seen in Smith's analysis of capital, when markets are free from distortions, the best return is initially in the home-trade circuit. When that circuit is overfull, capital naturally spills into that wider, somewhat slower and less secure circuit, the foreign trade of consumption, and then, in turn, into the carrying trade. As he analyzes the consequences of mercantile policies offered in the noble name of national interest, Smith employs his own analysis of optimal capital flows to demonstrate that these mercantile policies are a destructive distortion because unfettered capital finds its best advantage quite effectively, thank you. In doing so, it serves the national interest most efficiently, because the incentives always attract it to the place where it sets into motion the most productive labor.

Smith goes on to assert that any statesman who presumes that he could optimally micro manage the flow of capital is a dangerous, arrogant fool. Granting monopolies in the home market is, in effect, to do just this because it artificially channels capital. Similarly, regulations that artificially force capital into domestic circuits, producing commodities that could have been purchased more cheaply abroad, distort the flow of capital from "its natural course" (*WN*, 457) and reduce the productive power of the nation.

Who is behind these regulations?

[M]erchants and manufacturers, who being collected in towns, and naturally accustomed to that exclusive corporation spirit which prevails in them, naturally endeavour to obtain against all their countrymen, the same exclusive privilege which they generally possess against the inhabitants of their respective towns.[14] They accordingly seem to have been the original inventors of those restraints upon the importation of foreign goods, which secure to them the monopoly of the home-market. (*WN*, 462)

Smith's point is clear. Contrary to the mercantile view, trade is not an inherently a zero sum game. It can, however, be turned into a negative sum game if national policy is designed to "win" at trade by distortions that are nominally in the national interest, but are really in the interest of those who propose them. The real "winning" policy is a free and unfettered trade, for trade is naturally a positive sum game:

Nothing...can be more absurd than this whole doctrine of the balance of trade, upon which, not only these restraints, but almost all other regulations of commerce are founded. When two places trade with one another, this doctrine supposes that, if the balance be even, neither of them either looses or gains; but if it leans in any degree to one side, that one of them loses and the other gains in proportion to its declension from the exact equilibrium. Both suppositions are false. A trade which is forced by means of bounties and monopolies, may be, and commonly is disadvantageous to the country in whose favour it is meant to be established....But that trade which, without force or constraint, is naturally and regularly carried on between any two places is always advantageous, thought not always equally so, to both. (*WN*, 488–9)

Smith is careful to note that the gain must be measured by production, not bullion, and that, because the web of trade connections is very complex, tracing the ultimate incidence of gains from trade is very difficult. But there are mutual gains: "No goods are sent abroad but those for which the demand is supposed to be greater abroad than at home, and of which the returns consequently, it is expected, will be of more value at home than the commodities exported" (*WN*, 491). As the value of the nation's production is augmented by this exchange, so, too, is its capital stock and, thus, so, too, its capacity for growth in the progress of opulence. Free trade, therefore, enhances the wealth of the nation. Unfortunately,

nations have been taught that their interest consisted in beggaring all their neighbours. Each nation has been made to look with an invidious eye upon the

---

[14] Recall from Chapter 7 that these exclusive privileges were valuable to progress when they were a means for the king to collude with the towns against the lords, but by now they have long outlived their usefulness and have become a barrier to progress.

prosperity of all the nations with which it trades, and to consider their gain as its own loss. Commerce, which ought naturally to be, among nations, as among individuals, a bond of union and friendship, has become the most fertile source of discord and animosity. The capricious ambition of kings and ministers has not, during the present and the preceding century, been more fatal to the repose of Europe, than the impertinent jealousy of merchants and manufacturers.[15] The violence and injustice of the rulers of mankind is an ancient evil, for which, I am afraid, the nature of human affairs can scarce admit of a remedy. But the mean rapacity, the monopolizing spirit of merchants and manufacturers, who neither are, nor ought to be the rulers of mankind, though it cannot perhaps be corrected, may very easily be prevented from disturbing the tranquility of any body but themselves. (*WN*, 493)

Here we begin to hear the anger in Smith's voice as he not only disagrees with, but denigrates the purveyors of that mercantile system for transforming and misusing the philosophy of Locke to "confound . . . the common sense of mankind" (*WN*, 494).[16] The consequence of their sophistry is a Europe burdened by a system of restraints on trade that reduces the wealth of each nation and pits nation against nation.

Smith cites, as an example of this absurdity, the relationship between Britain and France. There is, Smith recognizes, a natural wariness of a strong, wealthy, close neighbor because such is a potentially formidable opponent. The mercantilists on both sides of the Channel exploit this, announcing "with all the passionate confidence of interested falsehood, the certain ruin of each, in consequence of that unfavorable balance of trade, which, they pretend, would be the infallible effect of an unrestrained commerce with the other" (*WN*, 496). But Smith sees the possibilities very differently. "If those countries . . . were to consider their real interest, without either mercantile jealousy or national animosity, the commerce of France might be more advantageous to Great Britain than that of any other country, and for the same reason that of Great Britain to France" (*WN*, 495).

---

[15] John Maynard Keynes echoes these words in his General Theory (1964). In the "Concluding Notes on the Social Philosophy Towards Which the General Theory Might Lead." he writes: "War has several causes. Dictators and others such, to whom war offers, in expectation at least, a pleasurable excitement, find it easy to work on the natural bellicosity of their peoples. But, over and above this, facilitating their task of fanning the popular flame, are the economic causes of war, namely, the pressure of population and the competitive struggle for markets. It is the second factor, which probably played a predominant part in the nineteenth century, and might again" (Keynes, 381) be, as Smith put it long before, "fatal to the repose of Europe." Prescient words from Keynes in 1936.

[16] In a letter of 26 Oct. 1780 to Andreas Holt, Smith refers to "the very violent attack I had made upon the whole commercial system of Great Britain" (*Correspondence*, 251).

France, he argues, offers a great opportunity because of its wealth and proximity. It is capable of demanding much, and the proximity means that the speed with which capital could complete that circuit is high and risk in the circuit is low. This, as we've seen, is the ideal case for trade and thus the trading condition that contributes most to the wealth of the nation.

These advantages make this potential trade with France much more lucrative than the American colonial trade, that circuit so very dear to the mercantilists. In making this contrast, Smith is preparing the reader for the story of the colonies he is about to tell. It is in that context that his attack on the mercantile interests becomes most virulent, because, according to Smith, for the sake of that colonial trade which served only those mercantile interests, Britain has paid most dearly in wealth and blood.

These fruitless colonial enterprises become the focus of Smith's thinking when he moves to London in 1773 to publish *The Wealth of Nations*.

SMITH'S SHARPENING VOICE

Smith had long appreciated that the character of political institutions has a dramatic impact on economic activity. This is reflected in his story of the emergence of European commerce. But it seems that only when he moved to London in 1773 to complete the *Wealth of Nations* did Smith become fully and acutely aware of a political dynamic in London:[17] the immense power the mercantile interests exerted over Parliament and how effectively they used that power to systematically shape policy, especially colonial policy, to suit their own advantage.[18]

---

[17] Indicative of Smith's own sense of distance from the heart of civic affairs and of his perception of those events, he writes to Lord Fitzmaurice in London on 21 February 1759: "This country is so barren of all sorts of transactions that can interest anybody that lives at a distance from it that little entertainment is to be expected from any correspondence on this Side of the tweed. Our epistles to our friends at the capital commonly consist more in enquiries than in information. I must therefore put your Lordship in mind of the promise you was so good as to make to me of some times letting me hear from you of what passes in the Great World, either at home or abroad. I hear there is no faction in parliament, which I am glad of" (*Correspondence*, 28). Rosenberg notes that "[t]he unreformed parliament was the instrument of the powerful and the privileged.... [I]t is worth recalling that during the years when Adam Smith was writing *The Wealth of Nations* it was still regarded as a breach of privilege for newspapers even to divulge the contents of parliamentary debates... prohibitions... evaded by a variety of journalistic subterfuges" (Rosenberg, 1979, 25).

[18] It is interesting to note that in the *Index to the Works of Adam Smith* (Haakonssen and Skinner) there is no listing for "mercantile system" in the index for the *Lectures on*

Faced with this heightened awareness, he spent several years in London transforming the *WN*.[19] The tone of this transformed presentation is angry. Its focus is on colonial policy and the advantages that merchants enjoy thanks to those policies:

> Of the greater part of the regulations concerning the colony trade, the merchants who carry it on, it must be observed, have been the principal advisers. We must not wonder, therefore, if, in the greater part of them, their interest has been more considered than either that of the colonies or that of the mother country. (*WN*, 584)

The general monopoly on colonial trade created "by the act of navigation" gave British merchants an advantage in that trade that led to profits "much above the ordinary level of profit in other branches of trade" (*WN*, 596). This, in turn, attracted capital from those other branches, a flow that continued until "the profits of all came to a new level, different from and somewhat higher than that at which they had been before" (*WN*, 596).

This distortion of capital flows benefited the merchants, but harmed the nation by artificially directing capital into circuits that were "more distant" (*WN*, 596) and thus slower and more risky. As a consequence, these navigation acts reduced the productivity of the nation's stock of capital. Ironically, they also adversely affected the nation's trade position.

"[L]essening the competition of capitals" in the colonial trade led to a rise in the rate of profit in all trades.[20] This raised prices and, in turn,

---

Jurisprudence, whereas there is a long listing under this title in the index for *The Wealth of Nations*. In *LJ*, Smith does discuss bounties, for example (*LJA*, 365), and does refer to "this system" (*LJA*, 381), but here it is the system of Mun and Locke...one that "has occasioned many errors in the practise of this and other nations...in endeavouring to raise the quantity of money" (*LJA*, 384). At the time when he is delivering the Lectures, Smith treats this system as a misguided philosophy creating "bad practicall effects" (*LJA*, 388), or "prejudicial errors in practice" (*LJB*, 509), but there is no anger. He writes of Law's disastrous scheme: "This scheme of Mr. Laws was by no means contemptible; he realy believed in it and was the dupe of it himself" (*LJB*, 519)...a la the "man of system...wise in his own conceit" (*TMS*, 233).

[19] In the course of his analysis of American colonial policy in *WN*, Smith references the time frame with comments like: "the present disturbances" (*WN*, 573) or "the late disturbances" (*WN*, 578) or "at present, October 1773" (*WN*, 581). All of these suggest that he is writing this after he arrived in London in the spring of 1773. This is consistent with the speculation that the mercantile policies and, most significantly, those with respect to the colonies that were being pressed upon the Parliament, were a story he did not fully appreciate before his arrival in London, but a story he could not, for both philosophical and practical reasons, leave out of his *Wealth of Nations*.

[20] He asserts that if rates of profit have fallen since the establishment of the act, "as it certainly has, [then] it must have fallen still lower, had not the monopoly established by the act contributed to keep it up" (*WN*, 599).

made the cost of living and thus the cost of labor higher. All of these effects combined to hurt the nation's competitive position in branches of trade that it did not monopolize:

[W]hatever raises in any country the ordinary rate of profit higher than it otherwise would be, necessarily subjects that country both to an absolute and to a relative disadvantage in every branch of trade of which she has not the monopoly.... Our merchants frequently complain of the high wages of British labour as the cause of their manufactures being undersold in foreign markets; but they are silent about the high profits of stock.... The high profits of British stock, however, may contribute towards raising the price of British manufacturers in many cases as much, and in some perhaps more, than the high wages of British labour. (*WN*, 599)

Unfettered capital naturally flows into the channels that offer the best advantage, which is synonymous with the most productive use. When capital is flowing to its most productive use, it is growing most quickly and so, too, in turn, is the wealth of the nation. Smith summarizes his concern about mercantile colonial policies as follows:

The monopoly of the colony trade ... by forcing towards it a much greater proportion of the capital of Great Britain than what would naturally have gone to it, seems to have broken altogether that natural balance which would otherwise have taken place among all the different branches of British industry.... Her commerce, instead of running in a great number of small channels, has been taught to run principally into one great channel. But the whole system of her industry and commerce has thereby been rendered less secure; the whole state of her body politick less healthful, than it otherwise would have been. (*WN*, 604)

This is the voice of Smith, the citizen, expressing concern about the state of his nation. As a philosopher, he enjoys system building for the wonder that is associated with imagining the invisible connecting principles of our world in his mind's eye. But while the wonder alone makes the enterprise fascinating and engaging,[21] he has a public purpose. In *WN* Book IV, Smith seeks to strip away the veil of "philosophy" that obscures the self-serving purposes of the mercantile system and to reveal its destructive implications.

In her present condition [having followed the dictates of the mercantile system], Great Britain resembles one of those unwholesome bodies in which some of the vital parts are over grown, and which upon that account, are liable to many dangerous disorders scarce incident to those in which all the parts are more properly proportioned. A small stop in a great blood-vessel, which has been artificially

---

[21] "Smith devoted a good deal of attention to the 'pleasing satisfaction of science.'..." (Skinner, 1979, 24)

swelled beyond its natural dimensions, and through which an unnatural proportion of the industry and commerce of the country has been forced to circulate, is
very likely to bring on the most dangerous disorders upon the whole body politick.
(*WN*, 604–5)

Indeed, he continues, Britain has become so dependent on the flow in this
one artificially enlarged vessel, the colonial trade, that "the expectation
of a rupture with the colonies... has struck the people of Great Britain
with more terror than they ever felt for a Spanish armada, or a French
invasion" (*WN*, 605).

So why did Britain get into this unfortunate situation? Because the
mercantilist sophistry with respect to colonial policy was very appealing.

At first sight, no doubt, the monopoly of the great commerce of America, naturally
seems to be an acquisition of the highest value. To the undiscerning eye of giddy
ambition, it naturally presents itself amidst the confused scramble of politicks and
war, as a very dazzling object to fight for. (*WN*, 628)

This "undiscerning eye of giddy ambition" allowed Parliament to be se-
duced by the prospects of wealth to accept and implement a doctrine that
enjoyed the philosophical imprimatur of Locke and that was offered by
those who know the subject most intimately, the merchants. Furthermore,
the initial cost to Britain of the colonial enterprise (discovery, reconnoi-
tering, and "fictitious possession" (*WN*, 614)) was, Smith suggests, pretty
meager, and the costs during peace were also modest.

However, since those early days, there had been two wars, a cost he
lays squarely "to the account of the colonies" (*WN*, 615). These were very
expensive, and to what end?

The whole expense is, in reality, a bounty which has been given in order to support
a monopoly. The pretended purpose of it was to encourage the manufacturers,
and to increase the commerce of Great Britain. But its real effect has been to
raise the rate of merchant profit. (*WN*, 616)

Under the present system of management, therefore, Great Britain derives nothing but loss from the dominion that she assumes over her
colonies. The only winners are the mercantile interests.

So how have the mercantilists maintained their grip on policy? With
sophistry and persuasion and, when those have failed, by intimidation:

This monopoly has so much increased the number of some particular tribes of
them, that, like an overgrown standing army, they have become formidable to the
government, and upon many occasions intimidate the legislature. The member of
parliament who supports every proposal for strengthening this monopoly, is sure
to acquire not only the reputation of understanding trade, but great popularity and

influence with an order of men whose numbers and wealth render them of great importance. If he opposes them, on the contrary, and still more if he has authority enough to be able to thwart them, neither the most acknowledged probity, nor the highest rank, nor the greatest publick services can protect him from the most infamous abuse and detraction, from personal insults, nor sometimes from real danger, arising from the insolent outrage of furious and disappointed monopolists. (*WN*, 471)

Because of these powerful interests, Britain is burdened by what should have been a wonderful opportunity: the globalization of trade.

The opening of the East and West gave Europe access to markets that spanned the globe. Because an expansion of the extent of the market is both a prerequisite for the ever-finer division of labor and an opportunity to generate the capital to finance those improvements, a new era of global trade for Europe could have been a great benefit, directly and indirectly, to all the nations of Europe.[22] However, while nominally meant to "enrich a great nation" (*WN*, 627), the mercantile colonial policies have, in fact, "frequently [been] more hurtful to the countries in favour of which they are established than to those against which they are established" (*WN*, 627).

After all the unjust attempts, therefore, of every country in Europe to engross to itself the whole advantages of the trade of its own colonies, no country has yet been able to engross to itself any thing but the expence of supporting in time of peace and of defending in time of war the oppressive authority which it assumes over them. (*WN*, 628)

Clearly, Smith asserts, free trade is a better policy. Unfettered capital generates the most production, in turn, the most accumulation, and so the most growth in the wealth of the nation. In this natural dynamic, the risk-adjusted profits of stock are the signal that directs this allocation of capital. Wherever there is an advantage, these profits will be higher and this "superiority of profit will draw stock . . . till the profits of all return to their proper level" (*WN*, 629).

---

[22] Opportunities opened "much about the same time" (*WN*, 448) in both America and the East. The nations of the East (China, Indostan, Japan) were much more advanced than those of America (Mexico, Peru), and thus more ripe for constructive engagement and mutual benefit. But, "Europe . . . has hitherto derived much less advantage from its commerce with the East Indies, than from that with America" (*WN*, 448–9). The reasons for this disparity are directly related to the completeness of mercantilist power in setting the policies for the trade relationship. The East Indian trade was initially monopolized by the Portuguese, but as the Dutch "began to encroach upon them, they vested their whole East India commerce in an exclusive company. The English, French, Swedes, and Danes, have all followed this example. . . ." (*WN*, 449).

That level is inversely related to the supply of capital stock. Because that supply will grow with each circuit of production, the rate of profit in a growing, healthy economy will fall until it just covers the cost of superintendence.[23] But this prospect brings us back to the mercantilists and their power over policy.

Clearly, it is in the interest of the mercantile class to insure that this dynamic is thwarted so that the rate of profit remains high. Controlling markets insures an advantage, so it is "[m]onopoly of one kind or another... [that] seems to be the sole engine of the mercantile system" (*WN*, 630). It is a system that undermines and destroys the lifeblood of material progress:

- reducing the productivity of capital by sending it into unnatural circuits, and
- destroying capital by
  - requiring national treasure to be spent on defending colonies and colonial trade routes, and
  - allowing companies (as in India) to act as sovereigns so that opportunities for corruption and oppression, both very destructive, abound (*WN*, 635–641).

This is where Smith leaves the subject of the mercantile system in the original edition of *WN* (1776). In 1784, he returns to the *WN* and makes significant revisions. The most significant of these is a new Chapter 8 for Book IV titled: *Conclusion of the Mercantile System* (*WN*, 642).

"CONCLUSION OF THE MERCANTILE SYSTEM"

Between the publication of the first edition of *WN* in 1776 and the "Additions and Corrections" published in 1784, Smith served as a Commissioner of Customs. As Ian Ross makes clear in his biography of Smith, this is a position that Smith pursued[24] and one for which "[f]inancial inducement

---

[23] Indicative of this is his assertion that "[t]he mercantile capital of Holland is so great that it is... continually overflowing...." (*WN*, 632) And in Holland, the country that is closest to having "acquired its full complement of riches,... the ordinary rate of clear profit... is very small, so that usual market rate of interest which could be afforded out if it, would be so low as to render it impossible for any but the very wealthiest people to love upon the interest of their money" (*WN*, 113).

[24] "Following the death in 1777 of Archibald Menzies, one of the Commissioners, Smith announced his candidacy to Strahan on 27 October 1777, and asked him to find out how matters stood at the Treasury Board, claiming, however: 'I am not apt to be over-sanguine in my expectations'" (Ross, 306), implying a desire for the position.

could not have been a strong factor ... [since] he offered to give up the pension ... he held from [the Duke of] Buccleuch on receiving the Customs appointment. ... " (Ross, 306)

So why did Smith seek and take this position? Ross suggests that Smith might have sought "structure" in his life or proximity to friends in Edinburgh (Ross, 306). While these are certainly plausible possibilities, I would suggest another incentive: Smith had become, as the original *WN* Book IV makes clear, fascinated by the dynamic nature of the mercantile system and very concerned about its impact on Great Britain. A position in the Customhouse offered him an ideal opportunity as a scholar to study the intricacies of commercial policy from the inside of the system, and the possibility as an active citizen to ameliorate some of the excesses of that system created by "[t]he avidity of our great manufacturers. ... " (*WN*, 643).[25]

Whatever his motive for working in the Customhouse, after years of work there, the new *WN* Book IV Chapter VIII, *Conclusion of the Mercantile System*, picks up where the strong criticism of mercantilism embodied in the original Book IV left off, sharpening that criticism into a scathing attack.[26]

It begins with a review of several laws the mercantile interests "extorted from the legislature" (*WN*, 643) that are especially interesting because of their peculiar character: They follow a plan that is "opposite" (*WN*, 642) from the normal logic of the mercantile system. These laws limit exports and encourage imports.

Peculiarity notwithstanding, as always with mercantilist advocacy, "[i]ts ultimate object [in advocating these laws] ... *it pretends*, is ... to enrich

---

[25] This job was an ideal window into the details of the mercantile system: "[T]he customs service in Great Britain during the time of Adam Smith's tenure as a commissioner functioned basically as an agent of English mercantilism and as a tax collection agency" (Anderson, Shughart, and Tollison, 745). And, Smith clearly immersed himself in the job: "[T]he author of the *Wealth of Nations* was a good bureaucrat ... various parts of Smith's correspondence indicate two central points: he enjoyed his customs work and found it relaxing, and the job occupied a lot of his time" (Anderson, Shughart, and Tollison, 750, 752).

[26] With respect to the "famous chapter of *Wealth*, 'Conclusion of the Mercantile System' ... [Anderson, Shughart, and Tollison] suggest two simple links between Smith's customs experience and this added material. First, Commissioner Smith must have acquired a detailed knowledge of the various statutes it was his job to enforce, given his evident diligence; the chapter is based on direct knowledge of relevant laws rather than on secondary sources. Second, Smith may have had ample opportunity as commissioner to observe interest group behavior at first hand as a determinant of economic policy" (Anderson, Shughart, and Tollison, 755).

the country by an advantageous balance of trade" (*WN*, 642, emphasis added). Smith proceeds, however, to strip away this guise of national interest, and to demonstrate that these new laws are not at all peculiar if one traces their origins and reveals their intended, rather than their pretended, purpose: to enrich their mercantile advocates.

Clearly well schooled in the history and intricacies of these laws thanks to his years at the Customhouse, as an example of an "opposite" policy at work, Smith analyzes the rules put in place to control the linen yarn market in some detail.[27] His point is clear:

It is not by the sale of their work [("our spinners... poor people, women commonly, scattered about in all different parts of the country, without support or protection." (*WN*, 644))], but by that of the compleat work of the weavers, that our great manufacturers make their profits. As it is their interest to sell the compleat manufacturers as dear, so is it to buy the materials as cheap as possible. By extorting from the legislature bounties upon the exportation of their own linen, high duties upon the importation of all foreign linen, and a total prohibition of the home consumption of some sorts of French linen, they endeavour to sell their goods as dear as possible. By encouraging the importation of foreign linen yarn, and thereby bringing it into competition with that which is made by our own people, they endeavour to buy the work of the poor spinners as cheap as possible.... [I]t is by no means for the benefit of the workman, that they endeavour either to raise the price of the compleat work, or to lower that of the rude materials. It is the industry which is carried on for the benefit of the rich and the powerful, that is principally encouraged by our mercantile system. (*WN*, 644)

One hears Smith's values and feels his outrage in these words. As described in Chapter One, Smith's metric of a good society is the well-being of the least among the working class. The mercantile system, so meticulously arranged to insure the control of the market for the "benefit of the rich and the powerful," has just the opposite effect. In extorting Parliament to serve its interests, the mercantilists exploit and impoverish workers who, being "scattered about in all different parts of the country, without support or protection," cannot resist.[28]

Smith, conservative by nature, does not favor radical change.[29] However, he cares about the working class and he cares about the prospects

---

[27] "The linen trade more than any other manufacture must have been the industry Adam Smith was most familiar with, as it was successful and widespread throughout most of the Lowlands, not least in the Fife villages near Kirkcaldy [Smith's ancestral home]. It was still a domestic and cottage industry . . ." (Smout, 63).

[28] This theme of the asymmetry of power between employer and worker is one Smith also highlights in *WN* Book I (*WN*, 83–4).

[29] Even Smith's belief that mercantile policies should be reversed is tempered by his concern for the displacement effect on "many thousands of our people" (*WN*, 469). "Humanity

of his nation. Writing in 1784, as he presents his analysis of the linen trade, he makes it clear that something can and should be done about this exploitation because he notes pointedly that the two of the bounties on which this system is built "expire with the end of the session of parliament which shall immediately follow the 24th of June 1786" (*WN*, 644).

Again, based on intimate knowledge of the issues gained from his service in the Customhouse, Smith follows his analysis of the linen trade with an analysis of the actions of

[o]ur woollen manufacturers [who] have been more successful than any other class of workmen, in persuading the legislature that the prosperity of the nation depended upon the success and extension of their particular business. . . . [After sympathizing with the view that some revenue laws seem unjust, he continues:] but the cruelest of our revenue laws, I will venture to affirm, are mild and gentle, in comparison of some of those which the clamour of our merchants and manufacturers has extorted from the legislature, for the support of their own absurd and oppressive monopolies. Like the laws of Draco, these laws may be said to be all written in blood. (*WN*, 647–8)

These linen and wool policies are but two examples of a mercantile system that evolved as an increasingly complex set of regulations advocated by the mercantile interests for the supposed enrichment of the wealth of the nation. In the course of this policy evolution, epicycle was set on epicycle, each offered with the promise that with this new adjustment, the system would yield even greater wealth for the nation. However, like that flawed philosophy of the Ptolemaic system for which epicycles were no solution, this system is fundamentally flawed. Also like the Ptolemaic system – a once honest, albeit misguided, philosophy later captured by particular interests to preserve the power of those interests[30] – by Smith's day the mercantile system had become a self-serving sophistry in the guise of a philosophy that, for the sake of the wealth not of the nation but of the merchants and manufacturers, made production, not consumption, the national purpose. According to Smith, this is backward.

Consumption is the sole end and purpose of all production; and the interest of the producer ought to be attended to, only so far as it may be necessary for promoting that of the consumer. The maxim is so perfectly self-evident, that it would be

---

may in this case require that the freedom of trade should be restored only by slow gradations. . . . " (*WN*, 469). Having revealed this concern, however, he goes on to suggest that the dislocations might "be much less than is commonly imagined. . . . " (*WN*, 469).

[30] The resistance of the Church to the Copernican system and its transformation of the conception of the order of the universe is a classic example of particular interest driving philosophical advocacy.

absurd to attempt to prove it. But in the mercantile system, the interest of the consumer is almost constantly sacrificed to that of the producer.... (*WN*, 660)

The consumer pays the price of the policies extorted from the parliament by the mercantile interests directly in taxes levied as protections and indirectly in higher prices caused by prohibitions or restrictions. In addition, in Smith's view, above and beyond these was the most egregious cost of the mercantile system: the treasure spent to defend the colonies for the benefit of the mercantile interests:

> For the sake of that little enhancement of price which this monopoly might afford our producers, the home-consumers have been burdened with the whole expense of maintaining and defending that empire. For this purpose, and for this purpose only, in the last two wars, more than a hundred and seventy millions have been contracted over and above all that had been expended for the same purpose in former wars. The interest on the debt alone is not only greater than the whole extraordinary profit, which, it ever could be pretended, was made by the monopoly of the colony trade, but than the whole value of that trade or than the whole value of the goods, which at an average have been annually exported to the colonies.
>
> It cannot be difficult to determine who have been the contrivers of this whole mercantile system; not the consumers, we may believe, whose interest has been entirely neglected; but the producers whose interest has been so carefully attended to; and among this latter class our merchants and manufacturers have been by far the principal architects (*WN*, 661).

Here, we hear Smith in his full fury.

FOLLOWING THIS VOICE TO 1790 – SMITH AND CIVIC HUMANISM

Smith's concern about the mercantile interests, their influence on parliament, and their impact on the British, if not the human, prospect lies at the heart of his revisions to the *TMS* published in 1790. This work mattered a great deal to Smith. By his own account, he worked on these revisions at great cost to his health, and, indeed, he died that year.[31]

---

[31] Twice, in his correspondence to Thomas Cadell (along with Strahan, Smith's publisher) regarding the revisions to *TMS,* Smith notes his health as an issue. On 15 March, 1788, he writes that he had take leave from his work to write: "My subject is the theory of moral Sentiments to all parts of which I am making many additions and corrections. The chief and the most important additions will be to the third part, that concerning *the sense of Duty* and to the last part concerning *the History of moral Philosophy*. As I consider my tenure of this life as extremely precarious, and am very uncertain whether I shall live to finish several other works which I have projected.... I am a slow a very slow workman, who do and undo everything I write at least half a dozen times before I can be tolerably pleased with it; and tho' I have now, I think, brought my work within compass, yet it will

As noted in Chapter One, there was no financial or reputational need for this effort, his income and his reputation being both long since secure. Smith's purpose was public.

Jerry Muller has it just right: "The design and the rhetoric of Smith's work reflect his intention not only to *instruct* legislators by enunciating general principles but to *motivate* them to pursue the common interest" (Muller, 1993, 54, emphasis in original). Smith's sense of urgency for achieving this goal grows with his sense of concern about the power of the mercantile interests.

In order to inspire this "motivation...[for] the common interest" Smith turns to a progressively more civic humanist voice extolling "citizenship...as an active virtue" (Pocock, 1983, 235). He appeals to today's and tomorrow's leaders to resist the seduction and pressures of partial interests and to "assume the greatest and noblest of all characters, that of the reformer and legislator of a great state; and, by the wisdom of his institutions, [to] secure the internal tranquility and happiness of his fellow-citizens for many succeeding generations" (*TMS*, 232).

It may seem an irony that Smith begins to see civic humanist leadership as the best hope for maintaining Britain's advancement toward a classical liberal ideal, the liberal plan. But while Smith is an idealist, he is also a realist and a pragmatist. The one thing Smith is not is a dogmatist, a "man of system...wise in his own conceit" (*TMS*, 233).

In the most significant revision to the 1790 edition of the *TMS*, the new Part VI titled "Of the Character of Virtue," Smith begins in Section I by reflecting on that dimension of our moral sentiments that directs us to care for our "own happiness" (*TMS*, 212): prudence.[32] Prudence is that expression of self-love that "is always both supported and rewarded by the entire approbation of the impartial spectator...[because is it

be the month of June before I shall be able to send it to you" (*Correspondence*, 311). About a year later, 31 March 1789, he writes Cadell: "Ever since I wrote to you last I have been labouring very hard in preparing the proposed new edition of the Theory of Moral Sentiments. I have even hurt my health...." (*Correspondence*, 319–20)

[32] In this context, Smith offers an interesting commentary on the prudence of an educated person in general and the scholar in particular: "The prudent man always studies seriously and earnestly to understand whatever he professes to understand, and not merely to persuade other people that he understands it; and though his talents may not always be brilliant, they are always perfectly genuine.... For reputation in his profession he is naturally disposed to rely a good deal upon the solidity of his knowledge and abilities; and he does not always think of cultivating the favor of those little clubs and cabals, who, in the superior arts and sciences, often erect themselves into the supreme judges of merit; and who make it their business to celebrate the talents and virtues of one another, and to decry whatever can come into competition with them" (TMS, 213–14).

self-love moderated and directed by] that proper exertion of self-command" (*TMS*, 215).

The prudent man "would prefer the undisturbed enjoyment of secure tranquility, not only to all the vain splendor of successful ambition, but to the real and solid glory of performing the greatest and most magnanimous actions" (*TMS*, 216). Nevertheless, Smith asserts, the good citizen, "[w]hen distinctly called upon, . . . will not decline the service of his country" (*TMS*, 216), for "[t]he wise and virtuous man is at all times willing that his own private interest should be sacrificed to the public interest" (*TMS*, 235).

Here, we begin to hear Smith's appeal to the civic leader to be, as the patriot, one who may prefer secure tranquility but is ready and willing to serve the nation. Self-directed prudence is, according to Smith, virtuous, but "[i]t commands a certain cool esteem . . . not . . . any ardent love or admiration" (*TMS*, 216). In contrast, he continues:

Wise and judicious conduct, when directed to greater and nobler purposes than the care of the health, the fortune, the rank and reputation of the individual, is frequently and very properly called prudence. We talk of the prudence of the great general, of the great statesman, of the great legislator. Prudence is, in all these cases, combined with many greater and more splendid virtues, with valour, with extensive and strong benevolence, with a sacred regard to the rules of justice, and all these supported by a proper degree of self-command. This superior prudence . . . necessarily supposes the utmost perfection of all the intellectual and of all the moral virtues. It is the best head joined to the best heart. It is the most perfect wisdom combined with the most perfect virtue. (*TMS*, 216)

The case of the great patriot is easily familiar and so it makes a valuable point of reference for Smith:

The patriot who lays down his life for the safety, or even for the vain-glory of this society, appears to act with the most exact propriety. . . . But though this sacrifice appears to be perfectly just and proper, we know how difficult it is to make it, and how few people are capable of making it. His conduct, therefore, excites not only our entire approbation, but our highest wonder and admiration, and seems to merit all the applause which can be due to the most heroic virtue. (*TMS*, 228)

Weaving his conception of civic virtue and its real, if intangible, rewards into the mind of his audience, Smith is preparing the way for his assertion that a great statesman is on a par with this great patriot. However, always wary of imbalance, Smith pauses to warn his reader against jingoism:

The love of our own nation often disposes us to view, with the most malignant jealousy and envy, the prosperity and aggrandisement of any other neighbouring nation. Independent and neighbouring nations, having no common superior to decide their disputes, all live in continual dread and suspicion of one another.... The regard for the laws of nations, or for those rules which independent states profess or pretend to think themselves bound to observe in their dealings with one another, is often very little more than mere pretence and profession. From the smallest interest, upon the slightest provocation, we see those rules every day, either evaded or directly violated without shame or remorse. Each nation foresees, or imagines it foresees, its own subjugation in the increasing power and aggrandisement of any of its neighbours; and the mean principle of national prejudice is often founded upon the noble one of the love of our own country... France and England may each of them have some reason to dread the increase of the naval and military power of the other; but for either of them to envy the internal happiness and prosperity of the other, the cultivation of its lands, the advancement of its manufactures, the increase of its commerce, the security and number of its ports and harbours, its proficiency in all the liberal arts and sciences, is surely beneath the dignity of two such great nations. These are all real improvements of the world we live in. Mankind are benefited, human nature is ennobled by them. In such improvements each nation ought, not only to endeavour itself to excel, but from the love of mankind, to promote, instead of obstructing the excellence of its neighbours. These are all proper objects of national emulation, not of national prejudice or envy. (*TMS*, 228–9)

This larger, international perspective reflects the character of Smith's moral philosophy. Even as he is writing out of an immediate concern regarding the current state of Britain and the perverse effect of the mercantile interests on that state, Smith's larger and more abiding concern is always the human prospect. He appreciates full well that, just as domestic distortions impede the progress of nations, national boundaries can engender jealousies that are a menace to the realization of that larger prospect: "The love of our own country seems not to be derived from the love of mankind. The former sentiment is altogether independent of the latter, and seems sometimes even to dispose us to act inconsistently with it" (*TMS*, 229).

Having made this global point, he then returns to the challenge of constituting a nation state that is consistent with progress, and the role of the statesman in meeting that challenge.

Given that "particular orders and societies" are inevitable in any nation, the challenge of progress is, according to Smith, to establish an order within which the "powers, privileges, and immunities" of the "particular orders and societies" are balanced such that no particular faction is privileged (*TMS*, 230). "[T]he particular distribution which has been made of their respective powers, privileges, and immunities, depends... [upon] what is called ... the constitution of that particular state" (*TMS*, 230).

A constitution is a delicate and contestable instrument, especially "in times of public discontent, faction, and disorder" (*TMS*, 231). It is in just

such times that the statesman can become, like the patriot, a person who
serves the nation and earns the admiration of the nation for all times.
What it the key to such nobility? The wisdom and self-command that
allow one to rise above the interests of faction, even one's own faction,
and to govern for the common good:

[A] wise man may be disposed to think some alteration necessary in that constitution or form of government, which, in its actual condition, appears plainly
unable to maintain the public tranquillity. In such cases, however, it often requires, perhaps, the highest effort of political wisdom to determine when a real
patriot ought to support and endeavour to re-establish the authority of the old
system, and when he ought to give way to the more daring, but often dangerous
spirit of innovation....

In times of civil discord, the leaders of the contending parties, though they may
be admired by one half of their fellow-citizens, are commonly execrated by the
other....

The leader of the successful party, however, if he has authority enough to
prevail upon his own friends to act with proper temper and moderation (which
he frequently has not), may sometimes render to his country a service much
more essential and important than the greatest victories and the most extensive
conquests [of the patriot]. He may re-establish and improve the constitution,
and from the very doubtful and ambiguous character of the leader of a party, he
may assume the greatest and noblest of all characters, that of the reformer and
legislator of a great state; and, by the wisdom of his institutions, secure the internal
tranquillity and happiness of his fellow-citizens for many succeeding generations.
(*TMS*, 231–2)

Clearly, Smith sees this wise "reformer and legislator" as essential
to civic well being because only such a statesman can ignore the en-
treaties, enthusiasm, and intimidation of factions and instead pursue policies for the well being of all citizens. The editors of *TMS* suggest that "[i]t
seems likely that Smith had the French Revolution in mind when writing
this...." (*TMS*, 231, fn.6). Certainly so, but this theme is also entirely
consistent with that growing concern we've seen in the pages of the *WN*,
that the mercantile faction "like an overgrown standing army,... [has] become formidable to the government, and upon many occasions intimidate
the legislature" (*WN*, 471).

Extolling the virtues of the civic humanist statesman in 1790, Smith
cites Solon, "one of the leading figures in the republican 'myth'"
(Winch, 1978, 160), as a model:

The man whose public spirit is prompted altogether by humanity and benevolence,
will respect the established powers and privileges even of individuals, and still
more those of the great orders and societies, into which the state is divided. Though

he should consider some of them as in some measure abusive [as Smith did the mercantile powers and privileges], he will . . . accommodate, as well as he can, his public arrangements to the confirmed habits and prejudices of the people; and will . . . [w]hen he cannot establish the right, he will not disdain to ameliorate the wrong; but like Solon, when he cannot establish the best system of laws, he will endeavour to establish the best that the people can bear. (*TMS*, 233)[33]

Solon is an ideal civic humanist model for Smith because, as Smith represents him, Solon's actions reflect active virtue tempered by the moderation that comes with humility. Smith reminds the current and future statesmen that, whereas wise leadership is a virtue, arrogant leadership is a vice. So beware becoming

[t]he man of system . . . very wise in his own conceit; and . . . often so enamoured with the supposed beauty of his own ideal plan of government, that he cannot suffer the smallest deviation from any part of it. . . . [Do not, he warns the leader] imagine that . . . the different members of a great society [can be arranged] with as much ease as the hand arranges the different pieces upon a chess-board. . . . [I]n the great chess-board of human society, every single piece has a principle of motion of its own. . . . (TMS, 234)

Then, apropos of his own enterprise and his own role in civil society, Smith reminds the leader that a system of philosophy can a valuable tool for policy, but only when it is applied with humility:

Some general, and even systematical, idea of the perfection of policy and law, may no doubt be necessary for directing the views of the statesman. But to insist upon

---

[33] This notion that new policy should cautiously ameliorate old errors is a theme that Smith had expressed in the original edition of the *WN*. Having noted that the distortions of mercantile policies have created a long period of trade constraints and that a new regime can open up trade, he warns that such a change should be done gradually. This is so because the mercantile distortions are built so deeply into the British system of commerce, that a quick solution would be very destabilizing. What is clear is the ultimate solution: "[T]he natural system of perfect liberty and justice ought gradually to be restored . . . [How,] we must leave to the wisdom of future statesmen and legislators to determine" (*WN*, 606).

Certainly one thing the legislator should not do is create more monopolies: "To expect, indeed, that the freedom of trade should ever be entirely restored in Great Britain is as absurd as to expect that an Oceana or Utopia should ever be established in it. Not only the prejudices of the public, but what is much more unconquerable, the private [mercantile] interests of many individuals, irresistibly oppose it. . . . The equitable regard, therefore, to his interest requires that changes of this kind should never be introduced suddenly, but slowly, gradually, and after a very long warning. The legislature, were it possible that its deliberations could be always directed, not by the clamorous importunity of partial interests, but by an extensive view of the general good, ought upon this very account, perhaps, to be particularly careful neither to establish any new monopolies of this kind, nor to extend further those which are already established. Every such regulation introduces some degree of real disorder into the constitution of the state, which it will be difficult afterwards to cure without occasioning another disorder" (*WN*, 471–2).

establishing, and upon establishing all at once, and in spite of all opposition, every thing which that idea may seem to require, must often be the highest degree of arrogance.... It is to fancy himself the only wise and worthy man in the common-wealth, and that his fellow-citizens should accommodate themselves to him and not he to them. (*TMS*, 234)

Smith's point is clear. If human progress is to proceed, we need leadership by wise statesmen[34] who:

- make policy based on general, rather than particular, interests, and
- are guided by a moral philosophy but are not slaves to any such system.

In order to recruit such leaders, Smith appeals to those who aspire to leadership to follow the civic humanist model of Solon.

To make that model appealing, Smith notes that although the short-term challenges are certainly many and significant, the long-term rewards – the adulation of the nation and the personal serenity of self-respect[35] – make virtuous statesmanship worth the challenges. If these rewards are not sufficient to persuade, Smith cites yet a higher calling that should compel one to transcend that cool prudence of self-love and spend energies on the well being of one's fellow citizens. Doing so serves "the will of the great Director of the universe" (*TMS*, 236), and for any-one who "is deeply impressed with the habitual and thorough convic-tion[36] that [there is] this benevolent and all-wise Being" (*TMS*, 235),

---

[34] "Natural liberty...will require a conscious act of the will of the virtuous legislator to bring it about" (Young, 205).

[35] In the significant 1790 amendments and additions to Chapter II of *TMS* Part III, Smith describes the wise man as one who loves praiseworthiness rather than praise. This com-plements his 1790 appeal in the new *TMS* Part VI to leaders to take the role of statesmen, because a statesman is a person of wisdom and virtue who, measuring self by praisewor-thiness, can ignore the clamor of faction that tries to seduce with the vanity of praise and intimidate with the threat of disapprobation. This is precisely the kind of leader necessary to deal with the strategy of the mercantile interests. Recall: "The member of parliament who supports every proposal for strengthening this monopoly, is sure to acquire not only the reputation of understanding trade, but great popularity and influence with an order of men whose numbers and wealth render them of great importance. If he opposes them, on the contrary, and still more if he has authority enough to be able to thwart them, neither the most acknowledged probity, nor the highest rank, nor the greatest publick services can protect him from the most infamous abuse and detraction, from personal insults, nor sometimes from real danger, arising from the insolent outrage of furious and disappointed monopolists" (*WN*, 471).

[36] As described in Chapter One, Smith takes the existence of this Deity on faith, as a "conviction" not a "Truth."

such a service is a moral imperative.[37] Active citizenship is our human responsibility:[38]

The administration of the great system of the universe, ... the care of the universal happiness of all rational and sensible beings, is the business of God and not of man. To man is allotted a much humbler department, but one much more suitable to the weakness of his powers, and to the narrowness of his comprehension; the care of his own happiness, of that of his family, his friends, his country: that he is occupied in contemplating the more sublime, can never be an excuse for his neglecting the more humble department ... The most sublime speculation of the contemplative philosopher can scarce compensate the neglect of the smallest *active duty*. (*TMS*, 237, emphasis added)[39]

---

[37] In those 1790 revisions to the *TMS* cited in an earlier footnote, as Smith extols the virtue of praiseworthiness over praise, he also warns his readers of the downside of not following this moral road: "To attain to this envied situation, the candidates for fortune too frequently abandon the paths of virtue; for unhappily, the road which leads to the one, and that which leads to the other, lie sometimes in very opposite directions. ... In many governments the candidates for the highest stations are above the law; and, if they can attain the object of their ambition, they have no fear of being called to account for the means by which they acquired it. They often endeavour, therefore, not only by fraud and falsehood, the ordinary and vulgar arts of intrigue and cabal; but sometimes by the perpetration of the most enormous crimes, by murder and assassination, by rebellion and civil war, to supplant and destroy those who oppose or stand in the way of their greatness. ... Amidst all the gaudy pomp of the most ostentatious greatness; amidst the venal and vile adulation of the great and of the learned; amidst the more innocent, though more foolish, acclamations of the common people; amidst all the pride of conquest and the triumph of successful war, he is still secretly pursued by the avenging furies of shame and remorse; and, while glory seems to surround him on all sides, he himself, in his own imagination, sees black and foul infamy fast pursuing him, and every moment ready to overtake him from behind" (TMS, 64–5).

[38] Referring to men he respects, Smith writes to Edmund Burke on 1 July 1782 that "[i]t must afflict every good citizen that any circumstance should occur which could make men of their probity, prudence and moderation judge it proper in these times to withdraw from the service of their country" (*Correspondence*, 259).

[39] Indicative of this emphasis on active virtue, he writes in another revision of 1790: "To compare, in this manner, the futile mortifications of a monastery, to the ennobling hardships and hazards of war; to suppose that one day, or one hour, employed in the former should, in the eye of the great Judge of the world, have more merit than a whole life spent honourably in the latter, is surely contrary to all our moral sentiments; to all the principles by which nature has taught us to regulate our contempt or admiration. It is this spirit, however, which, while it has reserved the celestial regions for monks and friars, or for those whose conduct and conversation resembled those of monks and friars, has condemned to the infernal all the heroes, all the statesmen and lawgivers, all the poets and philosophers of former ages; all those who have invented, improved, or excelled in the arts which contribute to the subsistence, to the conveniency, or to the ornament of human life; all the great protectors, instructors, and benefactors of mankind; all those to whom our natural sense of praise-worthiness forces us to ascribe the highest merit and most

By 1790, this civic humanist voice extolling "active duty" has become an important instrumental tool for Smith in realizing his classical liberal vision.[40] It is a voice he adopts not only in his public writing, the *TMS*, but also in his private correspondence: "In what remains of Smith's correspondence with leading politicians on questions of trade, it is striking how often he sought to stiffen their backbone, urging them to buck the pressure from particular interests for the sake of the common good" (Muller, 1993, 26).[41]

Smith's voice evolves, but his vision remains the same ... and, as we will see in the next chapter, that liberal vision informs Smith's conception of the role of government in society. Informs, but doesn't dictate ... Smith is never a "man of system," he is a practical philosopher with a vision.

exalted virtue. Can we wonder that so strange an application of this most respectable doctrine should sometimes have exposed it to contempt and derision; with those at least who had themselves, perhaps, no great taste or turn for the devout and contemplative virtues?" (*TMS*, 134).

[40] "In the historical ... process which was now man's habitat, republican citizenship was no more than a crucial episode ... [T]here was an alternative ideal of liberty and virtue, in which property and specialization were protected by authority and law, more appropriate to the commercial stage of history and perhaps ranking higher in the human scale" (Pocock, 1983, 243). Smith believed that to reach this new ideal, society needed to draw on some of the old political virtues, not from an elite of autonomous landowners but from the emerging political leadership. This instrumental adoption of a civic humanist voice is consistent with Pocock's observation that such a voice was still available to Smith: "[H]istorians are trained to think in linear, progressive and quasi-dialectical patterns ... [so i]t is conventional to think of the predecessor of a given paradigm as altogether superseded and submerged. But the civic humanist paradigm ... encourages us to think of the civic and commercial ideologies as struggling with one another at least down to the lifetimes of Adam Smith and John Millar.... (Pocock, 1983, 244). Further: "It is certainly not the case that the Scottish theorists in general regarded republican and jurisprudential language as distinct and ideologically opposite rhetorics" (Pocock, 1983, 251). "Neither of us [Quintin Skinner or Pocock] ... reaches the point – and it may be that I should have – where we must ask whether and if so how, the language of republican virtue ever combined with that of juristic right" (Pocock, 1981, 54). One can find that combination in Smith.

[41] There has been, in the literature, a debate about Smith's "location" relative to the classical liberal and civic humanist positions. The most clear demarcation of the sides in this debate are represented by a wonderfully thoughtful exchange between Donald Winch (*Adam Smith's Politics*, 1978; "Adam Smith and the Liberal Tradition," 1988) and Edward Harpham ("Liberalism, Civic Humanism, and the Case of Adam Smith," 1984; "The Problem of Liberty in the Thought of Adam Smith," 2000). I agree with Harpham that Smith was not a civic humanist. But I believe Winch is correct in suggesting that Smith adopted and adapted civic humanist ideas as instrumental tools to achieve the classical liberal end he envisioned.

NINE

On the Role of Government

Book V of *The Wealth of Nations*

Having described in *WN* Book IV the errors of government policy that follow from competing systems of political economy, in *WN* Book V, the last Book of *The Wealth of Nations*, Smith goes into great detail as he describes:

- what he believes government should and shouldn't do, and
- how it should and shouldn't do what it should.

All these "shoulds" should suggest that *WN* Book V is a prescriptive, policy-oriented ending to Smith's *Inquiry into the Nature and Causes of the Wealth of Nations*. And it is.

Smith wrote in the *Theory of Moral Sentiments*, seventeen years before the publication of *The Wealth of Nations*, that:

if you would implant public virtue in the breast of him who seems heedless of the interest of his country, it will often be to no purpose to tell him, what superior advantages the subjects of a well-governed state enjoy; that they are better lodged, that they are better clothed, that they are better fed. These considerations will commonly make no great impression. You will be more likely to persuade, if you describe the great system of public police which procures these advantages, if you explain the connexions and dependencies of its several parts, their mutual subordination to one another, and their general subserviency to the happiness of the society; if you show how this system might be introduced into his own country, what it is that hinders it from taking place there at present, how those obstructions might be removed, and all the several wheels of the machine of government be made to move with more harmony and smoothness, without grating upon one another, or mutually retarding one another's motions. It is scarce possible that a man should listen to a discourse of this kind, and not feel himself animated to some degree of public spirit.... Upon this account political disquisitions, if just, and reasonable, and practicable, are of all the works of speculation the most useful. Even the weakest and the worst of them are not altogether without their utility. They serve at least to animate the public passions of men, and rouse them to seek out the means of promoting the happiness of the society. (*TMS*, 186)

In the first four Books of *The Wealth of Nations* Smith describes the elegance and benefits of the "the liberal plan of equality, liberty and justice" (*WN*, 664) and exposes the mercantile "obstructions" that encumber the British experiment with that system. Now, in *WN* Book V, he presents his analysis of the role of government in a liberal system and a commentary on how that role can be most constructively carried out. His goal throughout his *Inquiry* is to accomplish what, by his own account, all "political disquisitions" should: to "animate the public passions of men, and rouse them to seek out the means of promoting the happiness of the society."

ON THE ROLE OF GOVERNMENT – AN OVERVIEW

Smith's analysis of government in *WN* Book V is framed by his four stages, but his primary focus is on the various roles he believes government should play in the last, commercial stage. These roles are distinguished in his analysis by the method of their provision and financing:

- Do they require public provision and government expenditure to insure provision?
- Do they require public provision, but can be self-financing? or,
- Can they be provided indirectly by an alignment of incentives generated by government regulations or tax policy?

In all cases, Smith emphasizes that these roles should be carried out in a way that represents good, efficient government, because this not only minimizes the cost of government, it also enhances the probability that citizens will value and be committed to their government. As we will see, this commitment by citizens is crucial to Smith's vision of a constructive liberal order.

In Smith's view, a good and efficient government:

- taxes fairly, and with the least intrusion and cost possible,
- taxes in ways that align incentives constructively rather than destructively,
- spends frugally and only when necessary to provide services and infrastructure that are requisites for a healthy society and that would not otherwise be provided,

- taxes and spends for the benefit of the general citizenry, not for the benefit of a particular faction, and
- borrows responsibly.

Smith lays all of this out in a series of analyses covering:

- government provision,
- tax systems, and
- public debt.

What follows are selections from these analyses that represent the central points Smith makes about the role of government.

GOVERNMENT MUST PROVIDE FOR THE COMMON DEFENSE

Defense, according to Smith, is the "first duty" (*WN*, 689) of government, and how government carries out that duty changes with the evolution of humankind through stages.

In the rude state, there is no government. Every man, as a hunter, is prepared for war, and all fight together when necessity requires that the tribe be defended. In the age of pasturage, practicing the arts of war is a constant entertainment for all and the sustenance for all is afoot with them, so all are prepared and provisioned at no expense to the sovereign in the event of a conflict. In the agricultural stage, practicing the arts of war is still a leisure pastime and every warrior can sustain himself from the fruits of his own fields. Only if the combat comes during planting or harvesting do the warriors need support for their lost labor in the fields. During the rest of the year, the major work is done by nature.[1]

Thus, in the first three stages of humankind's evolution, the expense of war borne by the sovereign is nothing or not very great. This burden remains light into the early commercial stage because the initial model for military organization in commercial society is that carried over and adapted from earlier stages, a militia. Under this model, "the trade of a soldier was not a separate, distinct trade, which constituted the sole or principal occupation of a particular class of citizens" (*WN*, 696–7). Every soldier has a productive occupation and needs public support only when called upon to serve in a conflict, so the burden on the sovereign is limited to these exigencies.

---

[1] "Without the intervention of . . . labour ["after seed-time"], nature does herself the greater part of the work which remains to be done" (*WN*, 694–5).

However, hand in hand with advancements in the arts of production in commercial societies come two dynamics that undermine this militia model of defense:

- advancements in the art of war, and
- a general neglect among the population of the art of war:

A shepherd has a great deal of leisure; a husbandman ... has some; an artificer or manufacturer has none at all. The first may, without any loss, employ a great deal of his time in martial exercises; the second may employ some part of it; but the last cannot employ a single hour in them without some loss, and his attention to his own interest naturally leads him to neglect them altogether ... [U]nless the state takes some new measures for the publick defence, the natural habits of the people render them altogether incapable of defending themselves. (*WN*, 697–8)

Ironically, the very commercial dynamic that leads to the erosion of this militia model of defense also makes these nations more inviting targets: "That wealth ... which always follows the improvements of agriculture and manufacturers ... provokes the invasion of all of their neighbours" (*WN*, 697).

Advancement brings challenges, but it also provides a solution through the very process that makes advancement possible, the division of labor:

The art of war ... as it is certainly the noblest of all arts, so in the progress of improvement it necessarily becomes one of the most complicated among them. ... [I]t is necessary[, therefore,] that it should become the sole or principal occupation of a particular class of citizens ... the division of labour is as necessary of the improvement of this, as of ever other art. (*WN*, 697)

This division of labor does not occur naturally, however, because soldiering is a public good:

Into other arts the division of labour is naturally introduced by the prudence of individuals, who find that they promote their private interest better by confining themselves to a particular trade, than by exercising a great number. But it is the wisdom of the state only which can render the trade of a soldier a particular trade separate and distinct from all others. A private citizen who, in time of profound peace, and without any particular encouragement from the publick, should spend the greater part of his time in military exercises ... certainly would not promote his own interest. It is the wisdom of the state only which can render it for his interest to give up the greater part of his time to this particular occupation. (*WN*, 697)

This analysis brings Smith to a longstanding eighteenth century British policy debate regarding the appropriate model for the defense of the nation: a militia versus a standing army.[2] The "essential difference between those two different species of military force" (*WN*, 698) turns, according to Smith, on his division of labor logic.

The character of the soldiers in a militia is determined by their primary job, which is not soldiering. In contrast, soldiering is the soldiers' primary job in a standing army and it defines their character. Smith goes on to make the case that the transformation of the technology of warfare, in particular "the invention of fire-arms" (*WN*, 699), makes strong soldiering characteristics ("habits of regularity, order, and prompt obedience to command" (*WN*, 699)) essential for a modern army to be successful. Those characteristics "can only be acquired... by troops which are exercised in great bodies [as in a standing army.][3] ... A militia [doesn't instill these characteristics and so it]...must always be much inferior to a well-disciplined and well-exercised standing army" (*WN*, 699).[4]

Here, as always, his analysis is evolutionary. Militias were fine when combat was done with swords and spears, but with the invention of firearms the nature of warfare was transformed and so, too, a nation's military force must be if it is to be competitive on the field of battle. On those old battlefields, individual dexterity was at a premium, but on a "modern [battlefield characterized by] ... the noise of fire-arms, the smoke, and the invisible death to which every man feels himself every moment exposed" (*WN*, 699), the premium on individual dexterity is replaced by a premium on "regularity, order, and prompt obedience" (*WN*, 699).

In keeping with Smith's natural selection/evolution/limit story, the societies that are most capable of taking advantage of this evolution in warfare by establishing such standing armies are those advanced commercial societies that have the technological sophistication to produce the most modern weaponry and that have the productivity to support a

---

[2] See (*WN*, 700, fn 31) for references to Smith's correspondence related to the militia question.

[3] "The soldiers, who are bound to obey their officer only once a week or once a month, and who are at all other times at liberty to manage their own affairs their own way ... can never be under the same awe in his presence, can never have the same disposition to ready obedience, with those whose whole life and conduct are every day directed by him...." (*WN*, 700). Some militias, like those of the Tartar, approach the standing army model more closely than others, like the Highlanders. Those more like the standing army are more formidable.

[4] Smith notes that if a militia stays in the field for any length of time, it may develop the characteristics of a standing army, and he continues: "Should the war in America drag out through another campaign, the American militia may become in every respect a match for that [valorous] standing army" of Britain (*WN*, 701).

division of labor that includes the unproductive labor of professional soldiers. Therefore, *ceteris paribus*, natural selection favors such advanced states. It does not, however, assure the perpetuation of such states because "states have not always had this wisdom [to support a standing army], even when their circumstances had become such, that the preservation of their existence required that they should have it" (*WN*, 697).

This assertion brings us to Smith the policy advocate. He argues that it is essential for the government of an advanced commercial society to maintain a standing army.

[A] well-regulated standing army is superior to every militia... [and] can best be maintained by [such] an opulent and civilized nation... It is[, furthermore,] only by means of a standing army... that the civilization of any country can be perpetuated, or even preserved for any considerable time. (*WN*, 705–6)[5]

Smith fully appreciates the republican fears that a standing army would be a threat to the very state it defends and to individual freedom:[6]

Men of republican principles have been jealous of a standing army as dangerous to liberty. It certainly is so, whenever the interest of the general and that of the principal officers are not necessarily connected with the support of the constitution of the state. [He cites Caesar and Cromwell as examples.]... But... where

---

[5] With respect to Greece and Rome: "Smith presents the causes of decline in terms of military weakness which is itself a function of economic growth. This suggests that more advanced societies are likely to be overwhelmed by the more primative...." (Skinner, 1979, 77). Their weakness was, indeed, related to economic growth, but not an inevitable function of it – rather it was a function of the system of military preparedness (or lack thereof) that depended on citizens in a commercial world to be volunteers: "[W]henever luxury comes in after commerce and arts, nothing but the most urgent necessity...could now induce men to leave their business and engage in war as a common soldier. The only people who could go out to war in this state would be the very lowest and worthlesest of the people. And these too could never be trusted, nor would engage in any services with spirit, unless formed into what we call a standing army and brought under military discipline" (*LJA*, 232). Skinner notes that comparing Greece and Rome with modern commercial society: "while there are important parallels to be found in the discussion of military problems, there are equally significant contrasts. The parallel... [relates to] a decline in the proportion of the population which is available for war, as well as in martial spirit.... [The difference lay in part in the] developing technology of warfare which, Smith believed, would help preserve modern society from the threat posed by more primitive peoples...." (Skinner, 1979, 89–90). "[E]conomic progress brings about the dissolution of the republics of antiquity, but this is due, or partly due, to the absence of standing armies" (Forbes, 199).

[6] Recall the image he uses as a criticism of the mercantile interests: "[L]ike an overgrown standing army, they have become formidable to the government, and upon many occasions intimidate the legislature" (*WN*, 471).

the military force is placed under the command of those who have the greatest interest in the support of civil society . . . a standing army can never be dangerous to liberty.[7] On the contrary, it may in some cases be favorable to liberty. . . . That degree of liberty which approaches to licentiousness can be tolerated only in countries where the sovereign is secured by a well-regulated standing army.[8] It is in such countries, only, that the publick safety does not require, that the sovereign should be trusted with any discretionary power for suppressing even the impertinent wantonness of this licentious liberty[9]. (*WN*, 706–7)

Smith advocates for a standing army for the sake of liberal society. But while security from external threats and from internal insurrection is a necessary function of government in a liberal system, it is not sufficient for that system to flourish. Government must also establish justice if liberty is to be secure for every citizen.

GOVERNMENT MUST ESTABLISH THE EXACT ADMINISTRATION OF JUSTICE

The second duty of the sovereign, that of protecting, as far as possible, every member of society from the injustice or oppression of every other member of it, or the duty of establishing an exact administration of justice, requires too very different degrees of expence in the different periods of society. (*WN*, 708–9)

The continuity of Smith's thought as his analysis moves from defense to justice is striking. Both focus on security. In both cases, the analysis is framed by the evolution of society through the "different periods." In both cases, with that evolution comes added complexity and, in turn, added expense for security.

A world without property lacks one of the major motives for interpersonal injury: gain. In contrast, where property exists, "[t]he benefit of the

---

[7] One of the advantages of history that England enjoys is that "a system of liberty has been established in England before the standing army was introduced; which as it was not the case in other countries, so it has never been established in them" (*LJA*, 269).

[8] Where public authority is fragile, "the whole authority of the government must be employed to suppress and punish every murmur and complaint against it" (*WN*, 707).

[9] Smith's reference to "the impertinent wantonness of licentious liberty" reflects a valuing of diversity in liberal society that John Stuart Mill expresses also: "No society in which eccentricity is a matter of reproach, can be in a wholesome state. . . . [The] multiform development of human nature, those manifold unlikenesses, that diversity of tastes and talents, and variety of intellectual points of view, which not only form a great part of the interest of human life, but by bringing intellects into stimulating collision, and by presenting to each innumerable notions that he would not have conceived of himself, are the mainspring of mental and moral progression" (Mill, 211).

person who does the injury is often equal to the loss of him who suffers it" (*WN*, 709). A thief, for example, enjoys the fruits of his injustice. Such injustices driven by passions for property "are much more steady in their operation, and much more universal in their influence [than other motives for injustice]. . . . The acquisition of valuable and extensive property, therefore, necessarily requires the establishment of civil government" (*WN*, 709–10).

In the rude state where there is insignificant property, there is no need for civil government, but with the evolution from hunting to pasturage, property wealth emerges. With the evolution from pasturage to agriculture, property wealth increases. And finally, with the evolution from agriculture to commercial society, property wealth reaches its greatest height. This expanding property must be protected and secured if each of the steps in the progress of opulence is to be sustained. Thus, the progress of opulence requires the emergence and maturation of civil government in order to insure the security of property and person through the administration of justice.

Smith's policy prescription for the proper administration of justice is based on the contours of natural jurisprudence that he culls from his analysis of the evolution of civil government. Chapter Three describes the story he tells in his *Lectures on Jurisprudence* of this evolution in England and the principles he culls from that history. The story he tells and the principles he cites in *WN* Book V (*WN*, 715–18) are essentially a brief review of that earlier presentation.

The central theme of the analysis Smith presents in *WN* Book V is that for the administration of justice to be consistent with a liberal system it must be impartial, and for that to be so the judicial system must be independent. Justice can only be securely independent, according to Smith, where judicial tenure and compensation are not dependent on the executive:

When the judicial is united to the executive power, it is scarce possible that justice should not frequently be sacrificed to, what is vulgarly called, politics. The persons entrusted with the great interests of the state may, even without any corrupt views, sometimes imagine it necessary to sacrifice to those interests the rights of a private man. But upon the impartial administration of justice depends the liberty of every individual, the sense which he has of his own security. In order to make every individual feel himself perfectly secure in the possession of every right which belongs to him, it is not only necessary that the judicial should be separated from the executive power, but that it should be rendered as much as possible independent of that power. The judge should not be liable to be removed from his office according to the caprice of that power. The regular payment of his salary should not depend upon the good-will, or even upon the good economy of that power. (*WN*, 722–3)[10]

Defense, justice – these first two duties of the sovereign are about security.

In the story Smith tells, security is not a birthright of humankind. Indeed, for most of humankind's history individuals have been very insecure. Where they exist, institutions that provide security are a dimension of human arrangements that have evolved across many generations of societal experiments. As we saw in Chapter Three, that evolution is driven by chance, circumstance, and the unintended and intended consequences of human actions.

The progress of this process, the movement toward institutional arrangements that allow "every individual [to] feel himself perfectly secure" in turn enhances the possibilities for material progress because, as we've seen, the more secure individuals feel the more they invest in bettering their condition.

Smith constantly reminds us that government is a very significant dimension of an evolving simultaneous institutional system.

GOVERNMENT SHOULD PROMOTE THE GENERAL WELFARE

[I]nstitutions which tend to promote the public welfare ... [t]he perfection of police,[11] the extension of trade and manufactures, are noble and magnificent objects. ... They make part of the great system of government. ... (*TMS*, 185)

In addition to those works and institutions that provide security from external and internal threats, Smith believes that it is incumbent upon

---

[10] Smith makes a similar point in his *Lectures on Rhetoric and Belles Lettres (LRBL)*: "This Separation of the province of distributing Justice between man and man from that of conducting publick affairs and leading Armies is the great advantage which modern times have over antient, and the foundation of that greater Security which we now enjoy both with regard to Liberty, property and Life. It was introduced only by chance and to ease the Supreme magistrate of this most Laborious and least Glorious part of his Power, and has never taken place until the increase of Refinement and the Growth of Society have multiplied business immensely" (*LRBL*, 176).

[11] Referring to "Smith's lectures of 1762–63," Pocock writes that "in observing that the word 'police' was so new that the English language had to borrow it from the French, he was indicating that this subject was historically recent. ... But the French 'police' was enlarging its meaning from that of government of large capital cities to that of ensuring that the produce of the countryside was conveyed into towns; and it was this crucial activity that *The Wealth of Nations* indicated was better left to civil society than transacted by the state" (Pocock, 1999, 321). "Police" is certainly a concept that becomes central to Smith, but it is more textured in Smith's hands than this laissez-faire suggestion.

government to provide those works and institutions that are necessary to unleash human potential within that secure setting, but which would not be privately provided. These include public works and institutions related to commerce and education.

On Public Works and Institutions to Facilitate Commerce

As described in Chapter Six, Smith's analysis of the material progress of society represents that process as based on circuits of capital. In the nascent state, a small capital stock supports a simple division of labor generating surpluses that can be vented in a small trading area. With each circuit, however, the accumulation grows. This accumulation can support an ever-finer division of labor, but the division of labor is limited by the extent of the market. In Smith's analysis, therefore, the progress of opulence is contingent on access to an ever more extensive market. So, in order for this human progress to unfold, avenues for extending trade must either exist naturally or they must be developed.

Smith takes the need for public provision of market access infrastructure ("roads, bridges, navigable canals, harbours, &c." (*WN*, 724)) as a given: It "is evident without any proof" (*WN*, 724) that the progress of a society requires "publick works which facilitate the commerce" (*WN*, 724). The challenge, according to Smith, is to determine the optimal system for financing these public works. His rule of thumb for determining the optimal method of finance is to trace the impact and the incentives, always asking: How does a particular financing scheme affect the consumers, the producers, the administrators, and the financiers? Who benefits? Who bears the burden? Is this outcome just? Are the incentives properly aligned to achieve the socially desirable outcome most efficiently and effectively?

The best case for financing, according to Smith, is user fees that cover the cost of constructing and maintaining these public works. If properly imposed "[i]t seems scarce possible to invent a more equitable way of maintaining such works" (*WN*, 725). The burden of these fees falls on the ultimate beneficiary, the consumer, and the net effect is positive because "the cheapness of the carriage" lowers the price much more than the fees raise it. However, such fees are not always possible. So what are the alternative methods of financing?

As he examines alternatives, Smith keeps a keen eye on the alignment of incentives generated by the schemes he examines or proposes. Here and always, alignment of incentives plays a central role in Smith's analysis of government policy.

For example, when examining alternative ways the government can provide avenues for trade, he distinguishes those that require constant maintenance – canals – from those that continue to be passable with minimal maintenance – high roads. The best way to insure proper maintenance for the former is to put the toll revenue into the hands of a private person because this person's well-being will depend on traffic and thus he will have a keen interest in maintenance to keep the canal passable. In contrast, a high road does not need such constant care, so in the hands of a private person it might be neglected while that person simply collects the tolls. Thus, it is seems that high roads would be better managed by a public commission of trustees under the watchful eye of parliament. But, he continues, be careful to follow the alignment of incentives to the end of the story. If, as suggested, the high road fees are to go to the government, it is essential that those fees be directed to a dedicated fund for maintaining the works that generate them. Allowing such fees to become a resource for the general budget invites abuse because the state will constantly look to those fees as a source of funds for other activities.

Smith's commentary on public works expands almost fourfold in the revision to the *WN* published in 1784.[12] Why?

He had long understood that government has the power to align incentives, and that sometimes this was done wisely and sometimes foolishly. But, as we've seen in Chapter Eight, what he came to appreciate more and more was that this power of government to align incentives gives interested factions the incentive to align government . . . to their advantage.

In his 1784 addition to *WN* Book V on *"Publick Works and Institutions which are necessary for facilitating particular Branches of Commerce"* (*WN*, 731), Smith notes that although there are, on occasion, good reasons to give particular companies special powers for a limited period of time (e.g., protection for nascent industries), invariably and unfortunately these advantages have been protected and maintained and even expanded at the encouragement of the private interests that have enjoyed the benefits of the advantages. This has, all too often, led to monopoly advantages, with very perverse consequences.[13] He cites as an example the British experience with the joint-stock companies that were established

---

[12] In a letter to his publisher William Strahan (22 May 1783), Smith describes this new section as "A short History and, I presume, a full exposition of the Absurdity and hurtfulness of almost all our chartered trading companies" (*Correspondence*, 266).

[13] Smith writes that: "It is found that society must be pretty far advanced before the different trades can all find subsistence. . . . To bring about therefore the separation of trades sooner than the progress of society would naturally effect . . . it was found necessary to give them a certainty of a comfortable subsistence. And for this purpose the legislature determined that they should have the privilege of exercising their separate trades without fear of

by the government with grants of limited individual liability in order to encourage disparate individuals to amass large capitals for big projects.

This total exemption from trouble and risk, beyond a limited sum, encourages many people to become adventurers in joint stock companies, who would, upon no account, hazard their fortunes in any private copartnery. Such companies, therefore, commonly draw to themselves much greater stocks than any private copartnery can boast of. (*WN*, 741)

Since individuals can enter and exit the joint stock enterprise quickly by buying or selling stock, the company is "managed by a court of directors" (*WN*, 741). This, according to Smith, leads to an agency problem. The incentive for careful management when the money is that of others is less keen, so "[n]egligence and profusion" are common in joint stock companies (*WN*, 741). As a consequence, they seldom prevail in competition with privately held companies "without an exclusive privilege; and frequently have not succeeded with one" (*WN* 741).

Smith cites the East India Company as a classic example. A conflict over the Company's charter rights (king and parliament each issued rights) led to a fierce competition that the Company bemoaned. Smith's comment on this says it all:

The miserable effects of which the company complained, were the cheapness of consumption and the encouragement given to production, precisely the two effects which it is the great business of political economy to promote. The competition, however, of which they gave this doleful account, had not been allowed to be of long continuance. (*WN*, 748)

In 1773, "[t]he distress which . . . accumulated claims brought upon them, obliged them . . . to throw themselves upon the mercy of the government" (*WN*, 751). Parliament made "alterations" (*WN*, 752) in the governing structure of the company to achieve better management, "[b]ut [,Smith concludes,] it seems impossible, by any alterations, to render those courts [of company directors], in any respect, fit to govern" (*WN*, 752). Caring only about their own pockets, he describes the appointees to these courts as "plunderers of India" (*WN*, 752).

No other sovereigns ever were, or, from the nature of things, ever could be, so perfectly indifferent about the happiness or misery of their subjects, the improvement

---

being cut out of their livelihood by the increase of their rivalls. That this was necessary therefore in the 1st stages of the arts to bring them to their proper perfection, appears very reasonable and is confirmed by this, that it has been the generall practise of all the nations in Europe. But as this end is now fully answered, it were much to be wished that these as well as many other remains of the old jurisprudence should be removed" (*LJA*, 86).

or waste of their dominions, the glory or disgrace of their administration; as, from irresistible moral causes, the greater part of the proprietors of such a mercantile company are, and necessarily must be. (*WN*, 752)

As described here in Chapter Three, the incentives were all aligned for short-term gain at the expense of long-term development. The inevitable outcome of these mercantile colonial policies in India that resisted competition and exploited subjects was failure, followed by pleading to the government for help: "[T]he company is now (1784) in greater distress than ever; and, in order to prevent immediate bankruptcy, is once more reduced to supplicate the assistance of government" (*WN*, 753).

Free competition is, as Smith describes it, "a species of warfare . . . [that, given] occasional variations in the demand . . . [and] much greater and more frequent variations in the competition . . . [requires] dexterity and judgment . . . [and] unremitting exertion of vigilance and attention. . . . " (*WN*, 755). Insulated from this warfare by monopoly, a joint stock company can survive for a while, but even this does not allow it to succeed over the long term. The very monopoly that makes its existence possible, by eliminating the discipline of competition, makes inefficiency and decline inevitable.

The lesson, Smith asserts, is clear. Mercantile proposals must be "listened to with great precaution, and ought never to be adopted till after having been long and carefully examined, not only with the most scrupulous, but with the most suspicious attention" (*WN*, 267).

Scrupulous policy to facilitate commerce is one way government can promote the general welfare. Facilitating education is another.

On Public Works and Institutions to Facilitate Education

"[I]n the barbarous societies, as they are commonly called, of hunters, of shepherds, and even [in an agricultural society] of husbandmen" (*WN*, 782), the division of labor is not so fine, and therefore each person must possess many skills to meet his needs. In learning and exercising these many skills, the mind is challenged and developed.[14]

---

[14] "The common ploughman, though generally regarded as the pattern of stupidity and ignorance, is seldom defective in his judgment and discretion. He is less accustomed, indeed to social intercourse than the mechanick who lives in a town. His voice and language are more uncouth and more difficult to be understood by those who are not used to them. His understanding, however, being accustomed to consider a greater variety of objects, is generally much superior to that of the other, whose whole attention from morning till night is commonly occupied in performing one or two very simple operations.

"In a civilized state, on the contrary, though there is little variety in the occupations of the greater part of individuals, there is an almost infinite variety in those of the whole society" (*WN*, 783). As a consequence, "great abilities ... [are developed in a] few ... [while] all the nobler parts of the human character may be, in a great measure, obliterated and extinguished in the great body of the people" (*WN*, 783–4). If this is a prospect for the masses in an advanced society,

> Ought the publick ... give no attention, it may be asked, to the education of the people? Or if it ought to give any, what are the different parts of education which it ought to attend to in the different orders of the people? and in what manner ought it attend to them? (*WN*, 781)

Smith's answer to the first question is: Yes, the government ought to play a role. When the division of labor that comes with humankind's advancement reaches that degree of refinement which is present in an advanced commercial society, it is essential, for both the private and public good, that government provide education to those perversely affected by that refinement.

> In the progress of the division of labour, the employment of the far greater part of those who live by labour ... comes to be confined to a few very simple operations. ... But the understandings of the greater part of men are necessarily formed by their ordinary employments. The man whose whole life is spent in performing a few simple operations ... has no occasion to exert his understanding, or to exercise his invention. ... He naturally looses, therefore, the habit of such exertion, and generally becomes as stupid and ignorant as it is possible for a human creature to become. ... [He is] incapable of ... bearing a part of any rational conversation ... of conceiving any generous, noble, or tender sentiment, ... of forming any just judgment ... [on the] duties of private life ... [or the] extensive interests of his country, [and] he is ... incapable of defending his country in war. ... [I]n every improved and civilized society this is the state into which the labouring poor, that is, the great body of the people, must necessarily fall, *unless government takes some pains to prevent it.* (*WN*, 781–2, emphasis added)

Thus, the provision of public education to "the far greater part of those who live by labour" is a public good:

> The state ... derives no inconsiderable advantage from their instruction. The more they are instructed, the less liable they are to the delusions of enthusiasm and superstition, which, among ignorant nations, frequently occasion the most dreadful disorders. An instructed and intelligent people besides are always more decent

> How much the lower ranks of people in the country are really superior to those of the town, is well known to every man whom either business or curiosity has led to converse much with both" (*WN*, 143–4).

and orderly than an ignorant and stupid one. . . . They are more disposed to examine, and more capable of seeing through, the interested complaints of faction and sedition, and they are, upon that account, less apt to be misled into any wanton or unnecessary opposition to the measures of government. In free countries, where the safety of government depends very much upon the favourable judgment which the people may form of its conduct, it must surely be of the highest importance that they should not be disposed to judge rashly or capriciously concerning it. (*WN*, 788)

Just at the safety of the people depends on the performance of the government with respect to defense and justice, so too, at least "[i]n free countries, . . . the safety of government depends very much upon the favourable judgment which the people may form of its conduct." Government can nurture this favorable judgment by exercising its power prudently and by empowering its citizens, through education, to assess its performance thoughtfully.

Smith has made his case for education, but why is public provision necessary? Because "[t]he most essential parts of education . . . to read, write, and account" (*WN*, 785) are beyond the means of "the common people" (*WN*, 784) who live from hand to mouth and must send their kids to work early in life to support the family. These essentials of education can and must be offered to the poor "[f]or a very small expence [to] the publick. . . . " (*WN*, 785).

The public good that comes from this education warrants this public expense. But to insure that incentives are aligned in the right general direction, Smith suggests that the public contribution to a child's education should not pay the full salary of the teacher. Some affordable portion should come from the student as a reward for the teacher's performance.[15]

This public provision is not necessary for those with greater means, but their children's education is no less important to the public. So in order to insure that every citizen does, indeed, master the basics, Smith suggests that "[t]he public can . . . oblig[e] every man to undergo an examination or probation in them [positions/trades] before he can obtain the freedom

---

[15] Smith spends many pages of *WN* Book V on the alignment of incentives in teaching – what works and what doesn't. For example, he argues that a system of salaries independent of performance is likely to lead to poor performance and this is all the more likely when the trustees of an endowment are themselves the teachers receiving the salaries. Such an incentive creates a collusion of apathy. This is the case he describes from his experience at Oxford: "In the university of Oxford, the greater part of the publick professors have, for these many years, given up altogether even the pretence of teaching" (*WN*, 761). On 24 August 1740, Smith wrote from Oxford to his cousin and guardian William Smith that "it will be his own fault if anyone should endanger his health at Oxford by excessive Study. . . . " (*Correspondence*, 1)

in any corporation, or be allowed to set up any trade either in a village or town corporate" (*WN*, 786).[16]

What Smith is proposing here is a screen on market access, the very kind of imposition that elsewhere he decries as illiberal. Again, we see that Smith is a man with a system, but is not a dogmatic "man of system." In this case, the screen is designed to secure a public good, an educated citizenry, not a private monopoly. But always wary of a perverse alignment of incentives, Smith is careful to design his plan such that the public and not the private good is served. Instead of a screen based on the educational inputs, a screen that could give monopoly advantages to those providers deemed acceptable, his screen is based on outcomes and thus is independent of the provider.

Indicative of his keen awareness of incentives, although Smith wants government to finance education for working class children, he is very much against government financing of that institution which provides the instruction of people of all ages: religion.

As described here in Chapter Four, Smith fears a government-established church as the republicans fear a standing army. He believes it is an institution that is a threat to individual liberty. The difference for Smith is that the standing army is essential for modern defense and can be placed under civilian control. In contrast, an established church plays no essential role in liberal society, and it is under no control except its own understanding of God's will.

ON REVENUE AND THE PROPER STRATEGIES FOR TAXATION

When policy requires public provision, Smith believes that simple justice suggests that, where possible, the beneficiary should bear the cost. This is also desirable for the sake of efficiency, because if the beneficiary bears the cost, he will hold the provider accountable for the quality of the provision relative to cost.[17] However, if what is provided is a public good, such as defense, justice, and education for children, then, according to Smith, the whole of the public should contribute to the provision, each "in proportion to their respective abilities" (*WN*, 814). This brings him to the issue of revenue and proper strategies for taxation.

---

[16] He returns to and expands on this scheme later (*WN*, 796).

[17] As Smith writes with respect to the church, "[t]he proper performance of every service seems to require that its pay . . . should be . . . proportioned to the nature of the service" (*WN*, 813).

Most government revenues, according to Smith, come from taxes on private revenues (wages, profit, or rent) or from taxes on consumption. Smith offers four general "maxims" (*WN*, 825) that should guide all taxation:[18]

- Taxes should be based on ability to pay. Those who "enjoy [more] under the protection of the state" (*WN*, 825) have a greater interest and thus should pay more.[19]
- Taxes "ought to be certain, and not arbitrary" (*WN*, 825). "[U]ncertainty of taxation encourages the insolence and favours the corruption" of tax collectors (*WN*, 826).
- Taxes should be levied with the convenience of the payer in mind.
- Taxes should be collected as efficiently as possible, so they are as light as the necessities of government allow and so that they distort market activity as little as possible. It follows, according to Smith, that government *should not*:
  - make tax collection unnecessarily expensive,
  - unnecessarily discourage commerce by the tax structure,
  - set taxes so high that they encourage perverse behavior (e.g., smuggling),
  - make tax collection an onerous experience for the payer,
  - farm out the collection of taxes.[20]

These maxims, Smith asserts, should guide tax policy because they achieve both "justice and utility" (*WN*, 827). Unfortunately, as he makes clear in many examples, tax policy has largely been a story of failure caused by governments following misguided principles and/or bending to self-serving pressures.

---

[18] Taxes are not inherently evil in Smith's analysis. Revenue is essential for government. What is evil is irresponsible taxation. He writes to Sir Grey Cooper on 2 June 1783: "I most sincerely congratulate you upon the new taxes, which are in every respect as happily devised as any thing I ever saw" (*Correspondence*, 266).

[19] Having made this assertion regarding distributive justice, he writes that "I shall seldom take much further notice of this inequality...." (*WN*, 825)

[20] "Even a bad sovereign feels more compassion for his people than can ever be expected from the farmers of his revenue. He knows that the permanent grandeur of this family depends upon the prosperity of his people, and he will never knowingly ruin that prosperity for the sake of a momentary interest of his own. It is otherwise with the farmers...." (*WN*, 903). This echoes his criticism of the East India Company as the governors of Bengal.

Taxing Rent and Interest

Smith cites the Physiocratic model for land rent as a plan based on misguided principles. "All taxes, they pretend, fall ultimately upon the rent of land" (*WN*, 830). But while he rejects their premise, Smith believes that taxing rents is just because rents represent unearned income and is efficient because it need not distort incentives. However, he notes, in this as in most cases, moving from principle to practice is a challenge.

The most obvious challenge involved in imposing and maintaining a rent tax is that the constant need to update the rent rolls and to estimate implicit rents leads to a very intrusive system, one prone to abuses of power by the agents who do the updates and the estimates. Making these measurement problems even more of a challenge is the fact that rent on improved land comes as a part of a joint revenue: rent and profit. The return to the land alone is the rent. The return to the improvements on the land is a profit. If these are confounded and all the return is treated as a rent and taxed as a rent, then "the sovereign, who contributed nothing to the expence . . . [of the improvements would] share[s] in the profit of the improvement" (*WN*, 833). This would discourage investment in such improvements to the detriment of society as a whole.

These problems notwithstanding, Smith basically likes the "variable land-tax" (*WN*, 833) because he believes it can be properly implemented, and if it were, its incidence would be on the monopoly return of the landlords, the rent. Since a tax on a monopoly return is no discouragement to improvement, it does not represent an "inconveniency to the landlord, except always the unavoidable one of being obliged to pay the tax" (*WN*, 834).

Similarly, ground rents (on the land under a building) are an excellent target for taxes. The entire burden of such a tax falls on the landowner "who acts always as a monopolist" (*WN*, 843), and since a consistent tax on a monopolistic return has no effect on incentives, "no discouragement will thereby be given to any sort of industry. The annual produce of the land and labour of the society, the real wealth and revenue of the great body of the people, might be the same after such a tax as before" (*WN*, 844). Furthermore, "[g]round-rents, so far as they exceed the ordinary rent of land, are altogether owing to the good government of the sovereign. . . . " (*WN*, 844). It is, after all, good government that "by giving both the most perfect security . . . ; and by procuring . . . the most extensive market" (*WN*, 833), makes the enjoyment of this rent possible.

Nothing can be more reasonable than that a fund which owes its existence to the good government of the state, should be taxed peculiarly, or should contribute something more than the greater part of other funds, towards the support of that government. (*WN*, 844)

Smith clearly believes that those who enjoy the benefits of the security provided by government should pay into the government that provides that security in proportion to those fruits which that security affords them.

His analysis then makes what seems like a natural transition from rent to interest. Because interest, "[l]ike rent on land," is a scarcity return and is not necessary "compensation . . . for the risk and trouble of employing the stock," it would seem to make sense to tax interest in the same manner as rent.

The interest on money seems at first sight a subject equally capable of being taxed directly as the rent on land. Like the rent of land, it is a neat produce which remains after compleatly compensating the whole risk and trouble of employing the stock. As a tax upon the rent of land cannot raise rents [because the farmer has no more to bid] . . . so, for the same reason, a tax upon interest of money could not raise the rate of interest; the quantity of stock or money in the country, like the quantity of land, being supposed to remain the same after the tax as before it. (*WN*, 847–8)

However, Smith recognizes that interest is, in fact, different because although interest is the same kind of return as rent, the commodities involved, liquid capital and land respectively, are very different.

Determining the amount of land an individual owns and the rent on that land is a manageable challenge according to Smith. Determining how much capital one holds and the interest he is earning on that capital is much more difficult. Furthermore, unlike land, liquid capital is mobile so, if treated harshly by the tax collector, it can flee the country:

The proprietor of stock is properly a citizen of the world, and is not necessarily attached to any particular country. He would be apt to abandon the country in which he was exposed to the vexatious inquisition, in order to be assessed to a burdensome tax, and would remove his stock to some other country where he could, either carry on his business, or enjoy his fortune more at ease. By removing his stock he would put an end to all the industry which it had maintained in the country which he left. Stock cultivates land; stock employs labour. A tax which tended to drive away stock from any particular country, would so far tend to dry up every source of revenue, both to the sovereign and to the society. (*WN*, 848–9)

Here, as always, Smith's policy analysis is grounded in reality. Taxing interest is just and could be fruitful, but it is not practical because capital is mobile and chasing it away is counterproductive. Smith does, however, note a case in which such a tax is successful.,

At Hamburgh . . . [e]very man assesses himself, and, in the presence of the magistrate, puts annually into the publick coffer a certain sum of money . . . without declaring what it amounts to, or being liable to any examination on the subject. This tax is generally supposed to be paid with great fidelity. In a small republick, where the people have entire confidence in their magistrates, are convinced of the necessity of the tax for the support of the state, and believe that it will be faithfully applied to that purpose, such conscientious and voluntary payment may sometimes be expected. (*WN*, 850)

This quotation is significant because it highlights Smith's view about the relationship between the citizen and the state in the civic enterprise. Citizens are much more likely to accept their responsibilities for acting according to civic ethics where they value and respect their government.

Taxing Wages and Consumables

Smith rejects taxes on wages. Unless the standard for subsistence is reduced, such a tax will cause a rise in wages. That rise will be more than proportional to the tax, because the incremental increase in wages to maintain subsistence will have to compensate both the tax on the base wage and the effect of that tax on the price of subsistence. These taxes, therefore, generally lead to "[t]he declension of industry, the decrease of employment for the poor, the diminution of the annual produce of the land and labour of the country . . . Absurd and destructive as such taxes are, however, they take place in many countries" (*WN*, 865).

In order to avoid the difficulties of taxing wages or other forms of revenue, some governments turn to taxing consumption as a proxy for what people earn. But, Smith asserts, simplistic versions of such a tax fail to take into account an important distinction:

Consumable commodities are either necessaries or luxuries. . . . By necessaries [, Smith writes,] I understand, not only the commodities which are indispensably necessary for the support of life, but whatever the custom of the country renders it indecent for creditable people, even the lowest order, to be without. (*WN*, 869–870)

His standard, then, for social subsistence, as opposed to "immediate subsistence" (*WN*, 691), is relative to "the established rules of decency" (*WN*, 870).[21] All beyond these necessities, he "call[s] luxuries, without

---

[21] He demonstrates the social relativity of this latter standard by contrasting the standards in England with those of France.

meaning by this appellation, to throw the smallest degree of reproach upon the temperate use of them" (*WN*, 870).[22]

"[A] tax on the necessaries of life, operates exactly in the same manner as a direct tax upon the wages of labour" (*WN*, 871) because the compensation of the laborer must, *ceteris paribus*, be sufficient to purchase those necessaries. Thus, for the same reasons he rejects a tax on wages, he rejects a tax on necessities.

"It is otherwise with taxes upon what I call luxuries; even upon those of the poor. The rise in the price of the taxed commodities, will not necessarily occasion any rise in the wages of labour" (*WN*, 871). And, always following the path of incentives, he notes that taxes on tobacco, tea, sugar, chocolate, and "spirituous liquors" (*WN*, 872) can "act as sumptuary laws, and dispose them [(the poor)] either to moderate, or to refrain altogether from the use of superfluities" (*WN*, 872).

Taxing Consumables and the Sad Story of Customs

Consumables may either be taxed once the consumer has them or while they are still in the hands of the dealer. More durable commodities, like a coach, are best taxed over time when in the hands of the consumer. Spreading out the burden this way creates less of an impediment to demand. With less durable commodities, on the other hand, it is generally better to get the tax from the dealer before delivery. This method leads to taxes that are more proportioned to use and more convenient.

Excise and customs are the most common ways to collect a tax from the dealer. Smith examines both of these, but his focus is on customs because of their important role in mercantile policies.[23]

Customs policy is supposed to provide revenue to the sovereign, but not so the customs policy of Great Britain, so strongly distorted by the mercantile interests:

The saying of Dr. Swift, that in the arithmetick of the customs two and two, instead of making four, make sometimes only one, holds perfectly true with regard to such heavy duties, which never could have been imposed, had not the mercantile system taught us, in many cases, to employ taxation as an instrument, not of revenue, but of monopoly. (*WN*, 882)

[22] Here, we hear the moral philosopher who values proper prudence giving room for indulgence so long as it is "temperate."

[23] It is likely that Smith wrote this section on customs, as with much of his Book IV critique of the mercantile system, in London between 1773 and 1775 as he was completing the *WN*. Indeed, in the course of his discussion here, he refers to "the year which ended on 5th of July 1775...." (*WN*, 888).

Mercantile customs policies not only reduce net tax revenue by discouraging trade and by diverting a portion of the gross revenue to drawbacks, they also undermined customs revenue by encouraging smuggling. Smuggling is, for Smith, a classic example of the consequence of a government policy that aligns incentives in a way that encourages destructive behaviors. Smith blames the government as much as the smuggler for the smuggler's destructive behavior.[24] The smuggler, he writes,

though no doubt highly blamable for violating the laws... would have been, in every respect, an excellent citizen, had not the laws of his country made that a crime which nature never meant to be so. In those corrupted governments where there is at least a general suspicion of much unnecessary expence, and a great misapplication of the publick revenue, the laws which guard it are little respected. (*WN*, 898)

Here, again, we hear Smith describing the relationship between the citizen and the state as a reciprocal obligation. If the state is to reasonably expect a commitment of the citizen to its laws, then the citizen has a right to reasonably expect that those laws are just and constructive, and are justly administered. Absent that relationship, the citizenry treats the laws scornfully and, as in the case of smuggling laws, the criminal often enjoys "the indulgence of the publick" (*WN*, 898).

Smith is not against customs per se, but a constructive customs system must be "an instrument of revenue and never of monopoly...[and] the duties of customs...[should exhibit] the same degree of simplicity, certainty, and precision, as those of excise" (*WN*, 885). So why hasn't such a system been adopted in Britain? Because policy is the subject of interested political participation and when that interested participation is skewed by factional power, the result is policy based on interest:

It was the object of the famous excise scheme of Sir Robert Walpole to establish...a system not very unlike that which is here proposed....But... [f]action, combined with the interest of smuggling merchants, raised so violent, though so unjust, a clamour against the bill, that the minister thought proper to drop it; and from a dread of exciting a clamour of the same kind, none of his successors have dared to resume the project. (*WN*, 886)[25]

---

[24] On 18 Dec. 1783, George Dempster writes to Smith for help with ideas to "prevent smuggling, which by all the Information we have received has come to an alarming height, threatening the destruction of the Revenue, the fair trader, the Health and moral of the People" (*Correspondence*, 273).

[25] Smith has obviously been thinking about this system for a while because references to Walpole's failed system can be found in his *Lectures on Jurisprudence* (*LJB*, 532).

Nevertheless, while "[o]ur state is not perfect, and might be mended;...it is as good or better than that of most of our neighbours" (*WN*, 899).[26] Indeed, the "freedom of interior commerce, the effect of the uniformity of the system of taxation, is perhaps one of the principal causes of the prosperity of Great Britain" (*WN*, 900). So, notwithstanding the absurd policies with respect to colonial and international trade, good tax policy within the most productive circuit of trade, the domestic circuit, has helped make it possible for Britain to prosper.

ON PUBLIC DEBT, THE GOLDEN DREAM OF EMPIRE, AND A UTOPIAN VISION

Britain is doing well but it is "not perfect, and might be mended" (*WN*, 899). Among those public ills that the mercantile policies have imposed on Britain, one of the most deadly, according to Smith, is the huge increase in the public debt incurred in the wars fought to preserve the mercantile advantages.

In the closing pages of *The Wealth of Nations*, Smith explores the reason debt so often becomes a common public policy tool as nations advance, and how mercantile policies have led Britain down this perilous path. He concludes with a utopian vision – a policy prescription as if interested factions wouldn't get in the way. Apropos of the civic humanist voice that, as described in Chapter Eight, he adopts as he gets older, it is a policy that would take the noble leadership of a statesman such as Solon to implement.

Smith's story of public debt begins, as so many of his stories do, in an earlier time, an earlier stage of humankind's evolution.

A Brief Background on the Emergence of Public Debt

As Smith tells the story, with little on which to spend except retainers and with "violence and disorder" (*WN*, 908) abounding, feudal lords initially had a strong incentive to hoard treasure. However, as we've seen in Chapter Seven, all this changed with the coming of commerce and the opportunity for conspicuous consumption. Sovereigns no longer saved.

---

[26] He contrasts the British system with that of France. In France, there is an army of officers to enforce this system at the international border as well as at every provincial border. This latter detachment is necessitated by the fact that tax schemes are not uniform across provinces. These many tax schemes enforced by many officers are "restraints upon the interior commerce of the country...." (*WN*, 901).

This "want of parsimony in time of peace, imposes the necessity of con-tracting debt in time of war" (*WN*, 909). In Europe, war became endemic as nations emerged and pursued mercantile policies aimed at vanquishing others in the competition for markets.[27] However,

[t]he same commercial society which . . . brings along with it the necessity of bor-rowing, produces in the subjects both the ability and an inclination to lend. (*WN*, 910)

The fruits of mercantile policies line the pockets of the merchants and give those merchants the means to provide for the financial need of the government when the wars caused by those policies dictate such a need. In Britain, the government incurs debt as it spends to protect its colonial empire for the mercantile interests, and those interests benefit from lending to the government to cover that debt. Smith describes this symbiosis (*WN*, 910) and notes that "[t]he merchant or monied man makes money by lending money to the government, and instead of diminishing, increases his trading capital" (*WN*, 910–11).

Secure in the knowledge that it can borrow as needed, the state "there-fore dispenses itself from the duty of saving. . . . The progress of the enor-mous debts which at present oppress, and will in the long-run probably ruin, all the great nations of Europe, has been pretty uniform" (*WN*, 911).

The Story of Great Britain's Debt and the Role of the Mercantile Interests

As Smith tells the story, British borrowing beyond the means of repayment meant that borrowing became a successive game of catch up with old loans. Over time it became impossible to repay the principle, so only the interest was covered. This "necessarily gave birth to the more ruinous practice of perpetual borrowing" (*WN*, 915) and short-term solutions:

To relieve the present exigency is always the object which principally interests those immediately concerned in the administration of publick affairs. The future liberation of the publick revenue, they leave to the care of posterity. (*WN*, 915)

Since peacetime budgets tend to use up available revenue, when war comes, the sudden surge in expenditure is well beyond the current rev-enue. Borrowing allows the government to acquire the funds it needs

---

[27] J. M. Keynes makes precisely this point in Section IV of his *General Theory*: "Concluding Notes on the Social Philosophy toward which the General Theory Might Lead" (Keynes, 1964, 381).

without a sudden, large increase in taxes. If the war is remote, then for the people, who feel no real sacrifice, the war simply becomes a fascinating "amusement" (*WN*, 920).

Smith asserts that in peacetime and even at the outset of war, government should finance itself on a pay as you go basis with taxes. Doing so diminishes the negative impact on capital accumulation.[28] Furthermore, under such a system of finance "[w]ars would in general be more speedily concluded, and less wantonly undertaken" (*WN*, 926) because, bearing the full and immediate burden or the prospect thereof, the tolerance of the people for the undertaking would be very closely associated with their perception of its necessity.

Responding to the popular assertion that the interest paid financing a public debt is not a national problem because, in effect, "it is the right hand which pays the left. . . . [Smith writes that t]his apology is founded altogether in the sophistry of the mercantile system. . . . " (*WN*, 926–7). There are, he argues, two problems with this logic. First, we often do borrow from and thus pay the interest to foreigners (e.g., "the Dutch" (*WN*, 927)). Second, in order to pay the debt, we must tax ourselves, which means fewer funds for capital improvements or circulation: "The industry of the country will necessarily fall with the removal of the capital which supported it, and the ruin of trade and manufacturers will follow the declension of agriculture" (*WN*, 927–8). It is for these reasons that "[t]he practice of funding has gradually enfeebled every state which has adopted it" (*WN*, 928).

He cites a litany of examples (e.g., "France, notwithstanding all its natural resources, languishes under an oppressive load" of debt. (*WN*, 928)) and asks rhetorically: Is there any reason to believe the experience of Britain will be different?

The system in Britain is, he asserts, more "just and equitable" (*WN*, 834) than others, and people operating in a just and equitable system can overcome innumerable obstacles. However, he wonders, when our debt pushes us to find more revenue, will the wisdom of our system be sustained? Can the success we have enjoyed in the face of our own fiscal foolishness continue?

At some point, he suggests, a nation's debt can become so large that it simply cannot be paid. When that happens, nations resort to bankruptcy or

---

[28] Recall that funds borrowed by the government for military expeditions are not funds committed to the circuit of production; they are spent on unproductive labor and, thus, they are not "capital" in Smith's analysis.

degrade their currency to cover the nominal obligations either by "direct raising of the denomination of the coin, . . . [or by t]he adulteration of the standard. . . . " (*WN*, 932). Smith refers to degrading the currency as "real publick bankruptcy . . . disguised under the appearance of pretended payment . . . , and the creditors of the publick would really be defrauded" (*WN*, 929–30). The cascading effect of such a fraud becomes a disaster for the economy. Better the state should declare its bankruptcy than disguise it with this "juggling trick" (*WN*, 930).

As he writes for this 1776 publication, the current British debt is so significant that it can only be addressed by "either some very considerable augmentation of the publick revenue, or some equally considerable reduction of the publick expence" (*WN*, 933). He cites several possibilities, but focuses on what he believes would be the most productive way to augment the national tax revenue: "[E]xtending the British system of taxation to all the different provinces of the empire inhabited by people of either British or European extraction. . . . " (*WN*, 933). He notes, however, that if this is to be consistent "with the principles of the British constitution" then each of these provinces must enjoy representation in parliament in "proportion to the produce of its taxes. . . . " (*WN*, 933).

While he appreciates that this is a very unlikely prospect given "[t]he private interests of many powerful individuals, [and] the confirmed prejudices of great bodies of people. . . . " (*WN*, 933–4), nevertheless, "in a speculative work of this kind" (*WN*, 934) it seems reasonable, he asserts, to imagine how such a system would play out. "Such a speculation can at worst be regarded but as a new Utopia" (*WN*, 934), and since there was no harm in imagining the old one, he proceeds to imagine this new one.

A Utopian Vision

The extension of the custom-house laws of Great Britain to Ireland and the plantations, provided it was accompanied, as in justice it ought to be, with and extension of the freedom of trade, would be in the highest degree advantageous to both. . . . The trade between all the different parts of the British empire would . . . be as free as the coasting trade of Great Britain is at present. The British empire would thus afford within itself am immense internal market for every part of the produce of all its different provinces. (*WN*, 935)

Smith calculates, admittedly grossly, the fiscal impact of the union he envisions by estimating the additional revenue as well as the additional

costs associated with the union.[29] Given his caveat that this is speculation,[30] he estimates that if the union were to unfold as he envisions, the
public debt might be retired and the empire reinvigorated. Further, the
enhanced revenue from these equally apportioned just taxes would make
it possible that:

> people might be relieved from some of the most burdensome taxes; from those
> which are imposed wither upon the necessaries of life, or upon the materials
> of manufacture. The labouring poor would thus be enabled to live better, to
> work cheaper, and to send their goods cheaper to market. The cheapness of their
> goods would increase the demand for them, and consequently for the labour of
> those who produce them. This increase in the demand for labour, would both
> increase the numbers and improve the circumstances of the labouring poor.
> (*WN*, 938)

Smith recognizes that the benefits he describes, which are focused, as is
his constant concern, on the "labouring poor," would not be immediate.
But he believes that the prospect of the policy he advocates is better for
and fairer to Ireland and to the British colonies in America, and better
for and fairer to the mother country:

> It is not contrary to justice that both Ireland and America should contribute to-
> wards the discharge of the publick debt of Great Britain. That debt has been
> contracted in support of the government established by the Revolution, a gov-
> ernment to which the protestants of Ireland owe, not only the whole authority
> which they at present enjoy in their own country, but every security which they
> possess for their liberty, their property, and their religion; a government to which
> several of the colonies of America owe their present charters, and consequently
> their present constitution, and to which all the colonies of America owe the liberty,
> security, and property which they have ever since enjoyed. That publick debt has
> been contracted in the defence, not of Great Britain alone, but of all the different
> provinces of the empire. . . . (*WN*, 944)

Turing to the Irish case in particular, Smith argues that Ireland would
not only gain the freedom of trade that would come with union. Also,
as it was in Scotland, so, too, in Ireland, with union, "the middling and
inferior ranks of the people . . . [would gain] compleat deliverance from

---

[29] In the process, he refers to data from "March 1775" (*WN*, 937), so obviously this section
was written in London.

[30] He suggests that he is purposely being conservative to give his case more credibility.
For example, he takes the low end of the estimate of the population of the American
colonies because "[t]hose accounts [he cites] . . . may have been exaggerated, in order,
perhaps, either encourage their own people, or to intimidate those of this country. . . .
(*WN*, 937).

the power of an aristocracy.... [An aristocracy] much more oppressive [than that of Scotland, because unlike that of Scotland, which was based on] natural and respectable distinctions of birth and fortune; ... [that in Ireland is based on] the most odious of all distinctions, those of religious and political prejudices...." (*WN*, 944). This kind of divide "animate[s] both the insolence of the oppressors, and the hatred and indignation of the oppressed" (*WN*, 944), thereby nurturing immense hostility. "Without a union with Great Britain, the inhabitants of Ireland are not likely for many ages to consider themselves as one people" (*WN*, 944).

As for the American colonies:

> No oppressive aristocracy has ever prevailed in the colonies. Even they, however, would, in point of happiness and tranquility, gain considerably by a union with Great Britain. It would, at least, deliver them from those rancorous and virulent factions which are inseperable from small democracies, and which have so frequently divided the affections of their people, and disturbed the tranquility of their governments, in their form so democratical. In the case of total separation from Great Britain, which, unless prevented by a union of this kind, seems very likely to take place, those factions would be ten times more virulent than ever. Before the commencement of the present disturbances, the coercive power of the mother-country had always been able to restrain those factions ... In all great countries which are united under one uniform government, the spirit of party commonly prevails less in the remote provinces than in the centre of the empire. The distance of those provinces from the capital, from the principal seat of the great scramble of faction and ambition, makes them enter less into the views of the contending parties, and renders them more indifferent and impartial spectators of the conduct of all. (*WN*, 944–5)[31]

So the colonies, being at a distance from London, would, in a union, be less plagued by faction and more likely to "enjoy a degree of concord and unanimity at present unknown...." (*WN*, 945). Although taxes would be higher, those taxes would go to bringing down the debt for the union as a whole. All of these revenues could be further augmented by higher tax revenues that could be generated by reducing the oppression and corruption in British India.

If not by his Utopian scheme, the only other way Smith can imagine to reduce the debt is to reduce expenditures. The only option Smith can imagine that would reduce expenditures significantly is letting go of the

---

[31] The point Smith makes here about small democracies and the probability of virulent factions destroying them anticipates the logic Madison offers in making his case in Federalist No. 10 for a federal union (Wills, 1982).

colonies. After all, the vast majority of the current debt has been incurred in wars defending those colonies.

> It was because the colonies were supposed to be provinces of the British empire, that this expence was laid out upon them. But countries which contribute neither revenue nor military force towards the support of the empire, cannot be considered as provinces. They may perhaps be considered as appendages, as a sort of splendid and showy equipage of the empire. (*WN*, 946)

The benefits of this empire have, Smith asserts, been an illusion: "It has hitherto been, not an empire, but the project of an empire; not a gold mine, but the project of a gold mine...." (*WN*, 947). It has been a project undertaken at immense public expense but which has paid no profit to the public because, as he has demonstrated again and again, the monopoly of the colony trade has not been maintained for the benefit of the people but for that of the particular mercantile interests.

> It is surely now time that our rulers should either realize this golden dream, in which they have been indulging themselves, perhaps, as well as the people; or, that they should awake from it themselves, and endeavour to awaken the people. If the project cannot be compleated, it ought to be given up. If any of the provinces of the British empire cannot be made to contribute towards the support of the whole empire, it is surely time that Great Britain should free herself from the expence of defending those provinces in time of war, and of supporting any part of their civil or military establishments in time of peace, and endeavour to accommodate her future views and designs to the real mediocrity of her circumstances. (*WN*, 947)

And so Smith concludes his *Inquiry into the Nature and Causes of the Wealth of Nations* on, in his own terms, a utopian note. He imagines and offers a vision of a grand union of the British empire in which all enjoy equal status and representation. Furthermore, in solving the problem of public debt that created the current crisis, this grand union could become an even more powerful example of the liberal plan that he envisions as the human prospect. But, as he wrote in Book IV when he first presented this possibility,[32] it is not the operational difficulties that are "insurmountable . . . [it is the] prejudices and opinions of the people both on this and on the other side of the Atlantic" (*WN*, 625).

As the 1790 revisions to the *TMS* described here in Chapter Eight make clear, Smith went to his grave concerned about the condition of

---

[32] Union is a vision he suggested earlier in Book IV: The "constitution . . . would be completed by it, and seems to be imperfect without it" (*WN*, 624).

Britain and hopeful regarding the human prospect. His legacy is his moral philosophy: his representation of the human condition, its nature, its dynamic, and the liberal plan as its prospect. How does that legacy relate to modern economic analysis that claims him as its parent? The next three chapters argue that Smith's complex being and multidimensional dynamic analysis can enhance these modern efforts in economics by reintegrating economic analysis into the social sciences more systematically.

PART THREE

ON ADAM SMITH'S MORAL PHILOSPHICAL
VISION AND THE MODERN DISCOURSE

TEN

"Chicago Smith" versus "Kirkaldy Smith"

The "Chicago School" of economics (Reder, 413), home of such leading lights as Frank Knight, Theodore Schultz, George Stigler, Milton Friedman, Gary Becker, and many other deservedly esteemed scholars, lays claim to Adam Smith as one of its own, for it traces its heritage directly to Smith.

The "economic approach to human behavior" (Becker, 1976) that is emblematic of the Chicago paradigm begins with the assumption that humans can be represented as *homo economicus*, beings driven by a single motive: personal utility maximization. Smith, according to his Chicago disciples, is the visionary who established this foundation and thus made the economic approach to human behavior possible.

Indicative of the admiration Chicagonians feel for Smith in appreciation for his founding contribution to the Chicago paradigm, George Stigler writes that while many of the theories embodied in the *WN* are failures because Smith's "successors [have] either ignored or rejected [them] out of hand. . . .

Smith had one overwhelmingly important triumph: he put into the center of economics the systematic analysis of behavior of individuals pursuing their self-interest under conditions of competition.[1] This theory is the crown jewel of *The Wealth of Nations*,[2] and it became, and remains to this day, the foundation

---

[1] In Stigler's taxonomy of success and failure, "[a] success or triumph is a proposition in economics that becomes a part of the working system (the so-called paradigm) of contemporary and subsequent economists" (Stigler, 1976, 1200 fn. 1). Clearly, establishing the founding assumption of his own Chicago paradigm is, for Stigler, among the greatest of all successes.

[2] Stigler writes that "*The Wealth of Nations* is a stupendous palace erected upon the granite of self-interest" (Stigler, 1975, 237).

of the theory of the allocation of resources.... [Smith's] construct of the self-interested individual in a competitive environment is Newtonian in its universality. (Stigler, 1976, 1200–1, 1212)[3]

The unabashed claim of Smith as the parent of the Chicago paradigm is reflected even more clearly in Gary Anderson's assertion that:

The bold extension of economic analysis ["models of rational maximizing behavior" (Anderson, 1066)] beyond the narrow confines of commercial exchange has been described by some of its leading proponents as 'economic imperialism'... Curiously, this movement had a famous early proponent who has been largely ignored by modern practitioners: Adam Smith... [was] probably the first 'economic imperialist.'... Obviously, Chicago economics was not invented in Chicago. (Anderson, 1066–7, 1084)

Hand in hand with this assumption that human beings are rational utility maximizers goes mathematical optimization analysis. Although Smith's work was too rudimentary for such an application of mathematical tools, those who share the Chicago interpretation of Smith as deductivist see the structure he offered as inevitably leading to that advancement in the economics discipline:

Smith's main objective in *The Wealth of Nations* was the formulation of a reform program on the basis of an analytical model of the operations of a capitalistic exchange economy.[4]... [This was informed by] understanding *origins* of... institutions[, which] could only be appreciated in terms of a historical

---

[3] Indicative of the widespread adoption of this view of Smith in the modern literature, Albert Hirschman writes that Smith followed Mandeville "in this retreat from generality [by focusing on one passion.]... *The Wealth of Nations*... [is] a work... wholly focused on the passion traditionally known as cupidity or avarice...." (Hirschman, 18). Smith made this focus more palatable by "substituting for 'passion' and 'vice' such bland terms as 'advantage' or 'interest.'... [This] harnessing idea... [became] a central construct of economic theory" (Hirschman, 19). Hirschman writes that in *TMS,* Smith "paves the way for collapsing these other passions into the drive for the 'augmentation of fortune'" (Hirschman, 108). He refers to Smith as a "reductionist" (Hirschman, 109). Nathan Rosenberg writes that Smith is consistent "because human behavior in all walks of life flows in a consistent way from these basic psychological impulses in which Smith believed. All men are economically motivated...." (Rosenberg, 1979, 30–1) Samuel Hollander writes that "[t]he theoretical models of *The Wealth of Nations* were based squarely on the behavioral assumptions characterizing 'economic man,' for the proposition that self-interest is the governing motive throughout time and space as far as it concerns man in his economic affairs is Smith's fundamental axiom" (Hollander, 72).

[4] "The famous invisible hand of *The Wealth of Nations* is nothing more than the automatic equilibration of a competitive market" (Grampp, 334). Grampp cites Frank Knight as follows: "'The mutual advantage of free exchange is the meaning of the 'invisible hand' directing each to serve the interests of others in pursuing his own'" ((Knight, 377) cited in Grampp, 334, fn 13).

account . . . [But t]he historical analysis is best viewed as a digression; since the recommendations for the reform of actual institutions and policies . . . are based upon a rather precise analytical model of the 'progress of society' applicable to a competitive capitalist exchange economy. The model of development used in this context is a classic example of hypothetical-deductive theorizing and cries out for mathematical formulation. (Hollander, 71–2, emphasis in original)

Chicago Smith . . . the *homo economicus*, history as "digression," and math as the language best suited for analysis of human behavior and modeling the human condition Smith . . . has become the accepted identity of Adam Smith among most modern economists. It should be obvious, however, that this Chicago Smith is not the same person as the 'Kirkaldy Smith' I have written about.

Kirkaldy Smith does not assume that we are one dimensional in our motives, does not see history as a "digression" in his analysis, and does not offer a deductive analysis that "cries out for mathematical formulation." Quite to the contrary, Kirkaldy Smith would reject a reductionist approach that:

- purports to explain all human behavior based on one dimensional motivation,
- claims to be able to capture the complexity of multidimensional human choice and of humankind's evolution in a matrix of equations based on such a reductionist assumption, and
- establishes its empirical credibility based on analysis that reduces the complex choices of multidimensional beings interacting in evolving social and political constructions to numeric proxies.

Kirkaldy Smith sees humankind as a uniquely complex realm of nature that does not lend itself to such reductionism. As explained in Chapter One, this complexity derives from the nexus of human reason and human frailty that puts humankind in a peculiar and problematic position. Our reason gives us dominion over the earth and the ability to transform nature into material wealth far beyond our requirements for survival. But that reason, when wedded to frailty, can lead to destructive interpersonal conflict; for, if unbridled, self-interest drives each of us to seek a larger share of the human bounty for ourselves, and our society degenerates into a "rent-seeking society" (Buchanan, Tollison, and Tullock, 1980). This dynamic is especially problematic in a liberal society where freedom of choice simultaneously unleashes both productive capacity and opportunities for rent-seeking.

This dilemma gives rise to what I referred to in Chapter One as the "cohesion question": If the productive potential of liberal society derives from individuals' freedom to pursue their own interests (the Physiocrats' "laissez-faire"), how does such a society offer that freedom without also unleashing a Hobbesian war of all against all? What cohesive force can hold liberal society together so that its potential – a good, secure life for each individual and the greatest possible wealth for the nation – can be realized?

The Kirkaldy Smith represented in the preceding chapters believes that constructive liberal society is possible because he believes that humans are capable of a multiplicity of motives including, if properly nurtured, justice.[5] In this chapter I'll distinguish my Kirkaldy Smith from the Chicago Smith by making the case that if we are in fact the beings that Chicago ascribes to Adam Smith's work and that Chicago takes as the foundation of the economic approach, then a constructive liberal society is theoretically impossible. Using Gary Becker's work as representative of the most powerful presentation of and the most expansive claims for the economic approach based on the standard economic assumption that we are constrained utility maximizing beings, *homo economicus*, I will make the case that there is no cohesive force in such a theory sufficient to hold society together in the face of the destructive power of rent-seeking.

I then turn to Amartya Sen and James Buchanan. Like Becker, Sen and Buchanan are Nobel Prize winning economists. Unlike Becker, Sen and Buchanan see the centrality of this liberal quandary and they each address this issue in thoughtful, detailed analysis.

Buchanan's "Constitutional Economics" enterprise envisions a dynamic development of constraints by consensus, the emergence of a civic ethic which, in turn, makes possible the establishment of a constitution that allows individuals to pursue their own ends with the security that there are boundaries on the behavior of all. Sen borrows Buchanan's conception of dynamic value development and, relaxing the *homo economicus* assumption, offers a synthesis in which developing values are embodied in humans whose behavior is shaped by a multiplicity of motives, including the capacity for ethical behavior.

As we'll see, both Sen's and Buchanan's solutions to the "cohesion question" bring us back to the moral philosophy of Adam Smith. Buchanan's Constitutional Economics and its relationship to Smith's moral philosophy will be examined in the next chapter. Sen's synthesis,

---

[5] Smith rejected the social contract of Locke and the *despotisme legal* (benevolent dictator) of the Physiocrats as the ultimate glue to hold liberal society together.

its relationship to Smith's work, and its implications for modern practice are the subjects of this chapter. However, first, to set the scene for Sen's relaxation of the *homo economicus* assumption, we must examine the limitations of the *homo economicus* assumption.

ON *HOMO ECONOMICUS* AND SOCIAL COHESION

Modern mainstream economic analysis is built on the assumption that human beings are motivated by utility maximization. The *New Palgrave* entries, "utility and decision theory" and "expected utility hypothesis," by Peter Fishburn (Fishburn, 779) and Mark Machina (Machina, 232) respectively, make it clear that although layers of sophistication have been added to utility theory, ultimately utility maximization is still neoclassical theory's standard assumption on human nature.

The classic statement of the power of economic theory based on this assumption is found in the work of Chicago's Gary Becker. Becker asserts that:

> The combined assumptions of maximizing behavior, market equilibrium, and stable preferences, used relentlessly and unflinchingly, form the heart of the economic approach as I see it. . . .
>
> Needless to say, the economic approach has not provided equal insight into and understanding of all kinds of behavior: for example, the determinants of war and of many other political decisions have not yet been much illuminated by this approach (or any other approach). I believe, however, that the limited success is mainly the result of limited effort and not lack of relevance. . . . I am saying that the economic approach provides a valuable unified framework for understanding *all* human behavior. . . . (Becker, 1976, 5, 9, 14, emphasis in original)

Indeed, Becker argues that the economic approach can address what is "[a]ccording to [Edward] Wilson, 'the central theoretical problem of sociobiology . . . : how can altruism, which by definition reduces personal fitness, possibly evolve by natural selection' (Wilson, 3)"? (Becker, 1976, 283). Citing "[s]ociobiologists . . . [efforts] to solve their central problem by building models with 'group selection'" (Becker, 1976, 283), Becker asserts that such "models of group selection are unnecessary since altruistic behavior can be selected as a consequence of individual ["utility maximizing" (Becker, 1976, 294)] rationality" (Becker, 1976, 284).

Altruism is modeled by Becker as a nested utility function. In sociobiological terms, I am altruistic if I derive utility from your fitness, or "i" am altruistic if:

$$U_i = U_i\,(f_i, f_u)$$ – i.e., my utility is a function of my fitness, f_i and also your fitness, f_u

This nested utility function of the altruist improves the fitness of the altruist because "[t]he beneficiaries of his altruism [those included in his utility function] are discouraged from harming him" (Becker, 1976, 291).[6] As a consequence, altruism enjoys a natural selection bias. Thus, as advertised, Becker's explanation for the existence of altruism based on natural selection in a world of Becker's *homo economicus* beings solves what is "[a]ccording to [Edward] Wilson, 'the central theoretical problem of sociobiology.'"

Clearly, if fitness is defined as the survival of our genes, the power of this effect is increased as the genetic relationship gets closer, because by improving the fitness of our close genetic relatives we enhance the survivability of our shared genes. But is Becker's altruism a strong enough bond to provide the solution to that question that confronted Smith and those other philosophers in the first ages of the liberal experiment – the cohesion question: How can a liberal society avoid the Hobbesian abyss of a war of all against all? How is *e pluribus unum* possible?

Becker chooses the realm of sociobiology to demonstrate the power of his "economic approach," so let's examine the cohesion question in sociobiological terms to see whether Becker's model does, indeed, offer a solution.

Edward Wilson, the parent of sociobiology, identifies the source of the cohesion problem very clearly:

During the past ten thousand years or longer, man as a whole has been so successful in dominating his environment that almost any kind of culture can succeed for a while, so long as it has a modest degree of internal consistency and does not shut off reproduction altogether. No species of ant or termite enjoys this freedom... Man has temporarily escaped the constraint of interspecific competition. (Wilson, 550)

Ironically, however, this escape has confronted humankind with an equally dangerous problem. Our dominion over our world has allowed us to generate surpluses, and now we are trapped in an intraspecific competition over control of these surpluses, a "rent-seeking society." In sociobiological terms, having escaped the "stabilizing selection" of interspecific competition (Figure 10.1) we have made ourselves vulnerable to the "disruptive selection" of intraspecific competition (Figure 10.2).

Unfortunately, Becker's altruism offers no solution to this human quandary. Beyond genetic connection, the altruism effect diminishes as social distance increases because the reciprocal benefit one can expect

---

[6] For a more complete analysis of Becker's argument see (Evensky, 1992).

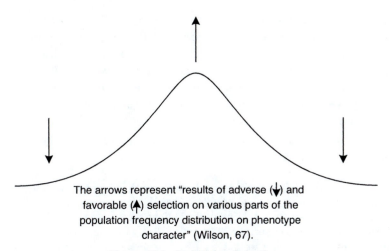

The arrows represent "results of adverse (↓) and favorable (↑) selection on various parts of the population frequency distribution on phenotype character" (Wilson, 67).

Figure 10.1. Stabilizing Selection.

to receive decreases. Adam Smith notes as much when, in the course of describing concentric spheres of relations, he writes that "affection gradually diminishes as the relation grows more and more remote" (*TMS*, 220). Diminishing with social distance, altruism rapidly loses the capacity to constrain the immediate and obvious incentive to create and exploit advantages that secure a larger share of the social surplus, the incentive to rent-seek. Clearly, the altruistic incentives of the corporate leaders at Enron, WorldCom, or Tyco, to name a few of the scandals at the turn of the century, did not constrain their pursuit of the rich returns of rent-seeking at the expense of millions of people those leaders never met.

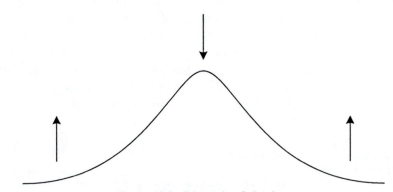

Figure 10.2. Disruptive Selection.

As Wilson makes clear, the solution lies not in Becker's self-interest but in societal constructions. Wilson writes that "[t]o counteract selfish behavior and the 'dissolving power' of higher intelligence, each society must codify itself. Within broad limits, virtually any set of limits works better than none at all" (Wilson, 562). So we are back to the cohesion question recognized in the first ages of liberal society: From whence the limits that make liberty work?

This is not just an abstract philosophical question. As Amartya Sen writes:

The trouble with reading much into ... [Adam Smith's] homely butcher-brewer-baker example [often cited as the classic statement of *homo economicus*][7] is ... that it downplays the function of *institutions* that sustain and promote economic activities. The concern of different parties with their own interests certainly can *motivate* people to take part in exchange from which each benefits. But whether the exchange will operate well will depend also on organizational conditions. There is a need for institutional development which can take quite some time to emerge – a lesson that is being learned [(his context is 1993)] rather painfully in Eastern Europe and the former Soviet Union. The importance of institutions was rather eclipsed there in the first flush of enthusiasm about the magic of allegedly automatic market processes.

The need for institutional development has some clear connection with the role of codes of behavior, since institutions based on interpersonal arrangements and shared understandings operate on the basis of common behavior patterns, mutual trust and confidence in the behavioral ethics of each other. The reliance on rules of behavior may typically be implicit rather than explicit – indeed so implicit that its importance can be easily overlooked in situations in which such confidence is unproblematic. But whenever it is not unproblematic, the overlooking of its need can be quite disastrous. (Sen, 1995B, 26)

In sum, if a liberal society is to be cohesive and constructive, human beings must have "mutual trust and confidence in the behavioral ethics of each other" because, absent ethics, rent-seeking can run amuck. A society populated by *homo economicus* does not have the capacity to establish this prerequisite for social cohesion. In his 1995 Presidential Address to the American Economic Association, Sen offers a vision of how modern economic analysis must evolve if is it to represent such a capacity and thus the theoretical possibility of constructive liberal society.

---

[7] One of the most often quoted lines in Smith: "It is not from the benevolence of the butcher, the brewer, or the baker, that we expect our dinner, but from their regard to their own interest. We address ourselves, not to their humanity but to their self-love, and never talk to them of our own necessities but of their advantages" (*WN*, 26–7).

SEN'S SYNTHESIS

Sen's Address, "Rationality and Social Choice," invites his colleagues in economics to set aside our "fight for basic principles" and transform competing paradigms into a synthesis. To make his case for synthesis, Sen invites his audience to join him in examining the following question:

How are we to view the demands of rationality in social decisions? How much guidance do we get from Aristotle's general recommendation that choice should be governed by "desire and reasoning directed to some end"?

Sen's point of departure into this inquiry is the problem raised by Arrow's impossibility result:

[W]hose desires, *whose* ends?... Kenneth Arrow (1951) has shown... that in trying to obtain an integrated social preference from diverse individual preferences, it is not in general possible to satisfy even some mild-looking conditions that would seem to reflect elementary demands of reasonableness.... Are the pessimistic conclusions that some have drawn from them [(these Arrovian "difficulties")] justified? Can we sensibly make aggregative social-welfare judgments? (Sen, 1995A, 1, emphasis in original)

Sen then introduces James Buchanan as counterpoint:

Buchanan... [has] argued that "rationality or irrationality as an attribute of the social group implies the imputation to that group of an organic existence apart from that of its individual components"... [and] that there was a deep "confusion surrounding the Arrow analysis" (not just the impossibility theorem but the entire framework used by Arrow and his followers) which ensued from the mistaken idea of "social or collective rationality in terms of producing results indicated by a social ordering...." (Sen, 1995A, 2)

Buchanan has "suggested" (Sen, 1995A, 5) that the notion of "social preference" implying an organic character to society should be dropped, and that with it would go the impossibility issue. Sen's response: "We certainly have to examine whether Buchanan's critique negates the impossibility result, but we must also investigate the more general issues raised by Buchanan" (Sen, 1995A, 2). This last line prepares Sen's audience for the transformation story he is about to tell: from competing paradigms to synthesis.

Sen's vehicle for developing his synthesis is a further exploration of the impossibility issue. He begins by "distinguish[ing] between two quite different uses of the notion of 'social preference,'... *decision mechanisms*" which reveal "the 'underlying preferences' on which *choices* actually made for the society... are implicitly based" and "*social welfare judgments* . . . [which reflect] some ranking of what would be better or worse for the society" (Sen, 1995A, 5, emphasis in original).

Responding to Buchanan's critique, Sen asserts that since "social welfare judgments [are made] by an individual or agency, [the relevance of] Arrow's impossibility theorem [to such judgments] . . . cannot be disputed on the ground that some organic existence is being imputed to society. . . . However, Buchanan's critique of Arrow's theorem would apply to mechanisms of social decisions (such as voting procedures)" (Sen, 1995A, 5). So if we follow Buchanan and drop any idea of social preference, does that eliminate the impossibility problem? No:

> The "impossibility" result identified in a particular form by Arrow can be extended to hold even when the idea of "social preference" is totally dropped and even when no conditions are imposed on "internal consistence" of social choice. (Sen, 1995A, 7)

"How might we then avoid that impossibility?" (Sen, 1995A, 7). Sen examines this question along the two dimensions cited previously.

With respect to social welfare judgments, Sen locates the source of the impossibility problem in overly narrow informational premises. "[B]ecause of its utilitarian form, traditional welfare economics had . . . been opposed to any basic use of nonutility information . . . [and t]o this was . . . added the exclusion of interpersonal comparisons of utilities. . . . [The result is a] barren informational landscape [that] makes it hard to arrive at systematic judgments of social welfare" (Sen, 1995A, 7).

> To try to make social welfare judgments *without* using any interpersonal comparison of utilities, and *without* using any nonutility information, is not a fruitful enterprise. . . . Once interpersonal comparisons are introduced, the impossibility problem, in the appropriately redefined framework, vanishes. The comparisons may have to be rough and ready and often open to disputation, but such comparisons are staple elements of systematic social welfare judgments (Sen, 1995A, 8, emphasis in original).

By introducing the notion that overly narrow premises can act as an artificial constraint on our vision, Sen establishes a frame for his synthesis case.

Next, he addresses the impossibility problem with respect to decision mechanisms. It has "greater resilience here" (Sen, 1995A, 9), and it is here that Sen's presentation takes its crucial turn. He begins the process of transforming the analysis by integrating the premises of social and public choice.

Rejecting the notion that analysis must begin with a choice between competing, incompatible premises, Sen makes the case that in order to address the question of decision mechanisms constructively, we must escape from the "dichotomy" (Sen, 1995A, 11) between *process-independence* identified with social choice and *consequence-independence* identified with public choice. After reviewing the cases for each, Sen concludes:

[I]t is not easy to believe that the public-choice approach is – or can be – really consequence-independent. For example, Buchanan's support of market systems is based on a reading of the consequences that the market mechanism tends to produce... While this is not in serious conflict with Buchanan's rejection of any "transcendental" evaluation of the outcomes..., nevertheless the assessment of outcomes must, in some form, enter this evaluative exercise.... [O]n the other side of the dichotomy: can we have sensible outcome judgments in a totally procedure-independent way? [No, argues Sen.] ...

The contrast between the procedural and consequential approach is, thus, somewhat overdrawn, and it may be possible to combine them, to a considerable extent, in an adequately rich characterization of states of affairs. (Sen, 1995A, 11–12)

Having opened the case for synthesis, Sen presses the issue. He looks to a melding of premises as a reasoned escape from the impossibility problem. In particular, the informational base can be expanded and the domain of impossibility can be contracted by taking into account the concept of a "'value restriction'" (Sen, 1995A, 9). This requires a synthesis of the social choice and public choice stories on the formation, role, and dimensionality of these value restrictions.

[C]oncern[ing] the role of social interactions in the development of values, and also the connection between value formation and the decision-making processes... [s]ocial choice theory has tended to avoid this issue, following Arrow's own abstinence: "we will also assume in the present study [Arrow's *Social Choice and Individual Values* (1951)] that individual values are taken as data and are not capable of being altered by the nature of the decision process itself" (Arrow, 1951, 7)....[8] On this subject, Buchanan has taken a more permissive position – indeed emphatically so: "The definition of democracy as 'government by discussion' implies that individual values can and do change in the process of decision-making...." (Sen, 1995 A, 3)

But while Sen asserts that social choice theory should open its mind to Buchanan's dynamic development of values, he believes that Buchanan

---

[8] Sen notes that "Arrow... himself points out 'the unreality of this assumption.' [(Arrow, 1951, 8)]" (Sen, 1995A, 3fn5).

and the public choice school should do the same regarding the nature of individual beings:

[T]he practical reach of social choice theory, in its traditional form, is considerably reduced by its tendency to ignore value formation through social interactions. Buchanan is right to emphasize [this] . . . However, traditional public choice theory is made unduly narrow by the insistence that individuals invariably behave as *homo economicus* . . . This uncompromising restriction can significantly misrepresent the nature of social concerns and values. (Sen, 1995A, 18)

Now, with an explicit melding of premises, Sen concludes with a call for the synthesis he envisions:

There are plenty of "social choice problems" in all this, but in analyzing them, we have to go beyond looking only for the best reflection of *given* individual preferences, or the most acceptable procedures for choices based on those preferences. We need to depart both from the assumption of given preferences (as in traditional social choice theory) and from the presumption that people are narrowly self-interested *homo economicus* (as in traditional public choice theory). (Sen, 1995A, 17, emphasis in original)

Sen envisions a synthesis model which "examine[s] value formation that results from public discussion . . . [and leads to] commitment on the part of citizens to do something. . . ." (Sen, 1995A, 17). It is a model of society in which civic values and their maturation play a central role in building a constructive liberal society. As I hope the preceding chapters have made clear, Sen's model addresses the cohesion question very much as Adam Smith's does in his moral philosophy.

ON MODERN SCOPE AND METHOD – MATHEMATICAL ANALYSIS

As Smith appreciated when he adapted Newtonian method to moral philosophy, scope and method are interdependent. If, then, following Smith and Sen, we expand the complexity of our analysis by expanding the dimensionality of the human nature we assume, does that have implications for the current privileged position of mathematics as the language of economic analysis?

The value of mathematics as a language for analysis is clear and compelling. It is a much more clean, crisp, unambiguous language than any other. Because ambiguity undermines and clarity enhances the persuasiveness of a model, Smith would appreciate and value this strength in mathematics. But Smith also understood that with any language's strengths come weaknesses.

As part of his analysis of the evolution of humankind, Smith explored the role of language in that evolution. Indeed, Smith's analysis of humans as social beings begins with the "first formation of languages"[9] because a means of communication is the first requisite and the foundation of all subsequent social constructions.

Clearly, different languages emerge in different times and places, and "[a]s [Smith] ... observes, depending on the special features of each language, various species of thought and intellect are produced.... [For] Smith ... language is a frame that sooner or later fixes the scope of our vision...."[10] (Becker, J. F., 17, 21). Thus, the price of using any particular language as the medium for our analysis is that with that language comes a frame that delimits the scope of that analysis.

Maurice Dobb makes precisely this point in response to Joseph Schumpeter's assertion in his *History of Economic Analysis* (1954) that, in contrast to the "history of Systems of Political Economy or ... [the] history of Economic Thought" (Schumpeter, 38), we can say with confidence that the history of economic analysis is a story of progress because our analytical "box of tools" (Schumpeter, 41) is better than that used in the past. Our "new apparatus [primarily mathematical modeling] poses and solves problems for which the older authors could hardly have found answers" (Schumpeter, 39). In response, Dobb writes:

A mathematical 'model' can be (and should be, *inter alia*) examined in its purely formal aspect, as a consistent structure. At the same time, *qua* economic theory, its very structure is relevant to the statement it is making about reality ... In choosing one structure in preference to another, the model-builder is not only providing a scaffolding or framework within which human thought can operate, but is laying emphasis upon certain factors and relationships and excluding others or casting them into the shadows; and in doing so he can be judged to be ... illuminating some corners or facets of reality, or certain situations that recur, at the same time as he is obscuring, or totally concealing others. (Dobb, 7)

Homo economicus, optimizing along a utility function subject to constraints, has proved an ideal assumption for mathematical analysis; and as our conception of this optimization problem has grown more complex so, too, have our mathematical tools and models. But is math a sufficient

---

[9] "Considerations Concerning the First Formation of Languages," Smith in (*Lectures on Rhetoric and Belles Letters*, 201).

[10] As noted in Chapter Two, this notion of frames and its application to language anticipates the work of Kahneman and Tversky (1984) on frames, Hirsch (1987) on schema, and Berger and Luckmann (1966) on the role of language in *The Social Construction of Reality*.

language to represent the complexity of a world in which multidimensional unique social beings interact and evolve within and in turn transform a multiplicity of multidimensional institutional constructions that
are all evolving along interactive non-linear paths? Math certainly sheds
much light, but we must also ask: What is lost in the shadows?[11]

ON MODERN SCOPE AND METHOD – EMPIRICAL ANALYSIS

Today's mainstream economics analysis begins with deduction. Given the
standard assumptions (e.g., *homo economicus*), an internally consistent
theory is established by building a mathematical model based on those
assumptions. The explanatory power of that model is then tested empirically by a regression analysis to determine to what degree the modeler
can be confident that the data (necessarily numeric) are consistent with
the hypothesized model. This is a very valuable technique for analysis
within a given social construction, but is it sufficient for understanding
larger questions of humankind's evolution, such as: What forces drive the
transformation of social constructions and the rise and fall of nations?

Smith's moral philosophy addressed these larger questions and his
method was very different. It did not involve "hypothetical-deductive
theorizing... [that] cries out for mathematical formulation" (Hollander,
71–2). He made this clear in his description of the proper method for
arriving at "general maxims regarding morality[:]

[A]ll... general maxims ["are formed"], from experience and induction. We
observe... a great variety of particular cases... and, by induction from this

---

[11] In a piece titled "Adam Smith's Theory of Inquiry," Ralph Lindgren (1969) argues that
Smith "adopted language, not mechanics, as the model of inquiry; and he drew a fundamental distinction between the methods of inquiry in the natural and the social sciences" (Lindgren 1969, 899). Deborah Redman (1993) makes the case that "the narrow,
technical, mathematical elements that Smith indirectly supported by labeling his method
Newtonian have become increasingly exaggerated in the course of the twentieth century"
(Redman, 226). Lindgren and Redman each assert that the conception of Smith as a lock-
step follower of Newtonian method has had perverse effects on Smith's heritage; and, in
fact, represents, as Montes makes clear (Montes, 2004), a misrepresentation of Newton.
Redman "conclude[s] that the richness of Smith's method lies not in the beauty of a precise mathematical theory or system like Newton's but in its *wide social emphasis* ... [and]
there would probably be no better antidote to the narrowness of economics' current
methods than a greater appreciation of and revival of the Scottish approach *in association* with today's analytical, theoretical approach" (Redman, 228, latter emphasis added).
Lindgren concludes that "[h]opefully, we can yet restore the vision of his genius and, given
time and similar motivation, put an end to that alienation which he aptly understood to
be the necessary consequence of insensitive and mechanical methods of inquiry in the
social sciences" (Lindgren 1969, 914).

experience, we establish...general rules.... It is by finding [a pattern] in a vast variety of instances...that we form the general rules... (*TMS*, 319)

Clearly, Smith is following Newton, who, in his *Opticks*, describes his method of analysis as follows:

As in Mathematics, so in Natural Philosophy, the...Analysis consists in making Experiments and Observations, and in drawing general Conclusions from them by Induction, and admitting of no Objections against the Conclusions, but such as are taken from Experiments, or other certain Truths. For Hypotheses are not to be regarded in experimental Philosophy. And although the arguing from Experiments and Observations by Induction be no Demonstration of general Conclusions; yet it is the best way of arguing which the Nature of Things admits of, *and may be looked upon as so much stronger, by how much the Induction is more general.* And if no Exception shall occur from Phaenomena, the Conclusion may be pronounced generally. But if at any time afterwards any Exception shall occur from Experiments, it may then begin to be pronounced with such Exceptions as occur. By this way of Analysis we may proceed...from Effects to their Causes, and from particular Causes to more general ones, till the Argument end in the most general. This is the Method of Analysis: And the Synthesis consists in assuming the Causes discover'd and establish'd as Principles, and by them explaining the Phaenomena proceeding from them, and proving the Explanations.... And if natural Philosophy in all its Parts, by pursuing this Method, shall at length be perfected, the Bounds of Moral Philosophy will also be enlarged. (Newton, 404–5, emphasis added)[12]

Smith shared with Newton this general conception of method. He also shared the view, reflected in Newton's suggestion that natural philosophy is perfectible whereas moral philosophy can only be "enlarged," that moral philosophy is distinctly different from natural philosophy. But, while Smith would agree that these realms are different, he would suggest that the difference is only a matter of degree: Moral philosophy is more messy due to human frailty, but, in Smith's view, neither is perfectible.

In any case, Smith followed Newton's method but adapted it to his different domain. For Smith, as for Newton:

- The establishment of "Principles" begins with "induction" based on "Observations" (Newton, 404), Smith's "experience" (*TMS*, 319).
- The generality of the principles is established by the scope of the particulars observed.

---

[12] My sincere thanks to Leon Montes for directing my attention to this quotation. Montes offers an excellent commentary on the relationship between Newton and Smith in Chapter 5 of his book, *Adam Smith in Context* (Montes, 2004).

- Confidence in the general principles one proposes is a function of the richness of the data one observes.
- From these general principles, we develop a synthesis to explain observed "Phaenomena."[13]

Observation is the key, and Smith believed that for the purposes of moral philosophy the richest source of observations lay in humankind's history.

Smith's inclination in the study of any subject was to approach it historically in the first instance and then to form his own ideas from reflections on past history.... [He] was an empiricist, a thinker who began with experienced fact and then produced a hypothesis to explain the facts.... In all of his work Smith followed the method of empiricism, of taking facts of experience as the basic data and reaching general propositions by induction from them. (Raphael, 1997, 18, 68, 83)[14]

Smith turned to narrative history as the data of choice for moral philosophy precisely because of humankind's peculiar nature. Due to the nexus of imagination, reason and frailty, the human condition presents an endless variety of irregular, cacophonous, distorted cases represented by the histories of humankind's various societies. As a consequence, the observational matrix facing the moral philosopher (here/there, past/present, varying degrees of distortion) is incredibly complex.

In order to "see" beyond the distortions of any particular time and place, Smith took an imaginary position outside of time and place and "observed" the overall flow of humankind's history as if he were an impartial spectator.[15] From this imaginary position he sought to cull those

---

[13] In Smith's case, this includes, as we saw in Chapter Seven, explaining the distorting effects of human frailty.

[14] "Smith and his contemporaries did not disregard the experience of ages and clearly accepted Aristotle's dictum that we can only understand what presently exists by first considering 'the origins from which it springs'" (Skinner, 1972, 317). "To them [the eighteenth century writers including Smith] the history of society was a philosophy of history. They took the view, without questioning it, that a philosophy of society must in method be historical. For societies themselves were natural growths in their own unique environments, and interpreting that growth implied a theory of growth" (Macfie, 14).

[15] The challenge is all the more daunting because we each stand in a singular, unique location (time and place) *inside* this complex matrix. That position both limits the scope of and distorts our vision. "One of the principal problems in learning indeed is how to destroy the illusions of perspective, the belief that faraway things are in fact small. We do this in the physical world through movement, which soon reveals to us that our own immediate view of the world, if taken literally, would be an illusion, and that far-off things only seem small" (Boulding, 253). Smith was very conscious of the role of perspective on judgment, as reflected in his spectator analysis. David Levy suggests that Smith's focus

patterns that transcend the peculiarities of any given society caused by its unique time, place, and set of distortions.[16] History – rich, textured narrative history[17] – offered Smith the closest approximation to that imaginary position from which to observe and analyze the complexity of humankind's evolution.

This exercise was more than a craft for Smith; it was an art of imagination.[18] In describing A. L. Kroeber's historical approach, Tim Ingold captures the spirit of Smith's:

[A] genuinely "historical" approach is integrative and totalizing rather than analytic and atomizing. Whereas scientists confront the whole already broken into discrete fragments that can then be strung out in temporal succession to reconstitute process, historians aim to grasp the movement of the whole by a direct leap of intuition, by living it in their minds. History in that sense is like art, and the task of historians is to describe, translate and interpret, but not to dissolve into elements. (Ingold, 76–7)

If it is successful, the fruit of such an approach is an analysis that describes relationships not as deconstructed discrete parameters on independent variables, but as a complex co-evolution of individuals and a simultaneous system of social, political, and economic institutions that

---

on perspective was influenced by his admiration for Berkeley's *New Theory of Vision* (Levy, 223–6).

[16] As noted in Chapter One, Smith focused on the flow. Analytical detail was not to be belabored. He often used terms, for example, the word nature, in many different ways, so one can only understand the meaning of any given use by its place in the flow of the analysis. Dickey makes this point about Smith by citing Arthur Lovejoy's work (Dickey, 600, quoting Lovejoy, emphasis added by Dickey): "[T]he sacred word 'nature'" was "probably the most equivocal in the vocabulary of the European peoples." He insisted that a "knowledge of the range of its meanings, *and of the processes of thought...by which one sense of it gives rise to, or easily passes over into, others* is an indispensable prerequisite for any discriminating reading" of the western intellectual tradition. I think Lovejoy's advice can be applied with profit to the conception of nature Adam Smith employs in different editions of *TMS*.

[17] As I use the term here, narrative history includes numeric history as a subset of the descriptive evidence. Smith appreciated very well that narrative history was not Truth about the past, but, along with anthropological and archeological sources, it is the data we have to work with. Smith often comments on the veracity of his sources, so he is well aware of the limitations of these data.

[18] "In modern economics, this [Smith's] procedure has been called *model building*; but Smith conceived it less mathematically as akin to the painting of a picture" (Thompson, 221, emphasis in original). Fleischacker argues that Smith emphasizes judgment over scientific calculation: "[I]n the philosophy of the social sciences, Smith's approach to the subject represents perfectly what a turn to phronesis over theoria has come to mean, what is urged by those who argue that human beings cannot be fitted to the numeric calculi of the physical sciences" (Fleischacker, 125).

contributes to our understanding of the flow of humankind's history, and its prospect.

ON HISTORY, INDIVIDUALS, AND INSTITUTIONS

Smith believed that if, from an analysis of history, we can approximate an understanding of the general principles that guide human events, then from those principles we can develop policy prescriptions that can foster the progress of society. It was to that end that Smith offered his moral philosophy.

As Nathan Rosenberg expresses very nicely, and contrary to the laissez faire caricature of Smith, many of the policy prescriptions Smith advocated involved the optimal arrangement of institutions:

Perhaps as a result of the increasingly formal nature of economics as an academic discipline, the institutional content and preoccupations of Adam Smith's *Wealth of Nations* have suffered prolonged neglect.... [J]umping directly from the conception of man as a rational creature to the policy recommendation of laissez faire and all that, it completely short-circuits much of the real substance of Smith's work. By visualizing the human agent as engaged in the effort to maximize a single, unambiguous magnitude, two aspects of Smith's book and the crucial importance of the interplay between them are ignored: (1) ... the *conflicting* forces which impel the human agent to action ..., (2) his sustained inquiry into the ultimate impact, in terms of human actions and its welfare consequences, of different kinds of institutional arrangements. (Rosenberg, 1960, 557, emphasis in original)

Institutions matter in Smith because "self-interest can be pursued in innumerable antisocial ways" (Rosenberg, 1960, 558). Citing examples of such human failings, Rosenberg writes that "[g]iven these human characteristics, it is plain that the mere absence of external restraints and the freedom to pursue self-interest do not suffice, in Smith's view, to establish social harmony or to protect society from 'the passionate confidence of interested falsehood.' What are required, above all, are institutional mechanisms which compel man, in his 'natural insolence,' 'to use the good instrument'" (Rosenberg, 1960, 558).[19]

---

[19] "The ideal institutional order for Smith is one which places the individual under just the proper amount of psychic tension ... to make possible the pursuit of self-interest *only* in a socially beneficial fashion" (Rosenberg, 1960, 559–60, emphasis in original). Rosenberg cites many of Smith's analyses of such constructions (e.g., in religion and in education) noting that "large portions of his *Wealth of Nations* are specifically devoted to analyzing the nature of the appropriate institutional framework" (Rosenberg, 1960, 559).

Rosenberg goes on to reject any significant role for ethics in Smith's analysis of the necessary constraints on man's natural insolence: "[I]t will be shown ... that [assigning any significance to moral constraints] ... is not only totally incorrect but does a considerable injustice to the subtlety and sophistication of Smith's argument" (Rosenberg, 1960, 559).

Rosenberg is absolutely correct that Smith's institutional analysis is significant, subtle, and sophisticated, but so, too, is Smith's ethical analysis. To dismiss it as insignificant in Smith's representation of the construction of social constraints is to do "a considerable injustice to the subtlety and sophistication of Smith's argument."

As described in Chapter Two, in Smith's vision of the ideal liberal society, individuals govern themselves because no government can both impose the requisite order and, at the same time, allow the freedom necessary for the liberal plan to be realized. However, this ideal is a limit. As explained in Chapters Three and Four, institutions are instrumental in Smith's story of humankind's evolution toward this limit, because progress is only possible where institutions that are appropriate to the stage of society's development insure social cohesion. But even as institutions play this essential, instrumental role, if the ideal is to be more nearly approximated, the power of government must continuously be shifting from external institutional government to internal ethical government based on a common commitment to shared civic ethics.

As we've seen, Becker's economic approach to human behavior cannot explain the existence of such a common commitment that secures social cohesion because the only bond it offers, altruism, suffers from a diminution with social distance. In contrast, Sen recognizes the necessity of this common commitment to civic values and makes it clear as to where that commitment must come from. Recall his assertion:

The trouble with reading much into ... [Smith's] homely butcher-brewer-baker example is ... that it downplays the function of institutions that sustain and promote economic activities. ... [And Sen continues, t]he need for institutional development has some clear connection with the role of codes of behavior, since institutions based on interpersonal arrangements and shared understandings operate on the basis of common behavior patterns, mutual trust and confidence in the behavioral ethics of each other. (Sen, 1995B, 26)

This brings us back to Rosenberg and institutions, but to a larger conception of the role of institutions than Rosenberg suggested is in Smith.

Adam Smith was not an economist offering a materialist two-dimensional analysis, modeling political institutions because they play an instrumental role in his representation of economic processes and progress. Smith was a moral philosopher modeling a complex co-evolution of individuals within a simultaneous system of social, political, and economic institutions in order to contribute to our understanding of the flow of humankind's history and its prospect.

Where modern economic modeling of institutions is richest, in the New Institutional Economics, institutions are modeled in the materialist two-dimensional 'Rosenberg Smith' tradition, not in the Kirkaldy Smith tradition.

The next chapter will examine:

- the New Institutional Economics' own self-conscious awareness of the limitations of the 'Rosenberg Smith' approach to institutions,
- James Buchanan's reach beyond this two-dimensional, political/ economic institutional analysis to include a marginal consideration of social institutional change, and
- the advantages of moving institutional analysis from Buchanan's constrained three-dimensional analysis to Smith's dynamic three-dimensional analysis.

ELEVEN

Toward a Dynamic Three-Dimensional Analysis

Oliver Williamson begins his September 2000 *Journal of Economic Literature* piece "The New Institutional Economics: Taking Stock, Looking Ahead" with the following reflection:

I open my discussion of the new institutional economics with a confession, an assertion, and a recommendation. The confession is that we are still very ignorant about institutions. The assertion is that the past quarter century has witnessed enormous progress in the study of institutions. The recommendation is that, awaiting a unified theory, we should be accepting of pluralism. (Williamson, 595)

The focus of Williamson's piece is on the progress he cites. My focus is on the ignorance.

Williamson represents society's institutional structure as having four levels. Level 1 encompasses the embedded "norms, customs, mores, [and] traditions" of society (Williamson, 596). Although these are institutionalized, they are not directly observable institutions. They are a "social stock of knowledge" (Berger and Luckmann, 42) that each new generation inherits and takes as representing the natural order of things, as tacit knowledge. Unlike a court system, a legislative system, a body of common law, or a constitution, one cannot examine this social construct directly. It is a substructure, an invisible foundation upon which all other institutions are constructed.

Level 2 of Williamson's social construction encompasses what Douglas North refers to as the "formal rules" of social organization, rules that include "constitutions, laws, [and] property rights" (North, 1991, 97).

Unlike Level 1, where, Williamson conjectures, the "informal institutions have mainly spontaneous origins – which is to say that deliberative choice of calculative kind is minimally implicated" (Williamson, 597), the formality of Level 2 institutions "opens up the opportunity for first-order economizing: get[ting] the formal rules of the game right" (Williamson, 597–8). Similarly, Level 3 – which Williamson refers to as the "play of the game" level (Williamson, 597) – involves "second-order economizing, get[ting] the governance structures [(e.g., contract)] right...." (Williamson, 599). Level 4 is that at which resource allocation and employment are determined – "getting the marginal conditions right" (Williamson, 597).

The institutions at both Levels 2 and 3 of the social construct have a major impact on the cost of economic transactions at Level 4 because the conditions governing exchange are defined by the rules and structures embodied in these institutions. "Effective institutions ... reduce transaction and production costs per exchange so that the potential gains from trade are realizable" (North, 98). Thus, institutional analysis is central to "transaction cost economics [which] subscribe[s] to the idea that the transaction is the basic unit of analysis, ... [and that] governance is an effort to craft *order*, thereby to mitigate *conflict* and realize *mutual gains*" (Williamson, 599, emphasis in original). To the degree that transaction cost analysis informs institution building at Levels 2 and 3, it offers a valuable tool to help a society get its institutional structure "right," as Williamson puts it (Williamson, 598). This promise of operationally practical benefits is, for Williamson, one of the great virtues of the New Institutional Economics, and it is this promise that explains the New Institutional Economics' focus on Levels 2 and 3. This focus comes with a caveat, however: "The institutions of embeddedness (Level 1) are an important but underdeveloped part of the story" (Williamson, 610).

Williamson and North clearly appreciate that understanding these social institutions of Level 1 – norms, customs, mores, and traditions – is essential to a complete model of economic intercourse. As North puts it, these social institutions exercise a "pervasive influence upon the long-run character of economics," and, he wonders, "What is it about informal constraints that gives them" such power? (North, 111). Williamson cites this quotation from North and writes: "North does not have the answer to that perplexing question, nor do I" (Williamson, 596). Ergo the confession of "ignorance."

North takes the question a step further. Not only does he wonder at the power of these social institutions, but also about their origin: "How does an economy develop the informal constraints that make individuals constrain their behavior so that they make political and judicial systems effective forces for third party enforcement?" (North, 111). Williamson reflects on this question also; then he leaves it behind.

James Buchanan's Constitutional Economics enterprise addresses North's question as he excavates the Level 1 social foundation of The New Institutional Economics and extends the dimensionality of that analysis from two-dimensions (political and economic) to include a consideration of marginal changes in the third dimension, social institutions (Buchanan 1991, 232).

FROM A TWO-DIMENSIONAL ANALYSIS TO A CONSTRAINED THREE-DIMENSIONAL ANALYSIS: JAMES BUCHANAN'S "CONSTITUTIONAL ECONOMICS"

Because institutions have power and because power can be used to generate a rent, a return to advantage, institutions themselves can and do become a locus of competition – a rent-seeking competition. Rent-seeking theory has led some to the pessimistic conclusion that there is no way to get the institutional structure necessary for a successful liberal order "right," that there is no feasible resolution to the "cohesion question." After all, where individuals are truly free to choose, there are countless opportunities to benefit from seeking institutional advantages, and utility maximizing individuals will seek those advantages.

Are liberal societies, therefore, inevitably trapped between the devil and the deep blue sea: the oppressiveness of the tyrannical state that can suppress unbridled self-interest and the Hobbesian war of all against all if those central controls are removed? Buchanan (1991, 245) expresses distress about the current state of the majoritarian democracies, but he rejects the pessimism. He believes it is possible to constrain rent-seeking without infringing on the sovereignty of the individual by establishing *constraints by consensus*.

In order to represent this possibly, Buchanan expands the dimensionality of modern economic analysis from the standard market question: What choices will be made given the extant set of constraints? to the more general question: What choices will be made including what system of constraints will be chosen?[1] This more general question

---

[1] "Constitutional economics directs analytical attention to the *choice among constraints.* Once stated in this fashion, economists will recognize that there is relatively little in

integrates Levels 2, 3, and 4 of the New Institutional Economics analysis.[2]

Given this point of departure, Buchanan turns to an obvious question: Why would autonomous individuals "choose to impose constraints or limits on their own behavior"? (Buchanan 1991, 5). Why would they be a party to a process of social construction given that any social construct implies some degree of constraint on individual choice? To answer these "whys," Buchanan cites Adam Smith: "Smith stressed [the] . . . properties [of the market] that allow for self-interested behavior of persons and yet generate socially beneficial results, require an environmental setting of appropriate 'laws and institutions'" (Buchanan 1991, 208).

Buchanan agrees. He rejects the "romantic ideal of laissez-faire, the fictional image of anarcho-capitalists, in which there is no role for the state at all" (Buchanan 1991, 35) for the same reason he rejects the socialist "romantic image of the state as an omniscient and benevolent entity" (Buchanan 1991, 35). "[O]rdinary humans" are not capable of either. Socialism is an invitation to the exploitation of centralized power, and anarchist laissez-faire is a path into the "Hobbesian jungle" (Buchanan 1991, 35).

Any plausibly realistic analysis of social order, whether positive or normative, must be bounded by the limits set by these ideological extremes. The state is neither omniscient nor benevolent, but a political-legal framework is an essential element in any functioning order of human interaction. (Buchanan 1991, 35)[3]

According to Buchanan, we will agree to be a party to social construction because we need such constructs, constraints by consensus, if society is to cohere.

But how can we, mortal humans, create a state that constrains our humanness and its destructive predilection for rent-seeking without

their established canon that will assist in analyzing choices of this sort. To orthodox economists . . . it would appear to be both methodologically and descriptively absurd to introduce the artificial creation of scarcity as an object for behavioral analysis" (Buchanan, 1991, 5). Buchanan notes the relationship between his enterprise and the work of Elster, Schelling, and Thaler and Shefrin. The focus of these efforts is on intrapersonally generated constraints, whereas he is interested in interpersonally generated constraints – specifically, constraints generated through a system of exchange (Buchanan 1991, 5).

[2] As with New Institutional Economics, Buchanan's premises are standard ones: methodological individualism, utility maximization, and rational choice. He rejects the notion that society has an organic existence that transcends individuals (Buchanan 1991, 14–15, 29).

[3] Recall Edward Wilson's assertion cited in Chapter Ten that "[t]o counteract selfish behavior and the 'dissolving power' of higher intelligence, each society must codify itself. Within broad limits, virtually any set of limits works better than none at all" (Wilson, 562).

tyrannizing over us? "'How can the controllers be controlled?' Hobbes responded with despair" (Buchanan 1991, 235). Buchanan turns to the contractarian tradition for an answer:

The elements of Adam Smith's intellectual enterprise become directly precursory to the research program of constitutional economics only when those elements are imbedded within the tradition of contractarian political philosophy . . . In agreeing to be governed, explicitly or implicitly, the individual exchanges his or her own liberty with others who similarly give up liberties in exchange for the benefits offered by a regime characterized by behavioral limits. (Buchanan, 1991, 12–13)

In order to demonstrate why the constraints must be constitutional, Buchanan uses the example of a poker game. Participants in a poker game face two choices: 'What will the rules of *our* game be?' and, once those rules are determined, 'What should *my* strategy be?'

The rules of the game define the constitution of the game. The various strategies available within that constitutional order represent the post-constitutional choice set any participant in the game faces. For the game to be played in a constructive environment, it is crucial that there be an impenetrable wall of separation between the rule setting stage, the constitutional construction, and the in-rule play, the post-constitutional strategic interactions. Any breech of that separation allows the strategic self-interested pursuits of individuals to be focused on rule manipulation.

In a poker game such manipulation would simply lead to a breakdown of the game: The "poker game is voluntary . . . [and] each player retains a low-cost exit option" (Buchanan 1991, 155). But "[t]he political game is compulsory, and we must all play" (Buchanan 1991, 155) because the cost of not playing is the high probability of a significantly smaller distributive share as others manipulate the rules to their advantage. In the politicized market game, micro-motives drive rent-seeking with its attendant macro, negative sum implications.[4]

To avoid this dilemma, we must appreciate the lesson of the poker game. We must create that wall of separation between the rule creation stage during which individuals function as a cooperative group interested in designing the best standards for play, optimal rules for commutative justice; and the in-rule stage during which individuals become players competing with one another within the context of the previously agreed upon rules.

Buchanan believes this is possible because he believes that two characteristics of the constitutional stage distinguish it from the

---

[4] See Schelling (1978) on *Micromotives and Macrobehavior*.

post-constitutional stage. First, any agreement at the constitutional stage requires a greater threshold of social consensus than majoritarian democracy: "At the constitutional stage of choice among rules, our argument does, conceptually, require unanimous agreement among all parties" (Buchanan 1991, 47). Second, the perspective of the participants is fundamentally different when constitutional as opposed to post-constitutional choices are involved:

> [A]greement on rules is much more likely to emerge than agreement on policy alternatives within rules because of the difficulties in precisely identifying the individual's economic interest in the first setting. The rule to be chosen is expected to remain in being over a whole sequence of time periods and possibly over a wide set of separate in-period choices during each period. How can the individual, at the stage of trying to select among rules, identify his or her own narrowly defined self-interest? ... He or she is necessarily forced to choose from behind a dark *"veil of uncertainty."*[5] In such a situation, utility maximization dictates that generalized criteria, such as fairness, equity, or justice enter the calculus rather than more specific arguments like net income or wealth. (Buchanan 1991, 47–8, emphasis added)

In effect, the "veil" masks what Buchanan refers to as the "interest" component in each individual's choice mechanism, obscuring questions like: 'What serves *me*?' What remains is the "theory" component, framing questions like: 'What kind of world will *our* choices create?' With questions like this driving the discussion, there is more of a possibility for a consensus because individuals are not engaged in conflict (What are *my* interests? *v* What are *yours*?), they are engaged in cooperative discourse (What system seems most likely serve *us* best?). Buchanan argues that in such a discourse the paramount *"concern for stability* ... will induce a concern for fairness" (Buchanan 1991, 57, emphasis in original).

Very nice in theory, but is this feasible? The process is not costless. Are the incentives sufficient to encourage a rational citizen to voluntarily participate in this conversation about the constitution? Buchanan's answer: No. The constitution, "the set of constraints that limit the choice options of individuals, that define the feasibility spaces, is public in the classic sense. This structure is both nonpartitionable and nonexcludable" (Buchanan 1991, 24). Consequently, individuals have the incentive to free

---

[5] Buchanan notes that "[i]n this construction [of the veil of uncertainty], our efforts were quite close to those of John Rawls [veil of ignorance]." (Buchanan 1991, 48) In effect, Rawls' ignorance is the limiting case. Buchanan's uncertainty veil seems to get thicker (approaches Rawls) as his argument develops, because he realizes that the demarcation of interests and theory (described in what follows) is crucial to the success of his enterprise (See Buchanan 1991, 56).

ride. So, from whence the motive for participation? Buchanan's answer: Ethics. – "[B]ecoming informed about, and participating in the discussion of, constitutional rules may require the presence of some ethical precept that transcends rational interest for the individual" (Buchanan 1991, 155), an "ethic of constitutional citizenship" (Buchanan 1991, 156).

However, this raises the obvious question: In a world of methodological individualism, utility maximization, and rational choice, where does this commitment to a civic ethic come from? Buchanan's answer: There are "economic origins of the ethical constraints" (Buchanan 1991, 180). Self-interested individuals have an incentive to inculcate ethics in others because these ethics solve externality problems that are not amenable to any other solution. He cites as an example the work ethic.

People who are willing to work hard at the tasks of society generate a positive work-supply externality because their effort contributes to increasing returns in production. This is a "genuine public good" (Buchanan 1991, 175) because the benefit of this exertion, the greater productivity, is nonexcludable and nonpartitionable – it benefits all consumers. If a work ethic is instilled in individuals, then all others enjoy the benefits of the externality without having to compensate the worker because he "senses no constraining influence at all ... [he] may not [even] be conscious of the ethical norms that guide the choices made" (Buchanan 1991, 174). This, in turn, moves the internalization of this externality from the realm of "Pareto-irrelevant" – a benefit not worth the cost, to the realm of "Pareto-relevant" – worth the expenditure of resources to instill the work ethic (Buchanan 1991, 174). As a consequence, "there is justification for both individualized and collective efforts to promulgate, maintain, and transmit this ethic throughout the culture as well as intergenerationally" (Buchanan 1991, 177).

Just as the work ethic allows us to internalize a positive externality, so, too, does the ethic of constitutional responsibility. It inculcates a commitment to the constitutional conversation and thus creates a potential for jointly produced and individually adhered to, well-defined and consensually agreed-upon rules of the game. Such constraints by consensus make feasible the realization of a "*social order* without conflict while at the same time achieving tolerably acceptable levels of well-being" (Buchanan 1991, 231, emphasis in original).

But, is there sufficient incentive for an individual to expend resources on the behavior modification of others when the product of such an investment is ethics? No, says Buchanan, "in *n*-person settings, where each person confronts 'all others' in some relevant sense ... [t]he results of such investment become genuinely public goods...and each individual will have familiar free-rider incentives to hold back on his or her own contribution" (Buchanan 1991, 188–9). Therefore, some form of "[c]ollective organization of the moral persuasion enterprise may be necessary" (Buchanan 1991, 189). Each generation must establish social norms that are inculcated into the next generation.

The analysis is consistent with the sociologists' criticism of the economists' hypothesis of operationally meaningful utility maximization. The preference orderings of individuals are subject to change brought about by the sociocultural environment within which choices are made and action taken. "Social norms" do, indeed, determine individual choice behavior, at least within limits. But the model supplies operational content to the sociologists' criticism; the origin of and the direction of the effects of social norms are themselves grounded in a calculus of self-interest. (Buchanan 1991, 193)

Here, Buchanan reaches the roots of his argument. The foundation of liberal institutional order is a civic ethic. Although "individuals are the ultimate sovereigns in matters of social organization" (Buchanan 1991, 227), they benefit from a mutual inculcation of a constitutional ethic: A commitment to a constitutional conversation that takes place behind a veil that obscures individual interest. In such a conversation, all value justice because no one can predict his position beyond the veil and because the just outcome will be the most stable. The focus of the discussion thus becomes the theory of rules, because justice and the stability of the constitution depend on the quality of the rule structure it embodies.

The agreed-upon constitutional "state provides and maintains the appropriate structural constraints (the 'laws and institutions,' rules of the game), [and within that context] individuals, as economic actors, can be left alone to pursue their own privately determined purposes, and in so doing enjoy the values of liberty, prosperity, and peace in reciprocal and mutual respect, one for another" (Buchanan 1991, 244).

It is a wonderful image and a source of hope – but not, Buchanan believes, a naive hope. He sees in history evidence that humankind has already made some progress in solving the problem of creating "moral communities" (Buchanan 1991, 189). "The emergence of the minimally cooperative norms that are necessary for the effective functioning of the extended economic nexus offers a good example of 'order without design,'...stressed by Hayek and attributed to the insights of the eighteenth-century Scots moral philosophers" (Buchanan 1991, 190).

Buchanan views his work as extending Hayek's analysis: "In channeling the discourse toward constructive choice among sets of rules, I am, as you will recognize, both modifying and going beyond emphasis on cultural evolution associated with the work of F. A. Hayek. I accept, of course, the importance of cultural evolution in the establishment of the rules of social order . . . I want only to suggest that, at least along some *relevant margins*, we can deliberately modify institutions that constrain our interaction, one with another" (Buchanan 1991, 231–2, emphasis added).

Buchanan treats the inherited "rules of social order," this social foundation, as he does the inherited distribution of the society's material endowment. With respect to the latter he writes:

In my enterprise . . . parties to a potential contract commence from some status quo definition of initial positions[6] because, quite frankly, there is no other place from which to start. This [is an] existential acceptance of the status quo . . . My emphasis is almost exclusively placed on the *process* through which potential changes may be made, rather than either the starting point or the end point of change. (Buchanan 1991, 205, emphasis in original)

The focus of Buchanan's enterprise is on the margin, on process: How does change occur? and, more importantly, as is Williamson's concern: How can we act to accomplish constructive institutional change? and How do we get institutions "right"?

Buchanan takes us beyond the orthodox confines of choice within constraints – the market dimension – to the broader story of choice within *and* among constraints – the political dimension. Furthermore, he extends the institutional reach of analysis into that Level 1, social foundation that the New Institutional Economists confessed ignorance about because his enterprise lays bare the ethical foundation of society's political and economic superstructure by making it clear that in a liberal system, social values – in particular civic ethics – do, indeed, matter. However, his analysis only partially answers North's question: "How does an economy develop the informal constraints that make individuals constrain their behavior so that they make political and judicial systems effective forces for third party enforcement?" (North, 1991, 111).

Buchanan offers an explanation of *marginal* change in social values. However, these "informal constraints" are not established *de novo* by each generation. If, as Buchanan argues, each successive generation

---

[6] "[T]he status quo distribution has been generated through a complex process of political-legal evolution . . . and social change" (Buchanan 1991, 205–6).

inherits a status quo of social norms and acts on it at the "relevant margins," questions remain:

- Where does the core of these inherited social norms come from?
- How is an evolving core of norms sustained across multiple generations?
- How does that evolving set of social norms relate to the evolution of the political and economic dimensions of the human condition?

FROM A CONSTRAINED THREE-DIMENSIONAL ANALYSIS TO A DYNAMIC THREE-DIMENSIONAL ANALYSIS: ON SOCIAL CONSTRUCTIONS AND HUMAN BEHAVIOR

In the *Social Construction of Reality*, Peter Berger and Thomas Luckmann (1966) represent the social foundation, Buchanan's inherited social "status quo," as a "social stock of knowledge" (Berger and Luckmann, 42) that is taken to represent the natural order of things,[7] as tacit knowledge[8] that defines and dictates the parameters of choice. In the short run or at the margin, defined by a generation, this set of commonly shared norms and understandings is typically fairly stable, because an institutional status quo is essential for social stability. It is *within* this extant schema or frame[9] that individuals act as the rational choice model describes.[10]

---

[7] "Through reification, the world of institutions appears to merge with the world of nature" (Berger and Luckmann, 90).

[8] "The validity of my knowledge of everyday life is taken for granted by myself and by others until further notice, that is, until a problem arises that cannot be solved in terms of it" (Berger and Luckmann, 44). As Buchanan puts it: "Empirically, ... [we seem to] go about making ordinary choices, which involve complex interactions with other persons and groups, within a framework or a structure of rules that we simply take as part of our environment, a part of the state of nature, so to speak...." (Buchanan 1991, 153).

[9] See Kahneman and Tversky (1984) on frames, and Hirsch (1987, Ch 11) on schema. Buchanan himself writes of "alternative 'windows' on the world.... [T]he process through which individuals choose among such windows remains mysterious...." (Buchanan 1991, 18).

[10] "Formally, a social action is ... taken to be the resultant of all individual actions. In other words, any social action is thought of as being factored into a sequence of individual actions.... I certainly do not wish to deny that such factoring takes place, but I do wish to emphasize that the partition of a social action into individual components, and the corresponding assignment of individual responsibility, is *not* datum. Rather, the particular factoring in any given context is itself the result of a social policy and therefore already the outcome of earlier and logically *more primitive social values*" (Arrow 1983, 64, latter emphasis added). "Arrow's ... formulation ... allows social considerations to influence the choices people make" (Sen 1995, 2).

Modeling human behavior within such a given frame is a valuable tool for understanding the actions of individuals *within that particular social construct*. However, to suggest that any such framed model is a general theory is to imply that there was, is, and always will be, in all places, only one social construct – the one that is assumed, often tacitly, by the model. Clearly, that is a strong assumption that severely limits the scope of such a model's applicability.

If a model of humankind is to be truly general, rational choice analysis must be set into a more general context. It must reflect the fact that social frames are core values and understandings of a society embodied in its institutions, that these frames vary across societies, and that every such frame has an evolving, organic existence.

Individuals are born into and socialized by an extant frame that shapes their initial values and understandings.[11] But the uniqueness of each individual's personal biography gives him or her a singular perspective from which to reflect on, to redefine, and to act on and affect that extant social construct.[12] Thus, social constructs shape and are shaped by the individuals who people those constructions.[13] In a general model, frames change, and they do so in large part because individuals are social beings *and* they are sovereign rational actors.

Is there a model that, by weaving this third, social dimension of institutional analysis together with the two dimensions of the 'Rosenberg Smith' analysis described in Chapter 10 (economic and political institutions), represents humankind as an evolving, simultaneous three-dimensional institutional system? There is. Kirkaldy Smith's moral philosophy does this.

---

[11] "Every morall duty must arise from some thing which mankind are conscious of . . . [yet] it is very seldom that one has a distinct notion of the foundation of their duties, but have merely a notion that they have such and such obligations. . . . [I]ndeed it will but seldom happen that one will be very sensible of the constitution he has been born and bred under; everything by custom appears to be right or at least one is but very little shocked at it" (Smith, 1978, 321–2).

[12] "Identity is, of course, a key element of subjective reality, and like all subjective reality, stands in a dialectical relationship with society. . . . If one is mindful of this dialectic one can avoid the misleading notion of 'collective identities' without having recourse to the uniqueness . . . of individual existence" (Berger and Luckmann, 174–5).

[13] Akerlof offers a compelling analysis as to how "some persons with unusual tastes" can set off "a sequence of increasing disobedience and erosion of belief that in the long run [can change] . . . the social custom[s]. . . . " and the role of "social sanction" in sustaining belief systems (Akerlof , 749–50). He concludes his piece with the observation that "[a] full explanation of social customs and economic equilibrium must describe not only how the system works with existing conditions, but also how such codes themselves evolve" (Akerlof, 773). Adam Smith's analysis captures the social sanction dimension of Akerlof.

As described in Chapters One through Nine, Smith's purpose is to explain the virtues and prerequisites of the "liberal plan of equality, liberty and justice" (*WN*, 664), and to describe how humankind has evolved toward this ideal prospect. In his *Theory of Moral Sentiments*, Smith represents the evolution of the social construction that provides the ethical foundation necessary for a liberal order. In his *Lectures on Jurisprudence*, he describes how systems of positive law and, in particular, those of England, have co-evolved with citizens' ethics in ways that sustain a liberal order. In *The Wealth of Nations*, he explains how the progress of opulence unfolds as the social, political, and economic dimensions of society simultaneously evolve toward a system consistent with the liberal plan.

The people in Smith's analysis are not *homo economicus*, they are social *and* sovereign beings. The story he tells is not of economics as a privileged, independent dimension of human endeavor, but rather as one dimension, along with the political and social dimensions, of a dynamic, simultaneous system in which the progress of the whole requires harmonic progress among those dimensions that make it up.

ECONOMIC ANALYSIS WITHIN A DYNAMIC THREE-DIMENSIONAL
INSTITUTIONAL FRAME: APPLICATIONS OF
ECONOMICS IN CONTEXT

Adam Smith held the Chair of Moral Philosophy at Glasgow University. There are few, if any, such Chairs anymore. Moral philosophy became thoroughly departmental when, as the social sciences, its dimensions were professionally divided and at most colleges and universities departmentalized into the disciplines of sociology, political science, and economics. Today, departments are the dominant organizational structure of academic institutions. Has this division of labor led to more productivity in the social sciences?

More production? Yes. More value? It has cast much light, but it has also left much in the shadows. Thoroughly departmental analysis leads to depth without dimensionality.

Modern economic analysis can benefit by setting itself into a larger context by making its assumptions about given social and political frames explicit,[14] by appreciating the constraints imposed by those assumptions,

---

[14] As it is incumbent upon a meteorologist developing theories about the weather to make his assumptions on climate explicit, similarly it is incumbent upon the economist developing theories about the market to make his assumptions on climate (in this case

and by encouraging some within the field to systematically explore the implications of relaxing those assumptions and allowing frames to change. Doing so makes possible a more general theory that enhances the dimensionality of policy analysis and offers exciting new opportunities in the economics classroom for exploration of the web of connections between the economy and its political and social context. What follows are some brief examples of these possibilities.

Economic Analysis and Emerging Liberal Experiments

Samuel Brittan writes:

The importance of moral aspects of economics should have been brought home by the events in the former communist countries, and especially the former Soviet Union. More thoughtful economists have always known that markets need a background not only of formal laws, but also of accepted rules of behavior, if the 'invisible hand' is to work.

Unfortunately . . . [t]he influence of beliefs on behavior has been confined to discussions over coffee, and their study left to sociologists and others, often unsympathetic to the market process. Yet it is just this aspect, which economists have neglected in their formal work . . . which have proved crucial in Russia and its neighbours, rather than the theorems which have been the predominant study of high-level professional economists. . . . So-called soft subjects, such as cultural history, may have more to tell us about the different outcomes of the breakdown of central planning in the Czech Republic, Russia, the outlying former Soviet republics and China, than mainstream economics. (Brittan, 2–3)

In a more general theory, institutional progress is modeled as a simultaneous system: social, political, and economic. Doing so brings to the fore the complex nature of societal change. As Buchanan makes clear, and Smith appreciated long before, simply opening up markets and letting prices fluctuate freely cannot create a coherent, constructive, cohesive liberal society. Such a society requires the institution of laws and the development and inculcation of civic ethics that are consistent with the freedoms of liberal society. Laws can be rewritten in a day. Ethics and values change more slowly. Effective policy requires an appreciation that a society can move toward a coherent, constructive, cohesive liberal order only as quickly as that social dimension is capable of change. In a time when great nations like Russia and China are trying to figure out

---

social and political climate) explicit. Explicit specification of the assumed climate matters precisely because the actual climate can change. The difference between natural climates and social/political climates is that the latter can change *much* more quickly, so taking social/political climate as given is a strong assumption.

how to join the global free market system, this larger frame should not be ignored.

On Invisible Boundaries and Economic Processes:
The Power of Language

Nancy Folbre and Heidi Hartmann write that:

Serious consideration of both the rhetoric and the ideology of economics can not only enhance an awareness of hidden assumptions, but also help to make those assumptions more realistic. The Hobbesian metaphor is wrong. Neither men nor women spring out of the earth as fully mature individuals, ready to exchange or fight. Rather, girls and boys are born into the care of people whose task is to find and to teach a balance between individual self-interest and collective responsibility. That balance cannot be achieved by simply assigning one to men in the marketplace and the other to women in the home. (Folbre and Hartmann, 198)

A general theory captures the effects of inculcating social definitions of being that are differentiated by an "index" (Spence, 11) such as gender or race; both the broad societal effects and the narrower market consequences. It can also model the incentives for and the effects of efforts to eliminate such index-based differences.

For example, did it matter that in all the books I read when I was growing up, "he" was a doctor and "she" was a nurse? Can such little pronouns affect the world in a big way?[15] A more general theory can address these questions. It makes possible a systematic exploration of the market effects of socially defined conceptions based on gender that are embodied in language.[16] Tracing the threads of such conceptions through a general theory identifies a systematic connection between these social definitions and distributive outcomes in the market.

Language frames expectations. When I was young, language taught that doctoring was appropriate for him and nursing was appropriate for her.

---

[15] In my introductory economics textbook, *Economics: The Ideas and the Issues*, every generic person (doctors, presidents, etc.) is a she, except nurses. It is not my goal in doing so to be "politically correct." Indeed, I reject the notion that I am bound by the latest fad in acceptable language, or that by adopting standard usage I am an enemy of progress. I do believe, however, that for a language to be alive, usage must be allowed to evolve and that there are some emerging usages that are helpful and that will stand the test of time. My students notice the non-standard usage in my text. This is an entrée to a conversation about the economic power of language.

[16] "[L]anguage is capable of becoming the objective repository of vast accumulations of meaning and experience, which it can then preserve in time and transmit to following generations" (Berger and Luckmann, 37).

When language does this in a way that channels half the population into a small sphere of the labor market called "women's work," leaving all other work in the "men's sphere," the consequence of this is, *ceteris paribus*, lower pay for women than men in occupations of comparable worth. Thus, tracing this thread reveals that these social definitions embodied in language do, indeed, create rent-generating market advantages.

These are particularly powerful rent-generating mechanisms precisely because they are imbedded in the social construction of reality. Representing tacit knowledge, part of the natural order that is taken as a given, they are invisible as they do their work. Indeed, for many women for many years, the movement into these crowded professions was, given the frame of their social construction, a voluntary choice.[17] Modeling this nexus, inequity in the market based on a social construction, raises all kinds of complex questions that are both important for policy and fascinating for the classroom.

Solutions based on market intervention can be quick (e.g., dictating that wages include a compensating variation), but they treat the symptom and not the disease. Such *ad hoc* solutions may cause distortions that can lead to perverse unintended consequences. On the other hand, given the inert character of social constructions, a solution based on changing those constructs is inevitably slow, and it may be intolerably so without market intervention.

Understanding the power of social definitions based on language also makes clear why some social/political actions are aimed at reconstructing language. For example, when I grew up down South in New Orleans "Negro" was a term of what I would call "diminished respect." For most whites, a Negro was to be respected, but only if he or she was in his or her "place."[18]

As the civil rights movement evolved, many in that movement began to reject the term Negro as a white community term that defined "place." Their response was to act on language, introducing the terms "black" or

---

[17] The experience of women in World War II, the classic Rosie the Riveter, reflects the constraints of social expectations. Given the exigencies of the war, there were new, high paying "men's sphere" jobs open to women, but the government had to convince many women that it was appropriate to take these jobs; ergo the Rosie the Riveter campaign. Interestingly, many of the women wanted to stay in those jobs after the war, but they were pushed out by institutional changes that gave preferences to men and redefined women's role; e.g., *The Feminine Mystique* (Friedan, 1963).

[18] The traditional southern white linguistic taxonomy of oppression included: "Negro" – respected, but only if s/he was in her/his "place," "colored" – quiescent and unrespected, and "uppity nigger" – a black person out of her/his "place."

"African American" in order to escape that "place" which, for several hundred years, had been a part of the natural order of the South. To the degree that this escape has been successful, the consequences show up not only in language, but also in the marketplace. There is a nexus here. It enriches our models and it should be in our classrooms.

The women's movement did something very similar. When I was growing up, "Master" and "Mr." defined a male based on age – youth and adult, respectively. "Miss" and "Mrs." sound like a parallel construction, but these terms did not have parallel purposes. Miss and Mrs. defined a female based on her custodial relationship to a man, under her father's (brother's, community's) or her husband's care, respectively. The women's movement introduced "Ms." as an escape from this "place." To the degree that this escape has been successful, the consequences show up not only in language, but also in the marketplace. There is a nexus here. It enriches our models and it should be in our classrooms.

In both cases, acting on language has been a part of a larger program by blacks and women respectively to liberate themselves from "place," and to enjoy more of the opportunities, including those economic opportunities, that society has to offer. This nexus between social and economic dynamics is invisible in a model that "sees" the world thoroughly departmentally.[19]

In the "Introduction" to his *General Theory*, John Maynard Keynes (1964) writes:

[I]f orthodox economics is at fault, the error is to be found not in the superstructure, which has been erected with great care for logical consistency, but in a lack of clearness and of generality in the premises.... Those, who are strongly wedded to what I shall call 'the classical theory', will fluctuate, I expect, between a belief that I am quite wrong and a belief that I am saying nothing new.... The ideas which are here expressed so laboriously are extremely simple and should be obvious. The difficulty lies, not in the new ideas, but in escaping from the old ones, which ramify, for those brought up as most of us have been, in every corner of our minds. (Keynes 1964, v, viii)

Today's economic orthodoxy faces a similar challenge. It must "escape from habitual modes of thought and expression" (Keynes, xiii) embodied in assumptions like *homo economicus*. Building on its Smithian legacy and expanding the "generality in the premises" to include the dynamic role of culture and values make possible a more general theory. Of course, there is a Catch-22 here. The fact that economic orthodoxy is, itself, an

[19] Robert Frost's poem, "Departmental," offers a wonderful image of such thinking (Frost, 1995).

extant social construction with all the attendant inertia of natural order thinking constrains its ability to "escape from habitual modes of thought and expression."

ECONOMICS FOR THE TWENTY-FIRST CENTURY – ADDING SMITHIAN DIMENSIONALITY

Introduction

The thoughtful reviewers of this work challenged me to speculate on what a Smithian economics for the twenty-first century might look like. My short response is that economics would look very much as it does today. It is and would remain high-quality work focusing on strategic optimization behavior and offering significant contributions to our understanding of the human condition. The standard economic approach does, after all, capture the vast majority of our individual choices, given societal context. Adding a Smithian dimensionality does not replace the economic approach, it contextualizes it.

Unfortunately, in its Beckerian 'we have discovered Truth' version, modern economics rejects the very notion that there is any larger context that matters. As a consequence, economics often appears isolationist and/or imperial with respect to its sister social sciences. In his delightful 1973 "anthropological" study of "Life Among the Econ," Axel Leijonhufvud describes the Econ as a tribe in which the "young are brought up to feel contempt for the softer living . . . Polscis and . . . Sociogs" (Leijonhufvud, 327). Although these tribes share a "common genetical heritage, relations with these tribes are strained" because the Polcis and Sociogs "'do not make modls,'" and "modls" are the "totem" of the Econ tribe (Leijonhufvud, 327, 330).

An isolationist/imperial attitude is reflected in George Stigler and Gary Becker's assertion in "*De Gustibus Non Est Disputandum*" that worrying about context is much ado about nothing. According to Stigler and Becker, the economic approach explains all, so better we should push ahead with our own tools rather than turn to sociologists or anthropologists or political scientists or historians to shed additional light on human events:

Our hypothesis is trivial, for it merely asserts that we should apply standard economic logic as extensively as possible. But the self-same hypothesis is also a demanding challenge, for it urges us not to abandon opaque and complicated problems with the easy suggestion that the further explanation will perhaps someday be produced by one of our sister behavioral sciences. (Stigler and Becker, 89–90)

Becker dismisses such efforts to move beyond the economic approach as a waste of intellectual energy:

With an ingenuity worthy of admiration if put to better use, almost any conceivable behavior is alleged to be dominated by ignorance and irrationality, values and their frequently unexplained shifts, custom and tradition, the compliance somehow induced by social norms, or the ego and the id. (Becker, 1976, 13)

Not surprisingly, this dismissive tone elicits a pained response from a scholar in a sister social science:

[While] political scientists try to give some account of preferences... [w]e do not believe that "there is no accounting for tastes." ... Political scientists as well as sociologists and anthropologists care about how societies select the kinds of tastes that they do. And this is obviously not just a rational process of choice taking place in the present time; it is a profoundly historical process....

So the preaching of economists about how to explain both dazzles and disillusions us. Many of us have been dazzled, and I think we have learned a lot by casting this reflected light, being the moon to the economists' sun. But eventually we become aware of the limitations of the approach, particularly its failure to consider culture, institutions, the sources of preferences, and historical process. Then the preaching seems too narrow, even a little bit like Savanarola, burning the books he didn't like. We don't burn the economist, but lacking a conversation, we may stop listening. (Keohane, 242–4)

A Smithian economics for the twenty-first century would be less arrogant. It would value analysis that factors in "culture, institutions, the sources of preferences, and historical process." It would enjoy and value engaging colleagues like Robert Keohane in a mutually respectful conversation exploring the web of connections that weaves economics into a larger societal dynamic. A twenty-first century Smithian economist would be the kind of scholar Keynes envisioned in 1924:

The study of economics does not seem to require any specialized gifts of an unusually high order. Is it not, intellectually regarded, a very easy subject compared with the higher branches of philosophy and pure science? Yet good, or even competent, economists are the rarest of birds. An easy subject, at which very few excel! The paradox finds its explanation perhaps, in that the master-economist must posses a rare *combination* of gifts. He must reach a high standard in several different directions and must combine talents not often found together. He must be mathematician, historian, statesman, philosopher – in some degree. He must understand symbols and speak in words. He must contemplate the particular in terms of the general, and touch abstract and concrete in the same flight of thought. He must study the present in the light of the past for the purposes of the future. No part of man's nature or his institutions must lie entirely outside his regard. He must be purposeful and disinterested in a simultaneous mood; as aloof and incorruptible as an artist, yet sometimes as near the earth as a politician. (Keynes, 1924, 321–2, emphasis in original)

Economists today are not trained to be, nor are they rewarded for being, this kind of scholar because economic thought today is framed by the "habitual modes of thought and expression" (Keynes, 1964, xiii) embodied in the *homo economicus* assumption that underlies the "*De gustibus*" assertion. Indeed, the acceptance of this assumption on human nature has become so habituated that it is no longer an assumption. It is canon, and the power of this canon is reinforced by the beauty that flows from it: the elegant mathematical modeling made possible by the belief in rational, optimizing man.[20]

This system of belief is inculcated into and becomes habituated in each new generation of the economics community by the process one must go through to become an official, continuing member of that society – to get a PhD and then to survive and prevail in the community by being tenured and promoted. Central to that process is the journal.

The Market Space in the Marketplace of Ideas: The Role of Journals

In economics, as in any scholarly discipline, the ultimate goal of the vast majority of the members of the community is to make a significant contribution to the community discourse and, based on that contribution, to advance to esteemed, senior status within this community of scholars.

For the professional economist, the path through tenure and promotion to such a contribution and, in turn, to personal advancement, lies through the pages of the professional economics journals. Journal publications are the coin of the realm and the more elite the journal, the more value in the coin. The gold standard in economics includes the *American Economic Review* and the *Journal of Political Economy*, to name two of this element.

Graduate students gain entry into economics PhD programs based, in large part, on the likelihood that they can master the theoretical modeling and the empirical analysis that represent the norms of the discourse because the mastery of these norms is essential if one is going to become a productive publisher in the journals. Since the primary language of this modeling and analysis is math, the essential screen for admission into an economics PhD program is high-order math skills.

---

[20] Recall Hollander's comment that the hypothetical-deductive theorizing "cries out for mathematical formulation" (Hollander, 71–2).

In graduate school, students are taught and mentored to master the application of this language to high-quality modeling and analysis.[21] If a student survives, receives a PhD, and moves on to an academic position, as a new assistant professor in almost any U.S. research university's economics department, she or he gets very simple marching orders: publish as much as you can in the best journals you can (and do a good job for your students, too), or perish. Thus the life of a research university economist:

- begins with from four to six years of graduate school training designed to prepare him or her to publish in the journals,
- proceeds to six more years as an assistant professor pursuing such publications in order to secure tenure and promotion rather than perish, and then
- continues with the pursuit of publications in order to establish one's "name," attain promotion to full professor, and enhance one's marketability. Very well published professors become very hot properties, or "stars." As in any labor market where there is free agency and where individual contributions are discernable and valued, these stars earn a significant premium.

The competition in the field can be modeled right out of the pages of an introductory economics textbook. As Deidre McCloskey writes in her *Rhetoric of Economics*:

It is a market argument . . . [and in this market t]he standards of "good" reasons and "warrantable" belief and "plausible" conclusions . . . come . . . from the conversations of practitioners themselves, in their laboratories or seminar rooms or conference halls. (McCloskey, 28–9)

In other words, the standards emerge from the community discourse and the primary medium for this discourse is the professional journals. Journal editors, themselves leaders in the community, ask other respected

---

[21] "The Education and Training of Economics Doctorates: Major Findings of the American Economic Association's Commission on Graduate Education in Economics," January 1991, reports that "Faculty members, graduate students, and 1977–78 PhDs exhibit complete agreement about the relative emphasis given in graduate training. . . . Economic theory leads the way, followed in order by econometrics, empirical economics, and applications-policy; institutions and literature reside at the bottom of the list" (Hansen, 1070).

members of the community to assess submissions based on these community standards. Editors choose from the submissions those pieces that represent the best work based on the reports of reviewers who are applying the community standards. In principle, this is a positive process that delivers the best work to the community discourse. But is it?

"To 'Exert a Wholesome Influence . . .'"

The institutionalization of the economics discourse took a significant step forward during the years from 1885 to 1892. The American Economic Association was established in 1885, the British Economic Association in 1890, and several of the leading journals in the field began publication during that period. The "Publications of the American Economic Association" were first issued in 1887. (This morphed into the *American Economic Review* in 1911.) The *Quarterly Journal of Economics* was established at Harvard in 1886, the *Economic Journal (EJ)* by the British Economic Association in 1890, and the *Journal of Political Economy* at the University of Chicago in 1892.[22]

The first pages of the first number of the *Economic Journal* report the minutes of the meeting at which the British Economic Association and the *EJ* were established. These minutes offer a fascinating insight into the role the founders believed their organization and its journal should serve in the discourse. It is worth reflecting on the issues raised.

The "meeting was held on the afternoon of November 21, 1890, at University College, London, under the presidency of Mr. Goschen"

---

[22] It was shortly after this (1903) that, under Alfred Marshall's leadership, Cambridge established "a separate School and Tripos in Economics," a seminal event in the establishment of "the Cambridge School of Economics" (Keynes, 1924, 365). "[A]fter his time Economics could never be again one of a number of subjects which a Moral Philosopher would take in his stride, one Moral Science out of several, as Mill, Jevons, and Sidgwick took it" (Keynes, 1924, 365). Marshall could do this without deconstructing the discourse because "[i]n that first age of married society in Cambridge, when the narrow circle of the spouses-regnant of the Heads of the Colleges and of a few wives of Professors was first extended, several of the most notable Dons, particularly in the School of Moral Science, married students of Newnham. The double link between husbands and between wives bound together a small cultured society of great simplicity and distinction. . . . [Reflecting on his boyhood in this world, Keynes continues:] I remember a homely, intellectual atmosphere which is harder to find in the swollen, heterogeneous Cambridge of to-day" (Keynes, 1924, 357). If that community of discourse across demarcated disciplines was beginning to vanish in the "swollen, heterogeneous Cambridge" of 1924, it's no surprise that it has largely vanished in the thoroughly departmental institutional cities that are the large universities of today.

(Edgeworth, 2). Alfred Marshall, who had called the meeting, spoke first and in the course of his address, he noted that:

he had received a great number of suggestions from persons who were not economists, some of which expressed the hope that the proposed Association would 'exert a wholesome influence.' That was one thing which he hoped they would not set themselves to do. Their desire was not to 'exert a wholesome influence' in the sense of setting up a standard of orthodoxy, to which all contributors had to conform; economics was a science, and an 'orthodox science' was a contradiction in terms. Science could be true or false, but could not be orthodox; and the best way to find out what was true was to welcome the criticisms of all people who knew what they were talking about.... The one influence which he hoped they would exercise would be that they would start from an absolutely catholic basis, and include every school of economists which was doing genuine work. (Edgeworth, 4–5)[23]

Mr. Goshen followed:

Warned by Professor Marshall, he would try to keep away from any question of 'wholesome influence.'... [Nevertheless, he expressed concern about] men who called themselves political economists, but who had not the slightest idea what economics were.... (Edgeworth, 7).

[After more discussion] Mr. Courtney proposed ... [a] resolution: "That any person who desires to further the aims of the Association, and is approved by the Council, be admitted to membership." ... [He continued:] But there were two or three words in it which apparently were not quite consistent with the catholicity which Professor Marshall had rightly demanded as the prime characteristic of the association. Persons were required not only to desire to further the aims of the Association, but to be approved by the council before they could be admitted to membership. Probably some gentleman present would like to have these words omitted.... But there must be some limitation, and it was necessary occasionally to exercise a little authority if they were going to conduct their business in a satisfactory manner. There were some things which must be taken to be finally fixed ... a mathematical journal would [for example] exclude contributions which affected to square the circle.... [N]otwithstanding what Mr. Marshall had said, he hoped the Association would exercise a wholesome influence....

[23] Its strong platform notwithstanding ("We regard the state as an educational and ethical agency whose positive aid is an indispensable condition of human progress.... [W]e hold that the doctrine of laissez-faire is unsafe in politics and unsound in morals...." (Ely, 6–7)), the "Report of the Organization of the American Economic Association" asserts that, in keeping with Marshall's view, "[I]t was not proposed to form a society of advocates of any political opinion or set of political opinions, as for example, free-trade or protection ... or a society to champion any class interests, either of rich or of poor, either of employer or of employe. What was desired was a society which, free from all trammels, should seek truth from all sources, should be ready to give a respectful hearing to every new idea, and should shun no revelation of facts...." (Ely, 5–6).

Professor Edgeworth defended the almost indiscriminate admission of members which was proposed, on the ground that it was impossible to find any satisfactory test of orthodoxy in economic doctrine. (Edgeworth, 9–10)

This conversation reflects a desire among these founders to avoid the trap of "habitual modes of thoughts and expression," the very trap that Keynes asserted the economics discourse had fallen into forty-six years later.

Marshall and his colleagues appreciated that given their control over access to the Association and to the pages of *The Economic Journal*, they could control the content of the conversation. To those, like Marshall and Edgeworth, who advocated that the Association and its journal should encourage a catholic discourse, this power made the prospect of exerting a wholesome influence appear to be a very slippery slope toward establishing an orthodoxy.

Deidre McCloskey's "market argument" is a reference to the belief that free and open markets serve all of us when they bring out the best in each of us through fair competition. The concept of a "marketplace of ideas" extends that logic to a free and open, catholic competition of ideas among us. There is, however, a problem with the application of this economic logic to the marketplace of ideas in economics, because market access to that discourse is not free and open. The market space, the journal page, is in private hands and access is screened by those who control that space.

In order to access a mainstream economics journal's pages, one's work must pass through an editorial process that exerts a "wholesome influence" by insuring that the work is consistent with the accepted norms of the community discourse. Those norms are determined by conversations that are mediated by those very journals. Those who master the application of the accepted norms become the leaders in the field, and it is these leaders who, in turn, become the editors and reviewers of the leading journals that define the community standards. Thus, as is inevitable in any community's culture, "wholesome" becomes endogenously defined as what "we" do.

Meeting these endogenous standards is a significant determinant of the success or failure of aspiring economists, so all are trained to meet the standards and the path to leadership lies in taking the modeling or analysis that derives from these standards to a new level of sophistication. It is this process of intellectual construction that takes concepts like *homo economicus* from the realm of explicit assumption to tacit assumption to canon.

From Canon to Catholicity

There is a lesson in all this from Adam Smith for the twenty-first century. As we've seen, in Smith's moral philosophy institutions are instrumental in humankind's evolution. They can be instruments that create impediments to progress or they can facilitate progress.

Journals are the framework that supports the entire institutional architecture of modern economics. If they are to facilitate progress, they must exert their wholesome influence with a very delicate (invisible?) hand that errs on the side of inclusion because, only then, can there be that catholic discourse that Marshall and Edgeworth envisioned as the path toward scientific progress.

Smithian scope and method can only flourish in the modern economics community if leading journals give such work access to the discourse. If Smithian work can gain access to gold standard journals, the norms of the economics culture will shift and the silver and bronze journals will follow suit. If journal access expands the dimensionality of acceptable thought, the training of economists will follow that trend. It might then become the case that the skills valued in a PhD program application include not only a high math GRE (Graduate Records Examination) score, but also a rich background in humankind's institutions and its history.

A Smithian economics for the twenty-first century would return to the role it played in Smith's moral philosophy – one necessary, but not sufficient, dimension of analysis in the social sciences.

TWELVE

The Liberal Plan and the Quandary of Capital

ADAM SMITH, THE LIBERAL PLAN, AND THE QUANDARY OF CAPITAL

One last issue that concerned Smith is worthy of note: The quandary of capital in a liberal, free market system.

This quandary can best be described as follows: The accumulation of the capital necessary for the progress of opulence, described in Chapter Six, seems to give rise to a class of accumulators who, being few in number, enjoy a concentrated of control over capital that empowers them to extort market advantages, either directly or through government, in pursuit of greater returns on their capital. This quandary became the foundation of Marx's critique of capitalism and was a central concern of such leading liberal economic lights as John Stuart Mill and John Maynard Keynes. Smith was concerned about this issue in 1776.[1]

In *WN* Book I Chapter 5, Smith describes how concentrated control over capital among a few "masters" makes it possible for "[m]asters [who] are always and every where in a sort of tacit, but constant uniform combination . . . sometimes . . . to sink the wages of labour below . . . [their natural] rate" (*WN*, 84). When the workers form a "defensive combination" and "clamour" for higher wages, "[t]he masters upon these occasions are just as clamorous upon the other side, and never cease to

---

[1] I agree with a reviewer's point that the traditional problem of capital, increasing returns to scale, was not an issue for Smith. I do believe, however, that capital was an issue in Smith. He was concerned with what he perceived as the asymmetric power in the market and in the political arena that comes with ever greater concentrations of capital in the hands of the mercantilists. The "economies of scale" issue complements Smith analysis of concentrated control over capital because these economies exacerbate the problem.

call aloud for the assistance of the civil magistrate, and the rigorous execution of those laws which have been enacted with so much severity against the combinations of servants, labourers, and journeymen" (*WN*, 84–5). Given their resource advantage, the accumulated capital they control, "in disputes with their workman, masters must generally have the advantage...." (*WN*, 85).

Smith saw very clearly that thanks to concentrated control over capital in their relatively few hands, masters can collude, can sustain themselves in labor disputes much more easily than their workers, and can mobilize political influence to their benefit.[2] Indeed, Smith considered the exploitation of workers in wage bargaining to be but one of the perverse consequences of a larger mercantile system built on the power that derives from concentrated control over capital.[3]

As a classic example of this power, in *WN* Book IV Chapter 8, Smith describes how, by mobilizing their resources and "extorting from the legislature bounties upon the exportation of ... [domestic] linen, high duties upon the importation of all foreign linen, and a total prohibition of the home consumption of some sorts of French linen" (*WN*, 644), the mercantile interests were able to exploit the "spinners ... poor people, women commonly, scattered about in all different parts of the country, [who worked] without support or protection" (*WN*, 644), and to minimize the competition from foreign producers. The fruit of this exercise of mercantile political muscle was a premium on their capital investment, an interest return which Smith considered a monopoly return like rent, not a return to effort or risk or superintendence (*WN*, 847–8).[4]

Smith recognized this perverse effect of the quandary of capital, but he seems to have seen the distributive injustice it causes as a transitory phenomenon within the commercial stage that is eliminated by humankind's progress.

---

[2] Recall from Chapter Eight that, according to Smith, this influence comes either from deference to the knowledge of capital markets based on their activity in those markets or, failing that, from intimidation by those who control capital.

[3] Being born into this concentrated wealth also had perverse effects: "[A] man born to a great fortune, even though naturally frugal, is very seldom capable. The situation of such a person naturally disposes him to attend rather to ornament which pleases his fancy, than to profit for which he has so little occasion" (*WN*, 385). See (Pack, 1991) for more on this.

[4] As described in Chapter Nine, apropos of the artificial and unproductive character of this return, Smith saw interest, along with rent, as an ideal source of public revenue because taxing it away does not reduce the incentive for productive activity. However, he also recognized that the global mobility of capital makes it, unlike rent, very difficult to tax because it can flee.

In the course of that progress, described here in Chapters Two through Four, as institutional and ethical systems establish and enforce ever more mature standards of commutative justice, the greater personal security this affords to individuals encourages increased accumulation. This leads to capital deepening. Capital deepening fuels the progress of opulence and, as described in Chapter Six, it also drives wages up and returns to capital down. So, in effect, Smith believed that in the natural course of humankind's progress, the quandary of capital and the associated problem of distributive injustice would be resolved by that progress.

By 1848, however, seventy-two years after the publication of *The Wealth of Nations*, the year Marx and Engels published their *Communist Manifesto* and the year John Stuart Mill published his *Principles of Political Economy*, Smith's sanguine hope had not been realized. Quite to the contrary, the quandary of capital seemed to be endemic to the liberal free market system and a potentially fatal flaw.

KARL MARX AND THE QUANDARY OF CAPITAL AS A FATAL FLAW OF THE LIBERAL PLAN

Karl Marx, following Smith, represented the accumulation of capital as a necessary condition for the ever-finer division of labor that leads to increasing productivity. Unlike Smith, however, Marx rejected the view that a liberal society based on private property could both accumulate and sustain itself. In the middle of the nineteenth century, Marx was one among many who, looking out at the immiseration of workers and the upheavals caused by that misery, asserted that the liberal, free market experiment was doomed.[5]

Marx argued that the quandary of capital, the concentration of capital that goes hand in hand with increased accumulation, is a fatal flaw in capitalism because it gives rise to a dynamic in the capitalist mode of production that inevitably leads to its own demise:

One capitalist always kills many. Hand in hand with this centralization [of capital]...develop, on an ever-extending scale, the co-operative form of the labour-process, the conscious technical application of science,...the economizing of all means of production...Along with the constantly diminishing number of the magnates of capital, who usurp and monopolise all advantages of this process...grows the mass of misery, oppression, slavery, degradation, exploitation...[But even as the misery of the] working class [increases, so too

---

[5] See Spiegel (1991), Chapters 19 and 20.

that class is]...always increasing in numbers, and [is] disciplined, united, organized by the very mechanism of the process of capitalist production itself. (Marx, 715)

This last line refers to Marx's view that the very increasing concentration of control over capital that goes hand in hand with the advance of capitalism transforms disorganized labor into organized labor. In miserable conditions, this organized labor ultimately exploits the very organization imposed upon it by the capitalist mode to turn on its oppressors and seize the means of production: "The expropriators are expropriated" (Marx, 715). Sweet revenge, according to Marx, and the beginning of a new, socialized mode of production and with it a more just distribution.

In two important respects, Smith, Mill, and Keynes shared Marx's view on the quandary of capital:

- They believed that there is, indeed, a tendency for control over capital in a liberal system to become concentrated.
- They saw this tendency as a significant threat to the liberal system.

However, in two equally important respects, they differed from Marx:

- They did not believe that this tendency is an inevitably fatal flaw.
- They valued the liberal experiment for the freedom it affords the individual, so in order to preserve and nurture that experiment, each of them addressed this quandary of capital.

As we've seen, Smith's concern about the quandary of capital lay in his fear that its embodiment, the mercantile system, would undermine the liberal experiment in Britain. His hope lay in the deepening of capital that would, he believed, come with the development of greater commutative justice, and in the emergence of civic humanist, active statesmen to lead society in that direction.

John Stuart Mill and John Maynard Keynes each wrote in times – 1848 and 1936 respectively – when the liberal experiment seemed to be on the verge of collapse. Both traced the problems of their respective times to the concentration of control over capital. The difference between them lay in the solutions they offered to this quandary of capital.

JOHN STUART MILL ON CAPITAL AND THE LIBERAL EXPERIMENT

As did Smith and, later, Keynes, John Stuart Mill wrote in a time when the liberal experiment seemed to be very much at risk. The first edition of his

Principles of Political Economy was published in 1848, the same year that Marx and Engels published *The Communist Manifesto*. It was, Mill wrote, "an age [of "revolutions in Europe"] . . . when a general reconsideration of all first principles is felt to be inevitable" (Mill, 202). The liberal experiment seemed to many to be a failure and alternative social constructions were being advocated. Two of the most popular were communal schemes: "St. Simonism and Fourierism" (Mill, 204).

In his *Principles*, Mill compares and contrasts the problems and the promise of these alternative, communal visions of society with the problems and the promise of the liberal experiment in order to make a reasoned judgment as to whether a communistic[6] or a liberal plan is the preferable path for society.

He begins by examining a series of problems commonly attributed to communism. He cites, for example, "[t]he objection ordinarily made to a system of community property and equal distribution of produce, that each person would be incessantly occupied in evading his fair share of work" (Mill, 204).

After each such objection to a communistic scheme, Mill offers an ameliorating consideration, most of which are a function of the fact that in a communal society all are constantly under the eye of all others. That constant eye of the community creates immense social pressure to conform to communal standards of behavior. Mill concludes that with this constant source of community enforcement "these difficulties [e.g., avoiding work or having more children than one can support], though real, are not necessarily insuperable" (Mill, 207). He then proceeds to compare all these problems with "the [present] institution of private property" (Mill, 208) and concludes:

If, therefore, the choice were to be made between Communism with all its chances, and the present state of society with all its sufferings and injustices; if the institution of private property necessarily carried with it as a consequence, that the produce of labour should be apportioned as we now see it, almost in an inverse ratio to labour – the largest portions to those who have never worked at all, the next largest to those whose work is almost nominal, and so in a descending scale, the remuneration dwindling as the work grows harder and more disagreeable, until the most fatiguing and exhausting bodily labour cannot count with certainty on being able to earn even the necessaries of life; if this or Communism were the alternative, all the difficulties, great or small, of Communism would be but as

---

[6] It is important to note that when Mill uses the term communism, he does so in the pre-Marxist sense represented by St. Simone of Fourier or "Mr. Owen and his followers. M. Louis Blanc and M. Cabet . . ." (Mill, 203).

dust in the balance. But to make the comparison applicable, we must compare Communism at its best, with the regime of individual property, not as it is, but as it might be made. (Mill, 208)

Mill wants to give the liberal experiment a full, fair hearing. Why? If the problems of communism are manageable and the problems of liberal society as it is are so insufferable, why not move on? Because, as did Smith before him and Keynes after, Mill deeply valued the liberal ideal:

[I]t is not by comparison with the present bad state of society that the claims of Communism can be estimated; nor is it sufficient that it should promise greater personal and mental freedom than is now enjoyed by those who have not enough of either to deserve the name. The question is, whether there would be any asylum left for individuality of character; whether public opinion would not be a tyrannical yoke; whether the absolute dependence of each on all, and surveillance of each by all, would not grind all down into a tame uniformity of thoughts, feelings, and actions. . . . No society in which eccentricity is a matter of reproach, can be in a wholesome state. It is yet to be ascertained whether the Communistic scheme would be consistent with that multiform development of human nature, those manifold unlikenesses, that diversity of tastes and talents, and variety of intellectual points of view, which not only form a great part of the interest of human life, but by bringing intellects into stimulating collision, and by presenting to each innumerable notions that he would not have conceived of himself, are the mainspring of mental and moral progression. (Mill, 210–11)

Mill valued liberal society for the sake of the individual, and he believed that a society that nurtures its individuals as individuals nurtures itself. He shared this value with Smith and he shared the same purpose. Mill's goal was to further the liberal experiment by analyzing the sources of its failures and prescribing solutions that would strengthen and sustain it.

In light of the miserable state of that experiment in 1848, Mill looked back on the course of the experiment and identified what he believed was the problem in its institutional structure, a bias toward the concentrated control over capital in particular and over private property more generally:

The principle of private property has never yet had a fair trial in any country; and less so, perhaps, in this country than in some others. The arrangements of modern Europe commenced from a distribution of property which was the result, not of just partition, or acquisition by industry, but of conquest and violence[7] . . . [Subsequently, t]he laws of property . . . have not held the balance fairly between human beings, but have heaped impediments upon some, to give advantages to others; they have purposely fostered inequalities, and prevented all

---

[7] Marx's "primitive accumulation" (Marx, 667).

from starting the race fair. That all should indeed start on perfectly equal terms, is inconsistent with any law of private property: but if as much pains as has been taken to aggravate the inequality of chances arising from the natural working of the principle, had been taken to temper that inequality by every means not subversive of the principle itself; if the tendency of legislation had been to favour the diffusion, instead of the concentration of wealth ... the principle of individual property would have been found to have no necessary connection with the physical and social evils which almost all Socialist writers assume to be inseparable from it. (Mill, 208–9)

Clearly, this "tendency of legislation" derives from two sources that Smith highlighted in his attack on the mercantilists (Described in Chapter Eight here.): An asymmetry of information about the markets tends to make legislators deferential to those who are major players in the markets, those who control large sums of capital. In addition, the power of large capital holders to put their wealth to work supporting those legislators who support their interests and destroying those who resist their interests bends the mind of many legislators.

So how did Mill propose to accomplish this "diffusion, instead of the concentration of wealth"? His policy prescription derives from a principle that he believed is fundamental to a liberal order. One's claim to property is established only by one's *own efforts.*

Private property, in every defence made of it, is supposed to mean, the guarantee to individuals of the fruits of their own labour and abstinence. The guarantee to them of the fruits of the labour and abstinence of others, transmitted to them without any merit or exertion of their own, is not of the essence of the institution, but a mere incidental consequence, which when it reaches a certain height, does not promote, but conflicts with the ends which render private property legitimate. (Mill, 209)

Given this principle, that one's "own labour and abstinence" establishes property rights in a liberal order, Mill asserts that although one can legitimately offer one's own property as a gift or bequest to another who did not produced that value, no individual has an unfettered claim to such accumulated property simply by virtue of a relationship to one who dies with wealth remaining. "It follows, therefore, that although the right of bequest, of gift after death, forms part of the idea of private property, the right of inheritance, as distinguished from bequest, does not" (Mill, 221).

Mill asserts that both in theory and in precedent, the state can limit accession from gifts without violating the principle of private property, and given that premise, he offers the following policy prescription:

> Were I framing a code of laws according to what seems to me best in itself, without regard to existing opinions and sentiments, I should prefer to restrict, not what any one might bequeath, but what any one should be permitted to acquire, by bequest or inheritance. Each person should have power to dispose by will of his or her whole property; but not to lavish it in enriching some one individual beyond a certain maximum, which should be fixed sufficiently high to afford the means of comfortable independence. The inequalities of property which arise from unequal industry, frugality, perseverance, talents, and to a certain extent even opportunities, are inseparable from the principle of private property, and if we accept the principle, we must bear with these consequences of it: but I see nothing objectionable in fixing the limit to what any one may acquire by the mere favour of others, without exercise of his faculties, and in requiring that if he desires any further accession of fortune, *he shall work for it.* (Mill, 227–8, emphasis added)[8]

Mill sees the liberal experiment at risk and he identifies intergenerational transfer laws that concentrate control over accumulated property – land and capital – as a key source of the problem. Instead of accumulation based on one's personal exertion, innovation, and risk taking, property can be inherited, and thus concentrated control of wealth is maintained from one generation to the next. This, in turn, provides the resources among that class of wealth holders for establishing political power to protect and enhance this unearned advantage.

As Smith made clear and Mill understood very well, concentrated control over property goes hand in hand with political power. "The laws of property ... [that] have purposely fostered inequalities, and prevented all from starting the race fair" are not an accident of history. They are the result of rent-seeking/rent-maintenance behavior by a class that enjoys power based on concentrated control over property – land and capital. For Mill, as for Smith, the concentrated control over capital was the most significant dimension of this problem.

Mill writes that the laboring class works "for the benefit of the possessors of capital ... paying ... a heavy tribute for the use of capital" (Mill, 773–4). The families in this "non-labouring," capital-holding class may

---

[8] On June 19, 1935, President Roosevelt sent a message to Congress that echoed Mill's concern and his solution, asserting: "'Our revenue laws have operated in many ways to the unfair advantage of the few, and they have done little to prevent an unjust concentration of wealth and economic power.... Social unrest and a deepening sense of unfairness are dangers to our national life which we must minimize by rigorous methods.' Accordingly, he asked for ... stiffer inheritance taxes, since 'the transmission from generation to generation of vast fortunes ... is not consistent with the ideal and sentiments of the American people'" (Kennedy, 275).

change as new fortunes are generated and old ones are squandered, but the interest and the power of the class itself remains the same. Mill considers this "non-labouring" class that controls capital a social "evil...[that] cannot be eradicated, until the power itself is withdrawn" (Mill, 754). In other words, the concentration of control over capital must be broken.

Mill's proposed intergenerational diffusion of property preserves what he believes is the essence of liberal property rights – one's right to enjoy the fruits of one's *own* labor.[9] It also reflects his belief, a belief Smith shared, that personal independence is the best condition for personal growth, and that rich personal growth makes one a more constructive contributor in all dimensions of societal intercourse, be it the race for wealth, participation as a citizen in the political process, social interaction, or artful creativity.[10]

Smith and Mill present a primarily micro analysis of societal processes with the goal of understanding and furthering the liberal experiment, and both saw the quandary of capital as a threat to that experiment. Keynes shared the same goal, but he analyzed the liberal system and this quandary of capital from a macro perspective.

JOHN MAYNARD KEYNES ON CAPITAL, EMPLOYMENT, AND
THE RENTIER CLASS

When Keynes published *The General Theory* in 1936, the liberal experiment was 160 years older than when *The Wealth of Nations* was published, but it was still a work in progress. In 1936, a Great Depression, war clouds

---

[9] Under Mill's policy, Bill Gates would be fully secure in the property he acquires through fair competition, but his children would only be able to inherit a "comfortable independence" from that wealth when Mr. Gates dies. They would be forced to start in their own generation's race for wealth at a starting line that is much closer to all others, and their achievements in that race would be much more their own.

[10] The corrosiveness of dependence is a constant theme in Smith. See his comments on slaves (*WN*, 386–8), or colonies (*WN*, 582, 615), or lords' tenants and retainers (*WN*, 335–6) as examples. It is, according to Smith, the freedom from this latter dependency that allowed towns to become an engine of growth (contrary to natural tendencies) and to ultimately undermine this unproductive feudal structure built on dependency.

Citing a model of independency, Smith writes that "[t]hose laws and customs so favourable to the yeomanry, have perhaps contributed more to the present grandeur of England than all their boasted regulations of commerce taken together" (*WN*, 392). Describing his late, dearest friend Hume, Smith wrote that "[h]is temper...seemed to be more happily balanced...than that perhaps of any other man I have ever known. Even in the lowest state of his fortune, his great and necessary frugality never hindered him from exercising, upon proper occasions, acts both of charity and generosity. It was a frugality founded, not upon avarice, but upon the love of independency" (*Correspondence*, 220–1).

over Europe, and disarray in the realm of economic theory[11] made it seem like an experiment that might not last much longer. As did Smith and Mill, Keynes valued the liberal experiment, and for very much the same reasons:

[A]bove all, individualism, if it can be purged of its defects and its abuses, is the best safeguard of personal liberty in the sense that, compared with any other system, it greatly widens the field for the exercise of personal choice. It is also the best safeguard of the variety of life, which emerges precisely from this extended field of choice, and the loss of which is the greatest of all losses of the homogeneous or totalitarian state. For this variety preserves the traditions which embody the most secure and successful choices of former generations; it colours the present with the diversification of fancy; and, being the handmaid of experiment as well as of tradition and of fancy, it is the most powerful instrument for human betterment. (Keynes, 380)

As with Smith and Mill, Keynes' work was an effort at preservation. He sought to show how liberal society could overcome its problems and progress. And again, as with Smith and Mill, Keynes believed that the source of these problems was concentrated control over capital, a control that Keynes believed was derived from the mistaken, and self-serving for those who advocated it, view that it is necessary for institutions to encourage such concentrations in order to create a pool of capital to fuel economic growth.

In the last chapter of *The General Theory*, with his theory now laid before his reader, Keynes offers some "Concluding Notes on the Social Philosophy Towards Which the General Theory Might Lead" (Keynes, 372). The first topic Keynes addresses is the "arbitrary and inequitable distribution of wealth and incomes" (Keynes, 372). He writes that although progress has been made in reducing the vast disparities in control over property, some of the tools for accomplishing this (such as "death duties" (Keynes, 372)) have not been pushed very hard. This is so because there is a widely held perception that the "growth of capital . . . is dependent on the savings of the rich out of their superfluity" (Keynes, 372).

Keynes asserts that, quite to the contrary, these concentrations of capital are not only unnecessary, they are an impediment to achieving full employment in society. He suggests that if his argument is correct "[o]ne of

---

[11] In his "Preface" to *The General Theory*, Keynes writes of "deep divergences of opinion between fellow economists which have for the time being almost destroyed the practical influence of economic theory. . . ." (Keynes, xxi).

the chief social justifications of great inequality of wealth is . . . removed" (Keynes, 373).

Keynes labels those rich who enjoy this "superfluity" and live off of the interest return from their capital the "rentier" class[12] (Keynes, 376). According to Keynes, their concentrated control over a large portion of capital in society gives them the power to restrict access to capital, artificially raising the interest rate and thereby enhancing their income. While this is good for the rentier, it has very significant perverse macroeconomic effects. It constrains the ability of society to push out along what in his *General Theory* Keynes refers to as "the schedule of the marginal efficiency of capital" (Keynes, 375). Unable to fully exploit efficiencies of capital due to the high cost of capital, investment is constrained and society suffers unnecessary unemployment.

So, Keynes argues, contrary to the common belief that the rentier class serves society by providing the capital it needs and that "a moderately high interest rate . . . [is necessary to provide a] sufficient inducement to save" (Keynes, 375), high interest rates really only serve the interest of the rentier class. He argues that government should eliminate this artificial constraint on investment by reducing "the rate of interest to that point relatively to the schedule of the marginal efficiency of capital at which there is full employment" (Keynes, 375). This would not only bring full employment,

it would mean the euthanasia of the rentier, and, consequently, the euthanasia of the cumulative oppressive power of the capitalist to exploit the scarcity-value of capital. Interest to-day rewards no genuine sacrifice, any more than does the rent of land.[13] . . . But while there may be intrinsic reasons for the scarcity of land, there are no intrinsic reasons for the scarcity of capital. (Keynes, 376)[14]

---

[12] The term Keynes applies to them, rentier, makes it clear that, echoing Smith, this interest return is not earned, it is merely a return to control like a rent on land. Smith refers to this group as the "monied interest" (*WN*, 351) and Mill calls them "the possessors of capital . . . [to whom workers pay] a heavy tribute for the use of capital" (Mill, 773–4).

[13] Here, he echos Smith. See Chapter Nine.

[14] Smith envisions something similar when he writes that with the growth of the capital stock, when a nation has "acquired its full complement of riches . . . the ordinary rate of clear profit . . . is very small, so that usual market rate of interest which could be afforded out if it, would be so low as to render it impossible for any but the very wealthiest people to love upon the interest of their money" (*WN*, 113). In his *Lectures on Jurisprudence* Smith anticipates Keynes' call for the euthanasia of the rentier class. Responding to the popular argument that so long as a nation's public debt is held by citizens of that nation it does no harm for "[i]t is just the right hand owing the left, and on the whole can be little or no disadvantage. . . . [Smith asserts that] <it> is to be

Keynes' prescription for breaking the grip of those who enjoy concentrated control and thereby increasing access to capital is "a somewhat comprehensive socialization of investment" (Keynes, 378). The state should insure that the level of "communal saving [is sufficient to] ... allow the growth of capital up to the point where it ceases to be scarce" (Keynes, 376). Keynes recognizes that this is a radical thought involving "a large extension of the traditional functions of government" (Keynes, 379), but he suggests that it need not be illiberal.

He is not, he makes clear, advocating government micro management of the economy. He is not suggesting that the government try to pick the winners and losers among the available investment opportunities. His concern is the aggregate level of economic activity:

I see no reason to suppose that the existing system seriously misemploys the factors of production that are in use. There are, of course, errors of foresight; but these would not be avoided by centralizing decisions. When 9,000,000 men are employed out of 10,000,000 willing and able to work, there is no evidence that the labour of these 9,000,000 is misdirected. The complaint against the present system is ... that tasks should be available for the remaining 1,000,000 men. It is in determining the volume, not the direction, of actual employment that the existing system has broken down. (Keynes, 379)

His point is that government should be concerned not with which investment picks are made, but with how many. These picks are made with capital and capital need not be scarce. The role of the state in his plan is to insure that there is sufficient capital available to make enough picks to use up the available resources, that a sufficient aggregate quantity of capital is available for full employment. Within that frame, all "the advantages of decentralization and of the play of self-interest" as envisioned in the micro analysis of his mentor Alfred Marshall would still be realized (Keynes, 379).

THE CAPITAL QUANDARY AND THE MODERN LIBERAL DISCOURSE

As economic discourse moves into the twenty-first century, is this quandary of capital still an issue in the literature? If we were to look for it, what signal should we look for in order to find it?

considered that the interest of this 100 millions is paid by industrious people, and given to support idle people who are employed in gathering it. ... Their industry [of the industrious] would not be hurt by the oppression of these idle people who live upon it" (*LJB*, 514).

The quandary of capital exists because there is a strong incentive for those who control capital to use the resources they have already acquired to, as Smith's mercantilists did, seek even greater advantages in markets. The incentive to do so is the distributive return to these advantages, a rent. So if we are to find a research program in the modern literature that is exploring this issue, we should look for one that is focusing on rent and, in particular, on the use of resources in pursuit of advantages for the sake of this rent.

There is, indeed, just such a modern research program. It is the rent-seeking literature of the Virginia School led by James Buchanan.

As described in Chapter Eleven, the concerns that motivate Buchanan's Constitutional Economics enterprise are very similar to those we've seen in Smith, Mill, and Keynes. Concentrated control over capital can be a resource for pursuing political power in order to gain, protect, or extend artificial advantages for a distributive benefit, a rent. These rent-seeking/rent-maintenance behaviors are destructive because they undermine the liberal order.

Buchanan's solution to this perverse dynamic follows Smith. Buchanan believes that we must establish constraints by consensus, a system of commutative justice. He argues that the liberal experiment is foundering because the rules of commutative justice, the rules that are supposed to define the terms of play, are, themselves, in play. This leads to "the investment in rent seeking by competing groups seeking to curry political favor" (Buchanan, 245) in order to have the rules rewritten for their distributive benefit – to generate a rent. According to Buchanan, by establishing rules of the market game that are fair and are not vulnerable to such manipulation, the opportunity for rent-seeking can be eliminated, and thus the power of accumulated capital to undermine the liberal system can be ameliorated.

Buchanan's enterprise moves beyond the scope of standard orthodox economics because he appreciates that if our model is to represent the full power of markets, it must include the market for power. Markets are opportunistic. They form wherever there is a return that attracts individuals' resources. Shaping the rules can generate a return that is well worth the allocation of accumulated resources, of capital, so markets invade the rule space if they are allowed to do so. Buchanan's proposed constitution would define the rules of commutative justice, the rules of fair play, and protect those rules from being in play.

But while Buchanan's approach to commutative justice is very innovative, his approach to distributive justice is quite standard. As does most modern theory, his begins with the assumption that initial endowments are a given.[15]

In my enterprise ... parties to a potential contract commence from some status quo definition of initial positions [(given initial endowments)] because, quite simply, there is no other place from which to start. This existential acceptance of the status quo, of that which is, has no explicitly normative content and implies neither approbation nor condemnation by any criterion of distributive justice.... I commence from the status quo distribution of rights, and I do not apply criteria of justice to this distribution. My emphasis is almost exclusively placed on the *process* through which potential changes may be made ["principles of social process fairness" (Buchanan, 207)], rather than on either the starting point or the end point of change. (Buchanan, 205, emphasis in original)

But can Buchanan's Constitutional Order, or any liberal order, function on such a basis? His Constitutional Economics enterprise makes a powerful case that an agreement on a set of process rules, on standards for commutative justice that all accept and follow, is a necessary condition for a constructive liberal society. He also implies that this is a sufficient condition. Is it?

Suppose that such a set of rules can be agreed upon, but that among the participants there are perceived injustices with respect to initial positions. Is a stable constitutional order possible without addressing such perceived injustices? Buchanan argues that it is, and to make that case he analyzes an extreme example – the relationship between a slave and a master:

Why [Buchanan writes] should a slave, who is coerced by the master in the preagreement equilibrium, agree on terms of a contract that will permanently preserve the prearrangement advantage of the master? ...
  [Buchanan responds to his own query:] Clearly, he or she is enslaved only because of some inability to enforce more favorable terms of existence ... [and

---

[15] In modern discourse, this issue of initial endowments is often set aside. Paraphrasing Joan Robinson's comment on measuring the value of capital: The student of modern economic theory is taught to take initial endowments as given and then is hurried on to the analysis in the hopes that she will forget to ask about the implications this assumption. Before she ever does ask, she has become a professor, and so the sloppy habits of thought are handed on from one generation to the next.
  In the context of the Cambridge Capital Controversy, Joan Robinson wrote that "the production function has been a powerful instrument of mis-education. The student of economic theory is taught to write $O = f(L,C)$ where L is a quantity of labour, C a quantity of capital and O a rate of output of commodities. He is instructed to assume all workers alike, and to measure L in man-hours of labour; he is told something about the index-number problem involved in choosing a unit of output; and then he is hurried on to the next question, in the hope that he will forget to ask in what units C is measured. Before he ever does ask, he has become a professor, and so the sloppy habits of thought are handed on from one generation to the next" (Robinson, 81).

so d]espite our civilized sense that the master's act of enslavement is un-just, hardheaded analysis here must conclude that an independent existence for the slave was not feasible...given the presence of the potential master. (Buchanan, 204)

In effect, Buchanan argues that the inability of the slave to successfully resist enslavement makes that condition a given, and what remains to be negotiated is an opportunity,

for both master and slave [to] improve their positions by a removal of restrictions in exchange for continued work for the master on the part of the slave.... [He then goes on to note that, of course, r]ecognizing the prospect that the slave might not rationally comply with an agreement, the master, before agreeing to terms, can communicate to the slave that any departure from the terms will bring punishment. (Buchanan, 204–5)

There is a structural problem here. In the process of developing an order to eliminate rent-seeking – the allocation of capital in pursuit of advantageous rules – Buchanan has introduced rent-maintenance. A "negotiated" social contract between slave and master requires the master to allocate capital to suppress resistance to the inherited power structure, the master/slave relationship.

Thus, although the establishment of the contract may, indeed, suppress the dynamically degenerative rent-seeking activity, it does so at the price of a social structure that remains both inefficient and unstable. Instead of diverting otherwise productive capital to the pursuit of advantage, capital must be allocated to the maintenance of advantage. Instead of the "churning state" in which all are insecure in their position, we have the simmering state in which those on top have good reason to feel insecure in their position.

Perceived injustices create a bubbling caldron of discontent. Under a rent-maintenance "lid," pressure builds. Escaping steam or even explosion is a constant threat. As the pressure grows, the risks and so, too, therefore, the costs of rent-maintenance grow.

Analyzing this structure in Buchanan's own terms, that is abstracting from "our civilized sense that the master's act of enslavement is unjust, hardheaded analysis here must conclude" (Buchanan, 204) that building a liberal order on such a distribution of rights (slave and master) sets the system on a very unstable foundation. But recall that, as Buchanan is careful to note, stability is essential for the success of his liberal enterprise.

He writes that in the pre-constitutional stage, during the discourse on the shape of the constitution, when the discussion turns to theories of commutative justice there will be a *"concern for stability"* (Buchanan 1991, 57, emphasis in original). He continues:

The purpose of entering a constitutional agreement is the prospect of realizing gains that can be derived from operating under the respective constitutional constraints. The possibility of realizing such gains is not just a matter of securing some initial agreement. Stability refers to the viability of a constitutional agreement over time...And to the extent that fairness and stability of constitutional arrangements are interrelated, the concern for stability will induce a concern for fairness. (Buchanan, 57)

In practice, however, as the slave/master case suggests, if the negotiated standards of commutative justice are to produce a stable state, the participants in the constitutional conversation must address not only commutative justice but also distributive justice: The fairness of the initial economic, social, and political positions.

This creates a dilemma for Buchanan's model: If the initial distribution of economic, social, and political positions is perceived as unjust, a stable constitutional state cannot be constructed on that foundation.[16] But if not that distribution, how can endowments be redistributed without creating a whole new set of problems?

[T]he status quo distribution has been generated through a complex process of political-legal evolution, deliberative political action, preference shifts, economic development, and social change.... [Any effort to identify the source of unfairness in that status quo presents a problem of infinite regress and any such] rectificatory redistribution...must, as a process, involve violation of the contractarian or agreement criteria for fairness, and it is on this process that my own emphasis lies. (Buchanan, 206)

Furthermore, opening up a redistributive debate in the pre-constitutional stage would almost certainly unleash the very kind of unending, degenerative rent-seeking struggle for advantage that paralyzes the "churning state."

So how can Buchanan's enterprise escape what appears to be an untenable choice between a pre-constitutional rent-seeking chaos or the necessity of an unstable post-constitutional rent-maintenance structure to protect a privileged "status-quo distribution"? If the liberal experiment is to succeed, if the cohesion question is to be resolved so that liberal society can be a constructive sustainable environment, the issue

---

[16] Recall Smith's assertion that social cohesion in a liberal order rests on reciprocal responsibility, and each is more likely to live up to its responsibility to the degree that the other does so.

of initial endowments of economic, social, and political positions must be addressed.

Buchanan recognizes this and, his "existential acceptance of the status quo" with respect to initial endowments notwithstanding, he identifies a solution that is very much in the tradition of John Stuart Mill:

> The demands of justice require, first of all, constitutional articulation and implementation of the rule of law, which itself embodies the principle of equality before the law. This basic precept must be extended to insure that all 'play by the same rules,' that differentiation or discrimination in political treatment is strictly out of bounds. Second, the demands of justice require that, upon entry into the 'game' itself, players face opportunities that are equalized to the extent institutionally possible. I have often suggested that this principle implies equal access to, and state financing of, education at all levels. Beyond these constitutionally implemented steps, *some rectification of the intergenerational transmission of asset accumulation may be dictated*, again to be secured only via constitutional procedures rather than through ordinary politics. (Buchanan, 246, emphasis added)

THE CASE FOR INTERGENERATIONAL DIFFUSION OF WEALTH AND EXPANDING EDUCATIONAL OPPORTUNITY

Smith, Mill, Keynes, Buchanan . . . they all value the liberal experiment, and they all identify concentrated control over capital and the pursuit/preservation of political power that springs from that control (rent-seeking/rent-maintenance) as a corrosive dynamic in liberal society.

As Buchanan's enterprise makes clear, commutative justice is necessary but not sufficient to solve the problem. Mill offers a solution that establishes distributive justice in order to give legitimacy and thus stability to Buchanan's and Smith's envisioned system of commutative justice.

Mill's solution, endorsed in broad outline by Buchanan, is to diffuse wealth as it passes from generation to generation. Doing so would insure that all individuals in each new generation start the race from similar initial positions, and thus with similar opportunities to succeed. As Mill asserts, doing so is consistent with liberal principles because it insures that, given choice and chance, individuals can generally expect to enjoy the full fruits of their *own* labor and sacrifice . . . no more, no less.[17] But, is this cure worse than the disease? Would such a diffusion policy kill the incentive to accumulate and/or reduce the keenness of the competition?

---

[17] Mill envisions all starting the "race" with similar, albeit not identical, initial positions. This does not imply that all will have similar positions after the "race" is underway. The position one would have along the way would depend on choice and chance.

No. Mill's policy allows intergenerational transfers "sufficiently high to afford the means of comfortable independence." Building a diffusion policy with this transfer opportunity maintains the primary intergenerational incentive for accumulation – to see that one's children are comfortable. Once this has been secured, the keenness of an individual's participation in the market nexus is not driven by a concern to have more wealth to pass on.

Accumulation for retirement may drive one's competitive juices up to a point, but beyond the threshold of Mill's "comfortable independence," one's perceived current and future needs (retirement, bequest) are largely met. At that point, the marginal utility of each successive dollar accumulated declines rapidly. As that occurs, one's participation in the market game is driven less by the desire to accumulate wealth and more by the very keenness of the competition itself, by the desire to "win."[18] As Keynes writes, in such a game,

it is not necessary for the stimulation of these activities and the satisfaction of these proclivities [playing the competitive market game] that the game should be played for such high stakes as at present. Much lower stakes will serve the purpose equally well.... (Keynes, 374)

It is, in fact, possible that Mill's policy could actually increase, rather than decrease, the keenness of the competition. This would be the case if intergenerational diffusion is accomplished by investing the financial capital of the passing generation in the human capital of the emerging generation to make possible Buchanan's "equal access to, and state financing of, education at all levels" (Buchanan, 246).

In that case, in each successive generation, every individual would enjoy a similar opportunity to richly equip herself to participate effectively in whatever pursuit she chose upon entering adulthood. Since competition is most keen when all participants enjoy an equal opportunity to prepare, and because the quality of play in any game is highest when the competition is most keen, such a diffusion of wealth into human capital would enhance the quality of "play" in the market game. If such a competition were also governed by commutative justice, then each individual's success would generally depend not on her advantages, but on her effort, her agility, and her creativity ... all of which serve the market.

---

[18] Is Bill Gates still pushing the prospects of Microsoft for the sake of his retirement, of his children's inheritance? It seems very unlikely. These needs can be sufficiently met by his first several billions. Recognizing that, and being caught up in the competition, he has enlisted his father to give some of his accumulation away.

ON THE INTERDEPENDENCE OF COMMUTATIVE AND
DISTRIBUTIVE JUSTICE

What can we learn from following this thread, the liberal plan and the quandary of capital, through the history of economic thought?

First, that the corrosive effect of exploiting concentrated control over capital to generate a rent, rent-seeking/rent-maintenance, is a constant theme. Second, that the quandary of capital, the necessity for accumulation giving rise to concentrated control, cannot be solved by establishing commutative justice alone, nor can it be solved by ensuring distributive justice alone. A solution requires both commutative justice and distributive justice, because these two dimensions of justice are interdependent.

A system of rules that is vulnerable to rent-seeking offers no hope of commutative justice, and it offers rent-generating possibilities that destroy any sense of distributive justice. However, even if, as Buchanan proposed, fair rules can be established and placed beyond the reach of rent-seeking games, a game that commences from a skewed initial distribution of endowments will break down. This is so because citizens' commitments to the rules of commutative justice are contingent on their sense that the initial conditions sanctioned by the state offer them a fair chance for personal success.[19] Where fair rules (commutative justice) and fair initial positions (distributive justice) both hold, the presence of the latter enhances the incentive of each individual to value and to commit to the former.

Thus, a solution to the quandary of capital requires a synthesis that includes distributive justice and commutative justice. When these are both in place, the competition in the race for wealth is most keen and serves us all. In such a competition, the outcomes will not be equal, but all have a reasonable expectation at the outset that their achievements will be relative to their own efforts and sacrifices. This is, I believe, just the outcome Adam Smith envisioned in that limiting case he valued so much: "the liberal plan of equality, liberty and justice" (*WN*, 664).

---

[19] Recall Smith's assertion that a citizen's commitment to the constitution of the state is contingent on a sense of reciprocal responsibly (Chapter Nine).

Epilogue

On the Human Prospect

In his *Principles of Political Economy*, having laid out those principles, John Stuart Mill stops to reflect on the human prospect:

The preceding chapters comprise the general theory of the economical progress of society, in the sense in which those terms are commonly understood; the progress of capital, of population, and of the productive arts. But in contemplating any progressive movement, not in its nature unlimited, the mind is not satisfied with merely tracing the laws of movement; it cannot but ask the further question, to what goal? Towards what ultimate point is society tending by its industrial progress? When the progress ceases, in what condition are we to expect that it will leave mankind? (Mill, 746)

Asserting the "[i]mpossibility of ultimately avoiding" it, Mill says that the human prospect is a "stationary state" (Mill, 746).

He notes that this image has represented "an unpleasing and discouraging prospect" "to the political economists of the last two generations" (Mill, 746) because they have envisioned this end in Malthusian terms[1] as a time when population growth finally outruns production growth. Then comes "doom...an 'end in shallows and in miseries'" (Mill, 747).

Mill includes among those political economists who have dreaded this prospect, "Adam Smith[, for, according to Mill, Smith] always assumes that the condition of the mass of the people...must be pinched and stinted in a stationary condition of wealth, and can only be satisfactory in a

[1] Mill is careful to note that this image is not, in fact, "a wicked invention of Mr. Malthus" (Mill, 747).

308

progressive state" (Mill, 747). Although, as noted in Chapter One, Mill appreciates the dimensionality of Smith's thinking much more fully than any other among Smith's most famous successors, I believe that on this point Mill has Smith wrong. Mill's vision of the stationary state is entirely consistent with Smith's image of the limiting case, the ideal liberal society.

Certainly, Smith did see the progress of opulence as good for the working class, but he also fully appreciated that the progress of every well-governed society must, given finite resources, ultimately bring it to that point when it has "acquired its full complement of riches" (*WN*, 113). Artificial limits on the progress of opulence such as those imposed by the absurd laws and institutions of China or Bengal (Described here in Chapter Three.) are certainly to be avoided, but the natural limit, the ideal limiting case of the human prospect, is not to be dreaded, according to Smith, it is to be desired.[2]

Smith only represents this ideal norm, "the liberal plan of equality, liberty and justice" (*WN*, 664), in it broad contours ... mature citizens, natural jurisprudence, secure tranquility for the working class. The liberal experiment is only in its nascent state in his day; the ideal prospect is far beyond the horizon he can see, so he never presumes to describe this limiting case in any more detail. But by 1848, Mill can see farther and in the chapter of his *Principles* titled "Of the Stationary State" (Mill, 746), Mill offers a more detailed vision of that ideal.

It is a description that Smith would, I believe, find quite compelling. The evolutionary images, the notion of a societal ideal, the concern for the least among the working class, the conception of the best of life as secure tranquility, not material wealth, the valuing of "mental culture, and moral and social progress," and the joy of solitary moments in nature; all

[2] It is the progress of opulence that, Smith believes, will ultimately bring distributive justice to the working class. But economic growth and the distributive justice it brings are not ends to be desired in their own right. They are instrumental in approaching that end which Smith envisions as the human prospect: secure tranquility for all individuals. Indicative of the instrumental role of economic growth and personal material progress, Smith quite specifically imagines the limit as a stationary state in which growth ceases: in a nation fully capitalized.... This is not a sad state.

The stationary state is entirely consistent with Smith's conception of the limit for, as Smith notes on a number of occasions, the ultimate joys of life are derived not from the baubles and trinkets we accumulate but rather from the joys of the heart, love and friendship, and from the joys of the mind, beautiful philosophical systems or music or art. Although in the stationary state, the progress of opulence may have ceased, the progress of humankind's joy's need not end.

are entirely consistent with Smith's vision of the human prospect, so I cite Mill's vision at length. Mill writes that, contrary to those who:

regard the stationary state of capital and wealth with . . . unaffected aversion . . . I am inclined to believe that it would be, on the whole, a very considerable improvement on our present condition. I confess I am not charmed with the ideal of life held out by those who think that the normal state of human beings is that of struggling to get on; that the trampling, crushing, elbowing, and treading on each other's heels, which form the existing type of social life, are the most desirable lot of human kind, or anything but the disagreeable symptoms of one of the phases of industrial progress. It may be a necessary stage in the progress of civilization . . . [b]ut it is not a kind of social perfection which philanthropists to come will feel any very eager desire to assist in realizing. Most fitting, indeed, is it, that while riches are power, and to grow as rich as possible the universal object of ambition, the path to its attainment should be open to all, without favour or partiality. But the best state for human nature is that in which, while no one is poor, no one desires to be richer, nor has any reason to fear being thrust back by the efforts of others to push themselves forward.

That the energies of mankind should be kept in employment by the struggle for riches, as they were formerly by the struggle of war, until the better minds succeed in educating the others into better things, is undoubtedly more desirable than that they should rust and stagnate. While minds are coarse they require coarse stimuli, and let them have them. In the mean time, those who do not accept the present very early stage of human improvement as its ultimate type, may be excused for being comparatively indifferent to the kind of economical progress which excites the congratulations of ordinary politicians; the mere increase of production and accumulation. For the safety of national independence it is essential that a country should not fall much behind its neighbours in these things. But in themselves they are of little importance, so long as either the increase of population or anything else prevents the mass of the people from reaping any part of the benefit of them. I know not why it should be a matter of congratulation that persons who are already richer than any one needs to be, should have doubled their means of consuming things which give little or no pleasure except as representative of wealth; or that numbers of individuals should pass over, every year, from the middle into a richer class, or from the class of the occupied rich to that of the unoccupied. It is only in the backward countries of the world that increased production is still an important object: in those most advanced, what is economically needed is a better distribution, of which one indispensable means is a stricter restraint on population.[3] . . .

[Then after supposing individual prudence and his diffusion plan are in place, Mill continues:] Under this twofold influence society would exhibit these leading features: a well-paid and affluent body of labourers; no enormous fortunes, except what were earned and accumulated during a single lifetime; but a much larger

---

[3] Keynes also expresses concern about "the pressure of population . . . [and envisions the] attain[ment of] equilibrium in the trend of . . . population" (Keynes, 381–2) as essential for humankind's peace and prosperity.

body of persons than at present, not only exempt from the coarser toils, but with sufficient leisure, both physical and mental, from mechanical details, to cultivate freely the graces of life.... This condition of society, so greatly preferable to the present, is not only perfectly compatible with the stationary state, but, it would seem, more naturally allied with that state than with any other.

There is room in the world, no doubt, and even in old countries, for a great increase of population, supposing the arts of life to go on improving, and capital to increase. But even if innocuous, I confess I see very little reason for desiring it. The density of population necessary to enable mankind to obtain, in the greatest degree, all of the advantages both of co-operation and of social intercourse, has, in all the most populous countries, been attained. A population may be too crowded, though all be amply supplied with food and raiment. It is not good for man to be kept perforce at all times in the presence of his species. A world from which solitude is extirpated is a very poor ideal. Solitude, in the sense of being often alone, is essential for any depth of meditation or of character; and solitude in the presence of natural beauty and grandeur, is the cradle of thoughts and aspirations which are not only good for the individual, but which society could ill do without.[4] Nor is there much satisfaction in contemplating the world with nothing left to spontaneous activity of nature; with every rod of land brought into cultivation, which is capable of growing food for human beings; every flowery waste or natural pasture ploughed up, all quadrupeds or birds which are not domesticated for man's use exterminated as rivals for food, every hedgerow or superfluous tree rooted out, and scarcely a place left where a wild shrub or flower could grow without being eradicated as a weed in the name of improved agriculture. If the earth must lose that great portion of its pleasantness which it owes to things that the unlimited increase of wealth and population would extirpate from it, for the mere purpose of enabling it to support a larger, but not a better or a happier population, I sincerely hope, for the sake of posterity, that they will be content to be stationary, long before necessity compels them to it.

It is scarcely necessary to remark that a stationary condition of capital and population implies no stationary state of human improvement. There would be as much scope as ever for all kinds of mental culture, and moral and social progress; as much room for improving the Art of Living, and much more likelihood of its being improved, when minds ceased to be engrossed by the art of getting on. Even the industrial arts might be as earnestly and as successfully cultivated, with this sole difference, that instead of serving no purpose but the increase of wealth, industrial improvements would produce their legitimate effect, that of abridging labour. Hitherto it is questionable if all the mechanical inventions yet made have lightened the day's toil of any human being. They have enabled a greater population to live the same life of drudgery and imprisonment, and an increased

---

[4] On 7 June 1767, Smith writes to Hume from his home with his mother and niece in Kirkaldy that "[m]y business here is Study in which I have been very deeply engaged for about a Month past. [(He is working on the *WN*.)] My Amusements are long, solitary walks by the Sea side. You may judge how I spend my time. I feel myself, however, extremely happy, comfortable and contended. I never was, perhaps, more so in all my life" (*Correspondence*, 125).

number of manufacturers and others to make fortunes. . . . Only when, in addition to just institutions, the increase of mankind shall be under the deliberate guidance of judicious foresight, can the conquests made from the powers of nature by the intellect and energy of scientific discoverers become the common property of the species, and the means of improving and elevating the universal lot. (Mill, 748–51)

"[I]mproving and elevating the universal lot." This was the raison d'etre of Adam Smith's moral philosophy. To this end, Smith imagined the invisible connecting principles and the possibilities. We too should "Imagine" (John Lennon, 1971).[5]

---

[5] There are certainly differences in what Adam Smith and John Lennon "imagine," but I would argue that these differences are small relative to the fundamental similarity: secure tranquility for all.

References

Akerlof, George. 1980. "A Theory of Social Custom, of Which Unemployment May Be One Consequence." *Quarterly Journal of Economics.* 94(4): 749–775.

Anderson, Gary M. 1988. "Mr. Smith and the Preachers: The Economics of Religion in the Wealth of Nations." *Journal of Political Economy.* 96(5): 1066–1088.

Anderson, Gary M. and Tollison, Robert D. 1982. "Adam Smith's Analysis of Joint-Stock Companies." *Journal of Political Economy.* 90(6): 1237–1256.

Anderson, Gary M., Shughart, William F. II., and Tollison, Robert D. 1985. "Adam Smith in the Custom House." *Journal of Political Economy.* 93(4): 740–759.

Arrow, Kenneth. 1951. *Social Choice and Individual Values.* New York, NY: Wiley.

Arrow, Kenneth. 1983. *Social Choice and Justice: Vol. 1 of Collected Papers of Kenneth J. Arrow.* Cambridge, MA: The Belknap Press of the Harvard University Press.

Becker, Gary. 1976. *The Economic Approach to Human Behavior.* Chicago: The University of Chicago Press.

Becker, J. F. 1961. "Adam Smith's Theory of Social Sciences." *Southern Economic Journal.* 28(1): 13–21.

Beer, Samuel. 1957. "The Representation of Interests in British Government: Historical Background." *American Political Science Review.* 51(3): 613–650.

Berger, Peter L., and Luckmann, Thomas. 1966. *The Social Construction of Reality: A Treatise in the Sociology of Knowledge.* New York: Doubleday.

Bittermann, Henry J. 1940A. "Adam Smith's Empiricism and the Law of Nature, I." *Journal of Political Economy.* 48(4): 487–520.

Bittermann, Henry J. 1940B. "Adam Smith's Empiricism and the Law of Nature, II." *Journal of Political Economy.* 48(5): 703–734.

Boulding, K. E. 1984 (1971). "After Samuelson, Who Needs Adam Smith?" Reprinted in *Adam Smith: Critical Assessments.* Vol. 3. John Cunningham Wood, ed. London: Croom Helm. pp. 247–256.

Brittan, Samuel. 1995. "Economics and ethics." in *Market Capitalism and Moral Values: Proceedings of Section F (Economics) of the British Association for the*

313

Advancement of Science, Keele 1993. Samuel Brittan and Alan Hamlin, eds. Hants, UK: Edward Elgar. pp. 1–22.

Brown, Vivienne. 1994. *Adam Smith's Discourse: Canonicity, commerce and conscience*. London: Routledge.

Bryson, Gladys. 1945. *Man and Society: The Scottish Inquiry of the Eighteenth Century*. New York: Augustus M. Kelly.

Buchanan, James. 1991. *The Economics and the Ethics of Constitutional Order*. Ann Arbor: University of Michigan Press.

Buchanan, James. 1994. *Ethics and Economic Progress*. Norman: University of Oklahoma Press.

Buchanan, James. Tollison, R. D., and Tullock, G., eds. 1980. *Toward a Theory of A Rent-Seeking Society*. College Station: Texas A&M University Press.

Buchanan, James and Tullock, Gordon. 1962. *The Calculus of Consent: Logical Foundations of Constitutional Democracy*. Ann Arbor: University of Michigan Press.

Caldwell, William. 1897. "Review of Smith's Lectures on Justice, Police, Revenue, and Arms, delivered in the University of Glasgow. Edited by Edwin Cannan." *Journal of Political Economy*. 5: 250–258.

Campbell, R. H., and Skinner, Andrew. 1976. "General Introduction." *An Inquiry into the Nature and Causes of the Wealth of Nations*. R. H. Campbell and Andrew Skinner, eds. Vol. 2. *The Glasgow Edition of the Works and Correspondence of Adam Smith*. Oxford: Clarendon Press. pp. 1–60.

Campbell, T. D. 1971. *Adam Smith's Science of Morals*. London: George Allen & Unwin Ltd.

Campbell, T. D. 1975. "Scientific Explanation and Ethical Justification in the Moral Sentiments." in *Essays on Adam Smith*. Andrew Skinner and Thomas Wilson, eds. Oxford: Clarendon Press. pp. 69–82.

Campbell, T. D. 1986. "Rationality and Utility from the Standpoint of Evolutionary Biology." *The Journal of Business*. 59: S355–S364.

Childe, V. Gordon. 1951. *Social Evolution*. New York: Henry Schuman.

Clark, Charles. 1990. "Adam Smith and Society as an Evolutionary Process." *Journal of Economic Issues*. 24(3): 825–844.

Coats. A. W. 1975. "Adam Smith and the Mercantile System." in *Essays on Adam Smith*. Andrew Skinner and Thomas Wilson, eds. Oxford: Clarendon Press. pp. 218–236.

Cropsey, Joseph. 1957. *Polity and Economy: An Interpretation of the Principles of Adam Smith*. The Hague: Martinus Nijhoff.

Davis, Ralph. 1966. "The Rise of Protectionism in England, 1689–1786." *The Economic History Review*. 19(2): 306–317.

Dickey, Laurence. 1986. "Historicizing the 'Adam Smith Problem': Conceptual, Historiographical, and Textual Issues." *Journal of Modern History*. 58(3): 579–609.

Dobb, Maurice. 1973. *Theories of Value and Distribution Since Adam Smith*. London: Cambridge University Press.

Dunn, John. 1983. "From applied theology to social analysis: the break between John Locke and the Scottish Enlightenment." in *Wealth and Virtue*. Istvan

Hont and Michael Ignatieff, eds. Cambridge: Cambridge University Press. pp. 119–136.

Dunn, William Clyde. 1941. "Adam Smith and Edmund Burke: Complementary Contemporaries." *Southern Economic Journal.* 7(3): 330–346.

Edgeworth, F. Y. 1891. "Report of the Proceedings at the Meeting which Inaugurated the British Economic Association." *The Economic Journal.* 1(1): 1–14.

Ekelund, Robert, and Tullock, Gordon. 1981. *Mercantilism as a Rent-Seeking Society, Economic Regulation in Historical Perspective.* College Station: Texas A&M University Press.

Ely, Richard T. 1887. "Report of the Organization of the American Economic Association." *Publication of the American Economic Association.* (now *American Economic Review*) 1(1): 5–32.

Evensky, Jerry. 1989. "The Evolution of Adam Smith's Views on Political Economy." *History of Political Economy.* 21(1): 123–145.

Evensky, Jerry. 1992. "The Role of Community Values in Modern Classical Liberal Economic Thought." *Scottish Journal of Political Economy.* 39 (1): 21–38.

Evensky, Jerry. 1993A. "Ethics and the Invisible Hand." *Journal of Economic Perspectives.* 7(2): 197–205.

Evensky, Jerry. 1993B. "Adam Smith on the Human Foundation of a Successful Liberal Society." *History of Political Economy.* 25(3): 395–412.

Evensky, Jerry. 1994. "The Role of Law in Adam Smith's Moral Philosophy: Natural Jurisprudence and Utility." in *Adam Smith and the Philosophy of Law and Economics.* Robin Malloy and Jerry Evensky, eds. Dordrecht, The Netherlands: Kluwer Academic Press. pp. 199–220

Evensky, Jerry. 1998. "Adam Smith's Moral Philosophy: The Role of Religion and Its Relationship to Philosophy and Ethics in the Evolution of Society." *History of Political Economy.* 30(1): 17–42.

Evensky, Jerry. 2001. "Adam Smith's Lost Legacy." *Southern Economic Journal.* 67(3): 497–517.

Evensky, Jerry. 2004. *Economics: The Ideas, the Issues.* Boston: Pearson Custom Publishing.

Firth, Roderick. 1952. "Ethical Absolutism and the Ideal Observer." *Philosophy and Phenomenological Research.* 12(3): 317–345.

Fishburn, Peter. 1987. "Utility and decision theory." in Vol. 4. *The New Palgrave: A Dictionary of Economics.* John Eatwell, Murray Milgate, and Peter Newman, eds. New York: The Stockton Press. pp. 779–783.

Fitzgibbons, Athol. 1995. *Adam Smith's System of Liberty, Wealth, and Virtue: The Moral and Political Foundations of The Wealth of Nations.* Oxford: Clarendon Press.

Fleischacker, Samuel. 1999. *A Third Concept of Liberty: Judgment and Freedom in Kant and Adam Smith.* Princeton: Princeton University Press.

Folbre, Nancy, and Hartmann, Heidi. 1988. "The rhetoric of self-interest: Ideology of gender in economic theory." in *The consequences of economic rhetoric.* Arjo Klamer, Donald McCloskey, and Robert Solow, eds. Cambridge: Cambridge University Press. pp. 184–206.

Forbes, Duncan. 1975. "Sceptical Whiggism, Commerce, and Liberty." in *Essays on Adam Smith*. Anderw Skinner and ThomasWilson, eds. Oxford: Clarendon Press. pp. 179–201.

Freeman, R. D. 1984 (1969). "Adam Smith, Education, and Laissez Faire." Reprinted in *Adam Smith: Critical Assessments*. Vol. 1. John Cunningham Wood, ed. London: Croom Helm. pp. 378–388.

Friedan, Betty. 1963. *The Feminine Mystique*. New York: W. W. Norton & Company, Inc.

Frost, Robert. 1995. *Collected Poems, Prose, & Plays*. New York: Literary Classics of the United States.

Ginzberg, Eli. 1979. "An Economy Formed by Men." in *Adam Smith and Modern Political Economy: Bicentennial Essays on The Wealth of Nations*. Gerald R. O'Driscoll Jr., ed. Ames: The Iowa State University Press. pp. 35–43.

Glass, Bentley, Ttemkin, Owsei, and Straus, William. L., Jr. 1968. *Forerunners of Darwin: 1745–1859*. Baltimore: Johns Hopkins Press.

Grampp, William D. 1948. "Adam Smith and Economic Man." *Journal of Political Economy*. 56(4): 315–336.

Griswold, Charles. 1999. *Adam Smith and the Virtues of Enlightenment*. Cambridge, UK: Cambridge University Press.

Griswold, Charles. 2001. "Reply to My Critics." *Perspectives on Political Science*. 30(3): 163–167.

Haakonssen, Knud. 1981. *The Science of a Legislator: The Natural Jursiprudence of David Hume & Adam Smith*. Cambridge, UK: Cambridge University Press.

Haakonssen, Knud. 1988, "Jurisprudence and Politics in Adam Smith." in *Traditions of Liberalism: Essays on John Locke, Adam Smith, and John Stuart Mill*. Knud Haakonssen, ed. St. Leonards NSW, Australia: Centre for Independent Studies. pp. 107–118.

Haakonssen, Knud, and Skinner, Andrew. 2001. *Index to the Works of Adam Smith*. Oxford: Clarendon Press.

Hansen, W. Lee. 1991. "The Education and Training of Economics Doctorates: Major Findings of the American Economic Association's Commission on Graduate Education in Economics." *Journal of Economic Literature*. 29: 1054–1087.

Harpham, Edward. 1984. "Liberalism, Civic Humanism, and the Case of Adam Smith." *American Political Science Review*. 78(3): 764–774.

Harpham, Edward. 2000. "The Problem of Liberty in the Thought of Adam Smith." *Journal of the History of Economic Thought*. 22(2): 217–237.

Harpham, Edward. 2001. "Enlightenment, Impartial Spectators, and Griswold's Smith." *Perspectives on Political Science*. 30(3): 139–145.

Hirsch, E. D. Jr. 1987. *Cultural Literacy: What Every American Needs to Know*. Boston: Houghton Mifflin Company.

Hirschman, Albert O. 1977. *The Passions and the Interests: Political Arguments for Capitalism before Its Triumph*. Princeton: Princeton University Press.

Hollander, Samuel. 1979. "Historical Dimensions of The Wealth of Nations." in *Adam Smith and Modern Political Economy: Bicentennial Essays on The Wealth of Nations*. Gerald R. O'Driscoll Jr., ed. Ames: The Iowa State University Press. pp. 44–67.

Hont, Istvan, and Ignatieff, Michael. 1983. *Wealth and Virtue: The Shaping of Political Economy in the Scottish Enlightenment*. Cambridge: Cambridge University Press.

Hopfl, H. M. 1978. "From Savage to Scotsman: Conjectural History in the Scottish Enlightenment." *Journal of British Studies*. 17(2): 19–40.

Hueckel, Glenn. 2000. "On the 'Insurmountable Difficulties, Obscurity, and Embarrassment' of Smith's Fifth Chapter." *History of Political Economy*. 32(2): 317–345.

Hume, David. 1947. *Dialogues Concerning Natural Religion*. Norman Kemp Smith, ed. Indianapolis: Bobbs-Merrill.

Hutchison, Terence W. 1976. "Adam Smith and the *Wealth of Nations*." *Journal of Law and Economics*. 19(3): 507–528.

Ingold, Tim. 1986. *Evolution and social life*. Cambridge: Cambridge University Press.

Jones, Peter. 1992. "The aesthetics of Adam Smith." in *Adam Smith Reviewed*. Peter Jones and Andrew Skinner, eds. Edinburgh: Edinburgh University Press. pp. 56–78.

Kahneman, Daniel, and Tversky, Amos. April 1984. "Choices, Values, and Frames." *American Psychologist*. 39(4): 341–350.

Kammen, Michael. 1970. *Empire and Interest: The American Colonies and the Politics of Mercantilism*. Philadelphia: J. B. Lippincott Company.

Kennedy, David M. 1999. *Freedom From Fear: The American People in Depression and War*, 1929–1945. Oxford: Oxford University Press.

Keohane, Robert O. 1988. "The rhetoric of economics as viewed by a student of politics." in *The consequences of economic rhetoric*. Arjo Klamer, Donald McCloskey, and Robert Solow, eds. Cambridge: Cambridge University Press. pp. 240–247.

Keynes, John Maynard. 1924. "Alfred Marshall." *The Economic Journal*. 34(135): 311–372.

Keynes, John Maynard. 1964. *The General Theory of Employment, Interest, and Money*. First Harbinger Edition. New York: Harcourt Brace Jovanovich.

Kim, Kwangsu. 1997. "Adam Smith: Natural Theology and Its Implications for His Method of Social Inquiry." *Review of Social Economy*. 55(3): 312–335.

King, M. L. Jr. 1968. *Chaos or Community*. London: Hodder and Stoughton.

Knight, Frank H. 1947. *Freedom and Reform*. New York: Harper & Brothers.

Kramnick, Issac. 1982. "Republican Revisionism Revisited." *American Historical Review*. 87(3): 629–664.

Laslett, Peter. 1957. "The Great Recoinage, and the Origin of the Board of Trade: 1695–1698." *The William and Mary Quarterly*. 3rd Series. 14(3): 370–402.

Leijonhufvud, Axel, Sept. 1973. "Life Among the Econ." *Western Economic Journal* (now *Economic Inquiry*) 11(3):327–337.

Letwin, William. 1964. *The Origins of Scientific Economics*. Garden City, New Jersey: Doubleday & Co., Inc.

Letwin, William. 1988. "Was Adam Smith a Liberal." in *Traditions of Liberalism: Essays on John Locke, Adam Smith, and John Stuart Mill*. Knud Haakonssen, ed. St. Leonards NSW, Australia: Centre for Independent Studies. pp. 65–82.

Levy, David M. 2001. *How the Dismal Science Got Its Name.* Ann Arbor: University of Michigan Press.

Lincoln, Abraham. "Second Inaugural Address." *Speeches and Writings 1859–1865.* New York: Literary Classics of the United States, Inc. pp. 686–687.

Lindgren, J. Ralph. 1969. "Adam Smith's Theory of Inquiry." *Journal of Political Economy.* 77(6): 897–915.

Lindgren, J. Ralph. 1973. *The Social Philosophy of Adam Smith.* The Hague: Martinus Nijhoff.

Lovejoy, Arthur O. 1964. *The Great Chain of Being: A Study of the History of an Idea.* Cambridge: Harvard University Press.

Macfie, A. L. 1967. *The Individual and Society: Papers on Adam Smith.* London: George Allen & Unwin Ltd.

Machina, Mark. 1987. "Expected utility hypothesis." in Vol. 2. *The New Palgrave: A Dictionary of Economics.* John Eatwell, Murray Milgate; and Peter Newman, eds. New York: The Stockton Press. pp. 232–239.

Malloy, Robin Paul. 1994. "Adam Smith and the Modern Discourse of Law and Economics." in *Adam Smith and the Philosophy of Law and Economics.* Robin Paul Malloy and Jerry Evensky, eds. Dordrecht, The Netherlands: Kluwer Academic Publishers. pp. 113–150.

Marshall, Alfred. 1936. *Principles of Economics*, 8th Ed. London: MacMillan and Co.

Marx, Karl. 1954. *Capital: A Critique of Political Economy.* Vol. I. Moscow: Progress Publishers.

McCloskey, Deidre. 1985. *The Rhetoric of Economics.* Madison: The University of Wisconsin Press.

Meek, Ronald L. 1971. "Smith, Turgot, and the 'Four Stages' Theory." *History of Political Economy.* 3(1): 9–27.

Meek, Ronald L. 1976. *Social Science and the Ignoble Savage.* Cambridge: Cambridge University Press.

Mill, John Stuart. 1929. *Principles of Political Economy: With Some of Their Applications to Social Philosophy.* W. J. Ashley, ed. Based on the 7th edition, the last revised by Mill. London: Longmans, Green, and Co.

Minowitz, Peter. 1993. *Profits, Priests, and Princes: Adam Smith's Emancipation of Economics from Politics and Religion.* Stanford: Stanford University Press.

Montes, Leonidas. 2003. "*Das Adam Smith Problem*: Its Origins, the Stages of the Current Debate, and One Implication for Our Understanding of Sympathy." *Journal of the History of Economic Thought.* 25(1): 63–90.

Montes, Leonidas. 2004. *Adam Smith in Context.* New York: Palgrave Macmillan.

Morrow, Glenn R. 1923. *The Ethical and Economic Theories of Adam Smith: A Study in the Social Philosophy of the Eighteenth Century.* Cornell Studies in Philosophy: No. 13. New York: Longmans, Green, and Co.

Morrow, Glenn R. 1927. "Adam Smith: Moralist and Philosopher." *Journal of Political Economy.* 35: 321–342.

Muller, Jerry. 1993. *Adam Smith in His Time and Ours: Designing the Decent Society.* New York: The Free Press.

Muller, Jerry. 2002. *The Mind of the Market: Capitalism in Modern European Thought.* New York: Alfred A. Knopf.

Myers, Milton. 1983. *The Soul of Modern Economic Man*. Chicago: Chicago University Press.

Namier, Sir Lewis. 1957. *The Structure of Politics at the Accession of George III*. 2nd ed. London: Macmillan, St. Martins Press.

Newton, Sir Isaac. 1952. *Opticks*. New York: Dover Publications, Inc.

North, Douglas. 1991. "Institutions." *Journal of Economic Perspectives*. 5(1): 97–111.

O'Driscoll, Gerald P. Jr. 1979. *Adam Smith and Modern Political Economy: Bicentennial Essays on The Wealth of Nations*. Ames: The Iowa State University Press.

Otteson, James R. 2002. *Adam Smith's Marketplace of Life*. Cambridge: Cambridge University Press.

Pack, Spencer. 1991. *Capitalism as a Moral System: Adam Smith's Critique of the Free Market Economy*. Aldershot, UK: Edward Elgar.

Pack, Spencer. 1995. "Theological (and Hence Economic) Implications of Adam Smith's 'Principles which Lead and Direct Philosophical Enquiries.'" *History of Political Economy*. 27(2): 289–307.

Paganelli, Maria Pia. 2003. "*In Medio Stat Virtus*: An Alternative View of Usury in Adam Smith's Thinking." *History of Political Economy*. 35(1): 21–48.

Phillipson, Nicholas. 1983. "Adam Smith as Civic Moralist." in *Wealth and Virtue*. Istvan Hont and Michael Ignatieff, eds. Cambridge: Cambridge University Press. pp. 179–202.

Pocock, J. G. A. 1975. *The Machiavellian Moment: Florentine Political Thought and the Atlantic Republican Tradition*. Cambridge: Cambridge University Press.

Pocock, J. G. A. 1981. "The Machiavellian Moment Revisited: A Study in History and Ideology." *Journal of Modern History*. 53(1): 49–72.

Pocock, J. G. A. 1983. "Cambridge paradigms and Scotch philosophers: a study of the relations between civic humanist and the civil jurisprudential interpretation of eighteenth–century social thought." in *Wealth and Virtue*. Istvan Hont and Michael Ignatieff, eds. Cambridge: Cambridge University Press. pp. 235–252.

Pocock, J. G. A. 1985. *Virtue, Commerce, and History: Essays on Political Thought and History Chiefly in the Eighteenth Century*. Cambridge: Cambridge University Press.

Pocock, J. G. A. 1999. *Barbarism and Religion, Volume Two: Narratives of Civil Government*. Cambridge: Cambridge University Press.

Pollard, Sidney. 1968. *The Idea of Progress: History and Society*. London: C.A. Watts.

Porta, Pier Luigi; Scazzieri, Roberto; and Skinner, Andrew. 2001. *Knowledge, Social Institutions and the Division of Labour*. Cheltenham, UK: Edward Elgar.

Raphael, D. D. 1975. "The Impartial Spectator." in *Essays on Adam Smith*. Andrew Skinner and Thomas Wilson, eds. Oxford: Clarendon Press. pp. 83–99.

Raphael, D. D. 1984 (1969). "Adam Smith and the 'Infection of David Hume's Society.'" Reprinted in *Adam Smith: Critical Assessments*. Vol. 1. John Cunningham Wood, ed. London: Croom Helm. pp. 388–409.

Raphael, D. D. 1992. "Adam Smith 1790: the man recalled; the philosopher revived." in *Adam Smith Reviewed*. Peter Jones and Andrew Skinner, eds. Edinburgh: Edinburgh University Press. pp. 93–118.

Raphael, D. D. 1997. "Smith." in *Three Great Economists*. Keith Thomas. ed. Oxford: Oxford University Press. pp. 1–104.

Raphael, D. D., and Macfie, A. L. 1976. "Introduction" and "Appendix II" to *The Theory of Moral Sentiments*. D. D. Raphael and A. L. Macfie, eds. Vol. 1. *The Glasgow Edition of the Works and Correspondence of Adam Smith*. Oxford: Clarendon Press.

Reagan, Ronald Jr. 2004. "Eulogy." http://www.washingtonpost.com/wp–dyn/articles/A36014–2004Jun11.html

Reder, M. W. 1987. "Chicago School." in Vol. 1. *The New Palgrave: A Dictionary of Economics*. John Eatwell, Murray Milgate, and Peter Newman, eds. New York: The Stockton Press. pp. 413–418.

Redman, Deborah. 1993. "Adam Smith and Isaac Newton." *Scottish Journal of Political Economy*. 40(2): 210–230.

Ricardo, David. 1911. *Principles of Political Economy and Taxation*. London: J. M. Dent & Sons Ltd.

Robbins, Caroline. 1959. *The Eighteenth–Century Commonwealthman*. Cambridge, MA: Harvard University Press.

Robertson, John. 1983. "The Scottish Enlightenment and the civic tradition." in *Wealth and Virtue*. Istvan Hont and Michael Ignatieff, eds. Cambridge: Cambridge University Press. pp. 137–178.

Robinson, Joan. 1953. "The Production Function and the Theory of Capital". *Review of Economic Studies*. 21.2(55): 81–106.

Rosenberg, Nathan. 1960. "Some Institutional Aspects of the Wealth of Nations." *Journal of Political Economy*. 68(6): 557–570.

Rosenberg, Nathan. 1976. "Another Advantage of the Division of Labor." *Journal of Political Economy*. 84(4): 861–868.

Rosenberg, Nathan. 1979. "Adam Smith and Laissez-Faire Revisited." in *Adam Smith and Modern Political Economy: Bicentennial Essays on The Wealth of Nations*. Gerald R. O'Driscoll Jr., ed. Ames: The Iowa State University Press. pp. 19–34.

Ross, Ian. 1995. *The Life of Adam Smith*. Oxford: Clarendon Press.

Rothschild, Emma. 2001. *Economic Sentiments: Adam Smith, Condorcet, and the Enlightenment*. Cambridge: Harvard University Press.

Rowley, Charles; Tollison, Robert; and Tullock, Gordon, eds. 1988. *The Political Economy of Rent-Seeking*. Boston: Kluwer Academic Press.

Samuels, Warren J. 1984A (1973). "Adam Smith and the Economy as a System of Power." Reprinted in *Adam Smith: Critical Assessments*. Vol. 1. John Cunningham Wood, ed. London: Croom Helm. pp. 489–501.

Samuels, Warren J. 1984B (1976). "The Political Economy of Adam Smith." *Reprinted in Adam Smith: Critical Assessments*. Vol. 1. John Cunningham Wood, ed. London: Croom Helm. pp. 698–715.

Samuels, Warren J. 1993. "Adam Smith as Social Constructivist and Dialectician: Aspects of Intergenerational Intellectual Relations." *History of Economic Issues*. I(1): 171–192.

Sanderson, Stephen K. 1990. *Social Evolutionism: A Critical History*. Cambridge: Basil Blackwell.

Schelling, Thomas. 1978. *Micromotives and macrobehavior*. New York: Norton.

Schneider, Louis. 1979. "Adam Smith on Human Nature and Social Circumstance." in *Adam Smith and Modern Political Economy: Bicentennial Essays on The Wealth of Nations*. Gerald R. O'Driscoll Jr., ed. Ames: The Iowa State University Press. pp. 44–67.

Schumpeter, Joseph. 1954. *History of Economic Analysis*. Edited from manuscript by Elizabeth Boody Schumpeter. New York: Oxford University Press.

Selby–Bigge, L. A. 1897. "Introduction." *British Moralists*. L. A. Selby–Bigge, ed. New York: Dover Publications.

Sen, Amartya. 1977. "Rational Fools: A Critique of the Behavioral Foundations of Economic Theory." *Philosophy and Public Affairs*. (6): 317–344. Reprinted in Amartya Sen. *Choice Welfare and Measurement*. pp. 84–106. Cambridge: MIT Press.

Sen, Amartya. 1984. "The Living Standard." *Oxford Economic Papers*. 36 (Supplement): 74–90.

Sen, Amartya. 1995A. "Rationality and Social Choice." *American Economic Review*. 85(1): 1–24.

Sen, Amartya. 1995B. "Moral codes and economic success." in *Market Capitalism and Moral Values: Proceedings of Section F (Economics) of the British Association for the Advancement of Science*, Keele 1993. Samuel Brittan and Alan Hamlin, eds. Hants, UK: Edward Elgar. pp. 23–34

Sharp and Dunnigan Publications. 1984. *The Congressional Medal of Honor*. Forest Ranch, California: Sharp and Dunnigan Publications.

Sher, Richard B. 1985. *Church and University in the Scottish Enlightenment: The Moderate Literati of Edinburgh*. Princeton. Princeton University Press.

Skinner, Andrew. 1972. "Adam Smith: Philosophy and Science." *Scottish Journal of Political Economy*. 19(3): 307–319.

Skinner, Andrew. 1975A. "Introduction." in *Essays on Adam Smith*. Andrew Skinner and Thomas Wilson, eds. Oxford: Clarendon Press. pp. 1–10.

Skinner, Andrew. 1975B. "Adam Smith: an Economic Interpretation of History." in *Essays on Adam Smith*. Andrew Skinner and Thomas Wilson, eds. Oxford: Clarendon Press. pp. 154–178.

Skinner, Andrew. 1979. *A System of Social Science: Papers Relating to Adam Smith*. Oxford: Clarendon Press.

Skinner, Andrew. 2001. "Adam Smith, the Philosopher and the Porter." in *Knowledge, Social Institutions and the Division of Labour*. Pier Luigi Porta, Roberto Scazzieri, and Andrew Skinner, eds. Cheltenham, UK: Edward Elgar. pp. 35–52.

Skinner, Andrew, and Wilson, Thomas. 1975. *Essays on Adam Smith*. Oxford: Clarendon Press.

Smith, Adam. 1976a. *The Theory of Moral Sentiments*. D. D. Raphael and A. L. Macfie, eds. Vol. 1. *The Glasgow Edition of the Works and Correspondence of Adam Smith*. Oxford: Clarendon Press.

Smith, Adam. 1976b. *An Inquiry into the Nature and Causes of the Wealth of Nations*. R. H. Campbell and A. S. Skinner, general ed.; W. B. Todd, textual ed.;

Vol. 2. *The Glasgow Edition of the Works and Correspondence of Adam Smith.* Oxford: Clarendon Press.

Smith, Adam. 1977. *The Correspondence of Adam Smith.* Earnest Campbell Mossner and Ian Simpson Ross, eds. Vol. 6. *The Glasgow Edition of the Works and Correspondence of Adam Smith.* Oxford: Clarendon Press.

Smith, Adam. 1978. *Lectures on Jurisprudence.* R. L. Meek, D. D. Raphael, and P. G. Stein, eds. Vol. 5. *The Glasgow Edition of the Works and Correspondence of Adam Smith.* Oxford: Clarendon Press.

Smith, Adam. 1980. *Essays on Philosophical Subjects.* W. P. D. Wightman and J. C. Bryce, eds. Vol. 3. *The Glasgow Edition of the Works and Correspondence of Adam Smith.* Oxford: Clarendon Press.

Smith, Adam. 1980. "Of the External Senses." in *Essays on Philosophical Subjects.* W. P. D. Wightman and J. C. Bryce, eds. Vol. 3. *The Glasgow Edition of the Works and Correspondence of Adam Smith.* Oxford: Clarendon Press. pp. 135–168.

Smith, Adam. 1980. "The Principles Which Lead and Direct Philosophical Enquiries; Illustrated by the History of Ancient Physics." in *Essays on Philosophical Subjects.* W. P. D. Wightman and J. C. Bryce, eds. Vol. 3. *The Glasgow Edition of the Works and Correspondence of Adam Smith.* Oxford: Clarendon Press. pp. 106–117.

Smith, Adam. 1980. "The Principles Which Lead and Direct Philosophical Enquiries; Illustrated by the History of Astronomy." in *Essays on Philosophical Subjects.* W. P. D. Wightman and J. C. Bryce, eds. Vol. 3. *The Glasgow Edition of the Works and Correspondence of Adam Smith.* Oxford: Clarendon Press. pp. 33–105.

Smith, Adam. 1983. *Lectures on Rhetoric and Belles Lettres.* J. C. Bryce, ed. Vol. 4. *The Glasgow Edition of the Works and Correspondence of Adam Smith.* Oxford: Clarendon Press.

Smith, Norris Kemp. 1947. "Introduction" and footnotes as Editor for *David Hume's Dialogues Concerning Natural Religion.* Indianapolis: Bobbs-Merrill.

Smout, T. C. 1983. "Where had the Scottish economy got to by the third quarter of the eighteenth century?" in *Wealth and Virtue.* Istvan Hont and Michael Ignatieff, eds. Cambridge: Cambridge University Press. pp. 45–72.

Sowell, Thomas. 1979. "Adam Smith in Theory and Practice." in *Adam Smith and Modern Political Economy: Bicentennial Essays on The Wealth of Nations.* Gerald R. O'Driscoll Jr., ed. Ames: The Iowa State University Press. pp. 3–18.

Spadafora, David. 1990. *The Idea of Progress in Eighteen-Century Britain.* New London: Yale University Press.

Spence, A. Michael. 1974. *Market Signaling: Informational Transfer in Hiring and Related Screening Processes.* Cambridge: Harvard University Press.

Spiegel, Henry W. 1979. "Adam Smith's Heavenly City." in *Adam Smith and Modern Political Economy: Bicentennial Essays on The Wealth of Nations.* Gerald R. O'Driscoll Jr., ed. Ames: The Iowa State University Press. pp. 44–67.

Spiegel, Henry W. 1991. *The Growth of Economic Thought.* 3rd Ed. Durham: Duke University Press.

Stein, Peter. 1980. *Legal Evolution: The Story of an Idea.* Cambridge: Cambridge University Press.

Stevens, David. 1975. "Adam Smith and the Colonial Disturbances." in *Essays on Adam Smith*. Andrew Skinner and Thomas Wilson, eds. Oxford: Clarendon Press. pp. 202–217.

Stewart, Dugald. (1793) 1980. "Account of the Life and Writings of Adam Smith, LL. D." W. P. D. Wightman and J. C. Bryce, eds. Vol. 3. *The Glasgow Edition of the Works and Correspondence of Adam Smith*. Oxford: Clarendon Press. pp. 269–351.

Stigler, George. 1975. "Smith's Travels on the Ship of State." in *Essays on Adam Smith*. Andrew Skinner and Thomas Wilson, eds. Oxford: Clarendon Press. pp. 237–246.

Stigler, George. 1976. "The Successes and Failures of Professor Smith." *Journal of Political Economy*. 84(6): 1199–1213.

Stigler, George and Becker, Gary. 1977. "De gustibus non est disputandum." *American Economic Review*. 67: 76–90.

Sudgen, Robert. 2002. "Beyond Sympathy and Empathy: Adam Smith's Concept of Fellow-Feeling." *Economics and Philosophy*. 18: 63–87.

Tax, Sol, and Krucoff, Larry S. 1968. "Social Darwinism." in *International Encyclopedia of the Social Sciences*. David L. Sills, ed. New York: Crowell Collier and Macmillan, Inc. pp. 402–406.

Teichgraeber, Richard F, III. 1986. *'Free Trade' and Moral Philosophy: Rethinking the Sources of Adam Smith's Wealth of Nations*. Durham: Duke University Press.

Thompson, Herbert. 1965. "Adam Smith's Philosophy of Science." *Quarterly Journal of Economics.* 79(2): 212–233.

Todd, W. B. 1976. "Text and Apparatus." *An Inquiry into the Nature and Causes of the Wealth of Nations*. R. H. Campbell and Andrew Skinner, eds. Vol. 2. *The Glasgow Edition of the Works and Correspondence of Adam Smith*. Oxford: Clarendon Press. pp. 61–66.

Vaughn, Karen. 1980. *John Locke: Economist and Social Scientist*. Chicago: University of Chicago Press.

Viner, Jacob. 1927. "Adam Smith and Laissez Faire." *Journal of Political Economy*. 35: 198–232.

Waterman, A. M. C. 2002. "Economics as Theology: Adam Smith's *Wealth of Nations*." *Southern Economic Journal*. 68(4): 907–921.

Watson, John Steven. 1960. *The Reign of George III, 1760–1815*. Oxford: Oxford University Press.

Werhane, Patricia H. 1991. *Adam Smith and His Legacy for Modern Capitalism*. Oxford: Oxford University Press.

West, E. G. 1979. "Adam Smith's Economics of Politics." in *Adam Smith and Modern Political Economy: Bicentennial Essays on The Wealth of Nations*. Gerald R. O'Driscoll Jr., ed. Ames: The Iowa State University Press. pp. 44–67.

Wightman, W. P. D. 1975. "Adam Smith and the History of Ideas." in *Essays on Adam Smith*. Andrew Skinner and Thomas Wilson, eds. Oxford: Clarendon Press. pp. 44–68.

Williamson, Oliver. 2000. "The New Institutional Economics: Taking Stock, Looking Ahead." *Journal of Economic Literature*. 38(3): 595–613.

Willis, Kirk. 1979. "The Role in Parliament of the Economic Ideas of Adam Smith." *History of Political Economy*. 11(4): 503–544.

Wills, Garry. ed. 1982. *The Federalist Papers by Alexander Hamilton, James Madison, and John Jay*. New York: Bantam Books.

Wilson, Edward O. 1975. *Sociobiology: The New Synthesis*. Cambridge: Belknap Press of Harvard University Press.

Winch, Donald. 1978. *Adam Smith's Politics: An Essay in Historiographic Revision*. Cambridge: Cambridge University Press.

Winch, Donald. 1983. "Adam Smith's 'enduring particular result': a political and cosmopolitan perspective." in *Wealth and Virtue*. Istvan Hont and Michael Ignatieff, eds. Cambridge: Cambridge University Press. pp. 253–270.

Winch, Donald. 1988. "Adam Smith and the Liberal Tradition." in *Traditions of Liberalism: Essays on John Locke, Adam Smith, and John Stuart Mill*. Knud Haakonssen, ed. St. Leonards, NSW, Australia: Centre for Independent Studies. pp. 83–106.

Wordsworth, William. 1985. *The Fourteen-Book Prelude*. W. J. B. Owen, ed. Ithaca: Cornell University Press.

Young, Jeffrey. 1997. *Economics as a Moral Science: The Political Economy of Adam Smith*. Cheltenham, UK: Edward Elgar.

Index

"The literature on Adam Smith has in recent years been growing at an exponential rate: Adam Smith has been celebrated as the first neoclassical economist, as a founder of institutional economics, as an early constitutional economist, as a prescient evolutionary economist, and even as a proto-Marxian economist. There is no better guide to this literature than Jerry Evensky, whose splendid book reveals its central message by its very title."
   – Mark Blaug, University of Amsterdam

"Evensky is something amazing – an economist who writes like an angel and thinks like a philosopher, but remains an economist. He knows Smith and he knows the ethical philosophy to which Smith devoted his life. Evensky is among the growing if select group of new readers of Smith who have discovered that Smith was a major ethical philosopher, and that 'Prudence only' is not his theme."
   – Deirdre McCloskey, University of Illinois

"Jerry Evensky presents an engaging survey of Smith's system taken as an integrated whole. Beginning with Smith's youthful writings on the philosophy of science, Evensky shows the interconnections Smith makes between moral philosophy, jurisprudence, and political economy. But Evensky's interest in Smith is not merely antiquarian. He believes that Smith's vision is still relevant, and he shows how it can inform a number of modern research programs. This book will be of interest to economists generally, and it should be widely read."
   –Jeffrey T. Young, St. Lawrence University

Adam Smith is the best known among economists for his book *The Wealth of Nations*, often viewed as the keystone of modern economic thought. For many, he has become associated with a quasi-libertarian laissez-faire philosophy. Others, often heterodox economists and social philosophers, on the contrary, focus on Smith's *Theory of Moral Sentiments*, and explore his moral theory. There has been a long debate about the relationship or lack thereof between these, his two great works.

   This work treats these dimensions of Smith's work as elements in a seamless moral philosophical vision, demonstrating the integrated nature of these works and Smith's other writings. Although many practitioners today see the study of Smith as an antiquarian exercise, this book weaves Smith into a constructive critique of modern economic analysis (engaging along the way the work of Nobel Laureates Gary Becker, Amarty Sen, Douglass North, and James Buchanan) and builds bridges between that discourse and other social sciences.

Jerry Evensky is Professor of Economics and Laura J. and L. Douglas Meredith Professor for Teaching Excellence at Syracuse University. He coedited *Adam Smith and the Philosophy of Law and Economics* (1994) with Robin Malloy and is the author of the textbook *Economics: The Ideas, the Issues* (2004). Professor Evensky serves on the editorial board of *The Journal of the History of Economic Thought* and has published articles in the *Journal of Economic Perspectives*, *History of Political Economy*, and the *American Journal of Economics and Sociology*, among others.

CAMBRIDGE
UNIVERSITY PRESS
www.cambridge.org

ISBN 978-0-521-70386-4

9 780521 703864 >

Cover design by James F. Brisson